WAR, REVOLUTION AND PEACE

Essays in Honor of Charles B. Burdick

Edited by Joachim Remak

UNIVERSITY
PRESS OF
AMERICA

LANHAM • NEW YORK • LONDON

Copyright © 1987 by

University Press of America,® Inc.

4720 Boston Way
Lanham, MD 20706

3 Henrietta Street
London WC2E 8LU England

All rights reserved

Printed in the United States of America

British Cataloging in Publication Information Available

"Winning the Battle at Home: The First World War and the Development of California's Sardine Industry." Copyright © 1987 by Steven M. Payne

"American Naval Rearmament 1930-1940: The Legislative Dimension." Copyright © 1987 by Michael West

"Preparing Teenagers in Hitler's Germany for War: The Training of the 12th SS Panzer Division "Hitler Youth." Copyright © 1987 by Craig Luther

"*Innere Führung* and the Problem of Tradition in the Emergence of the West German Armed Forces." Copyright © 1987 by Donald Abenheim

ISBN: (Cloth) 0-8191-6342-2 (alk. paper)

All University Press of America books are produced on acid-free paper which exceeds the minimum standards set by the National Historical Publication and Records Commission.

To Charles Burdick

and

the History Students of

San Jose State University

ACKNOWLEDGEMENTS

This festschrift originated as the idea of three former students of Charles B. Burdick. Sam Lewis took the lead with Jim Farr and Steve Payne. In 1982 they brought their wish to honor their mentor to Professor James P. Walsh who had succeeded Burdick as Chairman of San Jose State University's History Department. Because the three Burdick students had continued their doctoral work in history at the University of California, Santa Barbara, the group turned naturally to Professor Joachim Remak. Remak had chaired the U.C.S.B. History Department and was himself a long-time friend and professional colleague of Charles Burdick. Professor Remak immediately agreed to edit this collective work. He consumed more than one summer of his life at this task.

Besides each of the contributors, many others deserve acknowledgement. On the campus of San Jose State, Dean Charles Burdick's personal friends are numerous. As this project developed more and more of them became drawn into festschrift plans and production. Yet, the Dean remained unaware of its existence despite the fact that his secretaries directed his purchases of computer hardware and software in order to facilitate the book's production. Key conspirators include Lynn Cole, Leslie Brand, Linda Garcia and Emi Nobuhiro. Likewise, Associate Deans Billie Jensen and Lawrence Brewster knew when to look the other way--particularly when strangers were using the Dean's new laser printer.

The work of Richard Mills, graphic artist for San Jose State, is particularly appreciated. Not only for this book. His years of effort in support of numerous Burdick history projects have allowed the final touches to be worthy ones.

The encouragement and support of President Gail Fullerton, San Jose State, and her academic administration have always assisted the initiatives of the University's History Department and its students. This project is no exception.

Ken P. Ruinard's photo of Charles Burdick was supplied by the SJSU Office of Community Relations.

In the end, however, the work of three persons brought the festschrift to its proper conclusion. Professor George E. Moore, current Chair of San Jose State's History Department, performed the final organizational duties required to bring the work of love to completion. Mrs. Joan Block prepared the manuscripts and made them camera ready. Further, she coordinated publishing with University Press of America. Together with Dr. Jim Farr, co-chair of the festschrift presentation banquet, they have earned the gratitude of all of Charles Burdick's former students.

Whether one more acknowledgement is deserved or not will never be known. Because he is so knowledgeable about the work of his School, Dean Burdick may have learned in advance of this four-year surprise-in-the-making. Because he is so considerate he may have allowed us, his friends, to believe that we were successes at secrecy.

CONTENTS

	Introduction	ix
	JOACHIM REMAK	
I.	Charles B. Burdick and San Jose State	1
	JAMES P. WALSH GERALD E. WHEELER	
II.	Discordant Chorus: The United States and the European Revolutions of 1848	9
	JAMES FARR	
III.	The Kaiser's Yangtse Patrol	29
	DWIGHT R. MESSIMER	
IV.	The German Prisoners of War in Japan 1914-1920	47
	URSULA R. MOESSNER	
V.	American Military Attachés in Russia 1914-1917	59
	S. J. LEWIS	
VI.	Frank A. Golder, The Inquiry, and Soviet Russia	89
	ALLEN WACHHOLD	
VII.	Winning the Battle at Home: The First World War and the Development of California's Sardine Industry	117
	STEPHEN M. PAYNE	
VIII.	Hostages to Fortune: The Confrontation Over Wal Wal, Ethiopia, December 1934	135
	DOREEN GAMA FARR	

IX.	American Naval Rearmament 1930-1940: The Legislative Dimension	165
	MICHAEL WEST	
X.	The Second World War - A Problem in Research	185
	HANS ADOLF JACOBSEN	
XI.	The Evacuation of the Kuban Bridgehead: A Model Retrograde Movement	211
	DAVID MIDDLESWORTH	
XII.	Preparing Teenagers in Hitler's Germany for War: The Training of the 12th SS Panzer Division "Hitler Youth"	229
	CRAIG LUTHER	
XIII.	Innere Führung and the Problem of Tradition in the Emergence of the West German Armed Forces	251
	DONALD ABENHEIM	
XIV.	Burdick Bibliography	275
	NANCY J. EMMICK	
XV.	Contributors	285

INTRODUCTION

by JOACHIM REMAK

Sixty is a good time to remember, especially if one knew the new adult--everything is upscale these days--for more than half his life. Charles Burdick and I met over thirty years ago when both of us were Western Civ. instructors (no one ever called the course by its full name) at Stanford. He had arrived a year before I did, and hence was the veteran. But it was not just the deference due to such an old-timer which made me respect and admire him, and I hope become his friend. For what struck me immediately about him was that--long before that phrase became common coinage--he was a person who cared. Above all, of course, then and now, that meant caring for his students. Teaching was not a means to an end for him as it was for so many of us; it was his natural habitat. Others might be surrounded by notes and library cards; he was surrounded by undergraduates. But to a degree that fooled you, for the cards and notes were there too. And his interests went beyond the specialization imposed by working for a degree: German history was among them, and so were military affairs, and so was the Hoover Library. It all made for good talk, and good company.

Three decades later, the character has remained unchanged, although the list of publications has grown, to an extent that tests friendship. Books and articles continue to offer witness to both his scholarship and his exceptional range of interests. What is more, his teaching is as effective and special as ever. Students at San Jose certainly will give one no argument on that, having offered him the best teacher award more than once. And if ever there was an honest vote this one was. The test of this is as simple as it is startling: the full enrollments for his European survey course scheduled for 7:30 a.m. ("You want time for yourself, and no students?" a friend advised me on my first job away from Stanford, when I was feeling swamped. "No problem. Teach TThS or before 9:00.")

It was enough for one career, just as his writing was. But he added a third: his role in graduate education. Gerald Wheeler's and Jim Walsh's fine introductory essay gives the figures: Some 120 students did their work for the master's degree under his direction, and many of them went on into the doctoral program. Yet each of them received his full attention. To quote the most endearing, and revealing observation in Wheeler's essay, "When questioned, most of them believed he, or she, was getting the largest share of Charles' time that semester." Ten or twenty years from now, perhaps, he will tell us the secret of how he managed it, or how he continued to maintain the trust and affection of all who have come into contact with him, from German generals to American undergraduates to--was it the experience with the generals?--his academic colleagues.

But it is time to yield the floor to others, for the most part those who learned their craft from Charles Burdick. Their topics are a fair reflection of the scope of his interests. They range from the Revolution of 1848 to this century's two great wars, from the Russian Revolution to the American legislative process. James Farr shows how a supposedly isolationist America was affected by events in Europe, and both welcomed "the wonderful revolution" of 1848, and was bothered by some of its excesses. He also sheds light on one of that year's most curious episodes: the Frankfurt Parliament's negotiations for the services of an American officer to help in implementing its plan for creating a German navy. It was a different Germany, of course, that would actually build that navy, which then would serve in regions of the world undreamt of by the delegates in the Paulskirche. Dwight R. Messimer offers an intriguing description of the imperial navy's Yangtse Patrol at the turn of the century--not the softest of assignments for its men, but one that offered challenge and adventure. When war came in 1914, the crew, rather than falling into Japanese hands, managed to find refuge in China. Other German military men overseas, such as the defenders of Tsingtao, were less fortunate, and spent the war years in Japanese prisoner of war camps. But as Ursula Moessner, co-author of Charles' most recent book, shows us, their treatment was worlds removed from what befell Japan's p.o.w.'s a generation later. A decent regard for not only their physical well-being but for their morale as well took many practical forms, from allowing them to work for wages to letting them share their expertise with the Japanese in the surrounding countryside.

But if Japan in effect could sit out the war after 1914, Russia had no such luck. An American embassy in Petrograd, which by today's standards was almost unbelievably understaffed, did its best to keep Washington informed of events, from the country's early defeats to the two revolutions of 1917, and S. J. Lewis does a fine job of showing us the importance of the reports of the embassy member whose position was one of the most difficult of all to fill at the time, that of the military attaché. Woodrow Wilson, aware of the need for more knowledge about Russia as well as other foreign nations in connection with the coming peace treaties, set about creating a special intelligence-gathering commission. Allen Wachhold gives us an always interesting description of the work of its Russian expert, of his achievements and his more than occasional frustrations. He was Frank Golder, who would then go to play a key role in the establishment of the Hoover Library.

"Mr. Hoover must have been a very smart man," Trotsky reportedly said. (The story was told to us by Ralph Lutz.) "Else he would not have called it the 'Library on War, Revolution, and Peace,' for that is the order of events." But as we know, it was a fragile peace that followed war and revolution. Doreen Farr gives us an intimation of the bloodier conflict to follow between Italy and Ethiopia in her graphic description of the confrontation that took place at a border post a year before the invasion. The United States, which as we learned from Stephen Payne's chapter, had aided the Allied war effort in World War I in more than the familiar ways, still was very much on the sidelines in this incident. But it was aware of coming troubles, and of the need for naval rearmament. What was more, it was beginning to take some effective action, thanks in no small part to the skillful management of the House of Representatives' Naval Affairs Committee. As one reads Michael A. West's convincingly detailed description of its work, one is struck by how different the results might have been had it not had the good fortune of being under the chairmanship of a man who mastered the legislative process the way Carl Vinson did.

But while there were those who could see the need for preparedness, hardly anyone had even an approximate idea of how unprecedented the coming war could be in scope. Appropriately enough, the problems it left for historians have been equally immense, and among the very few who can claim to possess even an overview of it all is Hans-Adolf Jacobsen. His thoroughly documented essay on the Second World War in all its aspects offers the kind of survey that only the very brave and the very knowledgeable may try. Two of the war's little-known but intriguing special topics are covered next by David Middlesworth, who shows how organization and cool nerves kept a retreat from turning into disaster, and by Craig Luther, who gives a graphic description of how the Nazi regime managed to harness the enthusiasm of the young for its war effort. The very different mood of Germany's postwar armed forces, with their emphasis on reason rather than fanaticism, can be gleaned from Donald Abenheim's concluding chapter. In dealing with what has been perhaps the Bundeswehr's most vexing problem--of how to come to terms with the past, and of how to decide what traditions remained worth saving out of the wreckage--he leaves us with a heartening conclusion about what intelligence and good will can achieve.

There remains now but one final note. The book's chapters have offered us some reflection of Charles Burdick's many interests. But why should birthdays be a time for kind words only? Opportunities should be seized, and I should like to use the occasion to complain about a matter that has long weighed on my mind. It is this: For a good many years now, Charles has sent a number of graduate students to Santa Barbara for their doctoral work. They have been excellent people all, and that has been the trouble. For they were all so well trained in method, and as often as not arrived with most of the sources they needed, that it has given me the feeling of collecting my salary under false pretenses; there really was nothing left for me--their nominal supervisor--to teach them.

That then is the part I find hard to forgive, even on this occasion. But aside from that, I'd like to join in the truly best of birthday wishes. <u>Herzlichste Glückwünsche</u>, Charles!

CHARLES B. BURDICK AND SAN JOSE STATE

by JAMES P. WALSH and
 GERALD E. WHEELER

Hard work and enjoying good company have been well established hallmarks in the life of Charles Burdick. As the oldest of six depression era children he learned early which came first. As a friendly and highly considerate youngster he kept the second as close behind as possible. Among his boyhood recollections of San Jose, California, in the 1930s was his waiting in a grocery checkout line with his parents. The wait, aggravated by his wish to join young friends for an afternoon ballgame, seemed to be forever. When, at last, escape appeared at hand, the grocer told Charles' father (Donald L. Burdick) the reason for the delay. His box boy had failed to show up for work.

Then Charles' chance for freedom died in one quick exchange. "Young man," the family grocer asked, "would you like a job for the rest of the day?" Charles' mother (Inez Shields) had always taught him to be polite, so he said, "No thank you. I have a baseball game today." Donald, who understood the work ethic even after a Stanford bachelor's degree and a Harvard M.B.A., intervened most directly. "He'll take it." Baseball had to wait for another day when work was unavailable.

Instead of rebelling against such a regime Charles accepted it for his own. In time, determining what was more fun, work or play, became quite unnecessary. As the years passed and Charles made his way through San Jose's Hester Elementary, Hoover Junior High, and Lincoln High School, his surviving two sisters and two brothers followed along at two-year intervals. Janet came second, then Donald James, Sara, and William. Margaret had died at age seven months. Charles' recollections of these Burdick family school days prompted his subsequent initiative, the establishment at San Jose State University of a scholarship in the name of the fourth grade teacher. He concluded that Edith Smith had endured her share of Burdicks and earned this quiet tribute. Perhaps it would encourage other young students to follow in the field of elementary education with equal patience and understanding.

The San Jose of Charles Burdick's youth would not recognize the post-war metropolis which displaced it. The abundant orchards of the Santa Clara Valley impinged upon the town's very existence. "Silicon" was a scientific word reserved for the more authoritative chemistry texts. And "disks" (then spelled "discs") merely perpetuated tradition; they plowed the rich ranchlands every spring and contoured the topsoil into patterns through which the irrigation waters coursed. No matter. Burdick viewed all of this from the perspective of his after-school job at the service station. The summers he spent in the canneries. This routine, established at age fourteen, continued with a single interruption until academic advancement allowed more dignified (though not always more remunerative) alternatives.

The United States Army represented his single evasion of family responsibility and obligation. Underage, but with his father's approval, Burdick enlisted during World War II. His military affiliation and his later preparation for scholarship profoundly influenced his life.

Charles Burdick entered San Jose State College in the fall of 1946. Essentially a small college dedicated to preparing public school teachers, San Jose State was entering a period of growth and change. Though there was no History Department, there was a group of historians within the Social Sciences Division. From these professors Charles received an excellent education that culminated in his 1949 graduation "with great distinction" as a history major. As a reader for several faculty members, he developed a "feel" for the profession; and in one, Dudley Moorhead, he found a role model for excellence at the lectern. From him Charles also received strong encouragement to enter the graduate program in history at Stanford University. Besides an excellent foundation in history, San Jose State provided Charles with a wife--Kay Lutz, the daughter of Dr. Ralph Lutz, Director of the Hoover Institution of War, Revolution and Peace on the Stanford campus. They were married in 1948 in the Stanford Chapel though both were still undergraduates at San Jose State.

The five years that Charles Burdick studied at Stanford were packed ones and somewhat typical of graduate student life. Working with David Harris, he completed a master's degree and then a doctorate in modern European history. His order of scholarly interest was Europe, modern Germany, and Adolf Hitler's <u>Wehrmacht</u>. In preparation for his dissertation, "German Military Planning for the War in the West, 1935-1940," he opened an epistolary siege of the Reich's surviving generals and admirals. From this correspondence, and a year of research in Germany as a student, followed by a year there as a Fulbright-Hays Post-Doctoral Fellow, Charles developed the research base for almost a half-dozen books and a trove of articles. He also developed a fluency in German that opened no end of doors to him. These years, spent largely in the Rheinland, Stuttgart and Munich, educated his palate to German music, cuisine and, above all, to the glorious assortment of fine white wines produced along the Rhein and Mosel in that area known as the <u>Rheingau</u>. The spring vacation which Kay and Charles shared with the other Fulbright couples in 1955 remained forever memorable.

Following their post-doctoral study year in Germany, the Burdicks returned to Stanford for two years during which Charles served as an instructor in the University's highly respected Western Civilization Program. Here he benefited from teaching Stanford's well-selected freshmen and sophomores, and from associating with an interesting and challenging group of newly-minted Ph.D. holders. The appointment to this prestigious program was "terminal" from the beginning; none could expect to enter the University's History Department after two or three years of service. Yet the experience was invaluable. With the expanding market for academic historians in the late 1950s, a Western Civ internship was an excellent bargaining chip when one sought a permanent position. The appointment also meant that for several years Kay and Charles would have the stability so desirable when raising two young daughters (Karen and Marla). Even so, Stanford's salary in 1953 ($1,500) convinced Charles to retain his tenure at the San Jose service station where he continued to work on weekends. Besides that he took an additional night job.

As a Western Civ instructor, Charles was an absolute success. Though considered a bit shy by his mentors, he was warm and outgoing with his students. He found challenging topics for the day and developed the technique of posing the right questions to start an animated discussion. His command of the subject was secure and he brought the interesting topics into clearer focus because of his travels on the continent. What early became clear to Charles' students was that he respected them and was interested in them. The result was that many worked harder than they normally would have because they didn't want to disappoint him. His success in the classroom was noted by the supervising faculty and the result was a strong package of recommendations when he began thinking of permanent employment, for in the spring of 1957 it would be time to leave "The Farm."

In the fall of 1956, the administration of San Jose State College recognized the start of a period of accelerating growth. New buildings were planned and funding their construction presented no problem. In the next five years, President John T. Wahlquist was to add almost 500 new permanent faculty to the College. For the fall of 1957, Dr. Dudley T. Moorhead, the head of the Department of History, Economics and Geography, was told to plan on having five or six new full-time history positions. His first recommendation to President Wahlquist was that Dr. Charles Burdick be appointed an instructor. He would be expected to teach three classes of basic American History and one lower division class of European Civilization, all for $5232 per annum. Given the expected growth in the number of students at the College, and an even larger increase in the number of history majors, Charles knew that eventually he would be teaching all European History. But first he would have to develop several new courses, in a minor specialty, as well as create a year's course of lectures in his major field, European History. Fortunately his years as a Western Civilization instructor at Stanford had prepared him quite well for this new assignment.

The San Jose State College that he returned to in the fall of 1957 was a vastly different campus from the one he had left in June 1949. The enrollments were almost double. San Jose Junior College students who previously shared the facilities no longer were on campus. A graduate program boomed. And the administrative structure had been altered to prepare for a more sophisticated curriculum. Nowhere were the changes more obvious than in his new department. The Department of History, Economics and Geography was now housed in the new classroom building, Centennial Hall, later to be renamed Dudley Moorhead Hall. Dr. Leo P. Kibby, the Chairman of the Social Sciences Area (History, Economics, Geography; Political Science and Public Administration; Sociology and Social Work; and the Social Science Teacher Training Program), was the acting head of H.E. & G. as well, and Dr. H. Brett Melendy was the interim administrator of the History faculty. Charles was housed in Centennial Hall, as was Dr. Moorhead, now Dean of the School of Humanities and the Arts, the school to which Charles would owe allegiance. Change quickly followed change when President Wahlquist, at the opening of the spring semester 1958, authorized the history faculty to constitute itself as a separate department and to recommend one of its members to be head. Dr. Melendy was elected and Charles had his third "boss" within a year.

When Charles Burdick accepted appointment to the History faculty, there were 14 members; now, in the fall of the same year (1957), the number suddenly jumped to 20. Of the six who joined the faculty, "the class of 1957," Charles was the youngest and least experienced, but that in no way intimidated him. Within six years he would rise to the rank of professor, a considerable accomplishment, particularly since he began a rank below (instructor) the other five who came to the department with him. A year as an instructor, two years as assistant professor, three years as associate professor, and appointment as a professor for the fall semester 1963. Of the six who came in 1957, three became professors in 1963 and Charles was among them. How had he done it? The short answer is: by working extremely hard. By then too, Kay and Charles had two more daughters (Saral and Darcy).

During the summers Burdick exchanged work in the local canneries for lecturing at the Sixth United States Army Intelligence School located then at the Presidio of Monterey. His depiction of the grand strategy of World War II captured the enthusiasm of the officer-students and made him an instant success. Nonetheless, Burdick worked at getting acquainted with the student body after hours. After three summers of association with their favorite teacher, one class hosted an uproarious graduation party that all but rocked downtown Monterey. No officer could be content until he expressed his gratitude for Burdick's personal attention. Of course drinks had to be offered and taken.

Saturday morning's 0730 graduation ceremony was more than inconvenient for the students. For Burdick, the designated speaker of the day, it was acutely painful. His friends on the teaching staff claimed years later that they shaved him, arranged his attire, and pushed him out on the stage. His mere vertical presence aroused uproarious applause which rather bewildered the commandant in charge.

Whether accurate or not, the event's symbolism gives truth and understanding to Professor Burdick's frequently stated advice to students approaching their first public presentation. "Remember, everyone there wants to be somewhere else."

During the academic year 1957-58, San Jose State's History faculty began an intensive effort to renovate the undergraduate curriculum and to create a master's degree with its panoply of courses. Charles sat on innumerable committees and sub-committees, with more patience than the work deserved, but in the end his ideas were present at both the undergraduate and graduate levels. Not only did he help create the new curricula, but by the fall of 1959 his schedule was now completely European History, with a graduate offering each semester. He set aside his American History notes, permanently.

It is almost an iron law of academic practice that with curriculum development there must also be library development, or there is no quality in what is offered. Charles understood this relationship and joined the departmental campaign to upgrade the library's history collection. He regularly sat on the department's library committee and soon began a one-man campaign to create a collection of primary materials for European History that would make it possible for graduate students to do original research on campus for an M.A. thesis. Because of his special interest in military history, he was able to capture several large personal libraries for San Jose State and thus significantly improve the monographic holdings in this area. Not only did he acquire private libraries, he convinced several members of the library's staff that they should take master's degrees in the department. The end product of his efforts, by 1963, was a graduate level library collection capable of sustaining student primary research in a large number of areas of modern European History. As will be evident to the reader, most of the essays in this Festschrift began in document collections purchased on the recommendation of Professor Burdick.

One of the major changes that Charles noted when he returned to his alma mater was a new spirit of professionalism that infused the History faculty. While nothing had been set down in writing, he early recognized that members of the department were expected to engage in research, write books, articles and reviews, and be active in professional organizations. Because the department now was to engage in graduate education, the professional requirements seemed reasonable. In 1959 he published his first three articles and it has been a rare year that one or more have not appeared in print. Books take more time. His first was published in 1965 and since then he has published a dozen. That figure alone has put Charles Burdick in a class of historians made up of less than one per cent in the profession.

While his publications have created an international reputation for Charles, he has been known at San Jose State University for his mastery of the classroom. Though he knew that publication would be required of him, and he planned to fulfill the department's expectations, Charles felt instinctively that what counted would be his ability to teach. Here his apprenticeship at Stanford paid dividends. He quickly became an exceptionally able classroom lecturer. Organized, witty, and loaded with information, he brought a sense of high drama to his students. Voice, diction, and timing were used to keep them enthralled. Once student evaluations of their professors became de rigueur, the honor fraternity, Tau Delta Phi, voted him "King of the Classroom." Long before that, his seniors in the department had recommended him for early promotion because of his unsurpassed teaching skills. Even students with majors normally thought to be less intellectually demanding than history elected to take his 7:30 a.m. lecture course on Modern Europe.

But classroom lecturing is just one aspect of collegiate instruction. Teaching a seminar, guiding colloquium discussions, correcting and editing student papers, and guiding the tyro historian by means of countless one-on-one discussions in the office, also constitute academic teaching. And here Charles Burdick has been superb. Well over 120 students have written master's theses under his direction. When questioned, most believed he, or she, was getting the largest share of Charles' time that semester. Unlike most humans who possess a finite amount of time for any activity, he has appeared to have infinite time for his students. And, as many have testified, he also has time for letters of recommendation, phone calls to locate jobs, and calls and letters around the world to find some documentary materials for a thesis or research paper. This, of course, is what the professional academic historian should be doing. But few do it with the same flair and success.

Why success in the classroom and at publishing recommends university professors for administrative positions few really know. Presumably those successes are a better recommendation than failure, even though quite different skills are needed for administration. In Burdick's case he moved by degrees (but never completely) away from full-time teaching into administrative positions. First, he assisted his department chairman, H. Brett Melendy, in constructing the semester schedules which became expansive and complex. The lives of up to fifty historians, with all their preferences and fluctuating idiosyncrasies, became as important to the finished product as the new graduate and undergraduate curriculum which Burdick helped bring into existence.

During Melendy's leaves Burdick served as acting chairman. Later, and with the advancement of Gerald E. Wheeler to become Dean of the School of Social Sciences, Burdick's colleagues elected him chairman. By then, however, the glory days of university history departments were over. Little or no demand for new school teachers accelerated the shift of student interests. With plunging enrollments in history also came redistribution of assigned positions and the actual threat that tenured historians at San Jose State University would be let go because of insufficient students to be taught. Until this downturn in enrollments hit, department policy had been to enrich the curricular offerings to the greatest degree possible through hiring and tenuring to the maximum. When the downturn actually arrived San Jose State's History Department was specialized, diverse, productive, and quite overstaffed.

What prevented a most unwanted academic precedent (the termination of tenured faculty) from commencing at San Jose State University was the administrative ingenuity, personal generosity, and abundant good will which emanated from 134 Moorhead Hall--the History Chairman's office. Charles Burdick successfully guided the reduction of history faculty positions from thirty back to nineteen during a period of no retirements. To do so he identified teaching and administrative needs in the University which were outside History and satisfied them with qualified department members. In most cases his "foreign legionnaires" were led by senior full professors who could have demanded full teaching schedules within their self-defined fields. Under Burdick seniority never became an issue at re-assignment time; neither did it become a reality at any termination time. There was no layoff.

By the time Charles Burdick accepted appointment as Dean of the School of Social Sciences, his colleagues in History were returning to full-time teaching in their home department. History again was looking up and the former chairman's confidence in the scholarship of his colleagues was well rewarded. During l982-83 the faculty of San Jose State's History Department presented the scholarly community with the publication of twelve new books. Most were monographic studies in the histories of Asia, Modern Europe, Medieval Europe, Africa, Latin America and the United States. Besides these, five more books appeared during the same academic year written by former Master's students. Within this record total, Dean Burdick co-authored The German Prisoners at Bando, 1915-1920 which appeared in Japanese.

The professionalization and scholarly development of the University's History Department coincided with the academic presence of Charles Burdick. Several colleagues challenged his record in teaching, or in publishing, or in administrative matters. But they did so only for a while, and only in one of the areas of his success.

This Festschrift celebrates two landmarks in the career of Professor Charles Burdick: his 60th year on this earth, and his 30th as a faculty member at San Jose State University. It is appropriate that almost all of the writing in this celebratory volume of essays comes from his former students at San Jose State. From the day he began teaching in San Jose, Charles commenced building a loyal legion of students who would carry his name and reputation throughout the academic world. He also began a record of publication that has made his name known wherever historians gather to discuss European military history.

His career has had its rewards and recognitions, but San Jose State University will remember Charles Burdick, historian, for his excellence in teaching, his accomplishments in publishing, and his humanity in administration.

As colleagues (past and present) of Charles Burdick, we are proud to have served in the faculty with him and congratulate him on the occasion of his receiving this <u>Festschrift</u>.

DISCORDANT CHORUS
THE UNITED STATES AND THE
EUROPEAN REVOLUTIONS OF 1848

by JAMES FARR

> As flake by flake the beetling avalanches
> Build up their imminent crags of noiseless snow,
> Till some chance thrill the loosened ruin launches
> In unwarned havoc on the roofs below,
> So grew and gathered through the silent years
> The madness of a people, wrong by wrong.[1]

In the third week of February, 1848, the citizens of Paris rose in rebellion against the government of King Louis Philippe and, to the great amazement of all onlookers, toppled the French monarch. The King and Queen fled their kingdom in a fishing boat, finding refuge across the English Channel.[2] News of the uprising quickly spread and within weeks the shouts of revolution reverberated throughout the capitals of Europe. The government and people of the United States, confident of their political institutions and economic strength, generally welcomed the tide of republicanism that washed over the European continent seeing in these revolutions the opportunity to serve both the cause of republicanism and their nation's economic position in the new republics of Europe.

The fall of Louis Philippe meant that, for the third time in sixty years, the people of France had overturned their government. The Revolution of 1848, however, differed from the upheavals of 1789 and 1830. This time it was not the middle class but a developing proletariat that provided the driving force for change. Like England, France was in transition from an agricultural to an industrial society. Several years of poor harvest had driven many peasants in from the countryside, and the nation's rapidly expanding population added thousands to the city's unemployed.[3] In Paris, the displaced peasants and the unemployed challenged the economic order and threatened the stability of the city. Yet the dislocations of a changing economic order might have been overcome with more inspired leadership.

Citizen King Louis Philippe, though hardly a tyrant, had gradually dissipated the support of his people, and both the lower and middle classes grew discontented with his reign. The King's preoccupation with establishing a secure dynasty, the narrow voting franchise, and widespread charges of corruption disenchanted many of his subjects.[4] Apprehensive about the rising discontent, the King and his ministers attempted to muzzle critics of the regime. The government canceled a "reform banquet" planned for February 22 by members of the opposition in the nation's elected assembly. Thousands of Parisians rushed to the streets to protest the government's action. Attempting to avert a crisis and mollify his subjects, Louis Philippe dismissed his unpopular Prime Minister, Francois Guizot. However, the King's stratagem did not have the desired effect, for on the evening of the twenty-second of February a hostile crowd gathered in front of Guizot's residence and provoked a detachment of soldiers deployed to protect the ex-Prime Minister. The confrontation took the lives of several citizens and news of the deaths swept over the city. Paris rose in arms. Frightened by the hostility of the mob and distrustful of the National Guard, Louis Philippe fled his capital. In response to the King's sudden flight, the Chamber of Deputies, led by Ledru Rollin, Alphonse Lamartine, and Louis Blanc, dissolved the Chamber and formed a Provisional Government. On February 24, two days following the initial disturbance, the new government declared France a republic.[5]

The sudden collapse of the French monarchy left foreign diplomats in an awkward position; the government to which they were accredited no longer existed. American Ambassador Richard Rush, anxious to support the fledgling republic but concerned about the weeks long delay in trans-Atlantic communication, stepped forward to formally recognize the new Provisional Government of France. Lamartine and the new government leaders hailed the magnificent gesture of the American minister.[6] Across the Atlantic, U.S. President James Polk would soon endorse Rush's course of action.

The world's foremost democracy in the 1840s and a rising world power, the United States was confident, expansionistic, and pugnaciously egalitarian. The administration of James Polk extended the boundaries of the United States from the Atlantic to the Pacific, thus creating a continental nation. With mixed success, reformers worked diligently to transform American society to meet the changing demands of an industrialized-urbanized economy. Horace Mann struggled to extend public education. William Ladd spoke for world peace. And thousands of organizations formed to combat the wiles of John Barleycorn.

The 1840s first heard women speak out for equal rights. Intellectuals joined together in Fourier societies and experimented in communal living. William Lloyd Garrison and Wendell Phillips began to win soldiers in their war to abolish slavery. The prevailing faith in human nature and domestic institutions convinced Americans that society could be reorganized, improved, even perfected. In this dynamic atmosphere of possibilities, news of the French and other European revolutions produced great excitement. Unaware of the social and economic complexities of European nations, most Americans saw the contests as republicanism challenging monarchy, freedom defeating tyranny. Besides, they felt reassured by the thought that other nations would now join their democratic experiment.

Hence, Americans in all the major cities of the nation celebrated the revolution of 1848 and the creation of a new French republic.[7] Though Louis Philippe had been a popular figure in the United States, Americans generally did not lament his fall from power. The French king, it seemed, had abused his subjects. He had overtaxed them in favor of the aristocracy, and constricted their liberties. A faith in American institutions reinforced this belief in republicanism, and newspapers of the era frequently boasted of the leading role America would play in moving the world out of the darkness of monarchy. The most exuberant expression of this sentiment emanated from Chicago. A Chicago newspaper wrote:

> We are the model republic; the centre of civilization. From us in future will go forth the rays of virtue and intelligence that are to serve to warm into life the kingdoms of the world and enlighten the darkness that covers the majority of nations.[8]

The intellectual community in the United States generally joined in the chorus of approval for the new French republic and the republican agitation in Europe. James Russell Lowell and other poets celebrated the French uprising in verse; articles appeared in literary magazines praising the events in Europe.[9]

Not all Americans, however, added their voices to the Marseillaise. Ralph Waldo Emerson suggested withholding judgment on the revolution for a year to see if the revolution was "worth the trees" cut down to make barricades.[10] Even those newspapers and journals which saw the revolutions of 1848 as the natural and inevitable decay of monarchial institutions, harbored doubts as to the ultimate outcome of the upheaval. Many voiced the same question: "Will it last?"[11] Still other voices expressed hostility to the revolutions. Whig newspapers, like the <u>Washington National Intelligencer</u>, felt only dismay and sympathized with the government of Louis Philippe.[12] The French Provisional Government soon confirmed the doubts of many American conservatives when it challenged not only the old political structures, but attempted to restructure the social and economic order of French society as well.

Buoyed by a wave of popular enthusiasm, the new government within days after assuming power announced the abolition of capital punishment, and the termination of all titles and class distinctions. It then released all political prisoners, granted universal suffrage to males, and announced the preparation of an act to emancipate all slaves in the French colonial empire. What was even more significant, the government proclaimed its intention to establish "national workshops" to support unemployed workers.13 Ambassador Rush reported a great enthusiasm among the general population for the new government. Workmen, he wrote, donated part of their wages and peasants sold family heirlooms to help finance the early days of the republic.14

The social and economic reform undertaken by the Provisional Government divided American opinion decisively. American slaveholders saw the emancipation of slaves as a dangerous precedent and feared for the South's "peculiar institution." Some Southern newspapers, reflecting the opinion of the dominant planter class, quickly denounced the actions of the French republic.15 American political conservatives, skeptical of French ability to create a successful republic, assailed the new government. Daniel Webster dismissed the new French leaders as "poets and editors" and doubted their eventual success.16 Whig Senator John C. Calhoun expressed the apprehension of many conservatives while debating a Congressional resolution congratulating the French on the creation of a republic: "They have decreed a Republic, but it remains for them to establish a Republic . . . Great events are before us. Their lives not the man who can say what another year may bring forth."17

Since successful commercial relations depended on political and economic stability, many American businessmen greeted the news of the French and European turmoil with mixed feelings. The New York Stock Exchange experienced "a little panic" after receiving the first news of the revolution; the New York Tribune noted that the upheaval had made the "capitalists timid."18 This same panic spread throughout European financial communities, disrupting the normal course of business not only in France, but in England, Holland, Belgium, the Germanies and Austria. The Tribune discerned "the Derangement of Business the real danger" to the Republic, and expressed fears about the revolution's drain on the French treasury.19 But if some politicians and businessmen saw the potential liabilities, others could see opportunity.

James Buchanan, Secretary of State under James K. Polk, congratulated Ambassador Rush on his quick recognition of the new French republic. Americans, noted Buchanan, greeted news of the revolution "with one universal burst of enthusiasm . . . ."20 In a message to Congress, President Polk echoed these sentiments, describing the relatively bloodless revolution as evidence of "the great truth that in this enlightened age man is capable of governing himself." Polk went on to express his belief that republican France would find it in her interest to develop "the most liberal principles of international intercourse and commercial reciprocity" with the United States.21

To Polk and of his era, "liberalism" meant not only political liberty but free trade between nations with a minimum of government interference. Polk and Buchanan and many advocates of free trade saw in the sudden removal of Louis Philippe an opportunity to penetrate markets once held as royal monopolies. Buchanan, in his early correspondence with Rush, exhibited both a genuine concern for the successful establishment of a republic and an equally fervent plea for free trade. Buchanan warned of the danger of a coalition of European monarchies descending on France to halt the republican contagion as well as that of the centralization of power in Paris, which he felt exposed the nation's democracy to the travails of the capital. The Secretary also urged the Ambassador to seek the removal of the royal tobacco monopoly which weighed "onerously" on the merchants of Baltimore.22 Buchanan's orders to Rush reflected the aggressive, business-oriented stance of the American government towards foreign trade, and the Secretary saw the potential advantage in the revolutions' restructuring of the European continent.

The tumult of 1848 heralded the arrival of new forces on the European scene. Forces of nationalism appeared in Italy and in Hungary, eager to free themselves from the Austrian Habsburgs. The citizens of the German states wanted to identify themselves as a people and a nation. Poles, too, spoke again of a new nation. In many German states, political leaders promoted a liberal constitutionalism and had strong backing from a growing middle class. New ideas of socialism and communism announced themselves while the lower classes listened. This proletariat, cut off from the soil, dependent on a system of wages for survival, and concentrated in the cities, came of age politically in 1848. This new class represented the dislocated elements in a changing economic order. That Karl Marx and Frederick Engels published their Communist Manifesto in 1848 was no coincidence. Though the communist philosophers and the power of their ideas would not play a primary role in the turmoil, they recognized the growing strength of the working class, the dynamics of economic forces, and the coming class struggle.23

Discontent with the established order grew and festered through the 1840s. The new power of the working class evidenced itself in the English Chartist movement for political reform, nearly a decade old by the outbreak of the French revolution. The insurrection in Cracow in 1846 and the Swiss civil war a year later suggested the violence to come. Sicilian revolutionaries actually struck the first blow of 1848, forcing King Ferdinand II, King of the Two Sicilies, to surrender dominion over the island. Following the fall of Louis Philippe, no European monarch felt safe. The two societies least affected by events of 1848, Russia and England, represented the most reactionary and liberal elements in European politics. Russia, defiantly absolutist, stood prepared to use its military force to preserve the kingdoms of other European monarchs. England, though favoring a policy of moderate reform in its national affairs and even in foreign policy, grew alarmed at the extent of revolutionary turmoil. The British, therefore, threw their support against revolution and in favor of reaction as the lesser of two evils.24 Though many in England hailed the French revolution, conservatives quickly saw the potential danger at home. One commentator excoriated those who referred to the ouster of Louis Philippe as a "wonderful revolution": "If this foolish speech be persisted in, it will be difficult to convince unlettered men that what is accounted glorious in Paris can be treasonable in Dublin and Birmingham."[25] Such caution proved to be justified, as the Chartists and Irish revolutionaries took inspiration from the clash of arms on the continent and continued their challenge of the status quo. American newspapers reported disturbances in Ireland and England in considerable detail, and fully expected the revolution to spread to the British Isles.[26]

English leaders, however, rose to the threat posed by the Chartists and the rebels of Ireland. As the middle class had a firm hold on England's government, the working class chartists could look for little help from that quarter. The Chartists also challenged a government willing to use force quickly and effectively, which set an example for the reactionary movements in 1849.[27] But perhaps the most effective method of blunting the revolutionary impulse in England came not from the use of force but from conciliation. But the success the English enjoyed in containing the revolutionary impulse in the British Isles did not delude them about the state of European affairs, however. As The Times noted "the materials of combustion are already profusely strewn abroad . . . ."[28] An accurate observation, of course, and after the fall of the Citizen King, Europe erupted.

Royalty, foreign and domestic, ruled the Italian peninsula in the 1840s, but liberal and national sentiment was rapidly growing. Soon after assuming power in the Papal States in 1846, Pope Pius IX instituted a broad program of reform, including political amnesty and freedom of the press. A number of Italian princes followed the Pope's lead and these reforms, in turn, begat more change. A brief constitutional movement followed the success of the Palermo revolt in the Kingdom of Two Sicilies and the Pope, somewhat concerned about what he had started, reluctantly granted a constitution to the Papal States.

Simultaneously, civil unrest in Vienna emboldened revolutionaries in the Northern Italian provinces, then under Habsburg domination. Clemens von Metternich, Austrian Foreign Minister and architect of European stability since the defeat of Napoleon, fled Vienna when confronted by an angry mob of unemployed and disenfranchised workers. Metternich's sudden expulsion from the Habsburg capital ignited rebellion in the Italian provinces of Milan and Venice, driving Austrian troops out of the region.[29]

The political agitation along the Italian peninsula drew favorable comment in American newspapers, which saw the uprisings and reforms seen as part of the inevitable triumph of liberal principles.[30] As with France and later with Germany, some businessmen and politicians saw in the Italian transformation both a vindication of republicanism and an opportunity for improved trade relations. The reforms of the Pope in the Papal States proved so encouraging that the United States appointed

Jacob Martin as the first Charge d'Affaires to the Papal States. In his instructions to Martin, Secretary Buchanan had high praise for the "consummate wisdom and prudence" of the Pope, but also noted that America's relationship with the Papacy concerned merely temporal matters and "can only be of a commercial character." Buchanan advised Martin of the specific tariffs and duties the United States would like to have reduced or eliminated.[31]

The Polk Administration did not extend immediate recognition to all revolutionary governments as it had that of the Second French Republic. The Sicilian revolution in January 1848 did not win the approval of Secretary Buchanan and the United States, perhaps because the Administration did not expect the regime to survive for long. The United States Consul in Palermo, John Marston, perhaps inspired by the initiative of Rush, did extend recognition to the revolutionary government. Buchanan received notice of this gesture in July, but failed to respond until late October. Buchanan finally explained that, as a mere consul, Marston's authority could not extend beyond commercial matters and that the Secretary had decided the recognition was "a mere nullity in itself, would pass away & be forgotten."[32] In late July, Buchanan offered assurances to the Chevalier Martuscelli of the Kingdom of the Two Sicilies that the United States would not recognize the revolutionary government in Sicily, explaining that such a move would violate Washington's long-standing policy of non-interference in the domestic policies of other nations.[33]

The whirlwind of revolution touched the divided German states and produced demands for republican government as well as for national unification. Revolutionaries besieged the monarchies of the German Confederation, a loosely bound group of thirty small states. Prussian authorities, facing similar demands, repeatedly quelled riots in Berlin. To coordinate unification efforts, a Liberal Congress called for a parliament of all the Germanic states. This first German National Assembly met at Frankfurt in May, 1848. But creating a politically unified German state presented nearly insurmountable obstacles. Powerful conservative elements within the German Confederation, notably the state governments and the Catholic Church, stood in opposition to republicanism and the diminution of their power. Even within the Frankfurt Parliament itself there was little agreement over means and ends. Moderate liberals sought a united Germany under a constitutional monarchy as an attainable goal, while radical members favored a pure republic, without titles, classes, and monarchs.[34] The prospects of success never looked bright for the Frankfurt Parliament.

News reports of revolutionary activity in the German states produced an enthusiastic response in the United States. German-Americans, through their probity and industry, had earned the respect of their fellow citizens. And Americans took pride in the fact that a number of German theorists, to explore the means of creating a united and republican nation, were studying the United States Constitution.[35] Members of the Frankfurt Parliament sought the views of John C.

Calhoun, widely regarded as a constitutional expert. Calhoun, who had spent much of his political career assailing the expansion of federal authority at the expense of the rights of the individual states, advised Germans to avoid a powerful central government, offering the prescient observation that a strong central government would either dominate the separate states, or "more probably engender a conflict leading to dissolution." Having already publicly doubted the ability of the French to create a successful government, Calhoun contended that if any nation of Europe could create a successful republic, it would be Germany. The Senator then warned that if Germany fails, "all others probably will."[36]

The Polk Administration approached the proposed German nation in the same aggressive fashion it approached all opportunities in foreign policy. Polk had extended the nation's boundaries across the continent, made overtures to Spain about the purchase of Cuba, and pursued the best possible trade arrangements around the world.[37] When the Frankfurt Parliament presented the opportunity to bolster American commercial and ideological interests, Polk and Buchanan did not hesitate to court the German assembly. Secretary Buchanan authorized Andrew Jackson Donelson, minister to Prussia, to proceed to Frankfurt and recognize the Provisional Government of the German Confederation, "provided you shall find such a Government in successful operation."[38] This action represented a departure from the conventional procedures of the State Department, as Buchanan himself had declared that the United States recognized only those powers which had demonstrated an ability to maintain themselves in power. In this instance, the Secretary approved recognition of a government whose successful operation had not yet been demonstrated. The United States, in fact, would be the only world power to move to recognize the Frankfurt government.[39]

The move, Buchanan made clear to Donelson, was intended to facilitate the negotiation of trade agreements with a United Germany. Buchanan hoped that one central government would renegotiate tariff duties and eliminate the onerous transit duties paid by merchants moving goods between various states of the German Confederation. To this end, Buchanan advised Donelson that the tariff revision was the "most important object" of his mission. On August 7, 1848, Polk and Buchanan elevated Donelson's status from Diplomatic Representative to Envoy Extraordinary and Minister Plenipotentiary to the Frankfurt Parliament-- while holding the same rank in Berlin. The Secretary needlessly pointed out to Donelson that straddling the two positions between Frankfurt and Berlin required a certain finesse.[40]

As German theorists argued the merits of constitutional principles and various factions vied for dominance in the Frankfurt Parliament, the newly-elected French National Assembly wrestled with problems that would prove equally difficult. Radical republicans in France argued that the speed with which the elections were held, a mere two months after the fall of the King and the declaration of the Second Republic, had not allowed sufficient time to "educate" the newly enfranchised population about the issues and principles of government and economy. Their concern may have been justified, as the National Assembly voted into office by the people of France represented the traditional and conservative elements of society.[41] The differences in the aspirations of the Parisian working classes and those of the middle class of France would prove the greatest challenge to the young republic. Tribune correspondent Charles Dana observed this class animosity and believed that the middle class in France only sought political reform and greater influence in the government, not the republic which events so unexpectedly thrust upon it.[42] For their part, the workers and unemployed of Paris wanted a degree of economic security from the government and sought programs that were avowedly socialistic. To this end the Provisional Government of Lamartine and Rollin instituted the National Workshops to absorb the unemployed of Paris and reduced the workday to ten hours. These reforms proved enormously expensive and undermined the support for the Republic among the middle class.[43]

One development that sent a shudder through republican ranks in Paris was the election to the National Assembly of Louis Napoleon, nephew of the former Emperor. The name of Napoleon continued to hold magic for many Frenchmen, particularly in the provinces. The Executive Committee of the government, more liberal than the larger National Assembly, attempted without success to prohibit Napoleon from taking his place in the chamber. Even more disturbingly, a "Bonaparte mania" gathered momentum in Paris, encouraged by a nervous middle class as well as those enamored of his uncle's glory. Pamphlets and brochures boosting his qualifications for president of the republic flooded Paris, and journals dedicated to his political advancement appeared throughout the city.[44]

Working class Parisians grew increasingly restive in the month of May, as the National Assembly gave indications of rescinding measures of the Provisional Government. In early June the Assembly passed a conspiracy law more severe than any attempted under the reign of Louis Philippe; De Tocqueville would later write that the middle class felt more threatened during this period than at any time during the Great Revolution.[45] Charles Dana witnessed the tumult, indecision, and weakness of the republic in June and began to despair for France. "CHAOS" was the only word Dana felt might convey the situation in Paris during that fateful month.[46] Conflicting philosophies and class aspirations provided the underlying causes for the growing disharmony while, at the same time, the Assembly's intention to disband the National Workshops brought the hostility to the flashpoint. By June 1848, the National Workshops employed over 100,000 men and 50,000 more stood by, eager to take the pittance for any menial work offered. The National Assembly, reflecting the concerns of the middle class over the cost of the workshops and the potential dangers inherent in large labor organizations, voted to give workshop members the option of quitting the shops or joining the army and being sent to the provinces.[47]

> The brute despair of trampled centuries
> Leaped up with one hoarse yell and snapped
> its bands.

Lowell's verse vividly captures the desperation in the working class uprising known as the June Days. Threatened and angered by the reactionary spirit of the National Assembly, workers on June 23 began constructing barricades across the poorer sections of Paris, blocking narrow streets to limit the mobility and firepower of government troops. The National Assembly responded by declaring a state of siege in Paris and granting General Eugene Cavaignac dictatorial powers to end the insurrection. Some rebels challenged the government to protect the socialist aims of the Provisional Government; others fought simply to put bread on the table. Perhaps 15,000 workers took part in the uprising, which was at once vicious, bloody and heroic. After three days of fierce combat the troops of Cavaignac succeeded in suppressing the rebellion, at a cost of 500 insurrectionists slain and perhaps twice as many regular troops and National Guardsmen. Greater carnage followed the workers' defeat. The victors tracked down the scattered rebels and slew nearly 3000 in cold blood. Another 4,500 suffered jail sentences or deportation to work camps in Algeria.[48]

News of the June Days in Paris first reached American shores as did all other trans-Atlantic communications--delayed, fragmentary, and sometimes wrong. The northeastern states of America, with greater numbers of immigrants and more extensive commercial ties with the European nations, followed foreign news more avidly than other sections of the country. The region also, of course, enjoyed the quickest communications. But the sketchy nature of early reports and the delay of several weeks of foreign intelligence could only heighten the anxiety of those interested in European affairs. The rebels of the June Days had already been laid in their graves and General Cavaignac ruled as dictator over the French Republic by the time the first report reached New York: "There is no doubt that a conflict of a severe nature is actually going on."[49] Two days later the Tribune noted: "PARIS FLOODED WITH BLOOD". Bloody as the strife actually was, the story greatly overestimated the number of casualties. Southern and Western newspapers generally devoted less space to European affairs, though tragedies such as the June rebellion still aroused concern.[50]

Stories of European revolutionary activity filled American newspapers in July and left many readers wondering where the tumult would end. The New York Tribune on any given day might contain stories of military activity or civil unrest across Europe, from Ireland to Russia, from Prussia to Spain and Italy. Political conservatives saw in the June Days evidence that the French were not ready for self-government. Those concerned with business worried that the continued upheaval in Europe would further disrupt commercial activity. DeBow's Review voiced an attitude common among businessmen, condemning both the monarchy of Louis Philippe and the "excesses" of the Second

Republic. The monarchy, the journal conceded, had hampered industry and trade while the new government established programs "to pander to the passions of the dissolute, the idle and the turbulent."[51] Equally disturbing to businessmen was the militarization of the economies of Europe. The Merchant's Magazine voiced a criticism that had a timeless quality: "the swelling numbers of military idlers decrease the producers of wealth, and multiply its consumers, enterprise perishes, confidence disappears . . . ."[52] This journal also expressed the hope that civil war in France might be avoided through the efforts of the middle classes "whose interests are alike in all countries."[53] In fact, the worker's uprising in Paris did sound the tocsin for the European middle class everywhere, encouraging its alliance with the forces of absolutists against an emerging proletariat.[54]

The Second Republic did not die with the June Days, in the sense that the Great Revolution of 1789 did not end with the death of Robespierre. But for the working class in Paris the failure of the uprising in June meant the end to any socialist efforts on the part of the government. In December, Louis Napoleon won an overwhelming victory at the polls, though his commitment to republican values was at best doubtful.[55] The Republic gradually atrophied under President Louis Napoleon, until it bore only a superficial resemblance to the republic envisioned by the Provisional Government in the heady days of February 1848. On December 2, 1851, Louis Napoleon and the army seized control of the state, and proclaimed the Second Empire, with the former president assuming the position of Napoleon III, Emperor of France.

The fortunes of liberalism also suffered repeated setbacks in the German Confederation. The antagonisms of class divisions were not as apparent in Germany as in France, or at least shared the stage with political, religious and regional differences. The Provisional Government established by the Frankfurt Parliament brought together many of the society's disparate elements, whose only common bond was dissatisfaction with the old order.[56] With the moderate liberals favoring a constitutional monarchy, the radicals favoring the end to all monarchies, and neither group capable of commanding a majority within the Parliament, the government made negligible progress toward a united Germany. Occasionally elements within the provisional government did manage to function and attempted to further the interests of the proposed German nation. To this end the Minister of Commerce capitalized on his government's formal relationship with the United States and requested the services of an American naval officer to aid in the creation of a German navy.

President Polk and members of his administration immediately saw the potential for diplomatic difficulty in the request. Polk, supranationalist that he was, nevertheless had no desire to slip into any entangling association with a foreign power.[57] The President, however, wishing to encourage the proposed German nation, found a way to assist the Frankfurt Parliament without compromising American neutrality. In December the President and Secretary Buchanan sidestepped the question of constitutional legality by granting a leave of absence to Commodore Foxhall Parker for a period of two months. As a private citizen Foxhall explored the situation in Germany, found it precarious, and advised the United States not to commit itself to aid the proposed navy.

As German deliberations dragged on with no apparent success, Polk and Buchanan began to doubt the ability of the Frankfurt Parliament to forge a successful government and to unite Germany. In October and again in November Buchanan instructed Donelson that he would not yet be given authority to negotiate a treaty of commerce with the Frankfurt Parliament. He observed that no constitution had yet been written, and that the United States had already established favorable treaties with the most important maritime states of the German Confederation.58 During the following January the Polk Administration accepted Baron Von Roenne as Minister from the Provisional Government of the Frankfurt Parliament. However, several weeks later the administration directed Donelson to abandon altogether his efforts to negotiate a commercial treaty with the Frankfurt Parliament. Polk and the Democrats were about to leave office and Zachary Taylor and the Whigs were about to enter.

President Zachary Taylor, an opponent of Polk's adventures in foreign policy, immediately severed the United States' connections with the Frankfurt Parliament. Taylor ordered Donelson back to Berlin and ended America's ties with the German navy. Particularly offensive to the new President was the outfitting of the German steamer, United States which was overhauled by the Brooklyn Navy Yard as a warship for the proposed German navy. Taylor, appalled at what he considered a violation of American neutrality, scuttled the plan and demanded that the Germans post a bond guaranteeing the pacific use of the ship before it left American waters.59 The overhauling of the German steamer by the United States constituted, perhaps, the most controversial aspect of the relationship between the United States and the Frankfurt Parliament.

The Frankfurt Parliament survived for one glorious year and then dissolved as Germany's best hope for unification. The refusal of Prussia's Frederick William to wear the crown of a unified German state ended the effectiveness of the Frankfurt convocation.60 By the end of 1850 any hope for an independent, democratic Germany had succumbed to other realities. Many factions, many interest groups, many philosophies within the German states share responsibility for the ultimate failure of the parliament. Karl Marx, active in European radical circles during the revolutions of 1848, contributed articles on the German revolutionary movement to the New York Tribune. In describing German affairs for the Tribune, he wrote an epitaph for the Frankfurt Parliament that sums up rather well the obstacles to a united nation.

> When interests so varied, so conflicting, so strangely crossing each other, are brought into violent collision; when these contending interests in every district, every province, are mixed

> in different proportions; when, above all, there is no centre in the country, no London, no Paris, the decisions of which, by their weight, may supersede the necessity of fighting out the same quarrel over and over again in every single locality; what else is to be expected but that the contest will dissolve itself into a mass of unconnected struggles, in which an enormous quantity of blood, energy, and capital is spent, but which for all that remain without any decisive results?[61]

Certainly the Frankfurt Parliament produced no "decisive results," but it nevertheless offered the vision of a unified Germany, and among those observers deeply affected by the ideal was Otto von Bismarck.

    Italian nationalists confronted many of the same obstacles hindering German unity. Royalists and republicans feared each other, and the moderate constitutionalist attempted to hold the middle ground. Divided into many kingdoms and partly under the dominance of the powerful Austrian empire, the Italian peninsula nurtured widely disparate political groups. But the success of the Sicilian revolutionaries in January 1848 and the constitutional movement in central Italy encouraged a spirit of reform, and the quick and successful rebellion against Austrian troops in Milan and Venice in March of 1848 awakened Italians to the prospect of expelling the Habsburgs and unifying the nation. Yet beyond this general goal, Italian opinion differed markedly. Charles Albert, King of Sardinia-Piedmont, and in the best position to lead a coherent resistance effort, distrusted the revolutionary forces of Mazzini and Garibaldi, thus fatally weakening the Italian war effort in 1848. Pope Pius IX, fearful of the growing revolutionary sentiment, and intimidated by Austrian threats, also opposed war with the Habsburgs, thus undercutting support for Italian nationalism. The early success of Italian arms in March and April could not be sustained against the powerful, reinforced Austrian army of Count Joseph Radetzky. By the end of the year independence seemed unlikely, and by the following year, hopeless.[62]

    The Polk Administration did not embrace the revolutionary movements sweeping the Italian peninsula. Secretary Buchanan refused to recognize the insurrectionists in Sicily, supporting instead the claims of King Ferdinand II. In similar fashion, when the assembly of the Papal States declared a Roman Republic, Polk and Buchanan refused it recognition. Under pressure from New York Bishop John Joseph Hughes, and facing the potential displeasure of 1,500,000 American Catholics, the government held itself aloof.[63] Buchanan explained to Lewis Cass, the newly appointed Charge d' Affaires to the Papal States, that the Roman Republic faced "almost insuperable difficulties" and the administration considered the Pope's restoration "highly probable, if not absolutely certain."[64] Buchanan's judgment proved accurate, for in the spring of 1859, Louis Napoleon, President of the French Republic, ordered his troops to restore the Pope to his throne. After a heroic resistance from all classes within Rome, which was joined by republican idealists from all over Italy, the Republic fell.[65]

Of all the European nations riven by civil strife during 1848, Austria drew the least sympathy from Americans. Seat of reaction, commanding one of the most powerful military forces on the Continent, the polyglot Habsburg empire of Slavs, Magyars, Croats, and Italians, symbolized for Americans the tyranny of monarchy. Consequently, those who struggled against it naturally took on the the mantle of revolutionary heroes. Hungarians in particular won high praise from Americans when they broke away from the Austrian empire and under Lajos Kossuth's leadership, established a republic after Metternich's ouster from Vienna.

The Hungarian Republic survived only briefly, however, as Austrian military leaders, Prince Windischgrätz and Marshal Radetzky, reestablished the monarchy in Vienna and smashed the forces of Italian nationalists. The newly crowned Emperor Francis Joseph then turned his attention to Hungary once again. With the aid of Russian Tsar Nicholas I, who held in abeyance his distaste for the Habsburgs, Austrian and Russian armies crushed the Hungarian opposition in August, 1859. The conquerors executed many of the Hungarian leaders, but Kossuth escaped the firing squads. In the Turkish exile he sought, the Hungarian rebel came to symbolize for Americans the cause of European republicanism besieged by the forces of tyranny. The people of the United States hailed the Hungarian martyr, and American politicians, playing to popular sentiment, took up the banner of Kossuth and the fading republican cause.[66]

Lajos Kossuth, defeated on the battlefields of Europe, now came to the United States and conquered. Invited by Congress in early 1851, Kossuth arrived in the United States in December to receive a tumultuous welcome. After much acrimonious debate, a now-apprehensive Congress welcomed the Hungarian firebrand to the United States.[67] Kossuth came not as a traveler, but as a missionary, seeking American financial support and intervention in the Hungarian cause. With a wonderful command of the English language and powerful oratorical skills, the revolutionary won converts wherever he spoke. Not everyone embraced the Hungarian leader, however. Many Southerners, fearful of European retaliation against slavery, kept Kossuth at arms length. So, too, did the Catholic Church, which had suffered much at the hands of anti-clerical elements set loose by the European upheavals in 1848.[68]

An organization of Democrats called Young America managed to gain some political currency from the passions aroused by Kossuth's whirlwind tour of the United States. Driven by political self interest and the same faith and enthusiasm that powered the nation's sense of Manifest Destiny, Young Americans pushed for an aggressive foreign policy of European intervention. Championed by frontier politicians like Stephen A. Douglas, Young Americans favored the expansion of

America's overseas interests.[69] Young American leaders like George Sanders and Senator Pierre Soule maintained contacts with European revolutionary leaders plotting the end of European monarchy.[70] Whigs and conservative Southerners, however, lent their influence to deflating the schemes of the Young Americans, fearing that American involvement overseas would bring down the wrath of the European powers.

Popular enthusiasm for Kossuth and the interventionist Young Americans proved short-lived, supported as it was by merely a vague sense of international republicanism. Neither party could successfully mobilize American distaste for European despotism; the prevailing wisdom of the age upheld Washington's policy of neutrality. Gratified by the moral support engendered by his tour, but defeated in his grand design for American involvement in Hungary's struggles, Kossuth sailed from New York on Bastille Day, 1852, with little notice taken by the city which had, just eight months earlier, bestowed a rapturous welcome on the revolutionary leader.[71] The Young Americans, too, disappeared over the horizon, failing to place their candidates in office, and by 1854 had effectively disbanded.[72]

By the time of Kossuth's departure, American interest in European affairs had waned. Military might had suppressed the republican gains of 1848, and monarchy again prevailed. Though saddened by the conservative victory in Europe, Americans maintained a fervent belief that time favored the rebels and the republican cause. The rhetoric of international republicanism, of the indivisibility of liberty would be heard again, and with greater force, in the next century. Though American diplomatic efforts during the European turmoil came perilously close to abandoning the nation's traditional non-interference in European affairs, the government stopped short of active intervention. Had the United States given tangible aid to the rebels, certainly the nation would have been more vulnerable to foreign machinations during the coming Civil War. Slavery, and the threat of a divided nation, now absorbed the interest of Americans, and many European political refugees, like Germany's Carl Schurz, added their voices to the rising chorus of abolitionism.

Though the forces of reaction triumphed in the revolutions of 1848, Europe was forever changed. The thousand year reign of European monarchy was coming to an end, and all could hear the death knell of royalty in the din of that momentous year. "New faiths, new nations, new classes" made their presence felt and change could not be deferred forever.[73] Karl Marx would be heard from again, and republicans and philosophers of social reform would find their audience in later generations. Critics dismissed leaders of the revolutions as poets and philosophers, mere men of letters not public affairs. Perhaps it is fitting, then, to allow a poet the final word. Walt Whitman, whose cosmic vision of humanity looked beyond the travails of individuals and nations, saw in the failure of the revolutions the denial of liberty, but not its defeat. Liberty, the poet said, can never be defeated.[74]

> What we believe in waits latent forever through all the continents,
> Invites no one, promises nothing, sits in calmness and light, is positive and composed, knows no discouragement,
> Waiting patiently, waiting its time.

NOTES

¹James Russell Lowell, "Ode to France." in <u>The Poetical Works of James Russell Lowell</u>, (Cambridge, Massachusetts: Riverside Press, 1904), 1:257.

²<u>New York Daily Tribune</u>, 28 March 1848, p. 2.

³Thomas P. Kettell, "Money of Commerce," <u>DeBow's Review</u> 6 (October-November 1848): 245; Geoffrey Best, <u>War and Society in Revolutionary Europe, 1770-1870</u> (New York: St. Martin's Press, 1982), p. 274; and Henry Blumenthal, <u>France and the United States, Their Diplomatic Relations, 1989-1914</u> (Chapel Hill: University of North Carolina Press, 1970), p. 56.

⁴<u>New York Daily Tribune</u>, 20 March 1848, 2.; Beckles Willson, <u>America's Ambassadors to France, 1777-1927</u> (New York: Frederick A. Stokes Company, 1928), p. 218.

⁵<u>New York Daily Tribune</u>, 20-21 March 1848; Willson, <u>America's Ambassadors</u>, pp. 224-225.

⁶<u>New York Daily Tribune</u>, 28 March 1848, p. 2.

⁷<u>New York Daily Tribune</u>, 20 March 1848 and 3 April 1848; <u>Richmond Enquirer</u>, 31 March 1848; Blumenthal, France and the United States, pl. 58.

⁸<u>Weekly Chicago Democrat</u>, 4 April 1848, p. 1. For similar sentiments, see the <u>New York Daily Tribune</u>, 30 March 1848, p. 2, and the <u>Richmond Enquirer</u>, 31 March 1848, p. 1.

⁹Joseph R. Chandler, "Reflections on Some of the Events of the Year 1848," <u>Graham's American Monthly Magazine</u> 33 (December): 318-324; see also <u>Graham's Magazine</u>, 33 (July): 25-32.

¹⁰Quoted in Elizabeth Brett White, <u>American Opinion of France</u> (New York: Alfred A. Knopf, 1927), p. 120.

¹¹<u>New York Daily Tribune</u>, 20 March 1948; <u>Graham's Magazine</u>, 33: 319.

[12] Cited in Richmond Enquirer, 31 March 1848, p. 1. This issue of the Enquirer also quotes another Virginia paper condemning the "volatile and profligate community of Paris," on page one.

[13] New York Daily Tribune, 28 March 1848, p. 2.

[14] Willson, America's Ambassadors, p. 229.

[15] Eugene N. Curtis, "American Opinion of th French Nineteenth-Century Revolutions," American Historical Review, 29: 258. Not all southern newspapers joined this sudden reversal. The Richmond Enquirer praised "an immense throng" that gathered in Richmond to cheer the revolution weeks after the Provisional Government announced measures to emancipate slaves in the French colonies. See Richmond Enquirer, 28 April 1848, p. 4.

[16] Quoted in Curtis, "American Opinion," p. 261.

[17] Congressional Globe, 1st Session, 30th Congress, p. 568.

[18] New York Daily Tribune, 21 March 1848, p. 3.

[19] New York Daily Tribune, 29 March 1848, pp. 1-3.

[20] James Buchanan to Richard Rush, The Works of James Buchanan, ed. John Bassett Moore, (New York: Antiquarian Press Ltd., 1960), 3:32-33.

[21] Congressional Globe, 1st Session, 30th Congress, p. 579.

[22] Buchanan to Richard Rush, Works, p. 53.

[23] E. J. Hobsbawm, The Age of Revolution, 1789-1848 (New York: Mentor Books, 1962), pp. 45-57. See also Best, War and Society, p. 275.

[24] Francois Fejto, ed. The Opening of an Era: 1848, An Historical Symposium (New York: Howard Fertig, 1969), p. 424.

[25] Quoted in the New York Daily Tribune, 25 April 1848, p. 2.

[26] New York Daily Tribune, 28 April 1848, 0. 4.

[27] Ibid., 3 July 1848, p. 1.

[28] Quoted in the New York Daily Tribune, 21 March 1848, p. 4.

[29] New York Daily Tribune, 28 March 1848, p.1; Priscilla Robertson, Revolutions of 1848: A Social History (Princeton: Princeton University Press, 1952), pp. 331-345.

30New York Daily Tribune, 1 April 1848, p. 6. This edition carried a lengthy "Ode to Sicily" praising the island's revolutionary sentiment.

31Buchanan to Jacob Martin, Works, p. 42; see also John A. Dix, "The Papal States," DeBow's Review 6:72.

32Buchanan to John Marston, Works, pp. 234-235.

33Buchanan to Chevalier Martuscelli, Works, p. 140.

34Frank Eyck, The Frankfurt Parliament, 1848-1849 (New York: St. Martin's Press, 1968), pp. 23-26. In April, the New York Tribune offered an interesting insight into the geopolitics of this revolutionary era: ". . . there appears every probability of a war between United Germany and Russia, Poland being the battlefield. The great object of the Germans is to interpose an independent nation between themselves and Russia, and this object is distinctly avowed." What a difference a century makes. See the New York Daily Tribune, 25 April 1848, p. 3.

35Merle Curti, "The Impact of the Revolutions of 1848 on American Thought," Proceedings of the American Philosophical Society 93 (June 10, 1949): 209. See also John Gazley, American Opinion of German Unification, 1848-1871 (New York: Columbia University Press, 1926), pp. 26-27.

36John C. Calhoun, "John C. Calhoun to Baron von Gerolt," 28 May 1848, American Historical Review 40 (1935): 476-478.

37Buchanan to Romulus Saunders, Works, pp. 90-102.

38Buchanan to A. J. Donelson, Works, p. 130. See also Buchanan to A. Dudley Mann, pp. 71-72.

39Arthur J. May, "The United States and the Mid-Century Revolutions," Opening of an Era, Fejto, ed., p. 214.

40Buchanan to Donelson, Works, p. 151.

41Blumenthal, Reappraisal, p. 59; Fejto, Opening of an Era, p. 414.

42New York Daily Tribune, 14 July 1848, p. 2.

43Best, War and Society, p. 281; Fejto, Opening of an Era, p. 417.

44New York Daily Tribune, 3 July 1848 through 10 July 1848; see also Blumenthal, Reappraisal, pp. 62-63.

45Georges Bourgin, "France and the Revolution of 1848," Opening of an Era, Fejto, ed., p. 87.

46New York Daily Tribune, 3 July 1848, p. 2. Dana proved himself a keen observer of the Parisian scene. he saw the irony that universal suffrage would put Napoleon at the head of the republic "and after he has been President three years, it will be but a short step to an Emperor."

47New York Daily Tribune, 10 July 1848, p. 1; Bourgin, "France," p. 89.

48Peter N. Stearns, 1848: The Revolutionary Tide in Europe (New York: W. W. Norton & Company, 1974), pp. 89-92.

49New York Daily Tribune, 11 July 1848, p. 1.

50Gazley, American Opinion, p. 20.

51Kettell, "Money," Debow's Review, p. 251.

52The Merchant's Magazine and Commercial Review, 19 (October 1848), pp. 407-408.

53Ibid., 19 (July 1848) p. 82.

54A. J. P. Taylor, Introduction to Opening of an Era, Fejto, ed., p. XX.

55Willson, America's Ambassadors, pp. 232-233.

56Eyck, Frankfurt Parliament, pp. 394-396.

57James K. Polk, The Diary of James K. Polk (Chicago: A. C. McClurg, & Co., 19190), 4: 232-233.

58Buchanan to Donelson, Works, pp. 233,239.

59May, "United States," p. 215; Gazley, American Opinion, p. 26.

60Eyck, Frankfurt Parliament, p. 393.

61Karl Marx, Revolution and Counter-Revolution, or Germany in 1848 (London: George Allen and Unwin Ltd., 1891), p. 11.

62Delio Cantimori, "Italy in 1848," Opening of an Era, Fejto, ed., pp. 114-130.

63May, "United States," p. 210.

64Buchanan to Lewis Cass, Works, p. 332.

65Robertson, Revolutions, pp. 114-130.

[66] Best, War and Society, p. 290; May, "United States, " p. 205.

[67] Congressional Globe, 1st Session, 32nd Congress, pp. 5-92. See also Edward L. Pierce, Memoir and Letters of Charles Sumner (Boston: Roberts Brothers, 1894) 3: 269.

[68] Curti, "Impact of the Revolutions of 1848," p. 213.

[69] Merle Curti, "Young America," American Historical Review 32:43.

[70] Blumenthal, Reappraisal, p. 61.

[71] May, "United States," p. 220.

[72] Curti, "Young America," p. 54.

[73] Taylor, "Introduction," p. XV.

[74] Walt Whitman, "To a Foil'd European Revolutionaire," Leaves of Grass, ed. Sculley Bradley and others (New York: New York University Press, 1980), p. 250.

THE KAISER'S YANGTSE PATROL

by DWIGHT R. MESSIMER

"All ahead full." The engine telegraph clanged in response to the captain's order, both handles crashed against the forward stops, speeding the pointers to VOLL. SMS Vaterland shuddered under the strain of being driven at full power against the foaming river current.

"No change in bearing." The seaman's flat-voiced report was a disappointment, but no surprise to the captain. The seaman was telling the captain that the relative bearing from the ship to an object ashore had remained constant despite the full power thrust of Vaterland's twin screws.

Looking forward, the captain surveyed the rock-strewn, plunging rapids in which his ship was caught. SMS Vaterland was in trouble. Unable to move forward against the powerful current, she was using all her power just to hold her own. Without way her rudder was ineffective, which meant that it was only a matter of time until the current pushed the bow off to one side or the other. When that happened, she would be swept, sideways, down river. In that situation there was little hope that the ship could be brought about before she was driven broadside onto a rock. To survive, the ship had to make it through the rapids.

"Man poles, port and starboard." The order was quickly followed by the sounds of men shouting, and boots pounding along the side decks. SMS Vaterland's crewmen would add their brawn to the power of her engines in an effort to literally push the ship forward. Using long, steel poles, and working to the cadence shouted by petty officers, the sweating seamen rammed their poles into the rocky river bottom, and took four steps forward. Over and over the sequence was repeated--set poles, take four steps forward; set poles, take four steps forward; set poles, take four steps forward.

"Bearing change, 047; 049; 051." SMS Vaterland was inching forward. Slowly she crept through the worst of the rapids and into a section where the current was less powerful. Her straining crewmen felt the change first. It took less effort to take the four steps forward. The ship was moving, her engines driving her forward.

SMS SCHAMIEN 1899-1904
LENGTH 79' BEAM 12' DRAFT 4.5' DISP. 40 TONS

SMS VORWÄRTS 1900-1911
LENGTH 155' BEAM 25' DRAFT 5'-7'MAX. DISP. 446 TONS

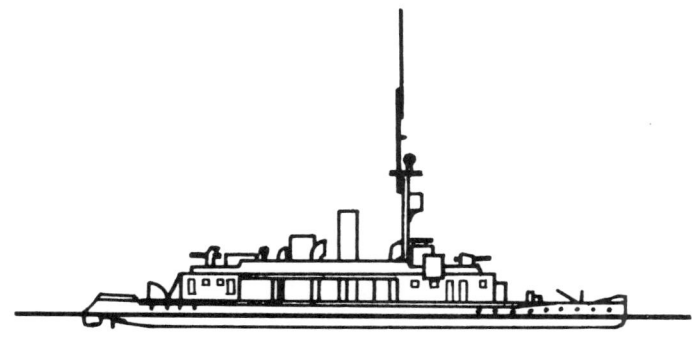

SMS TSINGTAU & SMS VATERLAND 1904-1914
TSINGTAU: LENGTH 165' BEAM 26' DRAFT 3' DISP. 308 TONS
VATERLAND: LENGTH 158' BEAM 26' DRAFT 3' DISP. 245 TONS

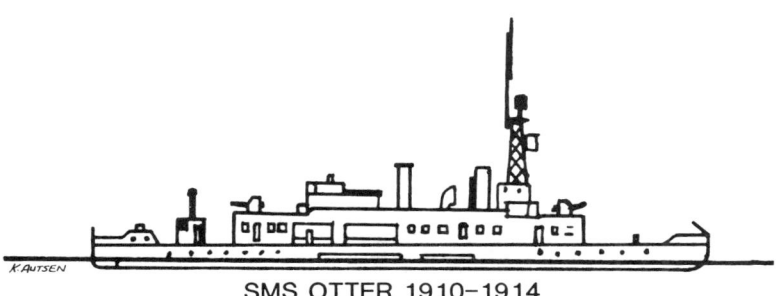

SMS OTTER 1910-1914
LENGTH 179' BEAM 29' DRAFT 3' DISP. 345 TONS

"Up poles. Stow poles." The order was heartily welcomed by the exhausted seamen. The order was also welcomed by the bridge crew. SMS <u>Vaterland</u> was underway again, She rudder controlling the ship. The danger past, the was soon clear of the rapids, steaming in quieter, deeper water. But the change was only a momentary respite. There would be more rapids; many more.[1]

SMS Vaterland was one of six, German river gunboats that operated on China's rivers from 1900 to 1914, protecting German interests in the interior of China. The river gunboats were long and narrow, with high superstructures so that the pilot and bridge crew could see over the dikes, levees, and riverbanks. They had a low freeboard and a draught of less than one meter.[2] The river gunboats could not work offshore, but could go up river as far a Kiating, nearly 1700 nautical miles inland. Starting at Shanghai, at the mouth of the Yangtse, and going up river, the ports which figured most often in German river operations were Nanking, Hankow, Ichang, and Chungking. German penetration beyond Chungking to Suifu and Kiating occurred much less frequently. Cruises up the Han River above Hankow were even more rare.[3]

In the South China area the Germans assigned only one river gunboat to the Si River, which opens at Hong Kong and Canton. Although larger ships of the German East Asia Cruiser Squadron paid regular visits to those two ports, no German warship other than the assigned river gunboat made a passage up river beyond Canton.[4]

The first river gunboat to enter service with the East Asia Squadron was the SMS <u>Schamien</u>. Privately built in 1899 as the <u>Tong Cheong</u>, she was designed to carry a few passengers and bulk cargo up river from Canton. In 1900 the German Navy bought the tiny steamer and modified it for use as a river gunboat. Twenty-four meters long and roofed over, the <u>Schamien</u> looked like the <u>African Queen</u>, or one of Disneyland's safari boats. Nevertheless, SMS <u>Schamien</u> served the purpose, operating on the SI River between Canton and Wuchow until 1904 when she was replaced by SMS <u>Tsingtau</u>.[5]

Kemp Tolly, in his book <u>Yangtse Patrol</u>, mentions a German river gunboat that was destroyed in the Kung Ling Tan rapids thirty miles above Ichang. The boat, identified as the <u>Sui Hsiang</u>, was making her maiden voyage as a German warship on 25 December 1900 when she was wrecked. There is no description of the boat, but she was probably a small vessel built by a private firm in China, and, like the <u>Schamien</u>, was bought and converted by the German Navy.[6]

That same year the German navy bought a vessel which became one of the prettiest river gunboats ever commissioned; SMS <u>Vorwärts</u>. She owed her pleasing lines to her builders, Farnham, Boyd, and Company in Shanghai, who designed her as a passenger steamer for the Hong Kong, Canton, and Macao Steamboat Company. Laid down in

1899, she was launched in 1900 as the ninety-nine passenger SS Woochow. But before she was completed, the German Navy bought the Woochow and put her into a yard at Shanghai for conversion to a river gunboat.[7]

Because the Germans were essentially tenants in the British Naval Yard, work on the boat was given a low priority. It was not until March 1901 that she was relaunched as the SMS Vorwärts. The Vorwärts, modern in every respect, was not a "make-do" boat like Schamien and Sui Hsiang had been. Her only drawback was that she was equipped with an underpowered engine, and could not overcome the rapids and river currents above Ichang. For that reason the Vorwärts spent her operational life confined to the middle and lower Yangtse.[8] Despite the drawback, she remained in service until June 1910 when she was sold in Shanghai.[9]

In 1904 two river gunboats designed and built specifically for use on the Yangtse were delivered. Both boats had been built in Germany by F. Schichau and then disassembled and shipped by freighter to China. One, SMS Tsingtau, went to Hong Kong for reassembly, and the other, SMS Vaterland, went to Shanghai.

They were identical boats each built with nine prefabricated hull sections and a separate prefabricated superstructure. Both were powered by two, three-cylinder, triple-expansion, steam engines developing a total of 1300 horsepower. Those powerful engines, plus twin screws housed in protective tunnels, and a draught of just .94 meter, made Tsingtau and Vaterland capable of working up river far beyond the previous operational limits. SMS Tsingtau spent her entire operational life on the Si River while Vaterland served on the Yangtse for which she, like Tsingtau , had been designed.[10]

In April 1910, SMS Otter, a bigger and more powerful river gunboat, arrived in Shanghai and was reconstructed. Like Tsingtau and Vaterland, she had been built in Germany and shipped in nine prefabricated pieces to China. She was similar in appearance to the two older boats and, though longer and heavier, had about the same draught. SMS Otter patrolled the Yangtse river with the Vaterland.[11]

The organization of the crews on the river gunboats was the same as found on every ship of the Imperial German Navy. The seamen were divided into port and starboard divisions, each division commanded by an officer who was responsible for training and discipline. The men in those two divisions were the people who stood the watches, and were responsible for the operation and maintenance of the ship. Both watches provided men to man the guns and form the landing parties, but those men were not exempted from the normal ship's routine and watch duty.

In addition to the seamen, there were the technical personnel. Much fewer in number, those specialists operated and maintained the steam machinery; an assignment that exempted them from watches on the bridge, or any other watch outside their special areas. They were never included in the landing parties or routine deck and hull maintenance. Understandably, the technical personnel considered themselves a cut above the seamen. In return, the seamen saw the engineers as a bunch of pampered slobs who made a regular practice of walking across freshly swabbed decks in their dirty boots.

Whether seaman or engineers, every man not on duty or standing watch made reveille, and took his morning bath. Reveille came with the shrill of the NCO's whistle, launching the scramble to roll and stow hammocks, and tumble out on deck. The scramble was for good cause. Watchful NCO's stood by the doors timing the men, assigning extra duty to the last few out. Additional goals of the race to the main deck were several small buckets of water. The first men to reach them had clean water for their morning bath. Those who were less swift, and the latecomers, made do with dirty, soapy water.

After the bath and morning inspection, the daily ship's routine began. When not standing a two-hour watch, the men performed maintenance, studied for promotional exams, and took part in the continuous training cycle. For most of the men a large part of their time was spent scrubbing the wood decks and repainting the hull and superstructure. German river gunboats, with their pale yellow superstructure and graceful white hull stripe, looked more like yachts than warships.

During the midafternoon, while the crew went about its duties, the captain handled the disciplinary problems which were too severe to be handled by the executive officer. Violators that could be given extra duty or restricted to the ship for short periods were not taken before the captain. He heard only those cases that could result in confinement to the ship's brig or a court martial. A man who was court martialed could be sent to prison or shot. Problems of that type were rare. When the captain did hear a serious case, he usually confined the man to the ship's brig; a decision that kept the crew from being a man short, and kept his problems on his own ship.

The brig on a river gunboat, a small metal cell in the boiler room, was particularly unpleasant. But the seaman assigned to guard the cell had it as bad or even worse than the prisoner did. Terrible heat, the clanging engine noise, mosquitos, and the dimly lighted area were suffered by both prisoner and guard. The prisoner could at least lie dow if he were tired, and strip if he got too warm. The guard on the other hand, was required to remain on his feet, fully dressed, and armed. While the prisoner could close his eyes and think about his sins, or more pleasant thoughts, the guard had to look in on the prisoner regularly and keep the brig log. Failure to perform those duties as required meant that the guard would be the cell's next occupant.[12]

Guarding the brig was an assignment that the seamen hated, but they were spared the equally onerous job of coaling the ship. That was done by Coolies.[13] Though they did not have to carry coal buckets, the German sailors still dreaded coaling. One of the worst features of the coal-burning era was the filth and grime of coal dust. On coaling day coal dust settled in great clouds over the ship. It covered everything, sifted through gratings, and choked the air in the lower decks. Coal dust collected in thousands of corners, cracks, and seams throughout the ship. The black grime was ground underfoot into the wood decks and made ugly smudges on the pale-colored deck houses. German sailors did not have to carry coal, but they did clean up the mess.

The Germans relied heavily on native labor for operating and maintaining the river gunboats. In fact, the river gunboats were designed with accommodations for Chinese crewmen who were divided into two categories; regular and special employees. The regular Chinese crewmen were long-term employees who filled slots as stokers, cooks, and stewards. The head Chinese crewman was the river pilot who, despite his title, never laid a hand on the ship's wheel. The steering was done by one of his two assistants.[14]

The Chinese pilot and his helmsman navigated the ship at all times except during an emergency, when transiting rapids, and when docking. During those three circumstances the German helmsman and the officer of the deck took over.

The Chinese who regularly served on German vessels spoke pidgin-english and a few knew a smattering of German. Almost without exception their native language was Cantonese, and so long as the boat remained in the assigned patrol area, that was good enough.[15]

But whenever the ship navigated outside its regular patrol area, special employees were taken aboard. Most often they were pilots, Mandarin-speaking interpreters, and photographers. The special employees were usually hired through the local German consulate, but in some cases the Germans relied on the British and French for recommendations.[16]

Without exception the interpreter, an unemployed government official, had the responsibility of selecting the pilot to guide the boat through the unfamiliar waters. He also conducted the negotiations for their fee--which meant that the job went to the pilot who offered the interpreter the biggest kickback.[17]

To pay the Chinese crewmen, buy coal, food, and anything else needed to operate a river gunboat on an isolated duty station, the captain was issued a strong box filled with Mexican silver dollars.[18] In fact, he used that money to pay for everything except ammunition and the annual yard fees.[19] As a result the river gunboat captains became experts at budget planning and barter.

The isolated position of the small boats also made their captains more self-reliant. They experimented with burning wood so that if their coal supply vanished they would know what to expect of their machinery.[20] They stockpiled coal reserves, supplemented their food supplies by hunting, and saved pilot expenses, whenever possible, by putting a leadsman out in a small boat ahead of the warship.[21]

Piloting on rivers, where the water level rose and fell as much as 15 meters on a seasonal cycle, was always a challenge. Generally, the rivers were high during the summer, with July and August being the best months. It was, however, never a sure thing, and the water level rose and fell from day to day, and even from hour to hour. To assist in gauging the water level, and the river's activity, the British had installed marker stakes from Shanghai to Kiating and Suifu.[22]

The gunboats operating in China were faced with all the problems normally associated with river navigation. There was, however, one feature on the rivers which presented the gunboat captains with a new, and different challenge--rapids.

Rapids existed between the coast and Hankow, and up to Ichang. They were a problem, but not insurmountable, and did not approach the ferocity of the rapids on the upper Yangtse.[23] As a gunboat went farther up river, the rapids became more vicious. At high water the boulder-strewn rapids became foaming cataracts, while at low water they were so shallow that even a leaf ran aground.

Transiting the rapids was not a straight line operation. The route lay between rocks, boulders, and also conformed to the twists and turns of the riverbed. There were times when full power could not overcome the surging current. When this happened the crewmen used steel poles, as was described earlier, to push the gunboat against the streaming water while the engines were run at full power.[24]

The river's power is evident when a boat developing 1300 horsepower had to use full power, and then flank speed, to breast the current. When one considers that there were times when human muscle had to be thrown in to the struggle to overcome the rapids, the magnitude of the problem comes into clear focus.

Rapids were not the only problems caused by the currents. The strong currents also cut and eroded the river bottom and its banks, scooping up millions of tons of soil and washing it down river. The result was that Chinese rivers were often characterized by a yellowish brown color. The muddy color meant special problems, and one of them involved getting an anchor up after it had been down a while. German river gunboat captains soon learned that an anchor had to be brought up and reset at least once every three days, or silt and mud buried them so deeply that they could not be gotten up.[25] In some cases, the anchor had to be resited each day. A captain could not afford to lose an anchor, and paid close attention to silting.

The same mud that buried anchors created new shoals and bars, and silted in channels. The strong current moved tons of mud and debris, and tumbled stones into new locations. The known obstacle which was here today was gone tomorrow, and a new one popped up where none had been before. The rise and fall of the rivers, their general shallowness, and the constantly changing character of the river beds made running aground a problem at any time of year.

The assistance of a good pilot, and careful attention to the French survey charts, reduced the hazard. But despite all the precautions, German gunboats got stuck. Getting unstuck was a matter of routine, the method used varying with the circumstances and the type of grounding. The method used to get off, and its success or failure, depended largely on the ingenuity and proficiency of the man in commend. It speaks well for the Germans that none of the four river gunboats that served between 1901 and 1914 were lost due to grounding. It is a record that the British cannot equal.[26]

When a German river gunboat went aground, the captain could usually expect one of the other foreign gunboats to help pull him off. There were enough of them on the river that one usually could be expected to come along before matters got completely out of hand. A full ration of good natured kidding went along with the assistance--but even the Germans could live with that.

In addition to foreign gunboats there were many steam-powered Chinese boats plying the rivers. Almost without exception they adamantly refused to help a stranded gunboat. The Chinese boaters' lack of cooperation may have resulted from what the Germans described as a total disregard for the law of the sea and rules of the road by the Chinese. More likely it was a matter that the Chinese boatmen did not like foreigners.

All those problems, and more, were covered in a publication put out by the German Admiralty called Das Yangtse Handbuch. Intended to assist the captain who commanded a boat anywhere in China, it was analogous to the United States Coast Pilot. Thought the Handbuch was updated every year, it was not entirely satisfactory. In fact, in 1914, Oberleutnant zur See Drehsler, commanding the Vaterland, described it as nearly useless. Conditions changed so often and so quickly, he said, that the Handbuch never seemed to have the right information. Most captains left the book in its locker, relying on their own seamanship and their pilot's knowledge.[27]

Rapids, shoals, rapidly changing conditions, and anchoring problems were things the German skippers took in stride. Surviving those natural hazards was a matter of seamanship. But surviving the rivers' human hazards was in the Germans' opinion, a matter of luck. As a result, the human hazards were the subject of much bitter comment.[28]

The rivers were always crowded with junks and sampans. And the number increased as the rivers rose, and trade picked up. River traffic was very heavy in September and October when the harvest was being brought in, and the junks and sampans were joined by a hoard of rowboats, punts, and towed boats. Congestion near any village, town, landing, or the confluence of two rivers was so bad that, in some cases, passage for large steam driven boats was impossible.

Among the lowest orders of life, in the eyes of a German river gunboat skipper, were the people who sailed sampans. Not much higher on the scale were the junk operators. Those Chinese craft sailed up, down, and across the river without regard to the "rules of the road," complained the Germans. What the Germans failed to realize was that the Chinese boatmen had no rules of the road. The thing which most annoyed the Germans was the way the Chinese boatmen rafted their vessels from the shore into the main channel. The result was a solid wall of boats around which the much bigger river gunboats could not pass.

German captains exercised the utmost caution when transiting heavily congested areas, but collisions with Chinese boats did occur. In some cases the traffic jam was so bad that a warship could not get through no matter how hard the steam siren was blown, or how menacing the bow looked as it nosed slowly forward. At about that point the Chinese police usually showed up in a steam launch to clear a path through the teeming mass of houseboats, junks, and sampans.[29] How they accomplished that seemingly impossible job is not explained in the German reports. But the Chinese police, less concerned about causing an incident than were the German captains, obviously had more options in the methods they could use. There were three reasons for the German's strong desire to avoid an incident.

In the first place the German navy was operating its base at Tsingtao as a model colony. The fact that the navy was running the colony was a major departure from the usual practice of leaving that function to the Ministry of Colonial Affairs. There were several reasons why the navy had taken control of the colony. In part it was because Navy officers were disgusted with the mismanagement which was evident in the German African colonies. They were particularly vocal about condemning the shoddy way the Africans had been treated by the German civilian administrators.[30] The Navy, intending to do better in Tsingtao, created the policy, and practice, followed by German gunboat captains, of respecting the Chinese and their property.

The second reason was based on Germany's exposed position in China. German officials and businessmen wanted to expand German influence and interests in China, but they had to be careful not to seriously upset the other foreign powers while they did it. They were, after all, operating 10,000 nautical miles from home. And if they got themselves into a shooting match there was no hope for relief. The Germans were literally out on a limb and they knew it. For that reason they usually backed away from any confrontation.

The Germans recognized that the situation in China would someday result in a military confrontation. But the Germans were not sure who would be on their side and who would not.[31] In any event, it would hardly do to overly antagonize the host, since if war came a neutral China would be the only place where the Germans could find a safe port. Their fears were well founded as the events in 1914 proved.

The German Navy held the view that its gunboats were in China to protect German commercial interests. To succeed in that mission they had to help provide the atmosphere in which German capital investments could prosper. Therefore any act by a German gunboat, or member of its crew, that caused a negative Chinese reaction interfered with the fulfillment of the mission. As antiforeign feeling in China became more intense, agitators were able to use just about any reason to work up a mob to attack foreigners and their property. Even a minor scrape with a Chinese boat could cause a full blown riot ashore. It was the desire to avoid that type of provocation that gave the German Navy the third reason for avoiding an incident. The collective result of those three concerns was that German navy officers showed more restraint in dealing with the Chinese than did their foreign counterparts.[32]

Though the Germans enjoyed good relations with the other foreign and Chinese gunboats, there are reports that the German crews got along better with the French and the Americans than with the British. The reason given for the bad German-British relations was the animosity caused by the growing naval rivalry between the two countries.[33]

On the other hand, there were claims that the Germans got along fine with the British but detested the French. In that case the blame was placed squarely on the French who, the story goes, wanted revenge for the loss of Alsace and Lorraine in 1871. Driven by their thirst for revenge, the French were rude to the Germans and caused all sorts of trouble.[34]

There was also an opinion that the Germans thought the British and the French were nice fellows, but the Americans were intolerable. The British and French were, afterall, Europeans suffering the same low pay as the Germans. The Americans, however, were loud-mouthed showoffs who were paid more money than they were worth, and bought up everything in sight.[35]

Each of those three views depended entirely on the attitude of the person telling the story. In part they are all correct, but none represents the prevailing German attitude at any time between 1898 and 1914. In fact, the Germans got along with everyone on about the same terms.

Despite the Cruiser Squadron's well deserved reputation for cooperation, there was one group with which they did not always see eye to eye. The group was the German Consular Corps in China. There was no open animosity between the two organizations, but just below the surface of their apparently cooperative relationship there was a ripple of disagreement. The rift, if it can be called that, centered on the issue of who had the final say about when and where the river gunboats would be sent, and for how long they would stay.

Both the Cruiser Squadron and the diplomats agreed that their joint function was to look after German interests. The diplomats argued, with some justification, that those interests were primarily a Foreign Office matter. The Navy did not object to that viewpoint. Next, the diplomats argued that the Cruiser Squadron was a military resource to be drawn upon. Again the Navy did not object. The diplomats, then took the position that since the squadron was a resource at the disposal of the Consular Corps, the river gunboats should be deployed according to the needs as seen by the diplomats. The Navy did not agree with that. Instead, the Navy argued that requests for deployment made by the various consuls would be accepted, but would be acted on only if the conditions for safety and tactical effectiveness were present. Therefore, decisions pertaining to time, place and length of deployment could only be made by the squadron planning staff.[36]

There was an annual plan for deployment which was arranged to give the maximum coverage with the few units available. The squadron planners felt that the schedule they used put the squadron in the best position to carry out its mission. The plan, which was set up on a quarterly basis, took into consideration several broad requirements as well as some which were specific. Among the broad requirements was the need to support the German diplomats. Also considered were seasonal changes in the rivers and the limitation they imposed on the boats. Within those requirements there was some flexibility in making assignments.

There were, however, three administrative considerations that made scheduling a rigid affair. Rarely could civilian demands be allowed to interfere with those three requirement. In order of importance they were: 1. the annual crew exchange, 2. annual haulout, and 3. annual individual ship's training. On the surface it would seem that the annual crew exchange would be of less importance than items two and three. Not so.

Every year, in early spring, replacements were sent from Germany to relieve the squadron personnel whose tours were up. Because every ship, from cruisers to river gunboats, replaced half its crew at the same time, the movement involved several hundred men.[37] The river gunboats, alone, received nearly one hundred new crewmen.[38] Getting hundreds of replacements to their ships was not a difficult thing to do if the schedule was kept.

The German Navy contracted with a German shipping line to carry replacements to Tsingtao. The trip from Germany to China took thirty-nine to forty-two days. Each spring, in anticipation of the replacement ship's arrival, the squadron's larger ships were deployed along China's coast from Hong Kong to Tsingtao, while the river gunboats moved down river, to Hong Kong and Shanghai.

As the steamer worked its way up the China coast, it put replacements aboard the waiting ships and took their returnees on board. By the time the transport docked in Tsingtao, the sailors still on board were the replacements assigned to the cruisers, and the returnees from the smaller warships.[39] The efficient system eliminated the expense and trouble of transporting replacements from Tsingtao to their ships. The system also allowed the larger ships to be dispersed along the coast, instead of being forced to group in one place at the same time. Understandably, the Navy opposed anything that interfered with that efficient plan.

For equally good reasons, the squadron planners were insistent that each ship follow a regular maintenance schedule. Without regular maintenance the ships would simply fall apart. Bottoms would become so fouled that speed would be dramatically reduced, boilers would cease developing the required pressures, and rust would eat up steel. Regular maintenance could be delayed for a while, but it could not be ignored. For the bigger ships it was a fairly simple matter of scheduling dry dock time in the German naval base at Tsingtao. For the river gunboats it was a wholly different matter.

The river gunboats were hauled out at two British yards; Hong Kong and Shanghai. The British gave priority to their own needs, and accepted all others, including the Germans, on a "space available" basis. The Germans had to make arrangements as much as nine months in advance, and even then the date was subject to change. Emergency repairs--short of avoiding a sinking--suffered equal delays.[40] As the boats got older, their yard time became more frequent and lasted longer.[41]

The third consideration, training, was handled in two ways. The first method, on-board training, was particularly intense after the new crews were received.[42] Such on-the-job training was continuous, and did not disturb the annual deployment planning. But the second type of training, individual training, involved exercises in infantry drill and landing parties. Every German sailor received infantry training when he was a raw recruit. For most of the sailors that initial experience was the first and last time they had anything to do with it, although from time to time they were again exposed to it. For the river gunboat crews infantry training was as regular as damage control, or man overboard drill.

The larger ships went to Tsingtao for one month each year to practice gunnery and amphibious assault. Naval infantry and civilian volunteers played the enemy role in those exercises. The river gunboats conducted the same annual training, but on the river. <u>Vorwärts</u> and <u>Vaterland</u> exercised their guns in the Wonson roads, and held mock landings in Shanghai and Hankow.[44] Their enemy was the volunteer German militia. When <u>Otter</u> replaced <u>Vorwärts</u> the routine was the same for her. SMS Tsingtau stationed in South China, did her gunnery in the mouth of the Si River, near Hong Kong, and her landing exercises were done without opposition on a beach near Canton.[45]

Though individual training was important, the German planners recognized that, if necessary, the schedule could be adjusted. They could also do some juggling when scheduling the haulouts. Those options, though undesirable, did give the planners some leeway when considering the demands made by the German diplomats. Still, German naval planners, victims of bureaucratic order, placed strong emphasis on keeping the three requirements of crew relief, haulout, and training according to schedule. Their insistance on that did not make the Consular Corps happy.

The argument between the Cruiser Squadron staff and the diplomats went on unabated until 1914. Each year the diplomats gained more ground while the Navy officers tried to convince themselves that the Navy view had prevailed. By the time the war started, the major decisions regarding gunboat and river gunboat deployment were being made by the German Consular Corps.[46]

The outbreak of World War I was not a complete surprise. But the alignment of sides--everyone against the Germans--had not been expected by the Germans.[47] The river gunboats, unable to leave their rivers, had no choice but to intern themselves in neutral China.

When the war started, Otter was on the upper Yangtse near Chungking, and Vaterland was patrolling the middle Yangtse between Ichang and Hankow. Both boats made it to Nanking where they interned themselves.[48] In order to keep the boats from being seized, should China declare war on Germany, the boats were "civilianized". This was done by selling them to a dummy German corporation. To complete the charade Vaterland was renamed Landesvater and Otter became München. Despite the ruse both boats were seized by the Chinese in Marach 1917. Vaterland was renamed Li Sui, and Otter became Li Tscheh. Both went into the service of the Chinese Navy on the Yangtse.[49]

Tsingtau , alone on the Si River, interned herself in Canton. There is no record of her having been "sold" as were Vaterland and Otter. In March, 1917, she was scuttled to prevent seizure by the Chinese.[50]

The Germans' river gunboat operations were never resumed, and today few people know that they even existed. But during the early years that foreign navies were operating fleets of river gunboats in China, the Germans were among the most considerate and efficient operators.

NOTES

[1]Deutsches Zentralarchiv, Potsdam, Microfilm OG. 02 "Verteilungspläne 1907-1914." (Hereafter cited as OG. 02 followed by the

specific document). The event described is based on reports taken from this microfilm.

2Erich Gröner, Die Deutsche Kriegsschiffe, 1815-1945 (Müunchen: J. F. Lehmann's Verlag, 1966), p. 203-204; and Dr. Werner Gast, "Erinnerung an China," Mitteilungsblatt N 58 (August 1978) p. 2-7.

3OG. 02, "Verteilungspläne 1907-1914."

4Ibid.

5Gröner, p. 205.

6Kemp Tolly, Yangtse Patrol (Annapolis: Naval Institute Press, 1971), p. 51.

7Gröner, p. 205.

8Ibid.; and OG. 02 Verteilungspläne 1907-1914." Vorwärts had two, 2 cylinder, upright, double expansion steam engines which developed a total of 500 horsepower.

9Gröner, p. 205-206.

10OG. 02 "Verteilungspläne 1907-1914."

11Ibid.; Otter had two, 3 cylinder, upright triple expansion engines which were the same type as were used on Tsingtau and Vaterland. Otter's engines developed 1718 horsepower and turned propellers which were 1.8 feet greater in diameter than those on the other two boats.

12Hans H. Matthiesen, "Meine Dienstzeit auf einem Kanonen-boot in Ostasian, 1910-1912." A typewritten narrative in the author's possession.

13Ibid.; and Marineschule Mürwick, Flensburg/Mürwick, Fritz Brehmer "Die Fahrt S. M. S. Tsingtau in die südchinesische Provinz Kuangsi, Juli-August, 1906." Die Flotte Nr. 1 (Januar-Mai 1908), p. 7.

14Gröner, p. 203-206. The Vorwärts had three Chinese, Tsingtau and Vaterland had nine, and Otter used three to five.

15Brehmer, p. 6. Whenever a gunboat, in nearly every case a river gunboat, made a trip beyond its normal patrol area, a special pilot was taken aboard. The pilots were usually Chinese, although the Germans sometimes used the Englishman, Cornelius Plant, for trips to Chungking. Plant was a French contract pilot who also operated a pilot firm in Chungking. If he was not available the Germans used one of his employees. On the Han River, above Handow, several pilots were hired from among the local boatmen. The pilot was taken aboard for a particular section of the river and then replaced by one who had knowledge about the next section. In this way a trip on the Han required the services of several successive pilots. The Han was particularly difficult to navigate, and, even with a pilot aboard, groundings were a regular occurrence.

16Ibid.

17Ibid.

18Matthiesen.

19Ibid.

20Ibid., Kapitänleutnant Brehmer found that he was able to get 250 rpm by burning just wood. A wood/coal mix increased the rpm to 270. The power developed was not enough to get him through the rapids so he saved his coal for that purpose. In practice German gunboats rarely burned wood. Coal was plentiful, and wood created spark showers that endangered the ship.

21An unfortunate event occurred shortly after Vaterland was ordered up river to Chungking in 1907. That summer one of the boat's NCOs took a few days leave and went hunting in the area around Kialing. He had been drinking and got into an argument with two Chinese. Things got out of hand and the sailor shot both Chinese in the face with his shotgun, blinding both of them. It was the sort of incident which the Germans wanted to avoid and resulted in tighter restrictions on hunting by anyone other than an officer. OG. 02 "Kaiserlich Deutsches Konsulat für die Provinze Szetschuan, Chungkin, Nr. 805, 8. Nov. 1907.

22OG. 02, "Kommando S.M.S. Otter: Reisebericht über die Fahrt Tschungking nach Suifu, 16-22 Juli, 1914." Because of the stakes, the Germans always reported the water depth in feet and inches. It is curious to read a German captain's report in which he says that he anchored in eight feet, three inches of water and put out sixty meters of anchor chain.

23Gast, p. 5.

24OG. 02, "Kaiserlich Deutscher Konsul an den Deutschen Gesandten in Peking, Bericht Nr. 2015, 13. Mai, 1907."

25Tolly, p. 62; and Bundesarchiv-Militärarchiv, Freiburg/Breigsgau, "Kommando S.M.S. Vaterland: Bericht über die Fahrt auf dem Han Fluss, April/Mai, 1914." (Herafter cited as Vaterland).

26Actually the German safety record was excellent during the time they operated in China. Despite the extraordinary navigation problems and dangers encountered in China's rivers they lost only two vessels in accidents between 1898 and 1914. They were the S.M.S. Taku and the S.M.S. Sui Hsiang. German captains used French charts almost exclusively while navigating on the rivers. The French had surveyed the Yangtse as far up as Chungking by 1903 and had made a rough survey from there to Kiating. The British and the Germans also made surveys but German emphasis was along the Chinese coast. Off shore surveys were part of the duties of the four big gunboats, <u>Iltis</u>, <u>Jaguar</u>, <u>Tiger</u> and <u>Luchs</u>.

27<u>Vaterland</u>.

28Nearly every report (Reisebericht) made by a German captain contains some comment on the problems encountered with Chinese boatmen. The best description is given by Brehmer, p. 22-23.

29Ibid., p. 22-23.

30John A. Moses and Paul Kennedy, ed., <u>Germany in the Pacific and Far East, 1870-1914</u> (Queensland: University of Queensland Press, 1977), p. 131. and pp. 189-195.

31Gast, p. 4.

32It is also interesting that among the many documents used for this research, there was virtually no mention of the Germans having used armed force against the Chinese. There is no doubt that the Germans landed armed sailors to protect German property when it was necessary. If during these landings they fired on the Chinese there was no mention of it. Both the Americans and the British write a great deal about their use of force.

33Gast, p. 6.

34Marineschule Mürwick, anonymous, "17 Kapitel."

35Matthiesen, p. 9. He does not come down quite this hard on the Americans but he does say that the American sailors' pay was much higher than that of the Germans. He suggests that the Ameraican insistence on paying for everything was more show-off than friendship.

36OG. 02, "Kommando des Kreuzergeschwaders Nr. 6536" and attached report from "Kommando S.M.S. <u>Otter</u>, 13 August 1910"; and "Kaiserlich Deutsches Konsulat für die Provinz Szetschuan Nr. 401, 18 April 1910," also "Kommando des Kreuzergeschwaders Nr. 68, 25 Oktober 1911."

37Matthiesen, p. 1; and OG. 02 "Ablösungspläne 1907-1914."

38Gröner, p. 203-207. The number is obtained by adding the crew figures and dividing the total in half. Each river gunboat carried forty-five to forty-seven German crewmen.

39Matthiesen, p. 2-3; and OG.02 "Ablösungspläne 1907-1914."

40 Moses and Kennedy, p. 115-116.

41 OG. 02 "Verteilungspläne, 1907-1914."

42 Gast, p. 3; and Matthiesen, p. 2-3.

43 OG. 02 "Verteilungspläne 1907-1914."

44 Ibid.; and Matthiesen, p. 8.

45 OG. 02 "Verteilungspläne 1907-1914."

46 Dwight Messimer, "Gunboats and Diplomats," <u>The American Neptune</u>, April 1980, pp. 85-99. Complete details of the dispute are described in the article.

47 Gast, p. 4.

48 Gröner, p. 206.

49 Ibid.

50 Ibid.

THE GERMAN PRISONERS OF WAR IN JAPAN
1914-1920

by URSULA R. MOESSNER

When war broke out in 1914, the world's interest focused on Europe. It was there that the battles were fought; it was on European soil where the powers decided the outcome of the struggle. In another part of the world, in China, German soldiers defended Tsingtao, port city of Kiaochow, the German leasehold colony, against the Japanese. The siege lasted from August to November 1914 and ended in a Japanese victory. The Japanese made 4,592 prisoners.

The story of these prisoners in Japanese prison camps is unusual. Compared with the hardships other nation's war prisoners experienced in Japanese prison camps during the Second World War, the picture that emerges is one of detention without malice. The tolerant attitude towards the German POWs expressed by the Japanese military authorities had many reasons but can most likely be attributed to the following circumstances.

Germany and Japan had never been enemies in the past. No war had ever been fought between the two countries and no deep-seated hatred or even animosity existed between the two countries. Japan respected Germany for her industrial expertise and her organizational talents. On the threshold of becoming an industrialized nation herself, Japan tried to emulate the advances Germany had made in the fields of modern technology and warfare. This became evident when in 1905 commanders of the Japanese Army invited representatives of the German Army to train the Japanese Army to fight a modern war.

The reason for the brief confrontation between Germany and Japan in August of 1914 was due more to immediate circumstance than to any long-range design. Japan, allied with England since 1902, saw the war as an opportunity to extend her territory into China. Germany held some such territory. It was Tsingtao, the port city of Kiaochow, which Germany had acquired in 1896 as a leasehold colony.

Encouraged by a promise of support from London, the Japanese on August 15 issued a demand to the German Governor of Tsingtao that called for the surrender of the German military forces in China and of the protectorship itself by August 23. The German Governor refused to comply with this demand, even though he had only a small force of men at his disposal to defend the protectorate. It consisted of approximately 3,500 colonial soldiers as well as about 1,000 reservists who arrived from all over Asia, and the crew of the ancient Austrian Cruiser <u>Kaiserin Elisabeth</u> (286 men) which happened to be in the harbor of Tsingtao.

In contrast, the Japanese had at their command 58,000 Japanese and 2,000 British soldiers. On August 27, 1914 they started a siege that lasted until November 7th, when the garrison at Tsingtao was forced to surrender.[1] The Japanese then took 4,592 prisoners. The prisoners were taken to prison camps on three of the four islands of Japan. Between October and December 1914, the Japanese military authorities had established 15 camps to house the prisoners, with 5 camps each on the islands of Kyushu, Shikoku and Honshu. The camps were located on the outskirts of 12 major cities.[2]

The captured Germans did not anticipate a long prison time. They believed that the war in Europe would be over soon, and that Germany would, of course, be victorious. It was this unshaken belief in German strength and in God, Kaiser and Fatherland (which many of their German comrades exposed to the horrors of the Western Front were soon questioning) that sustained many of the prisoners during the five years of their captivity.

The Japanese military authorities never discouraged the Germans' display of patriotism and, with an understanding for the importance of honor, they even permitted the German officers to keep their swords as a symbol of personal dignity.[3] Also, on a more pragmatic level, the officers were allowed to keep their orderlies.

Since a suitable locale for prison camps was not readily available in most of the twelve Japanese cities, housing was often poor. In Tokushima, for instance, the city's small municipal buildings had to serve as a prison camp. Osaka provided old wooden sheds, originally built as emergency shelter for fire victims. Kurume lodged the prisoners in an old army camp, which had detained Russian prisoners of war during the 1904-05 Russo-Japanese war. An old school building provided shelter for some of Oita's prisoners and the camps at Marugame, Matsuyama and Himeji, Asakusa and Nagoya had formerly been temples.

The rules and regulations issued by the Japanese military authorities to the camp commanders stressed the correct and humane treatment of the prisoners, and left it to the camp commander's discretion to interpret these rules with regard to the prisoners' daily activities.[4]

Most of the camp commanders, especially those of the smaller camps, were interested in an amicable relationship with the prisoners, and therefore tended to be lenient. The men could go for walks outside the camp, and do voluntary work inside the camp. In the camp of

Tokushima, for instance, the commander encouraged improvements of all kinds. He encouraged the craftsmen among the prisoners to repair the repairable, and to continue in their vocations if at all possible. Soon carpenters started to build furniture; a butcher started a butcher shop; bakers a bakery. Men with knowledge about the printing business set up a print shop and published a camp newspaper, and those with musical talents formed an orchestra.

With fine insight into the human psyche, the commander knew that an individual's self esteem pivoted around his ability to work, create and accomplish. Consequently, when a Japanese firm from the town of Tokushima needed some experienced machinists, the commander offered the positions to his prisoners. Six accepted. The firm offered permanent positions to the six men, and ultimately employed fourteen prisoners.[5]

The men who voluntarily worked in town received pay for their labor. The firm paid a salary which the men could use to supplement their daily food rations, since the amount contributed by the Japanese government did not adequately cover all the necessities. This was not a matter of ill will on the Japanese's part. The Japanese government did follow the rules promulgated at the Hague Convention of 1907, which specified that a country had to feed its prisoners according to the standards of its own army.[6] Since, however, a Japanese soldier's diet consisted mostly of inexpensive rice and fish, the bureaucracy allotted only a small amount of money for each enlisted man. The officers fared somewhat better. While the camp authorities received the money and in turn purchased food staples for the enlisted men's kitchens,[7] the officers among the prisoners received an amount equal to their Japanese counterparts, and were free to purchase their own food.[8] But all faced problems, since the Japanese contribution remained constant over the years, while prices increased tremendously in what was an inflationary period. Consequently, camp kitchens used much rice and fish.

To counteract this dietary monotony, each camp maintained a canteen, where the government sold the prisoners goods purchased from Japanese merchants. The canteen offered not only food, but everything else from stationery to socks. Japanese merchants advertised their wares, distributing among the prisoners flyers praising the goods the prisoners could purchase. One such advertisement for stationery read in part as follows:

> Wars are a matter between governments. We have no animosity in our heart against you. You have nothing to be ashamed about, since you fought bravely . . . .
> Since you have no pleasures other than writing letters, consider our envelopes. Extra strong, they will withstand the many miles they have to travel.[9]

The prisoners could buy goods freely, provided they had enough money. Those fortunate enough to receive salaries from their former places of employment in China or Japan could live rather well,[10] as could prisoners who received money from relatives at home.[11] The arrangement penalized the prisoners who had neither a bank account in China, nor relatives who readily supplied money.[12] Yet there was some help for them; prisoners who needed it could receive loans from German Aid committees which were formed in Japan by Germans living there. These committees had been organized as early as November 1914. They were especially helpful in distributing clothing, food, books, etc. to the prisoners. They also distributed money donations to the different camps on a monthly basis. By 1917, for instance, the monthly donations to the camps amounted to 48,000 marks.

The aid committees also provided an informational service, relaying messages from the prisoners to their relatives in Germany, China or Japan. Several of the prisoners' relatives moved from China to Japan to be near them, and to be able to help with the committees' work. The committees also bought food for the camps at wholesale prices, and at times acted as conduit for prisoner complaints to the Japanese War Ministry.[13]

Some of these complaints centered around restrictions, such as night-time roll calls, curfews and supervised walks. These restrictions were imposed on the prisoners of all camps after four prisoners had managed to escape from the mainland of Japan.[14] Many prisoners had made escape attempts--some to gain their personal freedom, others because they wanted to help fight the war in Europe. Supplied by the camp authorities with daily newsflashes from the European struggle, the men knew about the stalemate in France and the trench war, and many considered it their patriotic duty to escape. Most of them, however, were clearly conspicuous as Europeans, and often clumsy in their disguises, so that the Japanese authorities had little difficulty in quickly detecting and apprehending them.[15]

Punishment was swift, even though escape by itself was not an offense. According to the Hague Conventions of 1907, the escapee could not be punished by the host country except by a mild disciplinary penalty.[16] Out of necessity, however, escape from insular Japan usually involved other transgressions such as stealing or perjury. The Japanese prosecuted the escapees for these infractions and judged them according to Japanese law. In one case, for instance, an Austrian and a Bavarian had stolen a boat to cross a lake. Upon capture, the Japanese authorities punished them not for the escape, but for stealing the boat, a most serious offense in Japan. Interpreting the draconian Japanese law-code, the judge sentenced them to two and a half years in solitary confinement.[17]

Six men, however, did manage to escape from mainland Japan in 1915. Two of them were apprehended within days by Japanese plainclothes policemen--one of them in Mukden in Korea, and another in

Shanghai. The remaining four, however, all from the same camp, evaded the Japanese detectives and embarked on an adventurous journey with the hope of eventually reaching Germany. All four, without the others' knowledge reached Shanghai, where they had a chance meeting and discussed their future plans.

From Shanghai to Germany one could follow either of two routes through neutral or friendly countries. One involved crossing China and Persia to reach allied Turkey, and from there Germany. This route was time-consuming, but no more so than the second route that meant crossing the pacific for some west coast American port, crossing the United States, and then boarding a ship for Scandinavia. Another, more direct alternative, was the route through hostile Russia. But the passage by train would be very dangerous, since detection could result in a long Russian jail sentence.

The four men considered the possibilities and made their decisions. Two of the men, who had decided to travel together, chose the route through China, one chose the passage across the Pacific, and the fourth took the risk of traveling by train through Russia, which would take but two weeks.

The two men who had decided on China acquired the identity and passports of two German schoolteachers. For more than three months they traveled through China. Then one day when they were close to the Russian border, they received a warning that the Chinese government had ordered all provincial officials to prevent any suspect persons from traveling in Sinkiang province near the Russian border. Since they possessed German passports, they very likely belonged in this category,[18] so that they decided to turn back and return to Shanghai, where they arrived six months after the inception of their trip. Undaunted in spirit, they boarded an American ship for San Francisco, and crossed the United States by train in 1916. In New York, with the help of a Swedish steward, they boarded a European bound Norwegian passenger ship as stowaways. British naval officers searched the ship at the northernmost tip of Scotland, but did not discover them. At the last moment, however, a Norwegian steward informed on them. As a result, the two Germans, still posing as schoolmasters, were interned on the Isle of Man.[19]

A similar fate befell the third escapee. He had traveled on an old schooner to San Francisco, taken a train to New York, and with the passport of a Dutchman had boarded a Dutch vessel bound for Germany. When the captain of the ship broke the British blockade to deliver goods to Germany, the British apprehended the vessel, confiscated cargo and ship, and moved the passengers to the internment camp at the Isle of Man.[20] Thus the three escapees who had taken the relatively safe routes through neutral countries did not succeed in their quest of reaching Germany. Only the fourth escapee, the man who had chosen the most dangerous passage--the trip through belligerent Russia, was successful. After an adventurous train journey on the Trans-

Siberian Railroad, in a compartment which he, posing as a Norwegian businessman, had to share with a Japanese businessman, he reached Finland. Eighteen days after leaving Shanghai he touched German soil. Weeks later he fulfilled his patriotic pledge and departed for military duty on the western front.[21] He was the only escapee to reach Germany.

Over the years, meanwhile, the authorities were adding new camps and closing others.[22] In April of 1917 the military authorities consolidated three camps and established, on the island of Shikoku near a pastoral hamlet called Bando, a new prison-camp by the same name. Bando prison camp was particularly interesting, because it encompassed the Japanese authorities' general feeling towards the prisoners.

Five other camps existed in 1917. In one of those, the camp of Kurume, the lack of space prevented the creation of a satisfactory environment for the prisoners. Kurume camp, located outside the town of Kurume on the island of Kyushu, had formerly served th Japanese Army as a barracks. When in October of 1914 the Japanese, during the siege of Tsingtao, captured their first prisoners, they sent them to Kurume. From October to November 1914 the number of prisoners increased to 1,380 men, making Kurume the most populous and also the most overcrowded camp in Japan.[23] These were conditions that created an atmosphere of frustration for prisoners and guards alike. The guards, whom the camp commander had given permission to punish offenses such as smoking inside the wooden sheds on the spot, disciplined the smallest transgressions with undue harshness. They often withheld the prisoners' mail for months or prohibited their walks outside the camp for several days.[24]

Bando, however, was different. It consisted of 57,000 square meters of uncultivated land, nestled between gently rolling hills.[25] Over 900 prisoners could, within reason, develop their talents and hobbies. Bando's camp commander, who had previously administered the Tokushima camp, had a most lenient attitude towards his charges. He encouraged the building of a small village-like encampment with huts, where the prisoners could develop their own world. The encampment featured shops for carpenters, watchmakers, painters, mechanics, instrument-makers, locksmiths, bookbinders and more. There was a butcher shop, a bakery, a tailor shop and a fishmonger, who sold fish caught in Bando's own pond. The encampment had several restaurants, a sauna, a library, and three orchestras--a symphony, a string and a brass orchestra.

Bando also had its own hospital for mild illnesses. More serious cases were taken to the hospital in nearby Tokushima. When treatment in town was necessary, the prisoners had to pay for the treatment. So the prisoners devised a health-insurance plan. Funds for it came from those prisoners who could afford to contribute, from the proceeds of different sports competitions, and from the donations of the Tientsin/China Ladies Club and Aid Committees.[26]

Bando indeed resembled a village; a primitive settlement perhaps, with dirt roads and gray barracks. But the intense community spirit amply compensated for the lack of architectural beauty. It was a spirit that revealed itself in Bando's many sports associations, for instance; groups of soccer, stickball, hockey and handball fans formed leagues and played on fields situated outside the camps.[27] Those more interested in gymnastics joined one of several athletic groups. The groups participated in gymnastics competitions, and wrestling and boxing exhibitions. Money received from such activities helped to purchase, among other things, some farming equipment.[28]

And farming did play a major part in Bando. Most of it was done on land outside the camp's boundaries. The transformation of this land impressed the Japanese peasant, who tilled the land nearby. Many of the plants used by the prisoners were alien to the Japanese peasants, as for instance, the tomato, which, thanks to the excellent care given it, grew in profusion, as did other vegetables. Because the peasants showed interest in European farming methods, the prisoners shared their knowledge and instructed them in the application of modern agricultural methods.[29] A Japanese professor of agriculture, fascinated with the prisoners' work also offered his advice and inspired some of the Japanese officers to work alongside the prisoners to improve the countryside.[30] Working in unison, the Japanese officers and the German prisoners presented a living symbol of cooperation.

Such German-Japanese cooperation extended into many areas. While purchasing goods for their canteen in the hamlet of Bando, the prisoners invited some of the Japanese to visit the camp. The visits evoked a mutual interest in each other's culture and skills.[31] The Germans showed the Japanese several skills related to modern technology, and the Japanese in turn instructed the Germans in Japanese cuisine and crafts. During their outings to the sea the Germans observed the fishermen casting their nets. The fishermen sold their fish to the Germans and the Germans were much impressed by the Japanese's friendly demeanor.[32]

But most important to German-Japanese understanding was an exhibition of articles manufactured by the prisoners, which occurred several times during Bando's existence. The first exhibition, an exhibit of arts and crafts, took place on March 8, 1918. The exhibition grounds were located in the hamlet of Bando and consisted of a large hall and several temples. The villagers showed much interest in the planned exhibition. They even collected money for the renovation of the main hall, and displayed signs in their shop windows announcing the coming attraction.[33] The prisoners for their part worked for months to complete the exhibits, which included posters, woodcuts, oil paintings and photographs, as well as many technical items such as automatic coffee-brewers, rain-gauges, slide-rules, steam-engines, gas and electric motors, ship models and more.

When the exhibit opened, many of the Japanese villagers came with their families. They admired the exhibits and listened to lectures on botany, ornithology, chemistry and agriculture.34 Bando's orchestras played lively tunes and refreshments were served in the garden. The show lasted for twelve days and was a huge success. Almost all saleable items found buyers and many Japanese placed orders for items that sold out early.35 During the twelve days over 51,000 visitors, many of them from other towns such as Tokushima and Kobe, came to view the exhibits. One of the visitors was a Japanese prince, who purchased a painting of General Hindenburg.

Following Bando's example, the commanders of the other camps allowed their prisoners to hold similar exhibitions. Even the prisoners of Kurume, despite the notorious lack of space, organized one.36

The camp of Bando remained in existence until Christmas Day of 1919, when the prisoners were finally repatriated to Germany. Soon after the armistice in November 1918, the Japanese military authorities had indicated their desire to return the prisoners to Germany and Austria as quickly as possible. Several factors, however, delayed the implementation of this intention.

No repatriation could take place before the peace treaties had been signed. These treaties--the Treaty of Versailles pertaining to Germany and the Treaty of St-Germain pertaining to Austria--were signed in June of 1919. Some German and Austrian prisoners suddenly found themselves with a different nationality, because the treaties had shifted the boundaries and created new countries such as Poland, Czechoslovakia and Yugoslavia.37 Those who came from these newly established countries were the first to leave the camps for home.

One additional hindrance to the repatriation of the others was the circumstance that the German government had no ships at its disposal to bring the men home. The Germans had scuttled most of their fleet at Scapa Flow on June 21, 1919, two days before signing the Treaty of Versailles. The ships still at the disposal of the German Navy could not be used for any repatriation from Japan, since they patrolled the Baltic, supervising the return of refugees from West Prussia.38

Finally in December 1919 repatriation began. Japan had accepted the German government's suggestion that a private Japanese shipping firm provide the ships needed to bring the men back. Germany had negotiated the ships through the Swiss Legation. The Legation had handled diplomatic matters between Germany and Japan since March 1917, when the United States, Germany's previous diplomatic channel, had entered the war. Under the charter of the German government, six ships, with a Japanese captain and crew, sailed for Germany. The first ship left Japan in late December 1919 and the last in late March of 1920.39 When the first of the ships arrived at the German port of Wilhelmshaven, the Japanese captain gave a farewell speech, praising the Germans for their soldierly qualities, and stating that they could proudly stand before the world and proclaim their military and personal honor. Germany, the captain said, could be proud to welcome her sons back.

The welcome, however, was not what the men had expected. They remembered a young nation, humming with vitality, filled with pride in its social and economic stability. The Germany they found in 1920 was a nation sickened with fear and hunger. Communists fought in the streets and newspaper headlines screamed revolution. In the months after their return, many of the former prisoners realized that they had come back from another age. They were survivors from an age dominated by different ideals. They represented Imperial Germany and Imperial Germany was now an anachronism.

One of the returnees expressed his disappointment in a poem. He wrote:

> No church bells ring for us who now return.
> No maiden winds us twigs of roses.
> No festive goblet thanks the heroes.
> We come at night - the country lies in silence.

NOTES

[1] For a detailed account of the siege see Charles B. Burdick, The Japanese Siege of Tsingtao (Hamden: Archon, 1976).

[2] On Kyushu island, camps were located at Fukuoka (370 men), Kumamoto (500 men), Oita (215 men) and two camps at Kurume--a temple camp with 50 men and a barracks camp with 1,314 men. The five camps on Shikoku were located at Tokushima (208 men), Marugame (316 men) and Matsuyama (consisted of 3 separate camps with 395 men). Honshu housed camps at osaka (535 men), Himeji (400 men), Nagoya (506 men), Shizuoka (90 men), and Asakusa (300 men). Eduard Leipold, "Bericht über meine Jahre in Kriegsgefangenenschaft, p. 4.

[3] Otto Fliegelscamp, letter of November, 1971. Copy in the author's possession.

[4] The Japanese government issued rules and regulations regarding the treatment of prisoners, in addition to the rules promulgated by the Hague convention of 1907 to which Japan and Germany were both signatories. However, all rules were flexible and could be interpreted by the camp commanders. Hoover Institution of War, Revolution and Peace, Stanford. Government Documents Japan. Laws, Statutes, etc. Moral Regulations for Prisoners of War 1914, pp. 1-3, and Government Documents Japan. Législation Japonaise relative aux Prisonniers de Guerre. Bureau de Renseignements sur les Prisonniers de Guerre à Tokio, 1918, pp. 1-37.

[5] Leipold, pp. 12-13. The son of the owner spoke German and often conversed with the prisoners. After World War I he became president of the German-Japanese Association in Tokushima. In 1961 some of his former workers met with him at a reunion in Frankfurt. Ibid., p. 14.

[6] James Brown Scott, ed. The Hague Conventions and Declarations of 1899 and 1907 (New York: Oxford University Press, 1918), pp. 108-109.

[7] The Japanese government budgeted from 30-40 Sen a day per enlisted man, which had to cover food and heating expenses. The government allowed from 50 Sen to 5 Yen a month for clothing. Internationales Komitee vom Roten Kreuz, Dokumente herausgegeben während des Krieges 1914-1918. Bericht des Herrn Dr. F. Paravicini, in Yokohama, über seinen Besuch der Gefangenenlager in Japan - 30 Juni bis 16 Juli, 1918 (Basel: Verlag Georg & Cie, 1919), p. 6. The exchange rate dollar - yen from 1914 to 1920 was approximately 1 yen = 50 cents. A yen had 100 sen.

[8] Due to the rule of segregation between officers and enlisted men, the officers maintained their own kitchens run by their aides. Paul Kempe, "Bericht - Kriegsgefangenenschaft - ", p. 4; and German von Wenckstern, "Berichts - Kriegsgefangenenschaft - Chapter 5, p. 4.

[9] "Advertisement Z. Chujo Shoten", copy in the author's possession.

[10] Many of the prisoners had formerly worked in China and Japan. Some even owned businesses and factories. In many instances salaries continued to be paid. Dr. Kurt Meissner, "Bericht - Kriegsgefangenenschaft - ", p. 6.

[11] German von Wenckstern letter to his mother, April 4, 1915. Those of the prisoners with families in Japan were especially fortunate. In addition to monetary help, the families could come and visit the prisoners at the camp. The German government offered to repatriate German civilians during early 1915, but most families declined the invitation. Bundesarchiv, Koblenz, Microcopy R85/vorl. 3621. Cited hereafter as Microcopy R85/vorl.

[12] Microcopy R85/vorl. 4615.

[13] Microcopy R85/vorl. 3927 and Report from Herrn Hans Drenckhahn to Siemens-Schuckert, Germany, August 15, 1919, and Österreichisches Staatsarchiv. PK/MS 1920 8-4/5 Nr. 5843.

[14] Microcopy R85/vorl. 3623.

[15] Leipold, p. 18, and Kempe, pp. 6,7.

16Brown Scott, ed. The Hague Conventions, pp. 108, 109.

17Bericht - Kriegsgefangenenschaft - sailor Storff, p. 5.

18Fritz Sachse, "Meine Flucht durch China," Stralsunder Tageblatt. Unterhaltungsbeilage, March 14, 1938, Nr. 61. The Chinese government had received these instructions from the Russian Embassy. The Russians had reason to view German travelers in China with suspicion. In December 1914 and the early part of 1915, a small group of Germans and Austrians had crossed the Gobi desert for Lake Baikal in Siberia. For patriotic reasons they wanted to stop Russian troop transports from Siberia to West Russia by blowing up strategically important railroad tunnels of the Trans-Siberian Railroad near Lake Baikal (Manchuria). The group did not succeed. Shortly before reaching their destination they were murdered. Otto Prange, 14 Jahre Soldat im Land der aufgehenden Sonne. N.P.N.D., p. 8.

19Letter Heinz von Bassi to Dr. Charles B. Burdick, March 19, 1971.

20Letter Mrs. Carmen von Wenckstern to Dr. Charles B. Burdick, n.d.

21Kempe, p. 24.

22In 1915 Asakusa closed and the prisoners were transferred to the new camp of Narashino (near Tokushima). The prisoners of Oita, Shidzuoka and Fukuoka followed in 1918 increasing Narashino's inhabitants to 753 men. Aanogahara near Kobe, another camp erected in 1915, received the men from Himeji, and Kurume absorbed prisoners from Korodai and Kumamoto. When Osaka closed in 1917 the prisoners moved to Ninoshima near Hiroshima. In April 1917 three camps-- Marugame, Matsuyama and Tokushima merged into one camp--Bando. Six camps remained until the final dissolution--Aanogahara (477 men); Bando (1,028 men); Kurume (1,314 men); Nagoya (506 men); Narashino (753 men); and Ninoshima (536 men). Leipold, "Bericht," - list of camps.

23Microcopy R85/vorl. 4614.

24Ibid.

25Politisches Archiv des Auswärtigen Amts, Bonn, Politische Abteilung IV - Ostasien. Japan Pol. 13, No. 4, Band 1, 1920.

26Paravicini, p. 15. Good hospital care was especially important, since during the imprisonment wounded prisoners were not returned to Germany. Helene Luther, a Tsingtao citizen who had cared for the wounded during the siege, suggested the exchange of wounded prisoners to the Japanese in August 1915. On November 30, Mrs. Luther contacted the German government with the same request. The

Japanese replied to Mrs. Luther that an equal amount of wounded Japanese be exchanged for any Germans. The offer was futile, since the Germans held no Japanese prisoners. National Archives, Washington, German Naval Archive, Microcopy T-1022, Roll 724, PG 75225.

[27]Bando had a soccer field, tennis courts, handball and hockey fields. Leipold, p. 24.

[28]Die Baracke, Zeitung für das Kriegsgefangenenlager Bando, Japan, Band I, No. 17, January 20, 1918, pp. 1-4. Cited hereafter as Baracke.

[29]Leipold, p. 26.

[30]Paravicini, p. 14.

[31]Kurt Meissner, p. 9, and Tokio Saigami, Matsuyama Shuyosho (Tokyo: Verlag Chuo Koronsha, 1969), p. 4.

[32]Leipold, p. 28.

[33]Baracke I, Nr. 17, January 20, 1918, p. 12.

[34]The lectures were given in Japanese and German. Baracke I, Nr. 25, March 17, 1918, pp. 542-82.

[35]Baracke I, Nr. 25, March 17, 1918, pp. 579-80.

[36]Baracke III, Nr. 23, March 9, 1919, pp. 515-22.

[37]National Archives, Washington, Records of the Department of State relating to WW I and its termination 1914-1919. File No. 723.72114, Roll 315.

[38]Microcopy R85/vorl. 5143.

[39]Auswärtiges Amt, Band 1, 2, and 3. The Austrians were repatriated together with the Germans. In July of 1919 the Austrian government had authorized Germany to negotiate repatriation in the name of Austria. Österreichisches Staatsarchiv PK/MS 1919 VIII, 6/1 Nr. 9878.

AMERICAN MILITARY ATTACHÉS IN RUSSIA 1914-1917

by S.J. LEWIS

> West and away the wheels of darkness roll,
> Day's beamy banner up the east is borne,
> Spectres and fears, the nightmare and her foal,
> Drown in the golden deluge of the morn.
>
> A. E. Housman, Revolution

On July 6, 1918 President Woodrow Wilson authorized the dispatch of American troops to Russia. Notwithstanding Wilson's reservations and the narrow limitations he put upon the use of those troops, Americans were fighting Soviet troops in Russia within two months.[1] But other American soldiers had served in Russia before, although with a far different purpose. This study will examine the activities of a small group of professional US Army officers stationed in the Russian capital in the war's first three years, what they saw, how they functioned, and what recommendations they made to Washington, D.C.

The Department of State on September 2, 1914 requested the War Department to dispatch an officer to fill the position of military attaché in Russia. American attachés had served in Petrograd beginning in 1890, but the position had remained vacant since November 1913--the army possessed too few officers qualified for the post. But American diplomats in Petrograd, unable to enter into discussions with the Russian Ministry of War, now found it essential that a military attaché return to Russia. In Washington the Army War College Division, which oversaw military attachés and observers, was still hard pressed to find a suitable officer for the position, but on September 23, resolved to transfer First Lieutenant Sherman Miles from the Balkans to Petrograd.[2]

Sherman Miles arrived in Petrograd on October 16, 1914 but soon reported it unlikely that any of the military attachés would be allowed to leave the capital. The Russian government did not wish to risk exposing any of its secrets to the attachés of neutral nations, nations that could possibly join the ranks of its enemies. The lieutenant remained in

Petrograd until January 3, 1915 when the Russians unexpectedly allowed him to visit the Russian Army outside Warsaw.³

Once in Warsaw, Lieutenant Miles encountered a friend serving on the staff of the local Russian commander. That friend managed to secure permission for Miles to remain at the front. The Russian commander officially allowed Miles to observe Red Cross facilities in the area, but in reality permitted him to see practically anything he desired. Miles informed Washington that his position in Warsaw resulted from a personal favor and not official policy. He requested Washington not embarrass the Russian government by revealing his activities, for the majority of the neutral military attachés remained isolated in Petrograd.⁴ Miles spent the next two months observing the operations of the Russian Army. He roamed freely about the Russian positions dressed in the cap and overcoat of a Russian officer, carrying a Russian saber, and invariably accompanied by a Russian officer. This escort proved necessary to explain to the soldiers why Miles did not speak Russian, although dressed as one of their officers. The lieutenant returned to Petrograd in May in the belief that the United States would soon go to war against Germany.⁵

When his belief turned out to be wrong, Miles returned to the front for the summer, where he witnessed the battles leading to the Russian evacuation of Warsaw. He soon realized, however, that according to recent changes in army regulations he must return to serve with his regiment in the United States by the end of the year. He suggested that his replacement arrive by November 15, 1915 to meet several influential contacts. He added that it proved an embarrassment for the U.S. Army to be represented by a lieutenant and that his replacement should be at least fluent in French (assuming it was impossible to find a Russian speaking officer) and some German, although the Russian government would be offended if the officer was of German or Jewish descent. Miles also recommended that his successor be young and vigorous enough to withstand the rigors of accompanying the Russian Army in the field.⁶

In Washington the War College Division could not find a replacement for Miles. In mid November 1915 its Chief, Brigadier General M. M. Macomb, recommended that army regulations be circumvented to keep Miles in Petrograd. His superiors dismissed the idea, however, not wishing to draw the ire of Congress. In late November Macomb finally selected Lieutenant E. Francis Riggs to replace Miles. Macomb also directed Miles to return home via the Trans-Siberian Railroad. Miles' mother-in-law and infant daughter returned to New York by way of Norway in January, but the lieutenant and his wife could not depart until he had taken his formal leave of the Tsar and the imperial ministers. This proved no easy matter, for the officials were scattered over western Russia, and Miles spent several weeks calling on the far-flung dignitaries, finally quitting Petrograd on February 2, 1916.⁷

Lieutenant Riggs encountered a series of delays that prohibited his departure until Miles had already quit Petrograd. Miles' efforts to secure the same broad privileges for his successor came to naught. Upon his arrival, Riggs, like the other military attachés from neutral nations, found himself confined to the vicinity of Petrograd. Riggs nevertheless attempted to describe Russia's military situation, despite the shortage of reliable information. He summarized Russia's military operations during the summer of 1916 as a limited success with the army confident of victory and ammunition now in abundant supply. Riggs regretted that no information on the situation in Rumania could be obtained from Petrograd.[8] In November Riggs stated that he had no news from Rumania, but the Russian high command was attempting to prevent the Germans from dispatching additional troops to that country. Economic conditions in Russia continued to deteriorate, with increasing food shortages in the larger cities accompanied by labor disorders. Riggs also reported the latest mobilization of Russian reserves. The addition of these 18 and 43 year old recruits raised the number of Russians under arms to some 12-14 million, although only some 5 million were at the front. The lieutenant emphasized, however that Russia did not possess enough officers to lead such a large army.[9]

On January 10, 1917 Riggs reported the end of the Rumanian Campaign, with the victorious German Army in occupation of most of the country going over to the defensive and transferring their best troops for action on other fronts. Riggs stated that the inability of the Russian Army to intervene on behalf of the Rumanians resulted from inferior rail communication and faulty military organization. One particular flaw stemmed from a shortage of officers, necessitating the formation of large unwieldy battalions. He predicted that the Russian Army would be unable to resume offensive operations until later in the spring. Riggs described Russia's domestic conditions as deteriorating, with acute food shortages. These difficulties led to increasing criticism of governmental inefficiency and corruption in the Duma.[10]

The following month Riggs informed Washington of the continued scarcity of food and its effect in cities across Russia. Rumors in the capital attributed this dearth as a governmental ploy designed to prepare the people for a separate peace with Germany. The lieutenant thought the possibility of a Russian Army spring offensive unlikely; and for the moment the Tsar's generals remained preoccupied with blunting possible German offensives against Riga or Odessa. In the months leading up to the overthrow of the Romanov dynasty, then, Riggs succeeded in warning Washington of Russia's severe problems: the food shortages and the government's manifest inability to cope with the situation, the administrative inefficiency of the Russian military and bureaucracy, and the inadequate system of railway communication. In spite of these difficulties, Riggs concluded that the army and the majority of the people desired to see the war brought to a successful conclusion.[11]

Riggs' counterpart, the Naval Attaché Captain Newton A. McCully, painted a darker portrait of Russian conditions. In a report written only days before the Petrograd riots and the abdication of the Tsar, he concluded that Russia was rapidly approaching a climax in the struggle between the forces of liberalism and those of political reaction, and that as a result of governmental inefficiency, the nation stood on the brink of chaos. The naval attaché reported that the army's dependability remained questionable and that the bulk of the people desired peace. In addition, inflation had rendered Russian currency practically worthless, while English control of the Russian economy made it unlikely that Russia could extricate itself from its bleak economic situation. Furthermore, the railway network was on the verge of collapse. McCully stated that each railway station was clogged with broken down locomotives and cars without the personnel or materiel to repair them. Freight choked the port of Vladivostok, but only several trains a day could journey west with their vital supplies. This failure of the railway system resulted in a crisis in food distribution, with large amounts of perishable items rotting at the railheads for want of transport.12

The naval attaché also observed that the length and severity of the war had rent the fabric of Russian society--releasing moral restraint, creating a receptivity to spiritualism, and bringing about an alarming increase in crimes of violence. Although suicides had been numerous in Russia prior to 1914, they had increased during the war. The birth rate had declined and the death rate had risen since 1914. Armed robberies had become commonplace, often perpetrated by large bands of army deserters. McCully concluded:

> Combined with the general disturbance of moral ideas, uncertain means of existence, and loss of the sense of responsibility due to war conditions, the problem of preserving internal order becomes more and more difficult. An organized movement of any kind against the Government would find support from many elements in Russia. Flesh and blood is the cheapest thing in Russia.13

The news of the overthrow of the Russian monarchy, which came on the heels of this report, was well received in Washington; for already having broken off diplomatic relations with Germany, the American government could now argue that it was fighting a war against autocracy, unencumbered by the awkward presence of the despotic Romanov dynasty as a wartime ally. The American Ambassador to Russia, David R. Francis,14 66 years of age and at the end of a successful career both in business and Missouri state politics, gladly received the Department of State's approval of his request for prompt recognition of the new Russian government. On March 22, accompanied by the military and naval attachés, Francis officially relayed U. S. recognition to the Provisional Government headed by Prince G.E. Lvov.15

Captain McCully relayed his first observations of the Provisional Government to Washington on March 27, 1917. Its cabinet members impressed him as honest and patriotic men, particularly Paul Milyukov and Alexander Guchkoff. The naval attaché confessed surprise at the youthfulness of the cabinet (three ministers were under 36 years of age), and expressed concern only about Alexander Kerensky, the Minister of Justice and the sole socialist in the cabinet. He feared Kerensky's ability and the threat of the Workmen and Soldiers Deputies. McCully concluded that Russia would become a republic, mainly because the workers and soldiers, who were the most powerful forces in Petrograd, desired one. The captain on occasion would strike up conversations on the street with passers-by and, upon querying several soldiers as to what a republic actually was, one replied that it meant having a good tsar and another said he didn't quite know, although he knew it was something very nice.[16]

Ambassador Francis used Lieutenant Riggs to maintain contact with the Provisional Government during the first weeks of the new regime's existence, but with the approach of the United States' declaration of war against Germany, Francis sent him to the Russian Army headquarters (Stavka) at Moghilev. Riggs soon realized that if the American government intended to assume its responsibility in the effort to keep Russia in the war, the US Army would require authority greater than that of a lieutenant or captain. He consequently requested the War College Division on April 7, to dispatch a full military mission to Russia, one modeled on the large French and British missions already in Petrograd. Although Riggs did not know it, his superiors in Washington were thinking along the same lines. Within weeks, a group of distinguished US Army officers would tread the streets of Petrograd.[17]

The first such reinforcements to leave for Russia consisted of Majors Francis LeJau Parker[18] and Monroe C. Kerth.[19] The army had dispatched them to Rumania as military observers in October 1916. They had arrived in Bucharest in time to participate in the evacuation of the capital, missing the decisive German offensive. Even though the campaign in Rumania was ending, the Rumanian government still had no desire to reveal military secrets to attachés from neutral governments. Parker and Kerth consequently requested permission to return home. By the time their message arrived in Washington D.C., the United States had already declared war on Germany. The War College Division agreed that there was little reason for the two majors to remain in Rumania, but decided to send them to Petrograd, where a lowly lieutenant could no longer represent the US Army in the councils of war of the United States' newest ally.[20]

The US Army possessed few experts on its new ally, so any additional reports helped Washington piece together the Russian puzzle. On April 21, 1917 a particularly important report arrived from Baltimore, Maryland, where the senior engineer of the army's Eastern Division, Lieutenant Colonel William Vorhees Judson,[21] interrupted his work on harbor improvements to inform his superiors on Russia's new Minister of War and Navy, Alexander Guchkoff. They had become acquainted in 1904 on the train from Petrograd to Manchuria, when Judson was a military observer and Guchkoff a representative of the Tsar, both en route to observe the Russo-Japanese War. The War College Division found Judson's observations of sufficient importance to forward copies to the Department of State and the Army Chief of Staff. The following month President Woodrow Wilson (acting upon the advice of Judson's friend, the Postmaster General, Albert S. Burleson, who was also a close confidant of the president) requested Judson's participation in the Root Commission which was about to leave for Russia on a fact finding mission. Major General Hugh L. Scott,[22] Army Chief of Staff, on May 15, 1917 joined the Root Commission as its highest ranking military officer as the group left Washington.[23]

News of President Wilson's request for a declaration of war against Germany reached the headquarters of the Russian Army on April 5, 1917. America's entry into the war drew Lieutenant Riggs into the highest levels of the allied war councils in Russia. On April 17, he forwarded to Washington the Provisional Government's suggestion for Anglo-American military cooperation in Russia. Riggs reported that England and the United States could assist by helping to improve Russian railroads and by improving the harbor facilities at Vladivostok. Riggs awaited the arrival of his two superior officers from Rumania through mid-May, when he left for Vladivostok to greet the Root Commission.[24]

On June 3, 1917, he met the Commission's members as they arrived in Vladivostok. On the train journey to Petrograd, Riggs briefed General Scott and Colonel Judson on both the existing and planned American military aid to Russia, which consisted of: A.) stationing a military mission in Russia; B.) sending railway equipment to Vladivostok and the northern ports; C.) dispatching war materials; D.) sending special US Army units to serve on the Russian front; and E.) stopping the left-wing opponents of the Provisional Government from entering Russia from the United States. On Wednesday, June 13, 1917 as the former Tsar's train completed the eleven day journey from Vladivostok, Petrograd suddenly possessed a very distinguished group of US Army officers. Their mission was to evaluate Russia's remaining war potential to determine the extent of further American aid, a mission which would fail as significantly as the Root Commission itself.[25]

In his whirlwind tour of Russia and Rumania, General Scott, Chief of Staff of the US Army, recognized the two serious problems paralyzing the Russian Army--the inefficiency of the railways and the lack of discipline. He observed that the closer he traveled to the front, the better the discipline, and it appeared that the legions of deserters were returning to their units. He concluded that Russia would remain in the war if the United States provided more help. Scott justified further aid by explaining that the allies could ill afford Russia's departure from the conflict, for the release of 150 enemy divisions to other fronts would jeopardize the allied war effort. He recommended that the United States loan an additional one billion dollars and dispatch all available railway engines and rolling stock to Russia.[26]

General Scott saw what the Provisional Government wanted him to see, and perhaps what he himself wanted to see--a resolute ally in need of assistance. Historians have observed how the Wilson administration for the most part ignored Elihu Root upon his return from Russia.27 In point of fact, there was little reason to consult Root. Both Root and Scott sought to bolster the Russian war effort through increased aid, to improve the railways, and strengthen war morale. Both men were conservative Republicans who saw eye to eye on most issues; and they coordinated their reports on the return trip to the United States. General Scott's report was a different matter. It would carry considerable weight, since he possessed the special trust of the president, having been the first military man since the Civil War allowed to attend cabinet meetings.28

It would be altogether too easy to dismiss Root and Scott as two elderly men, unfamiliar with Russia, who after just one month's visit, failed to appreciate the thorough war weariness of the Russian people. But other individuals who were more familiar with Russia provided Washington with similar information on Russia's alleged desire to continue the war.29 What might have occurred had the US Army placed a senior officer in Petrograd through World War I remains open to conjecture. While it is possible that such a well placed expert on Russian affairs would not have altered the perceptions of the Wilson administration, it is certain that sending a mere lieutenant to Petrograd was a grave error. Riggs proved a capable young officer, but even if he had possessed the judgment of Solomon, it would not have changed the fact that he was a lieutenant, and hence excluded from the decision making process in Washington, D.C.30

Before departing Petrograd with the Root Commission on July 8, General Scott detailed Colonel Judson to remain behind to assume the dual responsibility of military attaché and chief of the American military mission in Russia. Military attachés were directly responsible to the resident ambassador, but as chief of the American military mission, Judson was able to report directly to the War Department, circumventing Ambassador Francis. Judson's reports and letters would reach not only the War Department, but the White House too, through his friend the Postmaster General.31

Colonel Judson found himself confronted with a multitude of tasks. To perform similar duties the British had over 60 officers, but Judson would have to make do with only three. He represented his government on the Michelson Commission (which regulated the shipment of allied goods to Russia) and used the recently promoted Captain Riggs as his deputy. He sent Major Parker to serve at the Russian army headquarters, and used Major Kerth to observe military operations at the front. One of Judson's most immediate concerns was the need for officers to perform counter-espionage work. He proposed to transfer the civilians who were performing similar duties on the embassy staff into the US Army.32

Following the collapse of the Provisional Government's military offensive and the unsuccessful revolt of the most radical elements of the Petrograd garrison and city workers, American officials by early August began to question Russia's viability as an ally. On August 3, Judson confided to Postmaster General Burleson that the Provisional Government was very weak, a sentiment echoed days later in a memorandum from Secretary of State Robert Lansing to President Wilson. Judson also warned Ambassador Francis of the weakness of the Russian Army, reporting that the lack of discipline was threatening to drive the corps of professional officers from the army. Judson believed that with the Russian Army thus incapacitated, Germany could quite possibly defeat the allies. He concluded that he and Francis should strongly urge the Provisional Government to restore discipline and warn it of the consequences of a German victory.33

Colonel Judson's difficulties increased through August, most serious being the recall of Major Parker to Washington. In addition the War College Division informed the colonel that neither funds nor personnel were available for service in Russia, although it authorized him to commission several American citizens residing in Petrograd.34 Judson also began to despair of the possibility of keeping Russia in the war. In early September in a memorandum for Ambassador Francis he lamented the absence of discipline not only in the military but throughout the nation. Nevertheless, he concluded that the army was the major problem; for without a reliable army the Russian government would be rendered impotent.35

The chaos within the Russian army was a grievous concern to the army's professional officers. The Provisional Government's unwillingness to discipline the army was a major factor that helped create a conflict with conservative elements of the officer corps. In early September this conflict resulted in the unsuccessful attempt by General Lavr G. Kornilov to overthrow the Provisional Government of Alexander Kerensky. Judson's allied colleagues favored Kornilov, but although Judson advocated many of Kornilov's proposed military reforms, he doubted the viability of a government headed by right-wing generals. Judson stated that even in the event of a Kornilov victory, the general would still be faced with the task of mollifying the Russian masses, who only desired to see the war end.36

The Provisional Government managed to quell the Kornilov revolt, but at a high price, for Kerensky was forced to arm the Petrograd workers and free his left-wing political opponents from prison. In the aftermath of Kornilov's failure Judson informed Washington that although the Provisional Government had survived, the real victor in the affair was the Petrograd Soviet, which now posed a threat to the Kerensky regime. Kerensky's position deteriorated even further as the Don Cossacks in southern Russia rose in revolt against the government. Judson concluded that Kerensky's regime was extremely weak and could be expected to move to Moscow soon in order to remove itself from both the Petrograd Soviet and the advancing German Army.37

Ambassador Francis received ample warning of the growing power of the Petrograd Soviet. On September 16, the Japanese ambassador, former Minister of War Alexander Guchkoff, and the President of the Duma Mikhail Rodzianko, each confidentially expressed the opinion in separate interviews with Francis that the Petrograd Soviet would eventually triumph over the Provisional Government. The ambassador, however, preferred to accept the views of Foreign Minister Mikhail Tereshchenko, who convinced him that Kerensky possessed the loyalty of the army and would defeat the Soviet in the expected test of strength.[38] Francis was still encouraged with the course of the revolution in spite of the threat from the Soviet. He informed the Secretary of State that the weakness of the Kerensky government was mainly the result of Russian exiles funded by Germany returning to their homeland from the United States, and agitating against the Provisional Government. Francis complained that the worst of these troublemakers was Leon Trotsky.[39]

The American government made a concerted effort to investigate the origins and activities of Trotsky and other Russian radicals who had lived in the United States. One search ultimately led to Muskogee, Oklahoma, where the government managed to find a no doubt surprised Dr. J.H. Stolper, Trotsky's cousin. Dr. Stolper provided the government with a list of his cousin's aliases and family background in Russia. He had last seen Trotsky the previous winter in New York City where he worked on a Russian language radical newspaper. Stolper described his cousin as a confirmed revolutionary of great audacity and energy, but a man with enough intellectual flexibility to compromise on issues in spite of his strongly held beliefs.[40]

The task of excluding such returning exiles from entry into Russia from the United States fell to Judson's military mission. The American embassy began the program at the request of the Provisional Government, organizing it into several passport control stations located at strategic cities across Russia. Each station possessed a representative of each major allied nation, and the allies hoped thereby to halt the influx of "political undesirables" into Russia. Judson retained the embassy personnel in their positions after having commissioned them as officers in the US Army. Ambassador Francis also requested Judson to observe the activities of selected American citizens in Petrograd. One such individual was the journalist John Reed. Judson informed the ambassador that although Reed openly associated with and supported the Bolsheviks he posed no threat to American interests, and to deport the young man would only serve to draw undue attention to Reed and perhaps make him a martyr. Judson suggested that Francis call in Reed and inform him that his actions were damaging the allied war effort.[41]

Throughout October Ambassador Francis warned Washington of the likelihood of an attempted *coup d' état* by the Petrograd Soviet instigated by the Bolsheviks. Allied concern with the weakness of the

Kerensky government manifested itself on October 9, when the British, French, and Italian ambassadors sent a joint protest threatening to stop all aid to Russia unless Kerensky strengthened the discipline and effectiveness of the Russian Army.[42] On the same day Francis informed the Department of State that the Provisional Government felt confident and looked forward to a test of strength with the Petrograd Soviet.[43] In an attempt to improve its relations with its allies, the Kerensky regime convened a meeting of the allied military attachés on the morning of October 18, at the home of the Russian minister of war. Minister Alexander Verkhovsky informed the allied officers of his measures to improve the quality of the Russian Army by reducing its strength from ten million to some seven million troops. The soldiers to be released were inductees from the older age groups, since there were too many troops in the army to be effectively led by the available number of officers. Indeed, the resultant lack of supervision was one of the major factors contributing to the poor state of discipline. The allied military attachés did not object to this reduction in the size of the Russian Army, nor to the remaining administrative reforms. Verkhovsky's proposal to abolish the death penalty in the army, however, met with howls of indignation from Generals Alfred Knox and Henri Niessel, the British and French Military Attachés. In the argument which immediately ensued the British and French generals convinced Verkhovsky that to abolish the death penalty would destroy the Russian Army. The minister of war reluctantly agreed but meekly added that he might not be able to prevent the measure from going into effect.[44]

On the evening of October 30, Ambassador Francis cabled Washington about his impressions of the situation. He reported that the Bolsheviks had cancelled their scheduled demonstration. Francis was disappointed, for he believed that Bolshevik's support was on the wane and that a confrontation would have provided the government with an opportunity to smash Lenin and his movement. Kerensky himself began on October 31 to prepare for the expected Bolshevik coup, massing loyal troops and developing contingency plans. The following week saw the two hostile camps maneuver and countermaneuver for tactical advantage as the Petrograd diplomatic community helplessly watched and waited.[45]

On November 2, Ambassador Francis informed Washington of the deteriorating political situation in Petrograd. He regretted that Kerensky had requested an additional loan from the American government, although he still held the opinion that Russia would eventually repay her heavy indebtedness. Francis reiterated the thought that his primary objective was keeping Russia in the war. He went on to say that the possibility existed that the Petrograd Soviet might gain control of the government, but he doubted its ability to stay in power for long. Francis concluded that following the inevitable failure of a Soviet government, a much stronger regime would assume power--a government with a greater potential for restoring order and continuing the war.[46]

Francis was less optimistic about the lack of cooperation among the allies. He expressed the opinion that the British government was more concerned with securing post-war economic supremacy in Russia than in seeking harmonious allied cooperation. He described British policy as selfish, grasping, and overbearing. The most recent incident which led to this denunciation involved American participation on the Michelson Commission. Judson (newly appointed brigadier general), perennially shorthanded, finally obtained permission to activate a former army lieutenant residing in Petrograd. Judson desired to employ the officer on the Michelson Commission, where his technical expertise and knowledge of Russian commercial life would be of great value. The British, however, refused to allow the lieutenant to join the commission, explaining that since the American was the representative of the General Electric Company in civilian life, that firm would benefit from his participation on the commission following the war.[47]

The following day the joint allied military attaché conference demonstrated the divided opinions and frustrations of the representatives. The British Military Attaché, General Knox, refused to consider the suggestion of Russian land distribution by the Kerensky government, roundly denouncing the Provisional Government. His French colleague, General Niessel, then joined in, describing Russian soldiers as cowards. At that point the two representatives of the Kerensky regime left in protest. General Knox, however, continued his diatribe, lamenting the failure of the Kornilov revolt and concluding that Russia could only be saved by a military dictatorship.[48]

The struggle between Kerensky's government and the Petrograd Soviet continued through the first week of November with an attempt by both sides to gain the loyalty of the Petrograd garrison. Kerensky publicly proclaimed confidence in his ability to defeat the Soviet, but his regime was weakened by a divided cabinet, and even the allied ambassadors expressed disenchantment with his leadership. Bolshevik maneuvering to gain control of the garrison convinced Kerensky of the necessity of arresting the Soviet Military Revolutionary Committee. Finally on the evening of November 5, Kerensky overcame the objections of his ministers and ordered his troops to arrest the Bolshevik military leaders and close the Bolshevik newspaper offices. By morning reliable government troops occupied the newspaper offices, but the leaders of the Bolshevik military forces remained free and were quick to respond. Bolshevik forces seized control of much of the city and forced Kerensky to flee the following day in an attempt to secure reliable troops. The final bastion of the Kerensky government, the Winter Palace, fell to the Bolsheviks in the early hours of November 8. The revolution succeeded practically without bloodshed, for at the decisive hour the Provisional Government's troops simply melted away.[49]

Ambassador Francis informed the Department of State of the ebb and flow of the struggle for Petrograd in spite of the unreliability of telegraphic service. Following the Bolshevik seizure of the telegraph network, the American minister in Stockholm kept Washington informed on the Russian situation. Francis, after initial uncertainty, told Washington that the Bolsheviks were in firm control and that Kerensky's return to power was very unlikely.50

General Judson's views remained strangely unaffected by the Bolshevik coup. He had previously maintained that the eastern front was of decisive importance to the allied war effort, so much so in fact that the allies should send troops to aid Russia. Elihu Root and General Scott had rejected his suggestion the previous June, but Judson raised the issue again on November 10 in a memorandum to Francis. In his ignorance of the Bolshevik party and its policies, Judson assumed that the new regime would welcome the prospect of allied troops serving in Russia. He believed that these troops would provide an example to the demoralized Russian Army. Judson further justified such action as a result of discussions with his allied colleagues; for since the fall of the Kerensky government, the British and French military attachés no longer objected to allied troops being sent to Russia.51

Ambassador Francis, however, took no action on the general's suggestion, for he had received no instructions from Washington since the revolution. He recommended on November 11 to the Secretary of State that the government cease loaning money to Russia. Two days later Francis reported that neither he nor his allied colleagues had received any form of communication from the new regime, but that the military attachés had paid an informal visit to the Bolshevik headquarters, where they were assured of the safety of foreigners residing in Petrograd.52

The full realization of the Bolshevik seizure of power gradually dawned on General Judson during the week following the revolution. On November 14, he cabled his revised estimate of the situation to the War College Division, with instructions that a copy be forwarded to the Postmaster-General, allowing Burleson to inform President Wilson of its contents. Judson stated that Russia was on the brink of anarchy and could be expected to abandon the war effort. He also forsaw the prospect of a world wide conflict between militant socialism and the forces of political reaction, a conflict which would constitute a dire threat to democracy. Judson believed that President Wilson could deal with the situation by suggesting acceptable peace terms. He concluded his report by stating that any Russian government formed in the immediate future must of necessity seek an end to the war, unless Germany demanded unjust terms.53

The following day Judson submitted a detailed report to Washington analyzing Russia's various political parties. He described the Bolsheviks as a group of extreme socialists, led by Lenin and demanding complete self determination of all nationalities in Russia, the nationalization of all large church and privately owned land holdings, state and communal control over production and distribution of goods, nationalization of banks, an immediate end to the war, and the implementation of a dictatorship by the peasants and workers.54

General Judson formalized his reappraisal of the strategic situation for Francis on November 16. He concluded that the Bolsheviks possessed sufficient military strength to remain in power in the immediate future and that Kerensky and the middle class were no longer factors in Russian politics. He did, however, believe that the remaining socialist parties would be of importance, and that these parties possessed three options: 1.) coalition with the Bolsheviks; 2.) non-cooperation with the Lenin regime in an attempt to sabotage the new government; and 3.) fighting the Bolsheviks in a civil war. Judson maintained that Germany would probably reject the Bolshevik peace proposal and that the allies therefore should not yet abandon Russia. The primary mission remained that of keeping Russia in the war in spite of its desperate domestic conditions. Furthermore it would be counterproductive for the allies to allow the non-Bolshevik socialists to resort to either of the two latter aforementioned options--for if the war was to continue on the eastern front, Russia must be unified behind one centralized government. Judson left the final conclusion unsaid, leaving the ambassador to infer perhaps that if the Bolsheviks could not reach a peace settlement with Germany, then it behooved the allies to assist the new Bolshevik regime.[55]

Francis remained unmoved by Judson's recommendations, for he disapproved of the Bolsheviks, and he had received no instructions from Washington regarding the new government. He even objected to the informal visits which Judson's personnel made to the Bolshevik headquarters, fearing that even such minor contact could imply American approval of the new regime. In response, the general informed Francis on November 19 that the efficiency of his office would be limited without the ability to contact the Bolshevik authorities in the capital. Francis, however, insisted that he be personally consulted prior to any meeting with the Bolsheviks; a proposal to which Judson stated he was willing to comply.[56]

Allied relations with the new government deteriorated through the following week, precipitated by the delivery by allied military representatives (excluding the United States) of a a joint note from their governments to the chief of staff of the Russian Army. The note protested the Bolshevik proposal of reaching a separate peace with Germany. Major Kerth delivered a similar protest at the request of Ambassador Francis several days later. In addition, on November 25, at the behest of the Russian Army chief of staff, Judson responded to a press report that the American government was stopping its exports to Russia until it could be determined that such goods would not end up in German possession. Francis and Judson had not received any such information from Washington, but the two were convinced that the press statement was genuine and that as a result of poor communications they simply had not yet received the message. Consequently Judson informed the Russians that the report was correct and that if the Bolsheviks continued to pursue peace negotiations the embargo would remain in effect. The cumulative effect of these allied messages to the Russian army chief of staff convinced the new Russian Commissar for

Foreign Affairs, Leon Trotsky, of Western hostility to the new government; and he responded by publishing the joint allied note and denouncing the allies.57

General Judson was taken aback by this rapid turn of events, for he believed that it was in the allied interest to cooperate with the Bolsheviks. On November 26 he informed Francis that the allies must change their present policy towards Russia--for it would soon be too late to alter the deteriorating situation. He suggested that it was time for a friendly outside force to assist in the formation of a unified Russian government, and that he believed the Bolsheviks could be persuaded to cooperate.58 The following day, after a meeting with Raymond Robins of the Red Cross, who also urged cooperation with Lenin, Judson wrote a letter to the Bolshevik government stating that the American government remained friendly towards the Russian people and that it had no preference as to which political party ruled Russia.59

Judson's letter did not have its desired effect, for it reached Trotsky at the same time as Major Kerth's protest note. In order to resolve this misunderstanding and to discuss the possibility of assisting in the upcoming negotiations with Germany, Judson decided to visit Trotsky. The British military attaché originally desired to accompany Judson, but the British ambassador prohibited Knox from seeing Trotsky. On the morning of December 1, with the blessing of Francis, Judson met with Leon Trotsky for some forty minutes. The general informed Trotsky that he came as an individual and not as an official of his government. He then suggested that allied and Russian interests still had much in common and that it was in the best interest of both Russia and the allies for Russia to secure a long armistice. Judson also requested that the armistice contain a provision prohibiting the Germans from transferring troops from the eastern front. In addition he discouraged Russia from exchanging prisoners of war and economic goods with Germany.

Judson stated that Trotsky was quite receptive to these suggestions, and authorized the general to tell Washington that the Bolsheviks would respect the interests of the allies as long as they did not contravene Russia's interests and its pursuit of peace. Trotsky stated that during the period of negotiations the allies were invited to examine provisions and to offer suggestions, but if the allies failed to participate, Russia would appeal directly to the people of the allied nations. Afterwards Judson expressed satisfaction with the interview, describing Trotsky as "the practical man of the Bolshevik administration." The general's impressions of Trotsky were as follows:

> Of medium stature and build; dark complexion, with a black mustached and small beard or goatee; wears glasses; nose slightly aquiline; complexion pale; eyes dark and penetrating; forehead high; of very intelligent appearance; manners quiet and pleasing; in perfect control of himself; might be taken for a

New York Eastside doctor or prosperous druggist; or even after intercourse for a small-college professor. Trotsky produces the impression of being a practical man able to do work without fuss or nervousness and without wasting words or energy.[60]

Although General Judson remained pleased, and did not mind even the Bolshevik press accounts of the interview, Ambassador Francis expressed regret the following morning over its treatment in the press. Francis, also apparently influenced by the British ambassador, reached the conclusion that Judson should not have seen Trotsky. Over the next several days Francis dispatched three telegrams to Washington, each giving a different version of the interview. His final version informed the Secretary of State that Judson's visit occurred without the ambassador's knowledge or approval. In fairness it should be noted that Francis was under a great deal of strain, for during the week he was forced to deal with the insubordination of several of his officials (the Foreign Service professionals had never liked him), and with other attacks upon his authority.[61]

Washington was quick to respond to the news of Judson's meeting with Leon Trotsky. Secretary of State Lansing on December 6 prohibited any contact between American officials and the Bolshevik government and on the following day discussed Judson's removal with the Secretary of War. The War College Division relieved Judson of his duties on December 24, and detailed his assistant, Monroe C. Kerth, to assume temporarily the duties of military attaché. At about the same time the allied governments were in the process of dispatching financial aid to the anti-Bolshevik movements in southern Russia, a policy to which Judson objected. The British government reached its decision to extend aid by December 8, with Lansing and President Wilson following suit on December 13, 1917.[62]

In Washington the War College Division in mid-December reevaluated its military policy in light of the Bolshevik seizure of power. The Acting Director of the War College Division, Colonel P.D. Lochridge,[63] closely examined the proposals of the military attaché in Rumania, who suggested that the Rumanian Army be evacuated deep into southern Russia in order to form the nucleus of an anti-German force. In Russia this force would, he thought, be joined by 400,000 Cossacks and an independent Ukrainian army. This plan had the support of the Department of State. The proposal also required the dispatch of American and Japanese soldiers to guard the Trans-Siberian railroad.

Colonel Lochridge balked at the idea of sending allied troops into Siberia, observing: ". . . the prospect of Japanese control of Siberia is hardly a pleasant one to contemplate." Lochridge believed that the situation of Rumania was intrinsically bound to conditions in Russia. He was concerned with Judson's warning that to aid any of the dissident national groups in southern Russia could force Russia into dependency upon Germany. Judson's cable of December 12 was even more ominous:

> Rumors circulating and alleged messengers from Cossack countries arriving, indicate approaching civil war. Many soliciting allied financial support. Can see no gain in fostering civil war. Do not believe success of either side would prolong war much, if any, and civil war perhaps most in German interest.

Lochridge was also concerned with the actions of certain Department of State officials in Russia who were in contact with anti-Bolshevik forces and requesting financial support from the United States. Lochridge weighed these conflicting views and in his formulations of the War College Divisions' position sided with the opinions of General Judson.

Colonel Lochridge's report recommended that the United States inform the Russian people that America urged them to resolve their own future and act as they saw fit, but that to conclude peace would increase American military problems. The United States should therefore prohibit the shipment of goods to Russia. He believed that the best course of action towards Russia was to restore confidence in American honesty and impartiality, which in the long run would ensure Russo-American friendship. Lochridge suggested that the Rumanians be urged to remain where they were and that no action be taken in southern Russia, where the future was entirely unpredictable. The report concluded that it was unwise to foster a civil war in Russia and that the American army should concentrate its efforts on the western front. The plans of the War College Division however had already been outdistanced by events, for President Wilson and the Secretary of State had already decided to ignore the Bolshevik government and secretly furnish aid to the anti-Bolshevik forces.[64]

General Judson discovered on December 10, that the Secretary of State had prohibited any further contact with the Bolshevik regime, a development which placed Ambassador Francis once more in firm control at the American embassy. Judson did not regret having seen Trotsky, and was even prepared to make another visit along with General Knox, who had now received permission to contact Trotsky. The two generals wished to reassure Trotsky that in the event of unacceptable German peace terms Russia could count upon the renewed assistance of the allies. Lansing's prohibition of contact with the Bolsheviks, however, quashed their plan. In the following days Judson lamented the news of the spread of civil war through southern Russia and attempted to answer Washington's request as to whether Germany was exchanging prisoners of war and economic goods with Russia.[65] On December 16, he replied that the two nations were not exchanging prisoners, although some smuggling was taking place between Germany and Finland. Judson requested authority to reinstitute contact with the de facto governments to prohibit Germany from securing economic materials. He also requested the power and finances to purchase war goods to prevent their purchase by German agents.[66]

Raymond Robins visited Judson on December 17 to inform him of Trotsky's perception of the situation. Robins had talked to the Bolshevik Commissar the previous evening; and Trotsky wanted the Americans to know that he was still attempting to comply with Judson's suggestions of December 1. Robins promised to remain in contact with Trotsky and the armistice negotiations. That evening Judson informed Washington that the Bolsheviks were threatening action against the allies if they continued to deal with the anti-Bolshevik groups in southern Russia. The general repeated his recommendation of maintaining friendly terms with the Bolsheviks, if only to keep Russian war materiel out of German hands. He then asked for permission to assure the Lenin-Trotsky regime unofficially of American support if the Russo-German talks broke down. The following day Robins returned with an assurance from Trotsky that Russia would not permit the shipment of war materials into Germany, although he requested assurance from the general that no American officers were serving with the anti-Bolsheviks.[67]

Washington directed Ambassador Francis on December 20 that the prohibition of contact with the Bolsheviks included Red Cross personnel (this was aimed specifically at Robins), thereby severing the last contact between Washington and the de facto Russian government. Two days later Judson and Colonel Kerth suggested to the ambassador that the allies should adopt a consistent Russian policy based on the following points: enter into helpful relations with all de facto governments including the Bolsheviks; attempt to stop a civil war in Russia; recognize that Russia could no longer fight Germany; recognize that the Bolsheviks were strangers to diplomatic etiquette and that the allies should not be offended by their behavior; and treat Russia with the sympathy it deserved. Judson and Kerth maintained that unless these principles were adopted Russia would be driven into dependency upon Germany.[68]

Ambassador Francis on December 19 confessed to the Secretary of State that he had sent no cables the day before because he was disgusted that the Bolsheviks had remained in power for so long. On December 24, however, he altered his views and suggested the possibility of recognizing the Bolshevik government. Francis acknowledged that Lenin and his followers controlled most of the nation and had remained in power for seven weeks. He feared the renewal of German economic interests in Russia and used Judson's argument that, by recognizing the Bolsheviks, the allies could at least have some influence upon the Russo-German peace talks. Francis concluded that it was of great importance to deny Germany access to war materials in Russia.[69]

The denial of such materials to Germany preoccupied the allied military attachés in Petrograd during the final weeks of 1917. The allied generals in Petrograd established a program to stop goods from entering German hands by stopping the shipment of materials into Russia, and by purchasing existing goods on the Russian market.70

The Secretary of State on December 29 implied to Ambassador Francis that Raymond Robins could resume his contacts with the Bolsheviks, so long as Robins understood that he did not represent the American government. So once again Francis and Judson possessed an unofficial link with the Bolsheviks. Robins immediately resumed contact with Trotsky at a critical moment in the Russo-German negotiations. On the afternoon of December 31, Robins arrived from the Bolshevik headquarters at Smolny to inform Judson that the negotiations would soon be broken off, and that the Bolsheviks were preparing for renewed hostilities against Germany. When Trotsky requested to know what action the United States would take if Germany renewed hostilities against Russia, Francis and Judson directed Robins to report that the American government would render all possible assistance to Russia. Later in the day Generals Knox, Judson, and Niessel met and agreed that in the event of renewed hostilities they would assure the Bolsheviks of their support, and that Judson would visit Trotsky to form a war council for coordinating military policy.71

Frenzied activity characterized New Year's Day at the American embassy in Petrograd as the allies prepared for the renewal of Russo-German hostilities. In the evening, however, the embassy received Washington's cable relieving General Judson and directing him to return to the United States. The following morning Francis received an enigmatic cable from Lansing, discouraging allied contact with the Bolshevik government, but allowing Francis to rely on his own judgment. In spite of this, on January 2, Francis gave Trotsky a written assurance of American support in the event of hostilities with Germany.72

Until his departure for Washington on January 21, 1918, General Judson devoted his energy to preventing the German seizure of Russian war materials, and the planning of military cooperation with the Bolsheviks. The program of preemptive purchases of war materials continued until the last US Army representatives departed Russia. Planning for Russo-American military cooperation occurred sporadically after Judson's departure, depending largely upon the exigencies of the situation, but reaching its high point in March 1918.73

General Judson returned to Washington in late February 1918. Secretary of State Lansing saw Judson on February 20, but the secretary was singularly unimpressed by the general's views on the Russian situation. Several days later Judson submitted to the General Staff the written views of his subordinates in Petrograd. Captain Riggs believed the Bolsheviks would remain in power for the immediate future, but would eventually fall as a result of Russia's dire economic conditions, which were compounded by the Bolshevik's unrealistic policies. He made no recommendations, but concluded that under certain circumstances the

United States and Russia could cooperate, but that it was foolish to believe that the Bolsheviks had any affection for the United States.[74]

Colonel Kerth wrote his report only weeks before his departure for France, where he was to hold several important staff positions in 1918. His credentials were impressive--he was known within the army as a remarkable officer who had already won the silver star for gallantry in action, and who was one of its most able staff officers--and he now stated that the Bolsheviks were firmly in control of Russia, and could be expected to remain in power. He recommended that the United States recognize the Bolshevik government.[75]

In Washington, General Judson continued to inform his superiors of his views on the Russian situation. The prospect of Japanese intervention in Siberia shocked Judson and on March 4, 1918, he drafted a memorandum explaining the repercussions of such an eventuality. He explained that Japanese intervention would alienate the Russian people not only against Japan but also against the allies and drive Russia into the arms of Germany. Judson believed that if the allies were compelled to intervene in Siberia, they should do so only with the approval of the Bolsheviks and that only a small American force should be used. He also stated that Japanese intervention could only be motivated by a desire for territorial aggrandizement.[76]

Judson found support for his opposition to intervention from a former military attaché to Russia, Lieutenant Colonel Sherman Miles, now serving on the General Staff. Miles did not object to a limited local intervention to protect supplies at Vladivostok. He did, however, fear that Japanese intervention would expand into an occupation of much of Siberia, which Russia could only interpret as an open invasion. Miles concluded that intervention would damage the allied war effort, and that the United States should restrain Japan to a limited "police patrol" of Vladivostok in order to assist Russia in the future.[77]

General Judson on March 8 recommended to the General Staff that the American government promise its support to Russia. Press reports indicated that Ambassador Francis had promised full American aid to Russia if the war on the eastern front continued. He urged that Washington fully endorse the ambassador's statement, for he feared that Russia would soon become a mere economic reservoir for Germany. Judson then repeated his view that Japanese intervention would drive Russia into reliance upon Germany. Believing that there was a possibility for renewed Russo-American military cooperation, he volunteered to return to Russia to continue his previous work.[78]

Judson never returned to Russia, and American policy remained unchanged. The American government continued to aid anti-Bolshevik factions and later sanctioned allied intervention into Russia--policies opposed by the Secretary of War, the Army Chief of Staff, the War College Division, and General Judson.[79] Judson apparently never discovered that President Wilson and the Secretary of State requested his recall from Russia as a result of unfavorable press commentaries of his meeting with Trotsky. Judson and his colleagues did not have a decisive influence on the course of events in Russia during their tours of duty. However, with his open mindedness and fundamentally sound judgment, Judson did help to establish a basis for cooperation between the Bolsheviks and the United States government. If President Wilson and the Secretary of State preferred to regard the Bolshevik government with a hostile neutrality rather than open and friendly cooperation, it was not the fault of the US Army officers in Russia.[80]

NOTES

[1]George F. Kennan, Soviet-American Relations, 1917-1920, The Decision to Intervene, Vol. II, (Princeton, New Jersey: Princeton University Press, 1958), 340-429.

All dates are based upon the Gregorian calendar, although Russia used the Julian calendar (13 days behind the Western calendar) until February 1918. For a view of military attachés in this early period, see T. Bently Mott, Twenty Years as Military Attaché, (New York: Oxford University Press, 1937); and Alfred Vagts, The Military Attaché, (Princeton: Princeton University Press, 1967).

The author is indebted to Dr. T.K. Nenninger of the National Archives for his kind help and to the Newberry Library for permission to cite from the Judson Papers.

[2]National Archives, record group 165, War College Division, Military Intelligence Division (hereafter MID), file 8747, document No. 1 of September 2, 1914 from the Secretary of State to the Secretary of War; document No. 6 of September 23, from the Secretary of War to the Secretary of State; and document No. 9 of October 5, from General W. Wotherspoon to the Adjutant General.

Sherman Miles was born in Washington D.C. on December 5, 1882, the son of Lieutenant General Nelson A. Miles. Following his graduation from West Point in 1905, he held successive positions with the field artillery until April 1912, when he assumed the post of military attaché in Rumania. Miles, although only a lieutenant, served as attaché to Rumania, Bulgaria, Serbia, Montenegro, and Greece and also served as military observer during the two Balkan Wars, George Washington Cullum, Biographical Register of the Officers and Graduates of the U.S. Military Academy, Supplement, edited by Wirt Robinson, Vol. VIb, (Saginaw, Michigan: Seeman & Peterson, 1920), p. 1204.

[3]MID file 8747, document No. 11, Miles No. 793 of October 16; document No. 16, Miles 808 of October 30, 1914; and document No. 22, Miles No. 880 of January 23, 1915. The Russian government allowed Miles to visit Warsaw as a result of recent improvement in Russo-American relations.

[4] MID file 8747, document No. 22, Miles No. 880 of January 23, 1915.

[5] MID file 38747, document No. 25, Miles No. 895 of March 3, 1915; and document No. 29, Miles No. 908 of May 19, 1915.

He requested the War College to allow him to return home in such an eventuality, to join the expeditionary force and make his experience available to the army. In addition, if the United States declared war against Germany, the Russian government would expect the American military attaché to join his allied colleagues at the Russian Army Headquarters where the lowest ranking allied officer was colonel. Miles' rank was of little importance so long as he remained at the front, but the presence of a mere lieutenant would undoubtedly create difficulties at a conference of allied generals.

[6] MID file 8747, document No. 32, Miles cable from Warsaw of June 19, 1915; document No. 34, Miles No. 943 of August 9, 1915; and document No. 35, Miles No. 951 of August 13, 1915. Miles also wrote that Petrograd, besides having very high cost of living, was a difficult habitat for a wife and children.

[7] MID file 8747, document No. 38, memorandum from Brigadier General A.S. Mills to the Adjutant General of September 22, 1915; document No. 47, memorandum for the Chief of Staff, Major General Hugh L. Scott, from Macomb of November 15, and General Scott's reply on same; and General Scott's memorandum of November 17, 1915.

E. Francis Riggs was a capable young officer born on June 16, 1887 in Washington D.C. He was a good horseman who had previously traveled in Europe and spoke fluent French. In addition, Riggs was unmarried and wealthy enough to afford the exorbitant cost of living in the Russian capital. Most officers selected to serve as military attachés were West Point graduates destined for distinguished military careers. Riggs, however, did not attend the military academy, graduating rather from Yale University in 1909 and obtaining his commission in 1911 and serving in the 5th Field Artillery Regiment, MID file 8747, document No. 51 of November 11, 1915; and US Army, Official Army Register December 1, 1918, (Washington D.C.: Government Printing Office, 1919), p. 362.

[8] MID file 9707, document No. 2 and No. 3 of October 2, 1916, Riggs No. 1093 and 1094. The Russian offensive jumped off to an auspicious start with General Alexey A. Brusilov's forces smashing the Austro-Hungarian Army on the South-West Front in the early summer. By the end of the summer, however, the Russian attacks bogged down in the face of stiff opposition and the Germans won a crushing victory in Rumania, which had injudiciously declared war on the central powers in August, see Norman Stone, The Eastern Front 1914-1917, (London: Hodder and Stoughton, 1976), pp. 232-281.

⁹MID file 9707, document No. 4, Riggs No. 1104 monthly report of November 1, 1916.

¹⁰MID file 9707, document No. 5, Riggs monthly report dated January 10, 1917.

¹¹MID file 9707, document No. 6 of February 12, 1917.

¹²MID file 6497, document No. 14 of March 6, 1917. Newton A. McCully was born on June 19, 1867 in Anderson, South Carolina and graduated from Annapolis in June 1887. He eventually became the Navy's authority on Russia. He retired as a Vice Admiral on July 1, 1931 and died on June 13, 1951, see Charles J. Weeks and Joseph O. Baylen, "Admiral Newton A. McCully's Mission in Russia, 1904-1921," The Russian Review, Vol. XXXIII, January 1974, No. 1, pp. 63-79.

¹³MID file 6497, document No. 14 of March 6, 1917.

¹⁴David R. Francis was born in Richmond, Kentucky on October 1, 1850, although he lived most of his life in St. Louis, Missouri, where he graduated from Washington University in 1870. He developed into a prosperous grain merchant, which assisted his entry into politics, first as the mayor of St. Louis, and later as governor of Missouri and United States secretary of the interior. Governor Francis (as he was addressed even while serving as ambassador) found himself a social outcast within the rarified atmosphere of the clannish Petrograd diplomatic community. Francis still possessed an active mind and he performed his duties energetically and to the best of his ability in this, his last and most difficult public post, despite his advanced age, his lack of diplomatic experience, and the enmity of his colleagues and subordinates. Allen Johnson and Dumas Malone (editors), Dictionary of American Biography, (New York: Charles Scribner's Sons, 1931), Vol. VI pp. 577-578; Kennan, Soviet American Relations, 1917-1920, Vol. I, Russia Leaves The War, (Princeton: Princeton University Press, 1956), pp. 34-41; and David R. Francis, Russia From the American Embassy 1916-1918, (New York: Arno Press & The New York Times, 1970), pp. 57-95.

¹⁵Francis cables, No. 1120 of 4 p.m. and No. 1124 of 9 p.m. of March 22, 1917, in United States Department of State, Foreign Relations of the United States, 1918, Russia, Vol. I, (Washington D.C: United States Government Printing Office, 1931-1932), pp. 12-14, (hereafter FRUS).

¹⁶MID file 6497, document No. 11 of Office of Naval Intelligence, March 27, 1917. The same day the American Consul in Petrograd, North Winship, issued Washington a more pessimistic report on Russian conditions. He stated that although the Provisional Government remained in control, the workers and soldiers of Petrograd posed an increasing threat to the new regime. He expressed concern over the demands of the Soviet for a forty-seven hour work week and the fact that

the local garrison had adopted an eight hour day, see MID file 6497, document No. 12, No. 179 from Petrograd, March 17, 1917 to the Secretary of State. See also Winship's cable No. 287 of April 10, 1917 in FRUS Vol. 1, Russia 1918, pp. 21-24.

[17]Riggs No. 2. April 7, 1917 to the Secretary of the War College Division, in the Papers of General Francis LeJ. Parker, Library of Congress, Manuscript Division, folder, "Rumanian Army Observer."

[18]Francis LeJau Parker was born on June 24, 1873 in Abbeville, South Carolina, He graduated from West Point in 1894 as a cavalry officer, serving in Cuba, Puerto Rico, the Philippines and China. He returned to West Point as an instructor, graduated from the Army War College, and served as aide de camp to no less than three generals before leaving for Rumania as military observer. Upon leaving Petrograd he served as regimental and brigade commander on the Western Front. He ultimately became Chief of the Bureau of Insular Affairs in 1929. He retired as a Brigadier General in 1939 to Charleston, South Carolina, where he died on May 16, 1966, Who Was Who in American History - The Military, (Chicago: Marquis Who's Who, 1975), p. 424; and Porter Williams, Jr., "Francis LeJau Parker," Assembly, Fall 1967, p. 93.

[19]Monroe C. Kerth was born in Cairo, Illinois on July 1, 1876 and graduated from West Point in 1898. He distinguished himself in the Philippine Campaign and later served in the General Staff in various capacities, Cullum's Register, supplement, Vol. VIa, p. 830; Vol. VII, pp. 460-461; and Vol. VIII, p. 113.

[20]MID file 9775, document No. 13 of April 16, 1917; and Parker Papers, Parker cable No. 4 1/2 of April 7, 1917 in folder "Rumanian Army Observer."

[21]William V. Judson was born in Indianapolis, Indiana on February 16, 1865. He graduated third in his class at West Point in 1888 and later served as Assistant Divisional Engineer of the Panama Canal and Director of Harbor Improvements for Lake Michigan. In 1901 he invented a revolutionary type of floatable concrete caisson for which he gained his fame in the engineering community. Judson was a quiet and intelligent man of average height, bespectacled, with a wife an family. George Kennan described Judson as the "finest type" of American officer, Kennan, op. cit., pp. 41-43; Cullums Register, Supplement, Vol. VI a, pp. 487-488, Vol. VII, pp. 168-179; Army Register 1922, p. 284; The Association of the Graduates of the United States Military Academy, Annual Report June 11, 1924, (Saginaw, Michigan: Seeman & Peters, Printers, 1924), pp. 74-83; and Who Was Who in American History - The Military, p. 297.

[22]Hugh L. Scott was born in Danville, Kentucky on September 22, 1853 and graduated from West Point in 1876 as a cavalryman. He spent much of his career in the American West, becoming an authority on American Indian culture and sign language. He was also a thorough

soldier, active, intelligent, and reliable. He served as Army Chief of Staff from November 1914 to September 1917, when he reached the mandatory retirement age. The Army retained him on the active roster through the end of World War I, however, and used him to observe operations on the West Front. In May 1919 he retired to Princeton, New Jersey, where he devoted his remaining years to his family, writing, and the New Jersey State Highway Commission, of which he was Chairman. He died on April 30, 1934, Who Was Who in American History-The Military, p. 413; and Hugh L. Scott, Some Memories of a Soldier, (New York: The Century Co., 1928).

[23] MID file 10055, document No. 1 of April 21, 1917, with enclosures; Richard W. Leopold, Elihu Root and the Conservative Tradition, (Boston: Little, Brown and Company, 1954), pp. 116-121

[24] National Archives, record group 120, Records of the American Expeditionary Force, entry 1553, box 72, Riggs letters of April 17, 1917 to Sir John Handbury Williams and General Frederick C. Poole; Op. cit., box 76, Riggs letter of April 5, 1917 to J. Butler Wright; William Appleman Williams, American Russian Relations 1791-1947, (New York: Rinehart & Co., Inc., 1952), p. 87; and FRUS, 1918, Russia, Vol. III, pp. 186-187.

[25] Parker Papers, Riggs memo for Colonel Judson of June 6, 1917, in folder "Rumanian Army Observer." Point "D" in all probability refers to aviation units.

[26] MID file 10063, document No. 3 of July 25, 1917 from Scott to the Secretary of War. The British military attaché drew precisely the opposite conclusions regarding the capabilities of the Russian Army viewing the same events as General Scott, see Alfred W.F. Knox, With The Russian Army, Vol. I, (New York: Arno Press & The New York Times, 1971), pp. 593-626.

[27] See Kennan, op. cit., pp. 19-26; Thomas A. Bailey, American Faces Russia Russian-American Relations From Early Times To Our Day, (Ithaca, New York: Cornell University Press, 1950), pp. 233-234; and Leopold, op. cit.., pp. 116-121.

[28] Scott, op. cit., pp. 570-593; and Mott, op. cit., pp. 190-210. For the Root Commission Report, see FRUS, 1918, Russia, Vol. 1, pp. 131-146.

[29] See for example MID file 6497, document No. 13, from the prominent lawyer Thomas N. Perkins, to General Joseph Ernst Kuhn, erroneously dated January 7, 1917. In all probability the letter was written on June 7, 1917.

[30] General Scott failed to mention Lieutenant Riggs in his report to the Secretary of War and in his memoirs. Nor did the general mention whether he conferred with naval attaché. Scott, op. cit.; and MID file 10063, Scott report of July 25, 1917.

[31] MID file 10166, document No. 12 of June 26, 1917, letter from Judson to General Kuhn. For a discussion of the problems presented by Judson's dual role see Kennan, op. cit., pp. 35-43. Francis and Judson received little if any guidance from their superiors in Washington.

[32] MID file 10166, document No. 15, Judson cable No. 1175 to Chief War College Division of July 19, 1917.

[33] N.A., record group 120, entry 1553, Judson memorandums for Francis of August 30, and 31, 1917; Williams, American Russian Relations, (New York; Rinehart & Co., Inc., 1952), pp. 96-97; and Robert Lansing, The War Memoirs of Robert Lansing Secretary of State, (New York: Bobbs-Merrill Col, 1935), pp. 337-338.

[34] MID file 10166, document No. 20 of September 3, 1917 Judson report No. 1209 to Chief of the War College Division. In early September Judson used Riggs to supervise passport control duties in Petrograd.

[35] N.A. record group 120, op. cit., Judson memorandum for Ambassador Francis of September 3, 1917.

[36] Ibid., Judson memorandum of September 11, 1917. On October 7, Judson informed the War College Division of the Provisional Government's decline in strength and inability to control separatist movements in Southern Russia and Finland. He also observed the increased popularity of the Bolshevik's demand for peace, FRUS, op. cit., pp. 204-205.

[37] MID file 6497, document No. 34 Judson cable No. 37 to War College Staff, and document No. 35 Judson cable No. 38 to War College Staff of September 15 and 17, 1917 respectively.

[38] FRUS, 1918, Russia, Vol. I, p. 192, Francis cable No. 1760 of September 16, 1917, 10 P.M. to Secretary of State.

[39] MID file 6497, document No. 64, Francis unnumbered cable of October 4, 1917 to the Secretary of State, printed in FRUS, 1918, Russia, Vol. I, pp. 202-203 as cable 1836.

[40] MID file 6497, document No. 171, Department of State periodical report on matters relating to Russia, No. 2 of December 1, 1917.

[41] N.A. record group 120, op. cit., Judson memorandum for Francis of October 4; MID file 10166, document No. 15, Judson cable No. 1175 to Chief WCD of July 19; document No. 18, Judson cable No. 1185 of July 31, document No. 20, Judson cable No. 1209 of September 3; and document No. 24, Judson cable No. 1216 of September 23, 1917. Francis apparently never contacted Reed.

⁴²William Henry Chamberlin, The Russian Revolution, Vol. I, (New York: The Macmillan Company, 1952), p. 296.

⁴³FRUS, 1918, Russia, Vol. I, pp. 208-209, Francis cable No. 1853 of October 9, 1917, 11 p.m.

⁴⁴Knox, With the Russian Army, Vol. I, pp. 697-698.

⁴⁵Robert V. Daniels, Red October The Bolshevik Revolution of 1917, (New York: Charles Scribner's Sons, 1967), pp. 112-113; and Francis cable No. 1935 to the Secretary of State of October 30, 1917 in FRUS, op.cit., p. 216.

⁴⁶MID file 6497, document No. 87, Francis cable No. 1948 of November 2, 1917.

⁴⁷Ibid.

⁴⁸Robert D. Warth, The Allies and the Russian Revolution, (New York: Russell and Russell, 1973), pp. 148-149.

⁴⁹Daniels, Red October, pp. 107-199; and Warth, op. cit., pp. 148-157.

⁵⁰MID file 6497, document No. 78, Stockholm No. 960 of November 8; No. 104, Francis cable No. 1964 of November 8; and No. 99, Francis cable No. 1968 of November 9, 1917, see FRUS, op. cit., Vol. I, pp. 226-228.

⁵¹N.A. r.g. 120, op. cit., Judson memorandum for Francis of November 10, 1917. Judson's proposal also allowed for the use of these troops to protect the allied embassies.

⁵²MID file 6497, Document No. 81, cables from Francis routed through Stockholm No. 970 and 972 of November 10 and 11; Francis cable No. 1985 of November 16, 6 p.m. of November 17, in FRUS, op. cit., pp. 233-234. Judson also received similar assurances from the Bolshevik military commander of Petrograd, Kennan, op. cit., I, 81-82.

⁵³The Secretary of War and Postmaster-General both relayed this and other Judson cables to President Wilson, MID file 6497, document No. 94, Judson No. 87 of November 14, 1917, 4 p.m.; and Kennan, , op. cit., I, fn. pp. 124-125.

⁵⁴Captain Eugene Prince assisted Judson in the compilation of this study, MID file 10212, document No. 13, Judson cable No. 1241 of November 15, 1917.

⁵⁵The General no doubt realized the awkwardness of his proposal, for he requested Francis not to reveal the contents to anyone;

N.A., r.g. 120, op. cit., Judson memorandum for Francis of November 16, 1917.

56Warth, op. cit., pp. 166-168; N.A., r.g. 120, op. cit., Judson memorandum for Francis of November 19; Francis memorandum for Judson of November 20; and Judson memorandum for Francis of November 21, 1917.

57The press report, as is now known, did not originate from the American government, Kennan, op. cit., I, 99-106; and Judson papers, the Newberry Library, Judson diary entry of November 27, 1917.

58N.A., r.g. 120, op. cit., Judson memorandum for Francis of November 26.

59Kennan, op. cit., I, 107-108. The letter was sent with the approval of Ambassador Francis.

60Judson Papers, diary entries for November 31 and December 1, 1917. The French military attaché expressed no interest in meeting Trotsky.

61Kennan, Russia Leaves the War, pp. 119-127.

62The French were already assisting anti-Bolshevik forces in southern Russia, Kennan, op. cit., pp. 123-128, and 169; U.S. Department of State, Papers Relating to the Foreign Relations of the United States: The Lansing papers, 1914-1920, Vol. II, (Washington D.C.: Government Printing Office, 1939-1940), pp. 345-346; and MID file 10166, document No. 27 with enclosures, memorandum from Colonel Lochridge for the Chief of Staff of December 22, and letter from the Secretary of War to the Secretary of State of December 24, 1917. One should note that Colonel Kerth did not assume the dual role of chief of the military mission, clearly placing him under the authority of Ambassador Francis.

63P.D. Lochridge was born on December 2, 1863 near Bexar, Alabama and attended West Point, graduating in 1887. He served as a cavalry officer in the West, the Caribbean area, and the Philippines before entering the General Staff. He retired from the army as a colonel in 1919, went into private business, and subsequently died in Washington D.C. on June 17, 1935, Who Was Who in American History - The Military, p. 334.

64MID file 8806, document No. 85, undated, date stamped January 14, 1918 memorandum for the Chief of Staff from the Acting Director of the War College Division, Colonel Lochridge. For the decision to oppose the Bolshevik government see Robert J. Maddox, The Unknown War With Russia Wilson's Siberian Intervention, (San Rafael: Presidio Press, 1977) pp. 34-41; and N. Gordon Levin, Jr., Woodrow

Wilson and World Politics America's Response to War and Revolution, (New York: Oxford University Press, 1968), pp. 64-73.

[65] Judson Papers, Judson Diary entries for December 10-12, 1917. Judson believed that the prohibition of contact with the Bolsheviks was largely the fault of the American correspondent of the Chicago Daily News in Petrograd, Louis Edgar Brown.

[66] Judson Diary, December 15; and MID file 10741, document No. 2, Judson cable No. 135 of December 15, 1917.

[67] MID file 9707, document 10, Judson diary entry for December 17; MID file 8806, document No. 85, Judson cable No. 138 of December 17; and file 9707, document No. 11, Judson diary entry of December 18, 1917.

[68] FRUS, Russia, Vol. I, p. 319, Lansing cable No. 1717; and Judson Papers, Judson diary entry for December 23, 1917.

[69] Kennan, op. cit., p. 205; Francis cable No. 2117 of December 17, 1917 in FRUS, op. cit., pp. 317-318; and Francis cable no. 2138 of December 24, 1917, 11 p.m., in FRUS, op. cit., pp. 324-326.

[70] MID file 10741, the entire folder pertains to the preemptive purchase of war materials in Russia. The War Department allocated $1 million to Judson for such purchases; and file 9707, document No. 11, Judson diary entries for December 24, 1917 through January 7, 1918.

[71] MID file 9707, document No. 11, entry of December 31, 1917.

[72] Judson diary entry of January 1, 1918; and Kennan, op. cit., pp. 236-241.

[73] Judson diary entry for January 6, 1918; and Kennan, op. cit., pp. 236-241. Judson dispatched Colonel Kerth and his aide to assist the Bolshevik military authorities at Moghilev.

[74] Kennan, op. cit., p. 476; the report of Major Henry C. Emery, former professor of political economy at Yale University, dealt only with the technical economic aspects of buying supplies in Russia. MID file 6497, document No. 367, Riggs report of January 22, 1918. Riggs remained with the military mission until the American representatives finally abandoned Russia. Riggs died in Puerto Rico, where as a colonel of the insular police, a Puerto Rican nationalist assassinated him on February 23, 1936, N.A.; r.g. 165, file 10110, document 2662, March 6, 1936 from Major J.N. Dalton to Colonel C.K. Nulsen, Headquarters Second Corps Area.

[75] MID file 6497, op. cit., Kerth report of January 22, 1918. Kerth served as professor of military science at the University of Missouri from 1925 to 1929, when he retired after thirty years in the army. He spent

the remainder of his life in Columbia, Missouri, devoting his efforts to youth activities, being an original member of the city parks and recreation board. After a short illness, he died at Walter Reed General Hospital on August 13, 1936; Cullums Register, Supplement, Vol. VI a, p. 830, VII, pp. 460-461, and VIII, p. 113; and West Point Annual Report, 1937, "Monroe Crawford Kerth," pp. 214-216.

76MID file 6497, document No. 433, Judson memorandum for the Acting Chief of Staff of March 4, 1918.

77MID file 6497, Miles memorandum to Judson of March 4, 1918. In his long and distinguished career, Miles served as Assistant Chief of Staff of the US Army during World War II, retiring as a major general in 1946 and dying in October of 1966, Army Register 1946, p. 477; and letter of January 13, 1977, GSA form 7093 to the author from the National Personnel Records Center, St. Louis, Missouri.

78MID, op. cit., Judson memorandum No. 3 of March 8, 1918.

79Peyton C. March, The Nation at War, (Garden City, New Jersey: Doubleday, Doran & Co., Inc., 1932), p. 126.

80General Judson's career did not suffer as a result of his recall from Petrograd; the recall was only a political expedient and Judson later received a distinguished service medal for his actions in Russia. He commanded the 38th Infantry Division for four months and later assumed command of the New York City port of embarcation on September 3, 1918. While serving in the latter capacity he contracted the flu in the influenza epidemic of 1918 and suffered irreparable heart damage. He spent much of the next several years under medical care. He retired from the army on August 31, 1922 when he could no longer perform his duties. Judson died on March 23, 1923 at Winter Park, Florida and was buried at Arlington Cemetery, Kennan, I, 123-128; Cullums Register Supplement, Vol. VIII, pp. 268-269; and West Point Annual Report June, 1924, pp. 74-83.

FRANK A. GOLDER, THE INQUIRY, AND SOVIET RUSSIA

by ALLEN WACHHOLD

> Amongst other infirmities of human nature is that mental blindness which not only forces man to err, but makes him hug his errors.
>
> Seneca

In September 1917, President Woodrow Wilson established a special organization called the Inquiry to prepare for the peace that might follow the First World War. To achieve this purpose, Wilson wished to establish a research organization, independent of the State Department, for collecting documents, writing reports, and presenting cartographic and statistical information in preparation for the United States' case at the peace conference. Wilson assigned his personal diplomatic advisor, Colonel Edward House, to select historians, economists, political scientists, and geographers as members of this research organization. Wilson hoped to keep the Inquiry a secret, but in september an Inquiry underling leaked the story to the press that a special diplomatic organization was being put together. Newspapers across the country printed the story on the front page. Dr. Frank A. Golder, an expert on Russian history, reading his newspaper in tiny Pullman, Washington, where he was a professor of history at Washington State College, learned about the Inquiry and decided that he would like to participate; scores of other intellectuals responded similarly. Golder's interest reflected fundamental patriotism, but scholarly considerations and his recent experience in Russia during the March Revolution prompted him to think that he might be able to assist the Inquiry. This decision eventually led to Golder's participation on the Inquiry, a participation neglected by historians.[1]

Golder's interest in Russia stemmed in part from the fact that he was born in Odessa in the Ukraine, a province of Tsarist Russia, of German-Jewish parents in 1877; at the age of eight, he and his parents immigrated to the United States to escape from Russia's toleration of the persecution of Jews. He grew up in poverty in New Jersey, but through the financial assistance of a Baptist minister, family encouragement, and

FRANK A. GOLDER

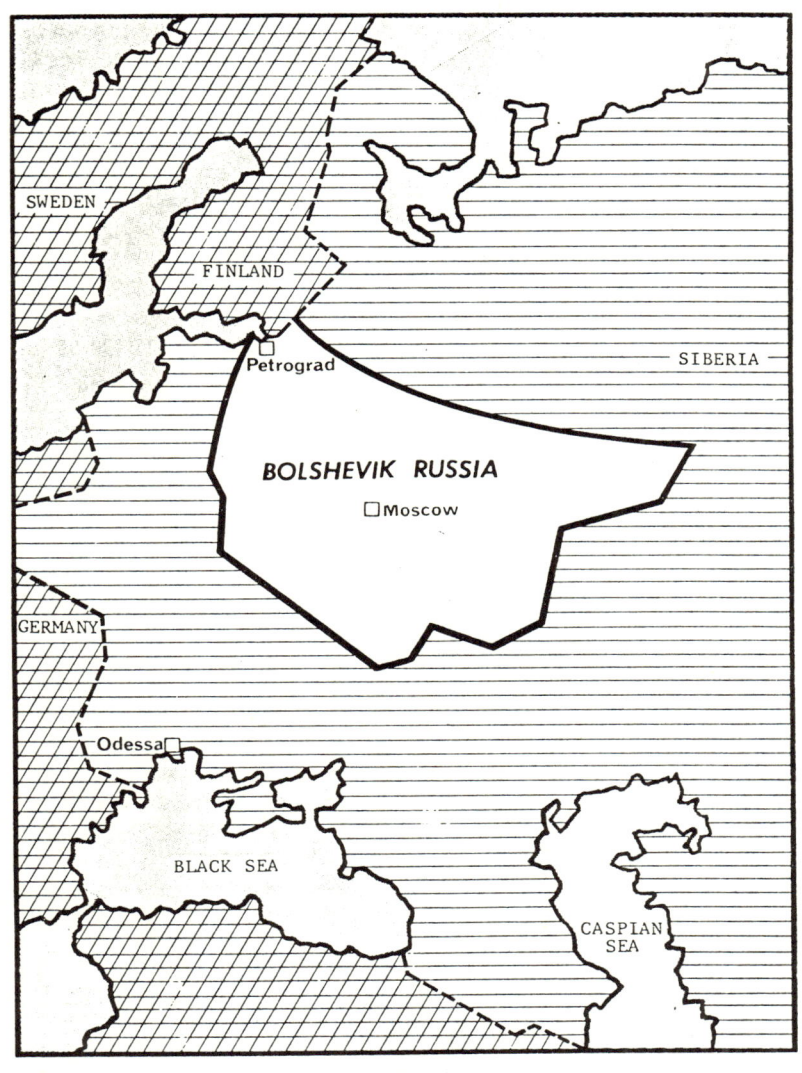

LIMIT OF THE AREA CONTROLLED BY THE BOLSHEVIKS
DURING THE HEIGHT OF THE SOVIET CIVIL WAR

self-reliance, Golder attended local schools and Georgetown College in Kentucky, a preparatory school. An impressive academic record at Georgetown College secured him admission to Bucknell University. After graduating in 1889, he sought adventure in Alaska, teaching native children for three years. The experience proved less a romantic adventure than a test of psychological adjustment to the loneliness of isolation. In spite of many depressing experiences, he learned forbearance and resolution, and appreciation for nature; more importantly, his contact with the Aleuts taught him to appreciate human values and cultures.

After Golder returned to the United States, he continued his education in 1902. He earned an M.A. in 1903 and Ph.D. in 1909 in history, both at Harvard University. His mentor, Archibald Cary Coolidge, a major figure in starting Russian studies in the United States, actively sought out students to train as experts in Russian and eastern European history, fields of study severely neglected in the United States.[2] Golder, who was fluent in Russian, fell under Coolidge's careful guidance. It was Coolidge who steered him through his Ph.D. program, a mixture of Russian, modern European, and U.S. history, and through his dissertation on Russian expansion in the pacific from 1641 to 1850. His mentor also believed in broad exposure to languages, knowledge, and the wider world, and had Golder study during his Ph.D. program at Paris and Berlin. Here he became fluent in French and German, took history courses, and expanded his knowledge of contemporary Europe.

With his Ph.D. in hand, Golder settled in Pullman, Washington as a professor of history at Washington State College; he preferred this institution over a more prestigious one because of its rustic environment and his fondness for the outdoors. In 1914, he traveled to St. Petersburg, Russia, and stayed there for six months as a research fellow for the Carnegie Institution, which commissioned him to put together a catalogue of archival materials in the capital's archival centers, which had a bearing on Russo-American relation, Russian exploration of the North Pacific, and Russian settlement of Alaska.[3] He also did research on his specialty, Russo-American relations. Golder was one of the earliest American historians to consult Russia's archives and to write on the foreign affairs between the United States and Russia. Golder's writings, though, were somewhat unsophisticated; he tried to describe what happened accurately and fairly, but without too much analysis, and with a preference for political and geographical over economic history. But he was becoming one of the leading American historians on Russian and Alaskan history, whose articles on the Russian fleet during the American Civil War, for instance, or on the purchase of Alaska in 1867, appeared in the prestigious <u>American Historical Review</u>.[4]

During his stay, Golder not only absorbed Tsarist Russia's archives, but also its theater, opera, politics, society, and intellectual life. He also saw the outbreak of the First World War, and witnessed Russia's nationalistic fervor and devotion to Tsar Nicholas II. When he returned to the country in 1917, this time as a research fellow for the National Geographical Society, he found the atmosphere very much changed. Petrograd (formerly St. Petersburg) was rife with dissension against the Tsar, upset over the country's military defeats, food and fuel shortages, and court corruption. In spite of this, Golder never suspected that he would find himself in the middle of a revolution. But just a few days after his arrival, the March Russian Revolution[5] broke out and on 15 March the Tsar abdicated; prior to this, Golder had seen huge crowds protesting in the streets, the police and Cossacks trying to restore order, and the defection of the Petrograd garrison that led to the Tsar's abdication. He also observed the festive atmosphere that accompanied the revolution. Golder shared the general enthusiasm for the fall of Tsardom; a strong believer in democracy, he favored the creation of liberal institutions in Russia.

For the next six months, Golder observed the revolution's degeneration as the Petrograd Government (PG), and its sometime ally and sometime rival the Petrograd Soviet, continued the war, which exhausted Russia's fighting morale and aggravated its serious socio-economic problems. Russians of every class, but especially the soldiers, wanted peace; Russians wanted food, but received inadequate food supplies due largely to transportation difficulties. The peasants, comprising around ninety per cent of the population, wanted the redistribution of land, which the PG had promised but failed to give them while the war was still on. In view of all this, Golder became very pessimistic over the PG's ability to stay in power. On 15 August 1917, he departed Russia, and three months later, in November, Vladimir Ilyich Lenin, and his radical Bolsheviks, seized power, withdrew from the war and began to reshape Russian society and politics in the Marxist image.

When Golder returned to the United States in September 1917, the American public regarded the Provisional Government as representative of the Russian people struggling for victory in the Great War for the cause of democracy. Most Americans did not suspect the PG's weakness and Russia's exhaustion and that the Bolshevik party moved closer to victory. President Wilson, along with numerous newspapers, inspired this false impression as they hailed the March Revolution as a victory for democracy and the PG as a suitable partner in the Allied coalition against the Kaiser of Germany rather than autocratic, Tsarist Russia. Wilson's view emanated from his moralistic crusade to rid the world of German autocracy, imperialism, and militarism (to be replaced by American globalism). But Golder, having just returned from Russia, knew that most Russians wanted peace and that the PG could not endure much longer because it had alienated the support of the soldiers, the workers, and the peasants.[6]

It was in the light of this experience that Golder solicited an Inquiry assignment. He wrote to a friend, John F. Jameson, Director of Historical Research for the Carnegie Institution, "that he would be delighted to be of service to our government."[7] Jameson had founded the National Board for Historical Service (NBHS), whose chairman,

James T. Shotwell, was an Inquiry leader. Shotwell enlisted NBHS's assistance in the Inquiry's work, and Jameson informed Shotwell of Golder's interest in participating on the Inquiry. Jameson, a leading historian, wrote Shotwell that:

> Golder speaks and writes Russian with facility, has a very exceptional familiarity with the history of the diplomatic relations between the U.S. and Russia, and has had excellent opportunities of observation during several of the earlier and several of the most recent months of the war. But what I should emphasize most, is, that he is an observer of extraordinary intelligence, insight, and good judgment, and that, being a man of catholic sympathies, he has put himself in contact with quite an unusual variety of people in Russia, so that he is exceptionally able to estimate the opinions and tendencies of different classes there.[8]

Shotwell, impressed by Jameson's opinion of Golder, sent Golder a telegram, asking him to join the Inquiry.[9]

After accepting this assignment, Golder secured a two month leave of absence from Washington State and left on the train for New York City in late November. When he arrived at New York, Golder visited Shotwell at the Inquiry's headquarters located in the building of the American Geographical Society on upper Broadway. There Golder discussed with Shotwell the Inquiry's organization, various planned assignments, and overall goals. Golder also found out that he would be working for $240 a month. He stayed in New York for a week, and then traveled to Harvard University, where he joined the other fifteen members of the Inquiry's Eastern European Division under the supervision of Archibald Cary Coolidge, Golder's mentor at Harvard. After moving into his living quarters at the Colonial Club, Golder began his sundry Inquiry assignments at Harvard's Widener Library, which had been established by Coolidge.[10]

The Inquiry hired over 100 scholars to fill positions in fifteen different divisions. The Eastern European Division had some of the best qualified Inquiry members, a tribute to Coolidge, who had a wide knowledge of eastern European studies. In other divisions, however, many of the members were not experts in the fields relating to their particular assignments; some members had been selected because of scholarly reputation or connections with an eastern university rather than acquaintance with world politics. The reason for this lay mostly at the door of American universities which trained few historians in the fields of contemporary history. The Inquiry's leaders had to rely on historians of ancient history or early American history, on archaeologists, medievalists, and experts in other fields that did not relate to contemporary European problems; even Coolidge relied on Samuel Eliot

Morison, who became an outstanding scholar on American colonial history. Morison had taken only one course from Coolidge on the Eastern Question and, although far from an expert on eastern Europe, had taught such a course at Berkeley in 1914; for the Inquiry, he wrote reports on Finland, Italian policy toward Albania, and on railways in the Balkans. Golder, however, even though he had a scholarly reputation, advanced degrees from Harvard, and connections with the Carnegie Institution and the American Geographical Society, contrasted sharply with others whom the Inquiry had chosen as members. His background of multi-linguistic skills and practical European experience, especially in revolutionary Russia, qualified him above scholars who were more brilliant perhaps but who were unfamiliar with contemporary Europe. Coolidge recognized this, writing, "I have not thought of any man better than Golder for Russia."[11]

At first, the Inquiry hired Golder for two months. On 17 December, he wrote Shotwell, asking if the Inquiry planned to extend his membership after January 1918 so that he could make arrangements with Washington State College. Shotwell sent Golder a contract that involved securing a leave of absence for six months, devoting all his time to research for the Inquiry, and accepting a monthly salary of $245. Golder signed the contract, but Washington State would not allow him a leave of absence with academic salary. E. Holland, President of Washington State, informed the Inquiry that the college had already committed its funds to special agricultural projects and could not pay Golder a salary while not teaching. As a result, Golder complained to Shotwell that he needed an increase in salary from the Inquiry to compensate for the loss of income from the college as well as from the public lectures he had planned to give. Shotwell, in reply, wrote that patriotism should be placed over financial reward: "May I point out that so far as I know every worker in this Inquiry is engaged upon it at some sacrifice to himself. It is not to be regarded as a purely business proposition."[12] Golder had to accept the financial loss, a decision which was made a bit more palatable by the special opportunity to engage in original research, to influence diplomatic policy, and perhaps to attend the actual peace conference in some capacity.

The Inquiry had chosen Golder as an expert on Russia. Its leaders, Sidney Mezes, a philosopher of religion and ethics, James T. Shotwell, a specialist in contemporary history, Isaiah Bowman, the director of the American Geographical Society, Walter Lippmann, a writer, and David Hunter Miller, a lawyer, did not directly charge the Eastern European Division with assignments regarding the new Bolshevik government. They had little knowledge of international affairs, and considered the Bolshevik government a transitory one; after the expected collapse, they believed that Russia would develop democratic institutions. Moreover, German, central European, Italian, and Turkish questions commanded a greater sense of urgency than questions involving Russia. The Inquiry reports, which numbered several hundred over the Inquiry's one year existence, had next to nothing to say about the Bolshevik government, with only one report actually considering the revolutionary situation.13

This lack of interest also stemmed from the fact that Wilson, with the State Department's aid, arrogated Russian matters to himself. Yet Wilson and Robert Lansing, the Secretary of State, although they were aware of the appeal and challenge of Bolshevism in a European society plagued by the war's political and economic disruptions, lacked the knowledge of Russian life and politics that might have enabled them to face the need of an accommodation with the Soviets.14 Instead the Wilson administration favored confrontation with Soviet Russia, and indicated this policy by refusing to recognize the Bolshevik government for a host of reasons: the Bolsheviks had withdrawn from the war in December 1917 and negotiated a separate peace at Brest-Litovsk in March 1918--treasonous acts according to the Wilson administration; they had divided the landlords' estates, nationalized land, banks, and factories--threats to capitalism; they had repudiated the Provisional Government's national debts--an act of international theft; they had confiscated church property--a symbol of their atheism. Wilson and Lansing thus viewed the Bolsheviks as the aggressive foes of capitalism, of morality, democracy, and international law, a new enemy as threatening to world stability as the Kaiser's Germany had ever been. It was this attitude that spawned the United States' ideological opposition to the Soviets, which prepared the way for global confrontation between these two countries.

Golder's views regarding the Bolsheviks were flexible, although they were basically antagonistic. In October 1917, just before the November Revolution in Russia, Golder wrote to Jameson: "Although I have no sympathy with the gang of anarchists and disturbers who are now at work in Russia, yet I occasionally catch a glimpse of their ideals and they are not at all bad."15 While working for the Inquiry, Golder's views on the Bolsheviks were hazy. But he appears to have favored cooperation between the United States and Soviet Russia. He pointed out that the Russians "trust the American government [since they believe that it] has no territorial ambitions and no exploitation projects."16 He seemed unaware of the possibility of United States' military intervention in Siberia against the Bolsheviks. However, Golder hoped that the United States would come to the aid of Russia and Siberia because of the First World War's immense destruction, but it was humanitarian aid he had in mind. "For the good of the world . . . [the Russians and the Siberians] must be helped to get on their feet, they must be assisted to govern themselves and to live together on a basis which will lead to their cultural and economic development."17

In 1919, after working for the Inquiry, Golder stated more directly his views on Bolshevism, Wilsonianism, and Leninist Russia in an article published in January 1920. In this article, he shows that he was thoroughly aware of the appeal of Bolshevism among Europeans. He wrote:

> The poor peasants [of Europe] are not interested either in cultural development or in national independence; many of them do not even understand the meaning of these words. What they want is steady work, good wages, and plenty to eat. They hate landlords of all nationalities, and they have no reason to think that a bishop of their own people would treat them with more consideration than one of another people. Ninety per cent of every nationality in Europe is more interested in social than national problems, in the question food and wages than in culture and independence. This explains the success of Bolshevism with its appeal to overthrow the clergy and the bourgeoisie because they are the landholder, the privileged classes, the capitalists, the reputed oppressors of the working class.[18]

He also understood the ultimate goals of Bolsheviks--ending states, governments, centralized power, class distinctions, political frontiers, custom barriers, economic jealousies, and making man more dignified, intelligent, and spiritual. He wrote, "Thoughtful people the world over are in sympathy with such a movement."[19] Golder further believed that Lenin, with his concentration on economic goals as embodied in Bolshevik internationalism, clashed with Wilsonian internationalism of national and cultural goals that would lead to a democratic, progressive, and liberal world order. Despite this, there were early hints that Golder was rejecting confrontation, and was favoring an attempt at cooperation. He took this attitude even though he had no illusion about Lenin, whom he viewed as a draconian revolutionary who was working for the social transformation of Russia by violent and brutal methods. He wrote:

> Since Lenin has been in power he has preached class war, he has poisoned the hearts and minds of thousands of ignorant people against their neighbors, he has killed, imprisoned, exiled, burned, destroyed, and has been directly and indirectly the cause of the death of tens of thousands. He and his adherents are as fanatic as the most zealous inquisitors, sow the same seed and reap the same harvest--hatred, intolerance, a spiritual and intellectual decline of mankind. Lenin's methods cannot bring about the ideal he has in mind. Mankind can advance just so fast and no faster; its speed, like that of a fleet, is determined by the speed of its slowest members.[20]

By 1922, Golder was elaborating on what he had hinted at earlier-- the idea of cooperation. At the time, he was in Soviet Russia as a member of Herbert Hoover's American Relief Administration during the great famine of 1921-1923 to investigate famine conditions in various parts of Russia. (He also was working for Hoover's Commerce Department as an informant on Soviet domestic and foreign affairs.) Because of his direct experience with Bolshevik leaders, Russians of every class, and with what he had seen of Russian agriculture and industry, Golder urged the Warren Harding administration to recognize the Bolshevik regime and to trade with the Soviets. He believed that trade and recognition would bring Soviet Russia out of its economic crisis resulting from war and revolution. He also thought that acceptance of Soviet Russia into the world community might perpetuate Lenin's New Economic Policy of permitting small business to flourish and farmers to trade on the free market while the Soviet government operated major industries. In other worlds, Golder reasoned that recognition and trade would make for a less revolutionary course in Soviet foreign and domestic policy; and that if the Soviets pursued a revolutionary course, the capitalist countries could exert strong economic and political pressure against them. But he also believed that such pressure would never eradicate the Bolshevik government. Conversely, Golder did not think that diplomatic and economic contact with the United States would lead to the supremacy of capitalism and democracy in Russia. No matter what capitalist nations did against or for Soviet Russia the Bolsheviks would always be there.[21]

Instead of being assigned topics by the Inquiry related to the new Bolshevik government, Golder received assignments that dealt with former Tsarist provinces--such as Lithuania, the Ukraine, and Siberia.[22] Wilson, in January 1918, had announced in his Fourteen Points' speech the principle of self-determination as the inherent right of all nations in a new world order of international cooperation. The speech made its mark on the Inquiry's assignments; the Eastern European Division handled, as Coolidge called the unit, Questions of Nationalities. Golder therefore researched territorial boundaries, and linguistic, ethnic, and cultural differences between Russia and its borderlands. His reports tended to be factual, concise in style, and illustrated with maps. He wrote approximately thirteen reports, and they varied in length, from over 100 pages to only a few pages. Of all those who submitted reports on Russia, Golder was the most productive.

In his reports regarding former Tsarist provinces, Golder recommended the independence of Finland. He wrote:

> Politically and economically the country seems comparatively well fitted for independent statehood; and its complete divergence from Russia in language, religion, and culture, its sad experience of a connection with Russia in the past, and its strong desire for independence would seem to make reunion with Russia inadvisable. Apart from the security of Petrograd and the question of a naval balance of

power in the Baltic, it does not appear that any essential Russian interest would be impaired by such a separation.[23]

For Lithuania, Golder believed that this state should be independent, while having certain reservations over a peaceful transition. He wrote:

> It is a debatable question whether an independent Lithuania state would be a success. Lithuania is not rich in natural resources, the Lithuanians constitute only about fifty per cent of the total population, and they have not been accustomed to govern. The Poles own large portions of the land and are the rulers. The Jews control the commerce. These are some of the handicaps to independence.[24]

He also wrote:

> To what extent the diversity of population (Lithuanians, White Russians, Jews, Poles, and Germans) will work against the success of the new state depends largely on the question whether the issues will be racial, religious, or social. If the class struggle (between socialists, who favored union with Russia, and nationalists, who opposed such a union) should get the upper hand, the ethnic confusion matters little; if the old prejudices should prevail, the prospects for the new state are not bright.[25]

But, he added, "even from the ethnic point of view the situation is neither unique nor hopeless."[26] Golder, however, was completely against union between Poland and Lithuania.

> All causes of hate and distrust must be removed, and among these are the large landholder's and privileged aristocracy, both in society and in the church. Polish and Polonized Lithuanian leaders must reconcile themselves to the fact that the old order of things is gone, that the old union of Poland and Lithuania, which was the union of reigning houses and ruling aristocracies is gone. It was never a union of people; their interests were never considered. It would be extremely unwise to force the Lithuanians, against their will, to unite with the Poles.[27]

In conclusion, he wrote, "The Peace Conference can merely lay down the lines of the future Lithuania. The real decision must be made by the

Lithuanians themselves."[28] If the socialists won and they brought about a union between Lithuania and Russia, Golder had no apparent reservation even against this outcome.

For Estonia, Golder wrote:

> While the Estonians form so compact and homogeneous a nation (85% of the population is Lutheran), while they are a sober, industrious and hard-hearted people, with an unusual thirst for education and almost the lowest percentage of illiteracy of all the nations in the Russian Empire, still it may be remarked that they have not been independent for seven centuries and have had very little political experience; that their numbers are too few to enable them to stand easily alone, and that there are very cogent economic reasons for advocating the inclusion of a self-governing Estonia in a Russian federation.[29]

For the Ukraine, Golder wrote:

> From the point of view of all concerned there seems to be but one honest solution to the Ukrainian question, and that is union with Russia. The causes (Tsarist autocracy) that have estranged them are now removed. There is no good reason why they should not live in harmony in the future, and there are many reasons why they would. The Great Russians and the Little Russians are of the same race; they have the same religion, the same general tradition, and . . . the same language. Then again they are economically dependent on another, and will continue to be so even more in the future than in the past. Now that the yoke of the autocracy is off, what will not a united Slavic race, with its high humanitarian ideals, with its fine artistic sense, with its unused powers, be able to do for the world! Russia and the Ukraine must be given a chance to show what they can do. It is, of course, out of the question to bring back the old union, but some other form of union or federation on more democratic lines could be and should be brought about.[30]

In another report, Golder wrote on the Ukraine:

> On the whole . . . Ukrainia is economically more important to the rest of European Russia than

> greater Russia is to Ukrainia. Ukrainia possesses most of the fundamental economic necessities of life. Russia without Ukrainia is inadequately supplied with wheat, sugar, coal, and iron. It is clear that economic factors weigh heavily against the political separation of Ukrainia from Russia.[31]

Golder did not consider the Ukrainian nationalist movement representative of the entire country. He wrote:

> In discussing the Russian situation a distinction should be made between the nationalists [in the Ukraine] who desire autonomy and those who claim independence. Until the coming into power of the Lenin government, the independence party had no strength. All that the prominent leaders desired was autonomy, but they disagreed among themselves on the question of how much autonomy. In order to rid themselves of the influence of the Bolsheviki, the Rada (Ukrainian government) came out for independence. So far as can be determined the great mass of the Ukrainian people were not interested in the [Nationalist] movement at the outbreak of the war. The leaders do not represent or come from the people; they are the socialists and the radical intelligentsia.[32]

For Siberia, Golder had no question that this vast body of land should not be an independent state. He wrote:

> As yet the Siberian population has no common purpose, no moral ties, no spiritual vision, no great leaders, no good outlet to the sea aside from Vladivostok (an uncertainty if the port would become Siberian in the case of independence), and all these are necessary for the formation of a healthy modern state.[33]

He also wrote, "It was Russia that made Siberia and not Siberia Russia."[34] He thought that Siberian federation with Russia sounded reasonable as long as Russia retained considerable control over Siberia "If Siberia is to have its own foreign policy and to cooperate or not with Russia as may be convenient, then the federation is not worth much, and for all practical purposes the two are independent states."[35]

In spite of Golder's recommendations, the Inquiry rejected his suggestions for Russian unification. Instead it recommended to Wilson the independence of Estonia, the Ukraine, and Siberia, along with every former Tsarist province, ideas which fit neatly into Wilson's conception of the fulfillment of national aspirations. Golder's recommendations, however, reflected his awareness of the problem of realism vs. idealism in a complex world.36

Golder, at this time was having some doubts about his role in the Inquiry. He wrote to Jameson, "I am wondering whether the United States government could not make better use of me in connection with some Russian work. I am writing this to you in the hope that you are in a position to learn whether the government has need of me for Russian work."37 But Jameson, who had connections with the Inquiry elite, could offer no advice.

Golder also complained about lack of information or sources for his reports. Being a thorough, careful and thoughtful researcher, he wanted the latest information, for example, from the State Department for his report on Siberia, since American observers had been sending data to the State Department. Walter Lippmann, the Inquiry's secretary, would not give him permission to use the State Department's files. Golder failed to receive permission because of friction between the Inquiry and the State Department over the Inquiry's independent diplomatic function. Moreover, Lansing and Wilson were considering the possibility of intervening in Siberia as an anti-Bolshevik measure, bringing self-determination to Russia through the victory of Russian right-wing armies and even American soldiers. After finishing his report on Siberia, Golder wrote Lippmann, "It is longer than it should be and not as good as it might be. The last part of it is incomplete owing to the difficulty of getting accurate information about the present situation in Siberia."38

In researching his other reports, Golder also sought out information beyond Harvard's Widener Library. This library, although rich in sources on western Europe, had few contemporary sources involving eastern Europe, the Baltic region, and Russia. As Golder found out in his determination to secure information, there did not exist a single archival center in the United States for the study of modern eastern Europe and Russia. Golder's difficulty in finding source materials brought him not only frustration but also irritation with an Inquiry member who critiqued his long report on Lithuania. Golder wrote Lippmann:

> The critic says there "must be somewhere in existence" better materials, better judgment, etc. Perhaps there is but I have tried hard, but in vain, to locate it. He says, "there are many studies in Russian of special aspects on the Lithuanian question: economic, linguistic, social, historical." If the critic would give us such a list and tell us where they may be obtained we would be very grateful to him.
> I have no controversy with the critic, but I wish you to know that I use the best data available and if it is a little old, it is because I cannot get anything more recent.39

Ironically, following his Inquiry stint, Golder contributed toward correcting this dearth of primary sources in the United States regarding modern eastern Europe. In 1920, he joined the history faculty at Stanford University, and there he became curator of the Russian section of the Hoover War Collection Library (now the Hoover Institution). Between 1920 and 1929, he collected millions of documents for it throughout Europe, especially on the Baltic region, eastern Europe, the Balkans, and Russia regarding the First World War and its aftermath. Golder was the first historian in the United States to collect and to make available for scholars archives involving Russian history--the largest outside Russia--for the study of both the Tsarist and the Provisional Government, and for the Soviet period as well. They were source materials that significantly aided the growth of Russian studies in the United States.[40]

Even though Golder had become dissatisfied with certain aspects of his work, he remained a loyal historian for the Inquiry. In March 1918, he received a letter asking him to accept a commission with the American Red Cross in France, a request which would place him in one of the countries that had suffered the most devastation during the First World War, since the German army had fought on French territory since 1914 and in fact was still doing so. Golder found it an exciting request, but first asked Lippmann if the Inquiry would require his services beyond June 1918. Lippmann responded:

> We are unanimous in wanting you to stay with us after June first . . . . Your very special qualifications and ability make you practically indispensable to us. We feel that there are few opportunities that might be offered you in which you could be of more immediate service to the cause.[41]

The response made Golder decide to stay with the Inquiry.

For the next several months, Golder labored over his reports in order to meet strict time schedules. Then, on 11 November 1918, Germany signed an Armistice with the Allies, bringing to an end the war that had brought about two revolutions in Russia, driven Germany's Kaiser into exile, slaughtered millions of young men, and turned democratic governments into instruments for encouraging sacrifice, hatred, amorality, and passion to win. Just before Golder had departed from Russia in August 1917, he wrote, "The thing to do now is to finish with this war and then let us all go to work to make this world a better place to live."[42] The Armistice meant to Golder the next stage of his role in the Inquiry--participating at the peace conference in Europe's reconstruction.

The Secretary of State, Lansing, established mechanisms for selecting the American personnel, from plenipotentiaries to advisors to clerks, to go to the international gathering, since only the State Department could handle the administrative, organizational, and personnel responsibilities for an entire delegation. Lansing, considering the Inquiry a competing diplomatic agency had insisted that Wilson reduce its membership for the peace conference. Wilson gave in to Lansing's recommendation. In conformity with the State Department's wishes, the Inquiry leadership whittled down its membership from 123 to 80. Only ten Inquiry members had been chosen by late November, as part of the United States' delegation for the voyage to Europe with President Wilson.[43] At that time, Golder learned that the Inquiry had omitted his name. The sudden realization that he would be left behind in the United States stunned Golder, since he expected to take the trip as the logical conclusion of his tenure with the Inquiry. Without question, Golder was the most qualified among the Inquiry's personnel on Russia; only Coolidge had better qualifications, but he had left the Inquiry to undertake another assignment for the State Department in Vienna. In a letter to Isaiah Bowman, an Inquiry leader, Golder wrote:

> Not that it will do any good . . . but in justice to myself I must protest at the way I am being treated. For a year I have given the Inquiry all my time and all my strength. It was done at a financial loss and an impairment of health, but it was done willingly.[44]

Golder also noted that he had decided not to take the assignment in France because of Lippmann's characterization that the Inquiry believed his work to be "indispensable," and mentioned that he should have negotiated a trip to the peace conference for his continued service with the Inquiry (Robert Kerner, a historian of eastern Europe, had done just that). Golder ended his letter, by stating, "I trusted the committee to do the right thing and as a result I have before me the humiliating position of having to answer the question--'Why are you not in Paris with the others?'"[45]

Golder may have fallen victim to a bureaucratic purge. Lansing, with the President's concurrence, in part perhaps reduced the Inquiry membership in order to clear the advisory group to Wilson of those opposed to the administration's policies. But there also was the fact that Coolidge had voiced criticism of Golder's Inquiry scholarship, although he had been helpful in selecting Golder to the Inquiry; he confided to Lippmann in February 1918: "Golder is not particularly skilled in presenting his results in such a way as to bring out and emphasize the important points . . .;[46] and in April, he informed Lippmann that, "I have never felt sure how much I should trust Golder without a little steering."[47] From another angle, Historian Lawrence Gelfand speculates, "My own view as to why [Golder] was not among those taken to Paris is that Bowman, then managing the Inquiry, did not want any Jews in the group going to Europe . . . ."[48] Whatever the reasons, Robert Lord, aged 32, (Golder was 41) who had replaced Coolidge as head of the Eastern European Division after Coolidge's departure for Europe to assume his new assignment, represented Russia and Poland. But Lord, a highly regarded expert on Polish history, was not a specialist on Russian history, even though he had studied in Moscow. His selection seemed to reflect the Wilson Administration's inclination to attach greater importance to settle outstanding issues with Poland than to find a modus vivendi with the new Soviet government.[49]

What was taking place between the United States' government, the Allied governments, and Soviet Russia before and during the Paris Peace conference in 1919 really was unofficial war against the Bolshevik government. In 1918, Wilson, a wavering moralist now, let his anti-Bolshevik sentiment compel him to participate with France and Britain in surrounding Soviet Russia in an effort to gain territory, to get revenge for Russia's withdrawal from the war and separate peace, to stop the spread of Bolshevism, to open up an eastern front against the Germans, and to help Russian anti-Communist forces in the overthrow of the Bolshevik government. The British established a blockade in the Baltic Sea, closing off Russia's ports. British, French, and American troops landed at Archangel, where they closed the Arctic Sea to the Bolsheviks and offered soldiers, war materials, food, and money to assist the White armies that were fighting the Red army in the Soviet Civil War that had begun at the end of 1917. The French who had an interest in Ukrainian coal and iron, occupied southern Russia, where they supported the White armies there and cut off Ukrainian resources to the Bolsheviks. The British also had an interest in the oil fields of the Caucasus, where again they supported the Whites and closed off the Black Sea. Contingents of British, French, Japanese, and American soldiers landed at Vladivostok, thus cutting the Bolsheviks off from the Pacific. This unofficial war, a war the Bolsheviks would rally to win, compelled the Soviet regime to impose on Russia repression, administrative centralization, and forced requisitions in the countryside. The price in human life and economic devastation, as in any war, was high.

In conjunction with American intervention, Wilson did try a diplomatic solution to the Soviet question. In 1919, he attempted to bring about a conference at Prinkipo or Prince's Islands in the Sea of Marmora close to Constantinople, between the United States, the Allied governments, and both the Bolshevik and White Russian governments, which had not been invited to the Paris Peace Conference. Wilson decided on this for a variety of reasons: Allied intervention had proved to be ineffective, more Russians than expected were supporting the Bolshevik cause, congressional opposition was increasing, and American troop morale was low and conscription was out of the question now that the war was over. Wilson also thought that a peaceful settlement might place Siberian territory in the hands of a de facto White government favorable to United States' interests there--a state hostile to the Soviets and to the spread of Japanese imperialism in the Far East as well. The United States had joined the Allied Governments in intervening in Siberia not only as an anti-Bolshevik measure, but also to oppose Japanese designs on Siberia, Manchuria, and China. (All were areas the United

States wished to dominate herself under the guise of an Open Door policy.)

From the outset, though, Wilson's solution with a conference at Prinkipo ran into difficulties. It was accepted by the Bolsheviks but rejected by the Whites, and vociferously opposed by the French government, which, in the false belief that it could crush the Bolsheviks, advocated a military solution. In the face of this, Wilson and House sent William Bullitt, an American diplomatic agent, on a special fact-finding mission to Soviet Russia, hoping to discover if there might still be a conference after all. But Bullitt, who favored a cooperative view toward the Soviets, returned instead with some conciliatory suggestions from Lenin's government for ending the Soviet Civil War. Wilson, not interested in a rapprochement with the Soviets, now withdrew his active support for a conference, and in March 1919 decided to continue the policy of intervention. This meant aiding Admiral Kolchak in Siberia as well as assisting counter-revolutionary forces in southern Russia, and the maintenance of an economic embargo against the Soviets. Wilson had qualms about supporting the reactionary Kolchak, but was persuaded to do so because of the admiral's rigidly anti-Bolshevik position, his willingness to pay Russia's old debts, and his opposition to the Japanese. Before long, of course, none of this mattered, as in January 1920 the Bolsheviks captured and executed Kolchak and forced the United States to withdraw its troops from Siberia.[50]

While the Allies were still intervening in Soviet Russia, Golder in December 1918 returned to Pullman with resentment and bitterness toward the Inquiry. Years later, Golder, in a more satirical than angry mood, wrote:

> The warring armies did not fight half as bitterly [during the First World War] over the frontier lines as did the peace experts. I had the best plan, which, I am grieved to say, aroused the jealousy of both Lansing and House, and they refused to take me to Paris. Had I been there to guide Wilson I am certain we would have made a better treaty than we did. After this fling in world politics, I returned to the mountains and prairies of the wild west and busied myself in criticizing the American and European statesmen.[51]

Golder had a point. The United States was badly prepared for making a sensible peace with the Soviets. Several factors accounted for this: an inadequate education in modern politics, especially concerning Russia, the existence of few professional historians in Russian history and contemporary problems, the inadequacy of primary and secondary source materials on eastern European history, and a State Department ideologically hostile to the Bolshevik revolution and a president preoccupied with his moralistic, ideological, and imperialistic priorities. In fact, Wilson never used any of the Inquiry's reports, numbering several hundred, at the Paris Peace Conference. The Inquiry, by and large, had been a waste of time, energy, and hope. And even if Golder had traveled to Paris with Wilson, one suspects that his advice, had it been contrary to WIlson's ideas, would have made little difference. As far as Soviet Russia was concerned, wrote historian John M. Thompson, Wilson followed his own dictates only: "There is no evidence that Wilson paid any attention to the suggestions of either his experts or his admirals."[52]

In spite of the Inquiry's futility, Golder's work for the organization did give him added awareness of the problems of Europe and of international politics. His experience deepened his interest in the wider world in which the United States had to play an intelligent role. He also thought that American universities had to accommodate themselves to a complex contemporary world. In the 1920s, Golder helped to transform American education and scholarship in that direction; he taught courses at Stanford University on the Russian Revolution which offered a balanced view of this great event; he established at Stanford an unparalleled collection of source materials on eastern Europe and Russia which broadened scholarship and awareness of international politics; he worked toward the establishment of United States-Soviet diplomatic and trade relations to lessen tensions within the USSR and the world;[53] and he created the first Russo-American Institute in the United States at Stanford for the study of the Russian Revolution. Until his death in 1929, at the age of 51, Frank Golder transcended the Inquiry's narrow approach toward Soviet Russia as he tried to enhance America's understanding of Soviet Russia, so that accommodation might replace recrimination. Others would follow him, but the aim would remain elusive.

NOTES

[1] Lawrence E. Gelfand, The Inquiry: American Preparation for the Peace, 1917-1919 (New Haven: Yale University, 1963), pp. 39-42, 181, 313-14. Cited hereafter as Gelfand, Inquiry. John F. Jameson to James T. Shotwell, 8 October 1917, p. 3, U.S. Department of State, Records of the American Commission to Negotiate the Peace, Record Group 156, National Archives, Washington, D.C. Cited hereafter as RG 256. Golder, in 1905, expressed interest in becoming a career diplomat before pursuing scholarly interests. See, William Allen White to Golder, 4 February 1905, pp. 1-2, Golder Papers, Box 13, Hoover Institution, Stanford, California. Cited hereafter as GP.

[2] There were so few American scholars in the field of Russian history because Russia, autocratic, isolated, and feudalistic, had little appeal to professors or students. American students who pursued European history studied England and France, and, to a lesser degree, Germany. In 1918, few American scholars had any understanding of the economic, social, and political origins for the dynamic changes taking

place in Russia. Coolidge helped to change this lack of interest, especially after his work for the Inquiry. Robert Byrnes writes, "Coolidge awakened American historical scholarship and teaching to many areas of the world, but his first and most important contribution was founding the professional study of Russia in the United States. He helped establish instruction in Russian and other Slavic languages and literatures at Harvard, and created the base for Harvard's great library collection on Russia and the other Slavic and East European peoples [in the 1920s]. He trained the able men who succeeded him at Harvard, and many who introduced the study of Russia (which Golder did in the 1920s after he became a faculty member at Stanford University) and other areas of the world into colleges and universities throughout the United States. The standards he set helped to give Russian studies a stamp of quality and distinction at their formative stage." See, Robert Byrnes, <u>Awakening American Education to the World: The Role of Archibald Cary Coolidge, 1866-1928</u> (Notre Dame: University of Notre Dame, 1982), p. 49. Cited hereafter as Byrnes, <u>Coolidge</u>. Philip E. Mosely, <u>The Growth of Russian Studies</u>, in <u>American Research on Russia</u>, Harold H. Fisher, ed., (Bloomington: Indiana University Press, 1959), pp. 1-2.

3This volume is Golder, <u>Guide to Materials for American History in Russian Archives</u> (Washington, D.C.: Carnegie Institution, 1917).

4Golder published his dissertation in 1914. This book is, <u>Russian Expansion on the Pacific, 1641-1850</u> (Cleveland: Arthur Clark, 1914). Golder was the first non-Russian scholar after Hubert Howe Bancroft to interest himself in Russian eastward expansion. Golder held that geographical considerations were behind the motivations for determining the separation of the continents of Asia and America. For years, Golder was the authority cited by non-Russian authors who wrote accounts of Bering's voyages. In the 1950s, Raymond H. Fisher began to challenge the traditional view, and in 1977, he published an excellent study on Bering's voyages. Fisher asserted that the geographical question was not the primary reason for the voyages: Peter the Great commissioned Bering to gather information in order to "establish Russian sovereignty in northwest America to the end of exploiting its fur and mineral resources." See, Raymond H. Fisher, <u>Bering's Voyages</u>: Wither and Why (Seattle: University of Washington Press, 1977), pp. 152, 18-19, 114-15. Fisher, "Seaman Dezhez and Professor Golder," <u>Pacific Historical Review</u> 25 (August 1956): 281-92.

Golder's two distinguished articles are, "The Russian Fleet and the Civil War." <u>American Historical Review</u> 20 (July 1915) and "The Purchase of Alaska," <u>American Historical Review</u> 25 (April 1920): 411-25). Thomas Bailey, "The Russian Fleet Myth Re-examined," <u>Mississippi Valley Historical Review</u> 38 (June 1957): 81-90.

5In Russia, the March Revolution is known as the February Revolution, since the country was using the Julian calendar until 1918. The March date follows the Gregorian calendar (new style), thirteen days behind the Julian calendar (old style) by the twentieth century.

6John F. Jameson to Hugh Gibson, 8 October 1917, pp. 3-4, RG 256. Golder, "Tragic Failure of Soviet Policies," Current History 19 (February 1924): 783. Golder had written the above article in order to develop interest in Russian studies in the United States; when he found out that the journal's editor had changed the original title to an inflammatory one, Golder reacted with anger. Dimitri von Mohrenschildt, "The Early American Observers of the Russian Revolution, 1917-1921," Russia Review 3 (Fall 1943): 64-74. Peter G. Filene, Americans and the Soviet Experiment, 1917-1933 (Cambridge: Harvard University Press, 1967), pp. 13-14. Christopher Lasch, The American Liberals and the Russian Revolution (New York: Columbia University Press, 1962), p. 57.

7John F. Jameson to James T. Shotwell, 8 October 1917, p. 1, RG 256.

8Ibid., pp. 3-4. Gelfand, Inquiry, pp. 44-45.

9James T. Shotwell to Golder, 15, 17 November 1917, RG 256.

10Robert Byrnes writes, "The division included ten men who had obtained their Ph.D.'s with [Coolidge]: Arthur Andrews, George Blakesless, Sidney B. Fay, Frank Golder, Robert Kerner, Robert Lord, Albert Lybyer, Henry Shipman, Lawrence Steefel, and Mason Tyler. In fact, all those in the Inquiry who wrote reports on Russia had studied with him." See. Byrnes, Coolidge, p. 166. Golder to E. Holland, 23 November 1917, p. 1, RG 256. James T. Shotwell to Golder, 3 December 1917, p. 1, Ibid.

11Quoted in Gelfand, Inquiry, pp. 56, 35, 48, 89, 211. Robert Byrnes writes that "the work of the Inquiry demonstrates how . . . few specialists the United States possessed on Central and Eastern Europe," since Coolidge had to rely so much on his own former graduate students for Inquiry assignments rather than on professionals who had been trained at other universities. "In 1920, only eighteen American historians had received Ph.D.'s for theses on Russia and Central and Eastern Europe." See, Byrnes, Coolidge, p. 67. Harold Coolidge and Robert Lord, Archibald Cary Coolidge: Life and Letters (Boston: Harvard University Press, 1932), pp. 158, 172-74.

12Shotwell to Golder, 3 January 1918, p. 1, RG 256. Golder to Shotwell, 17 December 1917, p. 1, Ibid. Shotwell to Golder, 20 December 1917, p. 1, Ibid. Mezes to Holland, 15 January 1918, p. 1, Ibid. Holland to Mezes, 1 February 1918, p. 1, Ibid.

13Gelfand, Inquiry, pp. 49-52, 55, 92, 212.

14Robert Lansing, the Secretary of State, set the tone for U.S. ideological opposition to the new Soviet government, an opposition which became an institutionalized policy in the State Department under his, Bainbridge Colby's, and Charles Evans Hughes' direction, and may still be seen to persist in the 1980s. Lansing wrote in a private memorandum, "Bolshevism is the most hideous and monstrous thing that the human mind has ever conceived. It appeals to the basest passions and finds its adherents among the criminal, the depraved, and mental unfit. It is opposed to nationality and represents a great international movement of ignorant masses to overthrow the government everywhere and destroy the present social order. According to this doctrine, life, property, family ties, personal conduct, all the sacred rights are subject to the arbitrary will of the proletariat." Quoted in Gelfand, Inquiry, pp. 212-13. For an excellent discussion of the clash between Wilsonianism and Leninism in the twentieth century see, Charles B. Burdick, Aesop, Wilson, and Lenin: The End of the World, Second Annual President's Scholar's Address, 23 April 1975, San Jose State University, pp. 3-15. For a penetrating study of United States-Soviet relations see, Joan Hoff-Wilson, Ideology and Economics: U.S. Relations with the Soviet Union, 1918-1933 (Columbia: University of Missouri Press, 1974). Cited hereafter as Hoff-Wilson, Ideology and Economics.

15Golder to John F. Jameson, 15 October 1917, p. 1, John F. Jameson papers, Library of Congress, Washington, D.C. Cited hereafter as JP.

16Golder, "Siberia," 25 May 1918, p. 146B, Inquiry Papers, Yale University Archives, New Haven, Connecticut. Cited hereafter as IP.

17Ibid., p. 146E.

18Golder, "Will the Unrestricted Self-Determination of all National Groups Bring World Peace and Order," Journal of International Relations 10 (January 1920): 284.

19Ibid., p. 186.

20Ibid., p. 287.

21Golder to Christian Herter, 10 August 1922, pp. 314-15, GP, Box 33. Golder to Herter, 1 August 1922, p. 298, Ibid. Golder to Herter, 18 August 1922, pp. 322-23, Ibid. Golder to Herter, 22 August 1922, p. 326, Ibid. Golder to Herter, 16 October 1922, pp. 391-92, Ibid. Golder to Herter, 25 December 1922, pp. 2-3, James P. Goodrich Papers, Russia: Golder, Herbert Hoover Presidential Library, West Branch, Iowa. Cited hereafter as HPL.

In one letter, Golder wrote after attending the Tenth All-Russian Congress of Soviets in December 1922, "Soviet Russia has the expenditure of a 20th century state and the income of a nineteenth. Industry and commerce of Russia of 1923 cannot bear much more taxation unless it is more highly developed. To do this, foreign capital must give a helping hand. In his speech, [Lev] Kamanev, indicated that Soviet Russia is kindly disposed towards foreign capital and was ready to go a long way to meet it. Foreign capital need not become frightened at the emphasis he laid on the government monopoly of foreign commerce. In any case the Soviet is always ready to make special arrangements." See, Golder to Herter, 25 December 1922, pp. 2-3, Goodrich Papers, HPL.

In October 1922, Golder also wrote to Herter, assistant Secretary of the Commerce Department, "I do not mind offering suggestions because I do not expect you to act on them. During the last two weeks I have mused over the Russian question . . . and I have come to the following conclusion: It would be best for Russia and the world to tie up with Soviet authorities. The Bolsheviks are very human and very parvenue. If the United States should give them some form of recognition and should send to Moscow one of our big-hearted Americans, a man with plenty of good sense, a true democrat, who would invite the Bolsheviks to his table and treat them as human beings, he would wield much influence for good. I know all the objections that will be raised but we can bury our pride and eat our words, if necessary, but we must save Russia and she is worth saving. I do not know any other way except the policy of waiting; if we wait . . . thousands of Russians will die, and millions of others will approach the state of savagery." See, Golder to Herter, 16 October 1922, pp. 391-92, GP, Box 33.

22Golder's reports for the Inquiry are located in Box 12 of his papers at the Hoover Institution, Stanford, California, among the Inquiry Papers in the Yale University Archives, New Haven, Connecticut, and in Record Group 256, National Archives, Washington, D.C.

23Golder, "Western Russia and Poland," no date, p. 3. GP, Box 12.

24Ibid., pp. 9-10.

25Golder, "Lithuania," 11 November 1918, p. 6, GP, Box 12.

26Ibid., p. 7.

27Golder, "Lithuania," 20 August 1918, pp. 66-67, GP, Box 12.

28Ibid., p. 94.

29Golder, "Western Russia and Poland," no date, p. 5, GP, Box 12.

30Golder, "Ukraine," 11 November 1918, p. 6, GP, Box 12.

31Golder, "Special Report on Russia: Ukraine, Economic Factors," no date, p. 4, GP, Box 12.

32Golder, "Ukraine," 15 February 1918, p. 74, GP, Box 12.

³³Golder, "Siberia," 25 May 1918, p. 146A, IP. Golder also wrote, "All this talk that the Siberian is self-reliant, liberty loving, progressive and superior to the Russian is not true and is based on the erroneous premises that the Siberian is like the American Westerner . . . ." See, Ibid., p. 146.

³⁴Ibid., p. 146E.

³⁵Ibid., p. 144, 143.

³⁶In 1920, Wilson abandoned his policy of self-determination in the Baltic and other former Tsarist provinces. Wilson's Secretary of State, Bainbridge Colby, who replaced Lansing, in his Note of 10 August 1920, announced that the Wilson administration would not allow the territorial dismemberment of Russia; Colby's Note was designed to prevent the Bolshevik government from strengthening itself through an appeal to nationalism during the Soviet Civil War; to uphold territorial inviolability and thus encourage the Russian people to revolt against Communism (and also keep the Japanese out of Siberia); to gain the gratitude of the Russian people; and to bring Russia intact into the fold of democracy and capitalism. But the policy failed to strengthen the hand of the anti-Bolshevik forces during the Soviet Civil War. When the Bolsheviks had won the civil war, the United States' government did recognize the independence of the Baltic States, thus following the French policy of establishing a cordon sanitaire from the Baltic Sea to the Black Sea to prevent the spread of Bolshevism into central and western Europe. See, Hoff-Wilson, Ideology and Economics, pp. 14-17, and Frederick Lewis Schuman, American Policy Toward Russia Since 1917 (New York: International Publishers, 1928), p. 182, 207-08.

³⁷Golder to John F. Jameson, 20 March 1918, p. 1, JP.

³⁸Golder to Lippmann, 25 May 1918, p. 1, RG 256. Lippmann to Golder, 17 May 1918. p. 1, Ibid. Jzlupa to Golder, no date, p. 1, GP, Box 2. Golder, "Siberia", 25 May 1918, pp. 1-184, IP. Golder did write to the former Russian Provisional Government's Embassy in Washington, D.C. (the U.S. government supplied the embassy with funds after the Bolshevik Revolution to keep it operational for political purposes, as an anti-Bolshevik propaganda center), but received only evasive responses.

³⁹Golder to Lippmann, 11 April 1918, p. 1, RG 256. William Bentinck-Smith, Building a Great Library: The Coolidge Years at Harvard (Cambridge: Harvard University Press, 1976), pp. 126-28.

⁴⁰For an excellent book regarding the development of the Hoover Institution see, Charles B. Burdick, Ralph H. Lutz and the Hoover Institution (Stanford: Hoover Institution Press, 1974). For a biography of Frank Golder see the author's, "Frank A. Golder: An Adventure in Russian History," (Ph.D. dissertation, University of California, Santa Barbara, 1984).

⁴¹Lippmann to Golder, 4 April 1918, p. 1, RG 256. Golder to Lippmann, 1 April 1918, p. 1, Ibid. Golder to John F. Jameson, 20 March 1918, p. 1, JP.

⁴²Golder to Holland, 16 July 1917, p. 1, E. Holland Papers, Special Collections, Washington State College, Pullman, Washington.

⁴³Gelfand, Inquiry, p. 162.

⁴⁴Golder to Bowman, 24 November 1918, p. 1, RG 256. Gelfand, Inquiry, pp. 162-63.

⁴⁵Golder to Bowman, 24 November 1918, p. 1, RG 256. Gelfand, Inquiry, p. 58.

⁴⁶Quoted in Jonathan M. Nielson, "American Historians at the Versailles Peace Conference, 1919: The Scholar as Patriot and Diplomat." (Ph.D. dissertation, University of California, Santa Barbara, 1985), p. 294.

⁴⁷Coolidge to Lippmann, 3 April 1918, Inquiry Files, General Correspondence, National Archives, Washington, D.C.

⁴⁸Lawrence Gelfand to author, 5 December 1984, p. 1.

⁴⁹John M. Thompson records that Wilson in 1919 at the Paris Peace Conference received a memorandum on the Russian situation from Robert Lord, his technical advisor on Russia, dated 16 January. Thompson states that "Lord's report, while full of accurate data, tended to stress Soviet weakness in its interpretations." In fact, at this time of the Soviet Civil War, as Thompson points out, the Bolsheviks were eager to be conciliatory to the Allies and to make peace, despite the fact that the Bolsheviks were gaining victories in the civil war over the Whites and their Allied backers, and were gaining growing support from those disillusioned with reactionary Russian policies or repelled by foreign intervention. See, John H. Thompson, Russia, Bolshevism, and the Versailles Peace (Princeton: Princeton University Press, 1966), p. 100, footnote # 62. Cited hereafter as Thompson, Bolshevism and the Versailles Peace. Robert Lord, in Some Problems of the Peace Conference (Cambridge: Harvard University Press, 1922), p. 171, did mention the problem of disposing of Russian territory without Soviet Russia's consent, but fell on the excuse that "there was no recognized Russian government which a voluntary settlement could be negotiated."

⁵⁰Adam B. Ulam, A History of Soviet Russia (New York: Praeger, 1976), p. 34. William Appleman Williams, American-Russian Relations 1781-1947 (New York: Rinehart, 1952). William Appleman Williams, American Intervention: Strictly Anti-Bolshevik, in Betty M. Unterberger, ed., American Intervention in the Russian Civil War (Lexington, Mass: Heath, 1969), pp. 83-97. Jerry Israel, Progressivism and the Open Door, America and China, 1905-1921 (Pittsburg: University of Pittsburg Press,

1971), pp. 160-65. William S. Graves, America's Siberian Adventure, 1918-1920 (New York: Jonathan Capte and Harrison Smith, 1931), pp. 191-95. Gabriel Kolko, Main Currents in Modern American History, (New York: Pantheon Books, 1984), pp. 58,61. Thompson, Bolshevism and the Versailles Peace, pp. 207-51.

[51]Golder, "Biographical Sketch," p. 2, Harvard University Archives, Cambridge, Massachusetts. In 1919, Golder wrote Lansing, asking for permission to publish the Inquiry reports he had written, one on Lithuania and one on the Ukraine. Lansing, perhaps for reasons of secrecy, did not give Golder the requested permission. See, Lansing to Golder, 18 August 1919, p. 1, GP, Box 19. Apparently, Golder felt confident that he could publish these studies and was not pleased with Lansing's response. See, Golder to E. E. Bernays, n.d., p. 1, GP, Box 2.

[52]Thompson, Bolshevism and the Versailles Peace, p. 48, footnote #35.

[53]During the non-recognition period, from 1922 to 1933, congressmen, businessmen, and editors traveled to Russia. After they returned to the United States, a number of them embarrassed the State Department by advocating trade with and even, on occasion, recognition of the Soviet government, although the majority of businessmen in the United States did not advocate recognition. Moreover, as Hoover's Commerce Department eased restrictions against trade with the Soviets in the mid-1920s, engineering companies, heavy machinery industries, and companies dealing with cotton, flour, automobiles, iron and steel traded with Russia. Golder's observation in 1922 proved insightful: "The only way [the Soviets] can save [Russia] is by calling in foreign capital and on the terms of the capitalists. The [party] will yield pretty much everything along economic lines . . . . I imagine foreign capitalists will have no quarrel with them on that score." Golder to James P. Goodrich, 17 September 1922, Goodrich Papers, HPL.

When Golder returned to the Soviet Union in 1925, he observed the positive effect of United States' economic contact with Russia; he wrote to the Commerce Department, "I think it may be said with safety that the population as a whole is as well off today as it ever was in its history." Golder to Christian Herter, 20 October 1925, p. 2, GP, Box 15.

Finally, in 1933, FDR circumvented public opinion, business opinion, and the State Department and granted recognition to the USSR as a counter-move to Japanese imperialism in the Far East. Joan Hoff-Wilson, "American Business and the Recognition of the Soviet Union," Social Science Quarterly 52 (September 1971): 368. But recognition proved to be a facade, as the State Department continued its ideological opposition against the Soviet Union. Hoff-Wilson writes of the contradictions of the non-recognition period and the persisting opposition during the period of recognition, "The policy of non-recognition . . . provides one of the best examples of twentieth century U.S. diplomacy at its worst because it fostered a lack of reconciliation and coordination between economic and political foreign policy. This inconsistency was the direct product of an ideologically based diplomacy that became bureaucratized and obsolete but nonetheless self-perpetuating. As such, it represents an endemic weakness in the subsequent conduct of a U.S. foreign policy that has not allowed the United States to achieve the humanitarian goals it proclaims and that, carried to its logical extreme during the Cold War, became an almost fatal liability in the United States' relations with foreign nations." See, Hoff-Wilson, Ideology and Economics, p. 132.

WINNING THE BATTLE AT HOME: THE FIRST WORLD WAR AND THE DEVELOPMENT OF CALIFORNIA'S SARDINE INDUSTRY

by STEPHEN M. PAYNE

The concept of war usually brings forth images of drilling armies, generals hunched over maps, and eventually combat. One concept that is usually minimized is the critical topic of food. In the wars of the twentieth century the availability of food for both the military and the civilian population has proved to be a crucial element in success. Most accounts of food in wartime are necessarily weighted toward the military with some thought directed toward the civilian population. If the topic is researched beyond the cessation of hostilities the emphasis has been toward the breakup of the wartime food supply network.

What researchers generally overlook in their accounts of the role of food during wartime is the effect that war production has on a given food related industry. While agricultural historians in the United States relate the effect of war production in wheat farming in the mid-west or the equally devastating surpluses created when California's orchardists planted excess acres in prunes and other fruits during the First World War little research has been undertaken in the effect that a war economy had on the nation's fishing industries. In California the fishery most affected by wartime expansion was the sardine.

By the time the California sardine fishery developed, at the turn of the twentieth century, most of the factors that played a part in the new fishery were well established. Canning, reduction, and the fishing gear all were commonplace in Europe and on the East Coast of the United States. While California's sardine was a different type of fish than either the Maine or Norwegian sardines, which were really herring and sprat, all these fish were very similar.[1] The state's early canners simply fitted the available technology to the conditions existing in California's sardine fishery.

In 1889 the Golden Gate Packing Company built California's first sardine cannery in San Francisco's North Beach. During the company's three years of operation, workers put up 20,000 cases of sardines in quarter-pound cans, 7,000 cases in one-pound cans, and 7,000 cases in two-pound cans. Because of the uncertainty of the catch and the unsightly appearance of the canned product, Golden Gate sold out to an East San Pedro firm, the Southern California Fish Company.

In December 1893 the new firm, under the management of A. P. Halfhill, started canning a small amount of sardines. Two seasons later, in 1895, another cannery began operations in San Pedro but a fire destroyed the plant the following year. The Southern California Fish Company continued to pack sardines caught by San Pedro's fishermen. The canned fish met a ready market in Chicago, Boston, New York, and other Eastern markets where they received the same price as European brands.

In 1906 the Southern California Fish Company started packing tuna and by 1909, due to the large profits, tuna was the only product the firm canned. With good prices and a ready market on the East Coast, tuna remained the mainstay of the Southern California canning industry until 1916.

Over the years several new plants came into operation in the southern part of the state: Lower California Fisheries Company, Pacific Tuna Canning Company, and Premier Packing Company, all in San Diego; Halfhill Tuna Packing Company, South Coast Canning Company, and Los Angeles Tuna Canning Company operating in Long Beach; and Van Camp Sea Food Company and White Star Tuna Packing Company together with Southern California Fish Company in San Pedro.[2]

By 1895 Northern California San Francisco fishermen caught almost as many sardines as the San Pedro fishermen. The fishermen sold the catch to fresh-bait fishermen and to fresh fish markets. While there were fish canners in the San Francisco Bay area, they made too much money in the lucrative salmon fishery to divert funds and time to sardines.[3]

In Monterey, however, things were different. The Central Coast port was located on the southern edge of the salmon run and by the turn of the twentieth century the fishermen began experiencing shortages of salmon.

In 1900 H. B. Robbins[4] built a fish packing plant on pilings next to the Pacific Steamship Company Wharf, now Fishermen's Wharf. Robbins was an established entrepreneur, who also operated a salmon cannery in Blaine, Washington, and the Twin Brothers Mush Company in San Francisco. The Monterey facility, measuring about forty feet by forty feet, canned smoked herring and sardines in spices.

The uncertainty of the catch, a problem that plagued the industry for some time, was the undoing of Robbins' Monterey enterprise. According to E. B. Gross, an early Monterey canner:

> Robinson [Robbins] sent out three or four small rowboats. They went to the edge of the wharf and delivered so many sardines from there that the place was swamped and there was no room to work. It broke him. 5

Robbins did not have a large enough canning facility to properly handle a large catch nor enough financial backing to pay the fishermen for the large sardine catch.

In the meantime another entrepreneur visited Monterey and decided to start up a cannery there. Frank E. Booth and his father owned the Sacramento Packers Association in Black Diamond, now known as Pittsburg, where they were engaged in canning salmon. During 1903 Booth visited the cannery operations in France to learn European canning techniques.

After returning to Monterey, Booth opened a small cannery near the present-day Fishermen's Wharf under the management of J. H. Madison. The plant put up 3,000 cases of salmon and sardines during the first year, paying out $12,000 for cannery labor and about the same to fishermen.6 Booth quickly established his plant as the forerunner of sardine canning operations in Monterey. The sardine industry quickly developed into the largest employer in the area.

The year 1903 turned out to be very eventful for Booth. Soon after the opening of his new plant a fire burned it to the ground. Local market fishermen did not like Booth for several reasons. They considered him an upstart and newcomer. They also, conservative fishermen that they were, did not take to his new sardine production and the smell from the cannery bothered many. Thus, they were the logical group to blame for the fire. Not dissuaded, Booth bought out Robbins' cannery, located at the foot of Alvarado Street, and operated there until 1940. Now located in a regular canning facility, Booth hired up to seventy workers during the sardine season, which ran from August 15th to December 15th.

While Booth intended to modernize his operations after his visit to France, a shortage of capital forced him to run the entire operation with manual labor. During the first three years of operation cannery workers scooped the fish from the boats, as the cannery did not have a power winch. The workers then cut the heads and other body parts off, using the French method of hand-flaking, before placing the sardines in the sun to dry. Workers put the dry fish in wire baskets and pushed them through troughs of boiling oil. After hand-packing the sardines in oval cans, the workers finally hand soldered lids on the cans before placing them in cookers.

Despite these labor intensive methods the new plant was a success, averaging four tons of sardines daily during the sardine run. The daily run of 110 to 166 cases of forty-eight one-pound cans per case represented a dramatic improvement over the daily 100 can capacity at the old lumberyard plant.[7]

Although Booth established himself in Monterey as a sardine canner, the work remained very labor-intensive and remained so until Knut Hovden came to work as the plant's manager in 1905. Hovden was born on January 3, 1880, in the shipping port of Bergen, Norway. As a young man he attended the National Fisheries College in Bergen. After two years Hovden graduated as a fisheries engineer and technician. For the next five years he lived in Liverpool, London, and in several Continental seaports while working for a steamship company as the supercargo. But chronic throat problems, caused by tuberculosis, forced him to return home where he engaged in fisheries work for six months before deciding to emigrate to the United States in 1904.

Upon his arrival in the United States Hovden visited several commercial fishing concerns. Hovden's next stop was on the Columbia River, where he engaged a horse seine net for salmon and worked for a short time for the Sanborn-Cutting Company as their superintendent. The horse-seineing method was an ancient European development consisting of placing a drag net with floats into the water, then hitching a horse at both ends of the net the fishermen pulled the catch onto the beach. After working for Sanborn-Cutting, Hovden started his own salmon smokehouse business in Kalama, Washington, along the banks of the Columbia River.

In November, 1904, while visiting San Francisco, Hovden met Frank E. Booth who promptly offered him a job. The young Norwegian decided to stay in the West although he did not immediately accept the Monterey position.

Instead, he went to Arizona, in an attempt to cure his tuberculosis. The dry heat of the desert became a mecca for those affected with "consumption", as tuberculosis was known, during the late nineteenth and early twentieth centuries. Hovden probably learned about Arizona while he stayed in Chicago, as many Chicagoans established winter homes in the Phoenix area during this time.

After a short time his condition indeed improved enough to allow him to return to San Francisco. In San Francisco Hovden worked briefly for the American Can Company. Late in May, 1905, Frank Booth again offered Hovden the Monterey position and this time Hovden accepted.[8]

Although Booth's plant remained the largest, other entrepreneurs became involved in the sardine industry. In 1906 Harry Malpas and O. Noda built the Monterey Canning and Fishing Company, also known as the Monterey Packing Company. Their small twenty-five by sixty foot building was the first to be built on Ocean View Avenue in New Monterey. Although abalone was the cannery's main product, cannery workers also canned sardines by hand.

Two years later James H. Madison, Booth's former superintendent, along with Benjamin Senderman, and Joseph R. Nichols, backed by several men, incorporated the Pacific Fish Company with $100,000 capital. The new enterprise bought out the Monterey Packing company and added several buildings and machines to the older operation in 1908.[9].

In 1910 Booth's plant put up 33,000 cases of sardines worth $225,000. The cannery employed 200 men during the sardine season. The Pacific Fish Company, whose major concentration was still abalone, packed about 4,400 cases, under the Del Monte label, valued at $30,000. This cannery hired as many as 150 men during the sardine season.[10] By 1913 the two canneries were processing three million pounds of sardines a year. Three years later Knut Hovden decided to open his own plant, Hovden Food Products Corporation, packing under the red Portola label. Hovden located his cannery on two acres at the far end of Ocean View Avenue. This cannery operated until 1973 and was the last still operating on what by then was known as Cannery Row.[11]

As the industry grew, so did the need to find new markets. Canners found that while Americans were willing to buy limited quantities of French sardines, the home packed product stayed on grocers' shelves even though it was of equal or better quality. Then in 1902, Captain Robert Dollar, a major shipper in San Francisco, made a trip to the Far East. In addition to sight-seeing, Dollar brought with him several cases of sardines. His objective was to introduce the California product to Japan, China, and the Philippines. Before long the Monterey one-pound oval cans were to be found in the Philippines and throughout the Orient, in Cuba, and in Southern and Northern Europe as well. Captain Dollar's efforts not only rewarded him, but the entire industry as well.[12]

Although the canners, like most businessmen shortly before the First World War, readily accepted technological innovations, their counterparts, the fishermen, were slow to adapt to change. Their catch still depended upon "the luck of the fisherman."

When Knut Hovden arrived in Monterey in 1905, the fishing fleet consisted of a motley collection: 3 gasoline-powered boats, 175 lateen rigged sailboats, and a few old whaling rowboats. Some days the fishermen would catch only a few tons, yet on another day they could swamp the canneries. While canners modernized their plants, the fishing fleet had hardly changed since the introduction of lateen rigged boats, which were a very old Mediterranean development.

Then in 1905, F. E. Booth's head fisherman, Pietro ("Pete") Ferrante remembered a net he used as a boy in Sicily, the lampara--the word lampara came from the Italian word <u>Lampo</u>, or lightning. In 1905, Booth sent to Tangier for such a net. Upon its arrival, Ferrante took his crew and the new net onto the bay. Unfortunately the cording was old and the new net tore when the men tried to capture the ever present sardines. Undaunted, Ferrante and his crew constructed another net, using the original as a pattern. This second net performed just as Ferrante predicted.13

In 1904 Monterey sardine fishermen caught 200,000 pounds of sardines for Booth's cannery, using the purse seine and gill nets. By 1920, the fishermen caught 3,000,000 pounds of sardines for Booth's plant using lampara nets. Until 1913, fishermen used the purse seine during the day as they spotted the schools by watching where the fish were jumping. At night the crews switched to the new lampara nets. A man stationed in the rigging could locate the sardines by the luminescence or phosphorescent glow given off on a moonless night. After 1913, however, the lampara entirely replaced the purse seine. This was partly due to the latter's expensive upkeep, but, more importantly, nine men with a lampara could do the work of twelve with a purse seine.14

The lampara nets were between 150 and 200 fathoms long and fifteen to twenty fathoms deep and had total capacities of twenty to thirty tons per catch. Launches carried the nets while the fishermen loaded the catch onto a barge rather than into a seine boat.

Although the crews could bring in as much as thirty tons of fish each night, the canneries were forced to impose a nightly catch limit of ten to twelve tons, as they were unable to process full loads from all the different crews. This catch limitation did not affect the earning power of the fishermen who worked for wages, not for shares, with both boats and gear being owned by the canneries rather than the fishermen.

Developments in motorized fishing craft toward the end of the nineteenth and the beginning of the twentieth century also affected the Monterey sardine fleet. The first steam trawler in California began to fish waters around San Francisco in 1885. By 1893 gasoline engines began replacing sails and from 1909 to 1915 most fishing boats either converted to or were built with gasoline engines. New five-ton boats powered with fifteen to twenty-five horsepower gasoline engines were expensive, costing up to $2,500. But the benefits outweighed the cost. Fishermen no longer were at the mercy of the ever-changing wind. They began making one day trips out to what were formerly remote fishing areas. Diesel-power engines, introduced in the 1920s, did not have the same revolutionary impact on the fisheries, but they did make the boats safer, since gasoline-powered craft occasionally blew up.15

During this time, Pietro Ferrante encouraged more and more of his countrymen to come to Monterey, writing to friends and relatives in Pittsburg and the Sacramento River fishery as well as in Sicily. The canneries, he wrote, always needed good fishermen. Before the First World War, Ferrante managed to save enough money to build a two-story home on Van Buren Street, overlooking Booth's cannery. He also took a trip home to <u>Isola delle Femmine</u> ("Island of Women") to marry. The Ferrantes boarded many of their countrymen until they too could buy homes of their own.16 Due to his activities in helping his fellow countrymen enter Monterey's fishery and his achievements in developing fishing techniques Pietro Ferrante became the patriarch of Monterey's Italian fishing community.

As Ferrante reported, fishermen in Monterey could make a good living. In 1909 Monterey's sardine fishermen made $15,000 for the season's catch from Booth's plant, while salmon fishermen took in $45,000 for their seasonal efforts. Booth's plant, which was the biggest, paid an additional $36,000 to cannery workers during the salmon and sardine season. This economic impact on Monterey's economy had an effect on city officials who were reluctant to do much about the constant complaints from citizens about the persistent odor problems around the canneries.

By this time Booth's cannery had a daily capacity of twenty-four tons of fish. The workers managed to can about 22,000 cases of fish in 1909. In 1915 Monterey's fishermen landed 2,000 tons of sardines and the cannery workers packed 75,000 cases of sardines in the one-pound oval cans, forty-eight cans to the case. Monterey's fishing fleet boasted 400 fishermen by 1916 in both the canning and fresh market fisheries. The following year Monterey canners, who were members of the National Canner's Association, established an inspection service to insure the quality of their product.[17]

In 1915, Frank E. Booth told a reporter that ninety percent of his business went to Germany. Indeed in most parts of the world one could find the oval cans containing Monterey sardines. While the sardine business was by 1915, already a sizable industry, world events would shortly affect this small California town of 6,000 people with such an impact that both the town and its main industry would never again be the same.[18]

The event that pushed the sardine fishery into the limelight of American and world fisheries was the outbreak of war in Europe. One might, at first glance, find it hard to associate a European conflict with the formation of a world-wide important fishery in the isolated and relatively unknown fishing port of Monterey. But, World War I did dramatically change the character of the West Coast sardine fishery, quickly transforming it from a small industry into a giant one. The reason was that food, for Europe's belligerents became a critical commodity. So vital was the need for new food sources that even neutral countries became involved.

France quickly moved to halt the export of sardines and other foodstuffs in order to feed its army. Soon the American consumer found grocers' shelves bare of French and then of Russian sardines. Also, in 1915, Norwegian canners in Stavanger found that they could command higher prices for canned sardines in Europe than in the United States. The following year became known as the "golden year" because of the high prices the combatants were willing to pay for the Norwegian canned product. This was also the year that saw the establishment of many new canneries in the Norwegian fishing ports.

Although the Norwegians took in even greater orders for their product over the next two years, 1917 and 1918, shipments actually fell off, due to the scarcity of materials--tin plate, olive oil, and fuel. In addition, labor unrest and the influenza epidemic of 1918 cut into the workforce. Finally, in a desperate attempt to get the Norwegian product to its army, Germany shipped some tin plate to Norwegian canneries. In the meantime, however, the Allied blockade took full effect and canners found that they were unable to get the tins of sardines back across the North Sea to Germany. By 1918, the new Norwegian canneries began to close, one after another.[19]

In Monterey the war resulted in a different scenario. Unlike Norwegian canners, who suffered from the British blockade, Booth was able to shift his sales to the home market to fill the gap left by French, Russian, and Norwegian sardines. Soon other canners in Monterey and Southern California joined Booth in the expanding sardine business. In 1915, one new cannery began packing sardines; the following year the eleven Southern California tuna canneries entered the sardine industry, and an additional three new plants entered the field. By 1919, a total of twenty-six new canneries were operating.[20]

Monterey's waterfront teemed with activity in 1916. Several canneries started processing sardines for the first time. These operators made their contributions to the existing canning and fresh fish industry in Monterey. E. B. Gross, who came to Monterey as a penniless San Juan Bautista farmboy, opened his cannery, which remained in business until 1940. The F. E. Booth plant expanded operations spending $9,000 for the construction of a new dock and a salmon splitting house, as well as for additional canning machinery and equipment. The Pacific Fish Company, under Benjamin Senderman's leadership, installed new machinery, and made several changes costing the firm $4,000. The owners of the San Francisco International Fish Company built a $3,000 building to handle fish on the city wharf. A. Napoli, a wholesale dealer, spent $1,000 for a collecting and shipping house, also on the city's wharf. Joseph Rodriquez spent $1,000 to build a sardine packing plant in New Monterey, where Hovden's cannery and the Pacific Fish Company were located. In addition, Bito Bruno's plans for a fish packing house on the city wharf were complete. The new plant, estimated at $1,500, would allow Bruno to move out of the Western Fish Company's facilities where he was then operating.[21]

In addition to expanding the market in the United States, California's sardine canners began a lucrative export trade with the Allies--Great Britain, France, and Italy. When the United States finally entered the war on April 4, 1917, citizens were asked to cut back on their consumption of beef and substitute fish which further bolstered the growing industry.

During the spring of 1917 consumers in the United States began experiencing food shortages. In addition, prices of staples--grains, breads, meats, oil, sugar, and milk--rose weekly. As wages and earnings stabilized, Americans found that their purchasing power was shrinking.[22] Bread, which had remained at a fairly constant price of between 5.4 cents to 5.6 cents per loaf from 1910 until the eve of the European war rose to 6 cents by 1915, and each following year rose another penny per loaf.[23]

On May 19, 1917, President Woodrow Wilson asked Congress to establish a food administration. Wilson had in mind a strong centrally controlled organization modeled after Herbert Hoover's Belgian food relief program, and hoped that Hoover might run the new organization.[24] Asbury F. Lever, the Chairman of the House Committee on Agriculture, introduced the Food Control Bill named after him in Congress. After three months of debate, the House passed "an Act to provide further for the national security and defense by encouraging the production, conserving the supply, and controlling the distribution of food products and fuel" on August 10, 1917, by a vote of 365 to 5. Two days earlier, on Herbert Hoover's birthday the Senate had passed the law by a 66 to 7 vote.[25] Wilson quickly appointed a willing Hoover to the new post of Food Administrator.

For Hoover food was the key to victory. He noted that demonstrations were taking place in major American cities over the high price of food and called the Russian Revolution a "Food Riot." Hoover felt that food was an international commodity, but was capitalist enough to call price-fixing or "profit-fixing . . . the most obnoxious job in history." However during the wartime crisis Hoover wanted the newly created Food Administration to have control of the nation's food supply "from the soil to the stomach."[26]

In an attempt to put a stop to runaway food prices, President Wilson issued an executive order to keep food at its pre-1914 profit level. In some industries this price control tended to limit production, and Hoover was forced to formulate a more flexible profit ratio to stimulate production.[27] Some food-related companies used this to make what were considered excess profits, and by mid-1918, the Federal Trade Commission stepped in to limit food packers' profits to nine percent.[28]

Hoover also set out to reorganize America's food system. The Food Administrator declared meatless and breadless days. Through newspaper advertisements and editorials as well as through posters Americans were urged to "win the battle at home." In California the Fish and Game Commission's journal, California Fish and Game, picked up the theme:

> The people of the Nation are being urged by the Food Administrator to use foods that are near at hand in order to relieve our congested railroads.

It is our patriotic duty, therefore, for the people of this state to use more of our fish which are here in such quantities close at hand.29

As early as 1916 canners were working with the United States Bureau of Fisheries and canning grayfish, or dogfish, for human consumption. This project was initiated by the Bureau of Fisheries with an appropriation of $25,000 to develop new food fishes. The canned grayfish sold well and by January 1917 several Pacific Coast canners were involved in the project. In addition to grayfish, the appropriation helped develop new markets for skates, rays, whiting, black cod, grindle, goose fish, Alaska herring, and other previously unused species.30

Responding to these wartime opportunities, California's canneries put up 150 million pounds of sardines in 1918. They did so even though, like other food processors, they were affected by government price controls. The price per case of sardines actually went down to $7.25 for one pound ovals packed in tomato sauce; while the price paid to fishermen was fixed at $15 per ton of delivered sardines. Canned sardines were thus the only food product that did not increase in cost during the war years.31

In Monterey's canneries government inspectors also insured that quantity and quality standards were met. This introduction of inspectors came about after increasing numbers of "swelled" cans began to appear, indicating spoiled contents.32

In a bid for new markets for sardines the California State Council of Defense's Committee on Zoological Investigations urged that sardines be utilized by consumers as a fresh fish as well as canned. They were one of the cheapest fresh fish consumers could buy--selling for only five cents a pound in the San Francisco markets.33

On August 10, 1917, a Presidential proclamation mandated licensing for all food packers, effective November 1.34 In response to this edict California's Food Administrator, Ralph Merritt, issued a proclamation on November 1, 1917, requiring all wholesale fish distributors, brokers, and commission men to obtain licenses from the agency. To further control the situation in California, the Food Administrator relayed a message from Hoover's office stating that all commercial fishermen must be licensed by the agency by February 10, 1918.35

In order to stimulate the fish catch, the Food Administration announced that it was removing local fishing restrictions that tended to hamper fishermen, and that the federal government was doing so as well.36 The action, the Administration announcement reported, was necessary because some states prevented non-residents and aliens from fishing in their waters. In addition, the agency abolished closed seasons and restrictions on purse seines legislated by some states. The Food Administration had the right to control state and local regulations under emergency war-time powers granting the federal government special powers over state laws during the war. These measures, the agency reported, "should largely increase the supply of seafood by spring of 1918."

In an attempt to placate state officials, the proclamation was tempered by the closing paragraph stating that it was the Food Administration's intent to protect the fish supply for the future and to prevent the extinction or reduction of the nation's valuable species of food fishes. Nonetheless the report caused a certain alarm in various California state agencies that were fearful of the consequences of any lessening of fishing restrictions.

To further explain their position in California, officials from the Food Commission and the Bureau of Fisheries met with the California Fish and Game Commission on March 2, 1918. After a presentation from W. C. Crandall, of Scripps Institute, on the conditions in California's fisheries, the California Food Administrator's staff declared that California's laws did not prevent or hinder the development of the state's fisheries. Only minor instances of local restriction were singled out for change by the Food Administration in California.[37]

During the war both industry and farmers created a tremendous demand for fish oil, fertilizer, and meal, resulting in a Congressional study on fertilizer and a study by the Department of Agriculture on fish oil by-products. An even more immediate consequence was a rise in prices, which led some canneries to install their own reduction facilities.[38] As for fish meal, prejudice and custom had prevented its use, even though studies in the United States and Europe had demonstrated its value as stock feed as early as 1875. But with the war-time demand for corn, barley, wheat, and other ingredients used in stock feed, farmers began to reconsider fish meal.

In Petaluma, California, poultrymen turned to salmon meal, but the Alaskan product's oil content was much too high, resulting in a fishy flavored fryer. The process utilized by both Frank Booth and Max N. Schaefer eliminated the oil problem for sardines, as the oil was too valuable to leave in the meal. Soon farmers began to feed the fish meal to cattle, swine, and chickens. In southern California orchardists used the meal for fertilizer in their orange groves.[39] The result was that sardine canners found that they could utilize the offal, spoilage, and catch-overage that they once dumped into the sea.

Meanwhile, however, the supply of sardines was felt by the State's fishery scientists to be diminishing to such an extent that they convinced the California Legislature to intervene. In 1915 and again in 1919 bills passed both houses authorizing the Fish and Game Commissioners to set catch limits on sardines and salmon. Both times, however, Governor Hiram Johnson vetoed the proposed legislation. The governor did, however, sign the 1917 State Fish Exchange Act, which was the first successful attempt to curb the runaway sardine fishery. The act was brought about by several factors: by the sale of fresh food fish to reduction plants, by the uncertainty of the fresh fish market, by the wartime desire to utilize fresh fish, and finally by the desire to stabilize fresh-fish prices. And although the act was later challenged and appealed in Paladini vs Superior Court, (178 California 3690), the State Supreme Court would uphold the constitutionality of the law.[40]

The act established the principle that the state, acting for all the people, had the "ownership and title to all fish found in the waters under the jurisdiction of the state." Hence it followed, the law declared, that the state had the right to regulate the taking of fish within its waters.[41]

Following this, the legislature passed the California Fish Conservation Act, also known as the Sardine Reduction Act, in 1919, as a result of which the Fish and Game Commission could report the following year that

> the direct fishing for reduction purposes which caused the passage of the law has been entirely stopped and over-catches and waste has been reduced to a low percentage.[42]

And more was involved than specific legislation affecting California's budding reduction industry; the overall concept of regulation and conservation was now being well established in the state.

With the end of hostilities on November 11, 1918, Monterey's canners could only wait for the expected collapse of their businesses, since they would soon be facing renewed competition from European canners. To add to their canners' woes, jobbers and other speculators had begun storing millions of cases of sardines in the last year of the war, to reap large profits if the war continued. Nor could the canners hope for any stabilizing influence on prices from Herbert Hoover's Food Administration, since Congress refused to extend that agency's life past its original July 1, 1919 deadline, although Hoover explained that a successful transition from a war-time economy to a peace-time economy depended upon a gradual shift.[43]

The result indeed was a serious depression for California's canned fish market. The number of fish canneries and packing plants in the state fell from fifty-seven in 1919 to forty-two by 1921, and finally to thirty-four by 1923. Not all of the canneries that went out of business were shut down, however. Some were bought out by other operators. Yet the shutdowns, coupled with increased labor unrest, caused the number of cannery workers to fall by fifty-five percent from 1919 to 1921. The situation in Monterey appeared grim.[44]

In response California canners began a practice that ultimately led to disaster--reduction. In 1919 canners claimed that most of the sardine catch was of inferior quality, and unsuitable for canning purposes.

Instead, they reduced most of the catch to oil and meal.[45] E. B. Gross, one of Monterey's early canners recalled:

> We threw away more than we saved. When the war was finished, we thought we were all through. Then we learned the lucrative reduction game. In order to get material for meal and oil, we needed the waste material, so we brought in all the fish we could and sold the canned goods for $2.16 a case....the low price acquainted the world with the best and cheapest food put up in a can or any other way.[46]

But this was a shortsighted solution which would lead to the ultimate destruction of the California sardine industry shortly after the Second World War. There was a repetition of California's mistake in Peru during the Second World War.

The high demands fostered by wartime needs for food staples led to the creation and overextension of Peru's anchovy industry. When the world returned to a peace-time economy the Peruvian anchovy industry, like its predecessor the California sardine industry, resorted to reduction of its fish. The result was overfishing, which, coupled with adverse ecological conditions, resulted in the demise of yet another of the world's major fisheries.[47]

What should be kept in mind, however, is that both situations had been caused not so much by the processors as by the government's pressure for increased war-time production. Hence one may well argue that where the government intervenes to alter economic situations the government also must take some responsibility to help an affected industry to return to something resembling its pre-war economic base. Herbert Hoover recognized this, but the legislative branch would not listen to him, and the long term result in the case of California's sardine industry was disastrous.

NOTES

[1]The California sardine is a true sardine, unlike the sardines found in Maine and New England which are a young herring, <u>Clupea Harengus</u>. The two species have different habits, biology, and flavor. Norwegian sardines are also not true sardines; they include not only young herring, but brisling, or young sprat, <u>Clupea sprattus</u>. Although these and other small fish were labeled "sardines" for years by canners, in 1916 English courts ruled that Norwegian "sardines" could not be sold under that label. True sardines in Europe are found in England, France, Spain, Portugal, and Italy. The Atlantic sardine is known as <u>Sardina Pilchardus pilchardus</u> while the Mediterranean type is called <u>Sardina pilchardus sardina</u>. Until 1929 scientists grouped all sardines under the

generic name Sardina. California sardines, ranging from Alaska to Baja California were known as Sardina Caerulea. Those along the coast of Peru were called Sardina sagax. The sardine found in Japanese waters were labeled Sardina melanostica, those in Australian waters Sardina neopilchardus, and the sardine found off the Cape of Good Hope in South Africa were labeled Sardina ocellata. (Will F. Thompson, "The Sardine of California," California Fish and Game, 7:4, 1921, pp. 193-194). In 1929 Carl Leavitt Hubbs successfully demonstrated that the Pacific sardine was different from the European sardine and placed all these in the genus Sardinops. California sardines were then renamed Sardinops caerulea. (Carl Leavitt Hubbs, "The Generic Relationships and Nomenclature of the California Sardine," California Academy of Sciences, 18:11, pp. 261-265). By the late 1960s scientists were again debating the nomenclature of the California Sardine and in 1971 Michael Culley reported that the California sardine will very likely be renamed yet again, this time as a sub-species of Sardinops sagax. (Michael Culley, The Pilchard: Biology and Exploitation, New York: Pergamon Press, 1971, p. 145). For the purposes of this paper the term Sardinops caerulea will be adhered to.

2William F. Thompson, "Historical Review of California Sardine Industry," California Fish and Game, 7:4, 1921, p. 195; W. L. Scofield, "Purse Seines for California Sardines," California Fish and Game, 12:1, 1926, pp. 16-19; Milner B. Schaefer, Oscar E. Sette, and John C. Marr, Growth of Pacific Coast Pilcard Fishery to 1942, United States Department of the Interior, Fish and Wildlife Service, Research Report 29 (Washington, D. C.: Government Printing Office, 1951), p. 2; Culley, Ibid., pp. 143-145.

3Schaefer, Growth of Pacific Coast Pilchard Fishery, p. 2.

4H. R. Robbins in some accounts.

5Monterey New Era, April 18, 1900 and February 19, 1902; Monterey Daily Cypress, August 22, 1912; Monterey Pacific Herald, February 28, 1952.

6Monterey Peninsula Herald, February 27, 1942; Monterey New Era, May 3, 1904; Earl H. Rosenberg, "A History of the Fishing and Canning Industries in Monterey, California," (M. A. thesis, University of Nevada, 1961), p. 70.

7Randall A. Reinstedt "Where Have All the Sardines Gone?" (Carmel: Ghost Town Publishing Company, 1978), p. 17; Rosenberg, p. 70-71; Monterey Daily Cypress, June 3, 1911; "West Coast Fisheries--San Pedro," pamphlet in California Room, Monterey Public Library, no date, no page; Thompson, p. 196; Monterey New Era August 9 and 13, 1904, reprinted in Monterey Peninsula Herald March 25, 1938; "Cannery Row, Number 2," article in California Room, Monterey Public Library, no date, p. 46.

[8]"West Coast Fisheries--San Pedro"; <u>Monterey Peninsula Herald</u>, March 7, 1947 and March 29, 1961.

[9]<u>Monterey New Era</u>, March 26, 1907 and February 20, 1908; Rosenberg, pp. 76-77; Thompson; <u>Monterey Peninsula Herald</u>, Rich Lovejoy interview with E. B. Gross, February 28, 1952.

[10]<u>Monterey Daily Cypress</u>, June 3, 1911; Rosenberg, p. 81.

[11]N. B. Scofield, "The Lampara Net," <u>California Fish and Game</u>, 10:2, 1924, p. 69; <u>Monterey Peninsula Herald</u>, March 29, 1961; Maxine Knox and Mary Rodriguez, <u>Steinbeck's Street: Cannery Row</u> (San Rafael, California: Presidio Press, 1980), p. 11.

[12]Robert Dollar, "Oriental Markets," <u>Outlook</u>, May 4, 1927, quoted in <u>California Fish and Game</u>, 13:3, 1927, pp. 218-219.

[13]Reinstedt, p. 13; "Cannery Row Industry Busted from 1900-1950," Cannery Row File number 2, p. 46, California Room, Monterey Public Library; Cannery Row file number 2, p. 46; Campbell, "Conservation of the California Sardine," (M. A. thesis, Chico State College), p. 23; Thompson, "Historical Review of California Sardine Industry," <u>California Fish and Game</u> 7:4, 1921, pp. 196-197; W. L. Scofield, "California Fishing Ports," California Department of Fish and Game, <u>Fish Bulletin</u> number 96, p. 95; N. B. Scofield, "The Lampara Net," <u>California Fish and Game</u>, 10:2, 1924, pp. 66-70.

[14]N. B. Scofield, p. 69; Thompson, p. 197; N. B. Scofield, "The Purse Seine," <u>California Fish and Game</u>, 10:4, 1924, p. 185; W. L. Scofield; Francis N. Clark, Measures of Abundance of the Sardine, <u>Sardinops caerulea</u>, in California Waters," Department of Fish and Game <u>Fish Bulletin</u> number 53 (Sacramento: State Printing Office, 1939), p. 11.

[15]Culley, p. 163; Clark, p. 10; Thompson; Harold B. Clemens and William L. Graig, "An Analysis of California's Albacore Fishery," <u>Fish Bulletin</u> number 128 (Sacramento: State Printing Office, 1965), p. 10; N. B. Scofield, "The Tuna Canning Industry of Southern California," <u>Twenty-Third Biennial Report of the Fish and Game Commission: 1912-1912</u> (Sacramento: State Printing Office, 1914), p. 116; Bureau of Commercial Fisheries, "The Commercial Fish Catch of California for the Year 1935," <u>Fish Bulletin</u> number 49 (Sacramento: State Printing Office, 937), p. 36.

[16]"Cannery Row Industry."; Knox and Rodriguez, p. 10.

[17]<u>California Fish and Game</u> 2:3, 1916, p. 154; Thompson, p. 203; Schaefer, p. 3.

[18]Thompson, p. 204; Campbell, p. 11.

[19]Thompson, p. 198-199.

[20]Ibid., p. 203.

[21]Monterey Peninsula Herald, February 18, 1952; California Fish and Game, 2:3, 1916, p. 154.

[22]Witold S. Sworakowski, "Herbert Hoover, Launching the American Food Administration, 1917, in Lawrence E. Gelfand, ed., Herbert Hoover: The Great War and Its Aftermath, 1914-1923, (Iowa City, Iowa: University of Iowa Press, 1979), p. 43.

[23]Annual Report, United States Food Administration for the year 1918, 65th Congress, 3rd Session, House Resolutions, House Document 1877, p. 47.

[24]David Burner, Herbert Hoover: A Private Life, (New York: Alfred Knoff, 1979), p. 97.

[25]Ibid.; Sworakowski, pp. 43-44.

[26]Burner, pp. 96, 99.

[27]Ibid., pp. 104-109.

[28]Ibid., p. 104.

[29]California Fish and Game, 4:1 (1918):49.

[30]H. M. Smith, Commissioner, Department of Commerce, Bureau of Fisheries, Washington, D. C., January 22, 1919, letter "Estimate of Appropriation to Reimburse Certain Fish Packers," in 65th Congress 3rd Session, House Resolution, Document 21736, pp. 2-3; William Redfield, Department of Commerce, Office of the Secretary, letter, "New Aquatic Food Fishes," December 28, 1916, 64th Congress, 2nd Session. House Resolution, Document 1871, p.1, Reintroduced: 65th Congress, 1st Session, Document 72, April 27, 1917.

[31]Twenty-Seventh Biennial Report of the Fish and Game Commission, 1920-1922, (Sacramento: State Printing Office, 1923), p. 63; Monterey Peninsula Herald, Ritch Lovejoy interview with E. B. Gross, 28 February 1952; Thompson, p. 204; Annual Report, United States Food Administration for the Year 1918, 65th Congress, 3rd Session, House Resolutions, House Document 1877, pp. 147-150.

[32]Wilfrid Sadler, "The Bacteriology of Swelled Canned Sardines," American Journal of Public Health 8 (1918):216-220 in Arthur Francis McEvoy III, "Economy, Law, and Ecology in the California Fisheries to 1925" (Ph.D. dissertation, University of California, San Diego, 1979), p. 369; Thompson, p. 203.

33California Fish and Game, 4:3 (1918):143-144.

34Reports of the United States Food Administration and the United States Fuel Administration, 1917, 65th Congress, 2nd Session, House Resolution, Document 7837, pp. 22-23.

35California Fish and Game, 4:2 (1918):94-95.

36Ibid.; Annual Report of the United States Food Administration . . . 1918, p. 34.

37Sadler, Chapter 803, California Statutes, 1917, p. 1673.

38Elbert H. Ahlstrom and John Radovich, "Management of the Pacific Sardine," A Century of Fisheries in North America, ed. Norman G. Benson, Special Publication number 7 (Washington, D. C.: American Fisheries Society, 1970), p. 186; McEvoy, pp. 370-371; Thompson, p. 195-206.

39William L. Scofield, "Fertilizer, Stockfood and Oil from Sardine Offal," California Fish and Game, 7:4 (1921):207-208.

40B. D. Marx Greene, "An Historical Review of the Legal Aspects of the Use of Food Fish for Reduction Purposes," California Fish and Game, 13:1 (1927):1-2, 5.

41Chapter 803, California Statutes, 1917, p. 1673.

42Twenty-Sixth Biennial Report of the Fish and Game Commission, 1918-1920, (Sacramento: State Printing Office, 1921), p. 73.

43Burner, p. 110.

44McEvoy, p. 332-333.

45Ahlstrom and Radovich; McEvoy, pp. 370-371; Thompson, p. 195-206.

46Lovejoy, 28 February 1952.

47For further information on the Peruvian Anchovy fishery see W. G. Clark, "The Lessons of the Peruvian Anchoveta Fishery," CalCOFI Reports, Vol. XIX, 1977, pp. 57-63; Gerald J. Paulik, "Anchovies, Birds, and Fishermen in the Peru Current," in Resource Management and Environmental Uncertainty: Lessons from Coastal Upwelling Fisheries, eds. Michael H. Glantz and J. Dana Thompson, (New York: A Wiley-Interscience Publication, John Wiley & Sons, 1981): pp. 35-80.

HOSTAGES TO FORTUNE
THE CONFRONTATION OVER WAL WAL, ETHIOPIA, DECEMBER 1934

by DOREEN GAMA FARR

> To cast an army of nearly a quarter million men, embodying the flower of Italian manhood, upon a barren shore two thousand miles from home, against the goodwill of the whole world and without command of the sea, and then in this position to embark on what may well be a series of campaigns against a people and in regions which no conqueror in four thousand years ever thought it worthwhile to subdue is to give hostages to fortune unparalleled in all history.
>
> Winston Churchill,
> The Second World War

Although historians have written volumes on the Italian-Ethiopian War of 1935-36, the preliminary skirmish at Wal Wal during December of 1934 usually receives only a paragraph or two in the opening chapters of such histories. Any known details of the battle itself are rarely explained by writers of Italo-Ethiopian history, and never studied thoroughly. Considering the significance of the event, this omission is surprising. The confrontation at Wal Wal has been called "the touchstone of appeasement" and singled out for its significance as a symbol of League of Nations' impotence during that era. And yet no one knows exactly what happened between November 22, 1934, the day Ethiopian and Somali troops and the Anglo-Ethiopian Boundary Commission confronted Italian irregulars at the oasis outpost in the Ethiopian Ogaden desert, and December 5 when both sides began shooting.

When the events which led up to and caused the confrontation and the circumstances of the skirmish itself are analyzed, the Wal Wal incident cannot be viewed as a planned outburst of Italian aggression as some writers would like us to believe. The fighting was the culmination of a long series of conflicts between Italians, Ethiopians, Somalis and British. The activities of these four groups prove that they were all giving "hostages to fortune" long before Winston Churchill so aptly coined the phrase.

The seeds of discord for the Wal Wal confrontation had been planted at the turn of the century when, in 1896, the Ethiopian forces of Emperor Menelik resoundingly defeated the Italian army in its attempt to colonize Ethiopia. The humiliation the Italians felt at losing the Battle of Adowa and their subsequent need for revenge manifested itself in Italo-Ethiopian relations during the ensuing forty years.

If Italy had not lost at Adowa, she would probably have become the conqueror of the last uncolonized country on the Horn of Africa. France was already ensconced on a piece of Somaliland, as were Italy and Great Britain. Great Britain also controlled the Anglo-Egyptian Sudan to the west of Ethiopia, and Italy proudly dominated her colony of Eritrea located to the north.

Luckily for Ethiopia, for thirty years following the Battle of Adowa no one seriously challenged the Ethiopian Empire's right to exist. This era of benign neglect finally came to an end in 1925. It was in that year that Italy's new Fascist dictator, Benito Mussolini, wrote an article which first discussed Italy's "pacific expansion in that vast world still enclosed in its prehistoric system and yet capable of great progress."[1]

The plan for the takeover of Ethiopia started off deceptively small. In 1929, the governor of Italian Somaliland, Guido Corni, initiated a plan of gradual encroachment into the Ogaden desert of Ethiopia which lay southeast of Italian Somaliland. Since the lives of the Somali and Ethiopian tribes who traversed the area depended on available water, whoever controlled the wells, controlled all the people. By entrenching Italian authority over the waterholes, Corni realized the whole area could become an Italian protectorate with very little effort and expense. And as the boundary between Ethiopia and Italian Somaliland had never been officially demarcated anyway, the governor of Italian Somaliland reasoned he could claim the land and justify the encroachment based on the vagueness of the demarcation--if he were ever questioned.[2] To bolster the small complement of military officers assigned to Italian Somaliland, Somali tribesmen were recruited to serve as irregular forces or dubats.[3] These dubats were organized into groups of forty to sixty men known as banda, each headed by an Italian officer.[4]

Beginning in 1929, detachments of banda roamed throughout the Ogaden in mobile patrols. As time went on these detachments set up semi-permanent camps in the vicinity of important oases and established regulations for the use of the water by the nomads. After some time, an officer in the Italian army would arrive to oversee the camp and cement Fascist authority over the various tribes that traversed that particular area.[5]

The Italian Somaliland government did not find much resistance to their encroachment from the desert's native inhabitants. From constantly warring over control of the water, the Somali and Ethiopian tribes had developed a strong hatred for each other. And even within each tribal group, there was no agreement. A tribe's allegiance could, and did, change daily. This lack of unity made them easy prey for the Fascist interlopers.

One by one the key oases in the Ogaden were taken over by the Italians. Most important of these oases was Wal Wal, a line of 359 wells which stretched in the shape of a crescent. Wal Wal was located about 250 miles inland from the Indian Ocean and about the same distance southeast from Harrar, the closest Ethiopian city of any size. In March of 1930, Wal Wal was added to the growing list of watering holes brought under Italian control. The Fascists, acknowledging the importance of these wells, erected a garrison post there, and a sector command post at Warder about nine miles away.

The Italian encroachment onto Ethiopian desert did not occur unnoticed by the government in Addis Ababa. Haile Selassie was particularly galled by the Italian incursion in the Ogaden, located in his home province of Harrar. One of his first goals after being crowned Emperor of Ethiopia in November 1930 was to try to push back the Italians to Somaliland.

Sometime during the first half of 1931, the Emperor unofficially suggested to the Deputy Governor of Harrar, Gabre Mariam, that the governor lead a large contingent of men through the Ogaden and retake the oases from the Italians. Mariam started marching south into the desert during August 1931. As his army approached each Italian-held oasis, the <u>dubats</u> melted away into the bush. The army continued to encounter no resistance for the next month and then began to turn back. Mariam and his men did not completely accomplish their original mission, however. The area they had covered neglected a very large section of the Ogaden between the undemarcated borders of British and Italian Somaliland and Ethiopia. Located in this triangular area was the large complex of wells at Wal Wal which, therefore, remained under Italian control.

Despite the partial success of Mariam's venture, the Ethiopian government remained silent on the issue of the Italian incursion. Haile Selassie realized his military force was still woefully inadequate to face a full scale battle with Italy over control of the Ogaden. To try to ensure Ethiopian sovereignty against current and future Italian aggression, Selassie knew he would need another, stronger country to champion his cause. He decided Great Britain was the most likely candidate. The Emperor's problem was how to convince the English to abandon their neutral status and openly support Ethiopia.

While deciding how to best lure the British into some kind of an alliance, the Emperor began to curry their favor. He agreed to the formal delineation of the boundary between Ethiopia and British Somaliland, a demarcation which the British had been hoping to accomplish for some years. In January of 1932, the newly created Anglo-Ethiopian Boundary Commission commenced work. During the course of the demarcation process, the Commission was denied access to several wells held by Italian <u>dubats</u> because the Commission ignored the Italian request to ask advance permission. The British Commissioners were under the mistaken impression that the Italian encroachment consisted of only infrequent visits to the wells by Somali <u>dubats</u>. To ask advance permission would imply that the Italian claim was valid. The Ethiopian Commissioners, who knew the true strength of the Italian hold on the area, remained silent on the issue.

By late 1932, Haile Selassie had decided on a possible way to tie British interests to those of Ethiopia. He would tempt them with a land trade. If the British showed interest in such a deal, they would naturally become more concerned about insuring Ethiopian independence. The Emperor planned to offer the British some territorial readjustments with his country in exchange for a piece of British Somaliland surrounding and including the port of Zeila on the Red Sea.6 A port of her own had long been a cherished dream of the landlocked Ethiopia. And, best of all, such a trade would bring closer ties with Great Britain.

When Haile Selassie broached the subject of the land trade to the British Foreign Office, via Sir Sydney Barton, the British Ambassador in Addis Ababa, the English were quite taken with the idea. The Colonial Office, in particular, showed a great amount of interest. If Selassie were interested in making some territorial adjustments in exchange for Zeila, then perhaps the Colonial Office could obtain a piece of the Ogaden and insure water and grazing for their Somaliland tribes throughout the year.

For the next two years, the British Foreign, Dominions, and especially the Colonial Offices would huddle over the Zeila scheme. The British government took pains to keep the whole matter very secret, with any papers concerning the possible trade "not touched by the Registry and their distribution strictly curtailed."7 England did not want France and Italy to know what she was contemplating until the trade had been assured.

While the British Colonial Office began to look more greedily at the Ogaden, the Italian government in Rome began to look more predatorily on Ethiopia. Among those at the Fascist Colonial Ministry, talk was rampant concerning Italy's future in East Africa. But Mussolini was worried about the international situation. In January 1933, Field Marshal von Hindenburg called Hitler to be Chancellor of the German Reich, and opened a whole new era in European politics. Il Duce began to slowly realize that if he contemplated military action in Ethiopia, it had better be in the near future before Germany became too powerful. By November of 1933, Mussolini had ordered money and material be made available to prepare the East African colonies for future military action.

For a good many logistical reasons, the Fascist generals decided that any possible future attack on Ethiopia should emanate from Eritrea, not Italian Somaliland. But when Eritrea was selected to received the majority of soldiers and armaments, one important point was overlooked. The Italian General Staff forgot that their policy of territorial aggrandizement in the Ogaden already demanded a need for better men and equipment to protect the gains made in recent years. No one in Rome seemed to be worried about another threatening encounter with the Ethiopians over the Ogaden. Italian Somaliland's need for better defenses was pushed aside when the military emphasis shifted to Eritrea.

On March 17, 1934, after warning the Ethiopian Emperor repeatedly of the extreme secrecy of the negotiations, Sir Sydney Barton announced the British terms for the Zeila offer. Great Britain was prepared to offer Ethiopia a corridor of land twelve miles wide to the port of Zeila, the port itself and eighteen miles of coastline. In exchange, the British had several counter-concessions to offer. These included an adjustment of the Sudanese and Kenyan frontiers, a treaty of commerce and amity, and a "readjustment of the British Somaliland frontier involving the cession to the Protectorate of a considerable area of Ethiopian territory...."[8]

The Emperor was unhappy after hearing the list of British demands. The size of the territory he would receive from the British would be dwarfed by the large pieces of land the British wanted in return. And they wanted part of the Ogaden! How could he cede a portion of the Ogaden when the Italians were once again camped all over it? He certainly did not want that problem to interfere with the rest of the Zeila negotiations. But when queried by the Emperor on that point, Sir Barton responded that his government would have to resolve _all_ the terms before Zeila could be ceded.

On April 13, 1934, when Sir Sidney Barton was called to the palace to discuss the Zeila plan again, Selassie brought up the subject closest to his heart. He asked what the British meant by a Treaty of Amity as described in their desiderata for the concession of Zeila. Was it a Treaty of Friendship? And if so, what would it mean "in the event of the independence of his country being threatened or attacked subsequently."[9] Barton, like the British Colonial Office, was very sympathetic to Selassie's position. When he recapped this conversation for the benefit of Sir John Simon at the Foreign Office, Barton pleaded the Emperor's cause as best he could.

> ... he is genuinely anxious to find means of reaching an agreement and that he would be prepared to meet even our present territorial desiderata provided he can see further into the future and be satisfied as to how far a settlement and friendship with us would operate as a guarantee of his continued independence. . . .

> Rightly or wrongly the whole country from the Emperor downwards is more convinced at present than at any time in the past that forward action by Italy inimical to Ethiopia's independence is only a question of time. . . .If we ourselves believe that the continuance of this independence is in the interest of British policy generally and that the objective of the proposed negotiations is of a nature to encourage indirectly such continuance, can any frank answer be given to the Emperor in his own justifiable anxiety as to the future?10

The answer which the Ambassador requested did not come for six long weeks. During that time, the Foreign Office in London was closely watching the growing rapprochement between Italy and France, and speculating on the implications of the forthcoming meeting between Hitler and Mussolini in June. With such events occurring in Europe, Sir John Simon decided that the time was not yet propitious for a major change in their Ethiopian policy. He cabled Barton not to say anything definite about a treaty of alliance yet.

Despite his disappointment with the British answer, Haile Selassie was not dissuaded from his plan. With strong encouragement from the British Colonial Office, he continued with the Zeila negotiations. As long as talks were going on between the two countries, there might yet be a chance for a treaty agreement.

The pressure was really on Selassie now to dislodge the Italians from the Ogaden. If this could not be done, not only would the Italians continue to control the vital wells, but the precious Zeila negotiations would come to an end. The wells were so isolated that it often took days for news from the interior of the desert to reach Addis Ababa. But the latest word Selassie had received was not encouraging. Although he had once again unofficially commissioned various Ethiopian and Somali tribesmen to attack the dubats and regain the wells, the results had been negligible. When Selassie's men raided an oasis, the dubats usually fled without a fight. But the Italian Somali irregulars would slowly filter back and reclaim the wells after the raiders marched on.

As time went on, Selassie found his situation becoming more and more dangerous. There was no doubt Italy was mobilizing against his country. He had come to hope that British support might be counted on to avert trouble, but instead he found himself in the middle of a very complicated and very vicious circle. The British Colonial Office had clearly stated that the Zeila negotiations could not be finalized unless Ethiopia could cede Wal Wal and Warder to them. By now the Colonial Office, as well as Selassie, knew that the Italians controlled Wal Wal and Warder. However, in the process of trying to dislodge the Italians, the Emperor did not want to become embroiled in an argument with Italy that the Fascists might use as a pretext to start a war--unless the Emperor knew he could count on British support. And yet there was not a chance of getting that support without the successful conclusion of the Zeila negotiations.

As he pondered his dilemma one day in late July 1934, the Emperor received news that Hitler's minions had assassinated Engelbert Dollfuss, the Chancellor of Austria and attempted to effect the Nazi dream of <u>Anschluss</u>. As subsequent events would prove, the assassination of Dollfuss proved to be a more immediate threat to the independence of Ethiopia than of Austria. As one writer said, Mussolini was "so depressed by Germany's power and initiative that he reacted not merely with a compulsive need for Italian feats of arms but also with the conviction that glory and influence must be sought outside Europe."[11] More than any other single incident, the assassination of Dollfuss solidified Mussolini's intention of conquering Ethiopia in the very near future.

The death of Dollfuss also profoundly affected the British, and they started to review their foreign policy toward the other Great Powers. For the first time, the Foreign Office began to worry that the Zeila corridor plan might seriously jeopardize their relations with Italy and France. In the past, the English attitude had been that the French and the Italians could be dealt with satisfactorily when the time came to publicize the final agreement. But now they began to shift their position. By September 1934, they began to intimate more strongly to the Colonial Office that they were seriously considering disengaging from the Zeila talks should events in Europe warrant such an expedient about-face in their policy.

The attempted <u>Anschluss</u> did not alter the narrow perspective of the Colonial Office however. They kept pursuing the Zeila negotiations even though the talks might impact unfavorably on British and Ethiopian relations with Italy. Although the Foreign Office kept the Colonial Office current on their change of feelings towards Ethiopia, the reverse was not true. The Colonial Office did not inform their sister Ministry of the extent to which they continued to push Selassie regarding the Zeila plan. So between the British Foreign and Colonial Offices, the rift regarding Ethiopian policy began to widen.

On September 6 , 1934 Sir Sidney Barton reported to his superiors in London that the Emperor

> . . . was most anxious to proceed with our conversations for a settlement but that these now seemed certain to involve him in a direct conflict with the Italians at Wal Wal and Warder and he begged for my advice as to the best course for him to pursue. I replied that in the first instance he should instruct the Ethiopian section of the Boundary Commission to agree at once to the British Section's proposal to start on the inspection of the eastern grazing areas . . .

and that as this inspection includes a visit to Wal Wal and Warder among other places in that neighborhood the Ethiopian Government will then be placed in possession of first-hand and accurate information of the actual situation obtained in strict pursuance of an agreement between our two Governments of which the Italian Government have notice, and to which no possible objection can be taken. The Emperor has agreed to this proposal and is sending instructions accordingly.[12]

In his response to the above communication, Sir John Simon reluctantly acquiesced to the proposed visit to the wells by the Anglo-Ethiopian Commission. But he warned Barton that the British Section of the Commission should proceed "very cautiously" on the general question to avoid the risk of "falling between the French, the Italians and the Ethiopians."[13]

Strangely enough, the only people who were not worried about a confrontation over Wal Wal were the Italians in Rome. They were so preoccupied with their military preparations in Eritrea, they were blind to the coming Ethiopian threat in the Ogaden. When Sir Eric Drummond, the British Ambassador in Rome, questioned Signor Guarnaschelli, the head of Italy's African department, the latter said he couldn't believe that Ethiopia was really that concerned about the Italian occupation of Wal Wal. The Ethiopians knew the Italians had been there for a long time already, and no reinforcements of "any considerable extent" had been made recently by the Italians.[14]

A later conversation between Drummond and Guarnaschelli in mid-November proved to be more unsettling for both parties. When Drummond broached the subject of the Anglo-Ethiopian Commission's imminent arrival at Wal Wal, Guarnaschelli "appeared to be somewhat disturbed at the prospect."[15] Later during their discussion, Guarnaschelli produced a new map of East Africa. On this new map the tentative boundary line which had always been drawn between Ethiopia and Italian Somaliland had been removed altogether.[16] When the members of the Foreign Office in London heard about this new map, they realized that allowing the British Section of the Commission permission to visit the wells had been a big mistake. There could be no doubt now that Ethiopia and Italy would clash in a territorial dispute over Wal Wal. Now the British ran the risk of becoming embroiled in an argument which would negatively affect Anglo-Italian relations.

But it was too late for the Foreign Office to change its mind. Colonel E. M. H. Clifford, the head of the British section, and his Commissioners had already left for Wal Wal. Since Clifford had not taken a telegraph set with him, nor made any arrangement for communication with his base in British Somaliland, any recall order would have to go by foot. Under such conditions the message would not reach Clifford before his arrival at Wal Wal. Only a few weeks earlier, Sir John Simon had confidently written Eric Drummond that he believed Colonel Clifford would be accorded at Wal Wal "the friendly and courteous welcome to which he is certainly entitled."17 Now he wasn't so sure.

The instructions given to Colonel Clifford by the Colonial Office covered several points. The most important of these ordered that he should obtain the fullest possible information as to the general situation at Wal Wal and Warder, that he should not discuss political questions with either the Ethiopian Commissioners or any Italians he might meet, and that should the Italians deny access to the area, Clifford was to lodge a formal protest and then retire to British territory.18

On November 7, 1934, Clifford sent the following wire to the Colonial Office:

> . . . leaving tomorrow without the Ethiopian Section. Anticipate they will follow in a few days. I have informed them I shall not delay my programme on their account but will carry on to the proposed limit waiting for them there if necessary. I am experiencing more than usual difficulty in getting them under way. They state that there is still a slight difference between their instructions and mine but I have not yet been able to ascertain what it is.19

No doubt the "slight difference" in instructions Clifford referred to was the news from Selassie that the Commission would be joined by a large "escort" of both regular and irregular Ethiopian and Somali forces. Unable to pin down the British on any type of alliance, the Emperor had continued to vacillate over the idea of trying to reclaim the wells at Wal Wal. However, he finally decided to go ahead and confront the Italians. If he didn't, the Zeila negotiations would end, and thus any possibility of British support against Italy. But if he tried, he might be successful. His spies reported that the dubats were not well-manned or well-supplied. He would use not only the Somali and Ethiopian irregulars who had already been fighting for him in the Ogaden, but some regular Ethiopian army troops as well. These last would be an important addition not only to increase the number of men, but also because they had been properly trained and equipped. As in the past, Selassie hoped his men would so badly outnumber their scattered Italian foes that the dubats would abandon their posts without a fight. But if the dubats and their officers held firm, there might be bloodshed and Fascism's ire was sure to be provoked. It was a risk Selassie decided he finally had to take.

On November 20, 1934, a contingent of approximately 200 regular Ethiopian soldiers under the command of Fitaurari Shiferra arrived at Ado, a town about eighteen miles distant from Wal Wal. They had in tow the Anglo-Ethiopian Boundary and Grazing Commission. Already waiting for the entourage were 350 Ethiopian and Somali irregulars.

If the British section of the Grazing Commission was surprised to find itself with a 600 man escort, they never showed it.[20] Lieutenant Curle of the British Commission described their new traveling companions thus:

> The escort amounted to some 600 men--these were not made up of soldiers in the European sense but of mixed elements. They were supplied with a rifle usually a Fusil Gras but had to provide their own ammunition which often did not fit the rifle and was sometimes without a charge of powder. They were not in uniform and many had paid substitutes to do duty for them. In some cases the quota had been filled with unruly youths who caused trouble in their villages. Donkeys and a motley crowd of servants and small boys came with them. There was nothing to carry water in and no arrangements for food beyond meat on the hoof.[21]

Although the possibility of a fight over Wal Wal now loomed ever larger, Clifford wholeheartedly threw in his lot with the Ethiopians. He neither made any protest concerning the size of his "escort," nor canceled his mission, nor even tried to inform Colonial Office headquarters. Clifford had not even reached Wal Wal and he had already violated his orders.

Two days later Fitaurari Shiferra and his army of 600 started marching towards Wal Wal. The Anglo-Ethiopian Boundary Commission delayed their departure for the disputed wells one day. The sun had only been up about two hours when a sentry posted at Wal Wal thought he saw a large group of men approaching the line of wells. The Somali dubat jumped down off his platform of tree limbs and hurried off to report his sighting to Alie Uelie, the dubat non-commissioned officer in charge. Fortunately for the Italians that day, Uelie was one of the bravest and best-trained examples of the dubat corps and a veteran of fifteen years service.

The news was unwelcome, but not surprising. Lieutenant Musti, Uelie's superior officer at Warder, had informed him just the day before that their spies reported the "Amharas" were marching towards the Wal Wal-Warder area. Since Musti did not know which Italian fort the Ethiopian army would approach, he did not reposition any troops. The dubats at Wal Wal numbered their usual sixty.

Alie Uelie quickly ordered all of his men out of the fort and spread them in a wide arc, attempting to shield the line of wells. Since there were so few men to cover such a large area, the dubats were spaced quite far apart. Once his men were in place, Uelie dispatched a runner to Lieutenant Musti to apprise him of the situation.

The soldiers had only a brief wait before the vanguard of Shiferra's group appeared. The Ethiopian forces advanced towards the line of wells until only a few yards separated them from Wal Wal's defenders. Behind them more and more men kept coming until all 600 were arrayed before the dubats. Without uttering a word, the army stopped and waited.

Having identified Shiferra as the one with which to parley, Uelie boldly stepped forward and asked him why he and his men had come to Wal Wal. Shiferra responded that his men were the escort for the Anglo-Ethiopian Boundary Commission which would arrive the following day. His men and the Commission needed to obtain water from the wells. Uelie replied that he had standing orders from the Italian officers at Warder to allow no one access unless they had received prior authorization. Shiferra retorted that the Italians had no right to make such restrictions because the wells were in Ethiopian territory. He and his men had every right to use them. Stalling for time, Uelie replied that if Shiferra was truly acting as a representative of the Ethiopian government, he should go through normal diplomatic channels and submit a written complaint.

The Ethiopian commander was taken aback by the calm, logical Uelie and abruptly turned and began conferring with his fellow chiefs. No doubt his feisty comrades all counselled in favor of an immediate attack, since the Ethiopian forces so vastly outnumbered the dubats. All Shiferra had to do was give the word.

But Shiferra would not give the word. The Emperor had ordered him to regain control of the wells, but had not specifically said to attack. Selassie had led him to believe that the presence of such a large force combined with the international authority of the Commission would scare the dubats into a quick retreat. When a handful of Somali soldiers stood firm and invoked diplomatic protocol, Shiferra lacked any guidance. He rebelled at the thought of retreat, however. And he knew that his other chiefs would never accept such a course of action.

Finally, Shiferra decided to do nothing for the moment. He would request new instructions from his Emperor and would play Uelie's diplomatic game while he waited for Selassie's response. The argument over the need for water had become meaningless anyway, as some of his men had already managed to gain access to a few of the wells without provoking any shooting.

After making his decision, Shiferra returned to Uelie and asked to speak to an Italian officer. Although he had already sent one messenger to Warder, Uelie quickly sent another. The "escort" stayed where they were, neither advancing nor retreating. For the moment, Shiferra's indecisiveness had averted a battle.

As each side began to settle into its lines the irony of the situation became obvious. On both sides Somalis faced their fellow tribesmen with hatred because of loyalty to a foreign rival. They were ready to kill their own kinsmen for the valuable water, only to give it to someone else. The Somali soldiers on the Ethiopian side took advantage of this situation by constantly haranguing the Italian <u>dubats</u> while each side built up its fortifications against the other. This harangue alternated threats and sarcasm with calls of loyalty to their common blood and their hatred of the Italians.[22] The <u>dubats</u> were not immune to this pastime of verbal harassment either. And so both sides flung insults and bribes across the defensive lines throughout the rest of the afternoon.

Eight miles away at the Italian sector command at Warder, an angry and scared Lieutenant Musti confronted a decision about the situation at Wal Wal. He had known something like this would happen eventually. For the previous two months he had been sending reports to Governor Rava in Mogadiscio concerning the movements of irregular Ethiopian troops. But Rava had done nothing. He thought Musti was overreacting to the small bands of Ethiopian and Somali brigands who had occasionally raided the area. Consequently, Musti's pleas for more men and armaments had gone unanswered. Now he found himself in the unenviable position of opposing a contingent of Ethiopians who outnumbered his <u>dubats</u> six to one.

Lieutenant Musti immediately began calling up more <u>banda</u> for active duty, using his radio to inform all Italian districts of the dangerous turn of events. He then answered Alie Uelie's note and told him that some of the 250 <u>dubats</u> stationed at Warder would be sent over during the night. Musti ended his letter by cautioning, "You will not fire any cartridges until the Abyssinians begin."[23] The Italian Lieutenant promptly readied a dispatch to Governor Rava relating the events of the day and requesting orders. Even before he received Rava's reply, Musti knew what his governor would say. Although Uelie's men were currently ill-equipped and drastically outnumbered for any battle with the Ethiopians, they would be ordered to stand and defend the wells, or die in the attempt. If Italy hoped to invade Ethiopia in the near future, they could not let themselves be forced into an embarrassing retreat now.

Rava's reply was as expected, stating that he was sending three airplanes, two tanks and several machine guns to Warder to be used to reinforce Wal Wal. He also told Musti to invite the Ethiopian chief to a meeting with him and ended by saying, "Refrain from any hostile act whatsoever; but if armed men attack our positions, counter by defending them,"[24]

Lieutenant Musti proceeded to write a letter directly to Shiferra asking him to not let the escort "aggravate the situation. If he had anything to say to the Italians to write to him directly that he would fix a meeting with the Italian authorities."[25]   Upon receiving Musti's letter, Shiferra immediately wrote back and said yes, he really did want to talk with the Italians. He complained that "thy askaris have come to us and are seeking a quarrel. Speak thou to thy askaris, when we will talk together, that is withdraw thy askaris."[26]   The Lieutenant decided to postpone composing the expected diplomatic response, and turned his attention to more pressing matters. As night fell, some 190 <u>dubats</u> from Warder stealthily bolstered the number of Wal Wal defenders. Although the still greatly outnumbered <u>dubats</u> maintained their vigilance, all became calm in the Ethiopian camp. On the Italian side, Alie Uelie was still in charge.

Towards evening of the following day, Captain Roberto Cimmaruta arrived at Warder. He had no sooner alighted from his vehicle than several <u>dubats</u> excitedly informed him that a large force of Ethiopians and Somalis was threatening Wal Wal. And, according to the excited babble of voices, the army troops had brought with them some machine guns, in addition to the traditional weapons of the Ogaden tribesman. The existence of the Ethiopian army troops was greatly distressing to Cimmaruta.[27] He realized that he and his men had not encountered a previous challenge quite like this one. Not only was the group larger than usual, they were better armed and better organized due to the addition of the regular army troops. This was meant to be a serious threat to the Italian positions in the Ogaden. And Cimmaruta knew the Italians were woefully unprepared for it.

The Captain searched out Lieutenant Musti who gravely verified the report. In addition, Musti confided he was worried about the loyalty of the <u>dubats,</u> particularly the Majerytens. The latter were of the same tribe as Omar Samantar, one of Shiferra's chiefs, and the Lieutenant was afraid they would desert to join their clan.[28] The hour was growing late, but Cimmaruta had still another surprise awaiting him that day. Another messenger arrived from Wal Wal, this time bearing a note from the Anglo-Ethiopian Commissioners.

The Commission had arrived at Wal Wal about 11:30 that morning, and had re-enacted a scene with Uelie and his men, similar to that of Shiferra the day before. Once permission to use the wells was denied, Clifford should have "lodged a protest" and then had the Commission leave the area. But Clifford did not follow orders. Both the British and Ethiopian sections of the Commission stayed and made camp at Wal Wal, separated from Shiferra's men by about 500 yards.

The presence of the Commission at Wal Wal was another surprise beyond Cimmaruta's anticipation. Although Guarnaschelli in Rome had been told by Eric Drummond in October that the Commission should be expected at Wal Wal, the news had not been relayed to Mogadiscio until November 22, the same day that Shiferra's troops arrived at Wal Wal. The Italian officers in the Ogaden had no advance notice of their arrival. The British members of the Commission were unaware of this mistake, as they had been told by the Colonial Office that the Italians would have prior warning of their visit.29

Early the next morning, Cimmaruta heard the sound of rifle fire coming faintly from the direction of Wal Wal.30 The dubats on duty immediately began to get very nervous, and sounded the alarm to awaken the others. Even though the volley of shots had not been repeated, Cimmaruta decided to leave immediately for Wal Wal and find out what was happening.

Once the Captain entered the beleaguered fort, he quickly singled out a dubat he recognized and asked him about the rifle fire he had heard from Warder. The soldier obliged and told him that a small patrol of dubats had been attacked by a band of Ethiopians and rebel Somalis. Although shots had been exchanged, there had been no casualties.31

While Cimmaruta and his men had been talking and inspecting their lines, a few Ethiopian soldiers began walking parallel to them on the other side of the brambles, shouting insults. The dubats' rude rejoinders were silenced by Cimmaruta. He understood how precarious their position was and that they must keep the peace pending additional help. He also realized that the hostility over ownership of the wells was an ancient one between the various tribes. Feelings were running very high and soldiers on both sides were spoiling for a fight.

Later that morning Cimmaruta arrived in front of the spacious tent occupied by the British section of the Commission. After the Italian Captain and the Commissioners had settled into some camp chairs, the Commissioners came to the point. They had been stopped from obtaining water from the wells by the intransigent Uelie and his men, and forced to camp in an uncomfortable spot. Cimmaruta did not answer their accusation. Instead he countered their complaint with one of his own. "How come the British Ethiopian Commission got so close to Italian possessions with such a large number of armed men without even notifying the Italian Authority?"32

Avoiding Cimmaruta's question, the Ethiopian Commissioners immediately protested that Wal Wal and Warder belonged to Ethiopia, not Italian Somaliland. The Italians should not be camped in this part of the Ogaden. Cimmaruta replied that the wells were very definitely in Italian Somaliland and had been occupied by the Fascist forces for many years now. However, their question was a political issue, not a military one. They should go through the proper channels to discuss it. As a military man he had no jurisdiction to decide territorial matters.

The Ethiopian Commissioners continued to insist that Wal Wal and its environs were Ethiopian territory, and there was no need to forewarn the Italians of their intention to use the wells. Cimmaruta once again changed the subject to that which was most worrisome to him--the close proximity of the two forces. He proposed that they all go for a walk along the lines and agree to some type of provisional arrangement to reduce the chance of a clash. The Commissioners hesitantly agreed and the party moved out into the hot afternoon sun.

As they walked around the lines, Cimmaruta proposed that marks be made on various tree trunks, denoting the position of the lines, and that his and the Commissioners signatures be affixed to these marks. This idea was not warmly received. Claiming that it "might create an undesirable precedent as regards Italian territorial claims," the Commissioners said the request was "inadmissible."33 The Ethiopian Commission went on to suggest that Cimmaruta withdraw his men a few yards so that the Commission could draw all the water it needed. Cimmaruta was starting to get angry, but replied that he would permit the Commission to draw as much water as it required from any well selected behind the line of his banda. His permission would be given once and for all.34

The Ethiopians immediately turned down Cimmaruta's offer, and with that a heated argument began. The British alternated between trying to convince Cimmaruta to give up the wells, and cajoling the Ethiopians into an agreement. Neither effort was successful. With feelings of mutual hostility, the meeting was about to break up when two Italian airplanes were sighted by the angry group. The two military aircraft, armed with cameras and machine guns, had left Mogadiscio that morning under orders from Governor Rava to do aerial reconnaissance of the area. As one of the pilots flew over Wal Wal, he could see that the dubats were enormously outnumbered, and Captain Cimmaruta was standing on the Ethiopian side surrounded by a group of men. Afraid at first that his fellow officer had been taken prisoner, the pilot put his plane into a steep dive to get a closer look.35 Second-guessing the pilot's fears, Cimmaruta began waving his arms to show them he was in no danger. The two planes made several more dives over the Ethiopian camp before they flew back to Warder.

The appearance of the two planes caused quite an uproar. Ethiopian soldiers and Commissioners alike claimed to have seen one of the aircraft's guns trained on the Commission. Colonel Clifford, however, was the most shaken by the incident. He angrily told Cimmaruta that the actions of the planes "was clearly a deliberate provocation by the Italian authorities."36 He then announced that to protest the hostile demonstration by the Italian aircraft, the British Commission would withdraw to Ado as soon as possible.37 Cimmaruta icily asked why the presence of the planes was considered a "provocation," when the presence of an "escort" of about a thousand armed men was not. Then he told Clifford to take his Commission and leave if he wanted. He certainly did not care one way or the other. Then, Lieutenant Curle noted, the Italian Captain "walked off in a rage, having made of himself, to use an Italian expression, a bruta figura."38

With the conclusion of this angry exchange, each side returned to its respective camp. Gradually the lines of Ethiopian soldiers and Somali dubats settled into their routine exchange of insults. But Colonel Clifford was worried. He was finally beginning to understand the delicate position in which he had placed his country by camping at the Italian-occupied oasis. If the Italian planes had used their guns, the presence of the British would have made an international incident out of a border skirmish. He regretfully decided that he could no longer risk involving himself and his government in what would have to remain an Ethiopian problem. The Zeila negotiations would simply have to be postponed until the Ethiopians could clear the Italians from their territory. In the morning the British Commission would beat a dignified but hasty retreat back to Ado, a safe eighteen miles away.

True to his word, Clifford led his Commissioners and the Ethiopian Commission in a single convoy of trucks and camels away from Wal Wal the next morning. At Ado they would await a response to their protests to the Italian government. Their "escort," which was about 900 strong by now, did not move when the Commission departed.

Two days later, Cimmaruta wrote an unconciliatory letter to Shiferra demanding to know "what you intend to do with all these armed men" and "whether you intend to remain in the positions where you are now, and beyond which I would advise you not to go."[39] After he read it, Shiferra sent a copy of Cimmaruta's letter on to the Commission. Clifford drafted a reply haughtily stating "We note the terms and the general tone of your letter, which we shall without delay communicate to our respective governments in London and Addis Ababa."[40]

With the Commission refusing to intervene and recall their "escort," Cimmaruta felt there was little left to do but wait for the inevitable Ethiopian attack. Even if the Ethiopian commanders did not order an attack, the atmosphere was becoming so tense that shooting might easily erupt at any moment. The Ethiopian troops, particularly their Somalis, were becoming even more belligerent and Cimmaruta was finding it increasingly difficult to restrain his own men.

The Italian Captain continued to do what he could in preparation for an armed confrontation. He ordered that a landing field be made ready at Warder for use by the three Italian planes sent by Governor Rava. The balance of the armaments Rava had promised--the armored cars, machine guns and extra ammunition--had still not arrived. Cimmaruta and Musti also tried to recruit more natives for service under the Italian flag. But these efforts fell quite short when matched against those of the Ethiopians. Their numbers were still steadily increasing, swelled by the irregular bands which continued to converge on the area.

The standoff dragged on. By December 1, the tenth day of the confrontation, life at Wal Wal had settled down into somewhat of a routine. Although each side continued to verbally harass the other, there were places where a certain esprit de corps had developed across the lines of soldiers. One Ethiopian soldier went so far as to say that they had become on "good terms" with the dubats, and although occasionally a "rifle went off accidentally, either in the Italian camp or in our own . . . no one thought of an attack."[41]

On December 2, the long-awaited supplies from Governor Rava arrived at Warder. The two armored cars, three machine guns and additional ammunition were a welcome sight to Cimmaruta and Musti, even though Rava had not sent any reinforcements. Cimmaruta ordered the machine guns sent on to Wal Wal, but was afraid that the Ethiopians might start shooting if the armored cars were moved there also. Instead, he ordered their crews to remain at Warder.

By December 3, the strain of the long series of sleepless nights and tension-filled days were starting to take their toll on both the Italian and Ethiopian contingents. Dubats and their officers were exhausted by the need to remain constantly vigilant. Men under Shiferra's command were becoming ill, and his army's supplies were running low. When Cimmaruta arrived at Wal Wal that day to make his daily inspection, his first news was that the opposing forces seemed to have stepped up their harassment of the dubats, and had attempted to infiltrate the Italian defenses in some spots. The Captain's fears of an imminent attack proved unjustified though, as the night of December 3 passed without incident.

The next morning Cimmaruta reconnoitered the lines again to see what Ethiopian infiltration might have occurred unnoticed during the previous night. The Captain ordered two of the pilots to fly over the armed camps and determine the relative positions of the two forces. In addition, the planes would act as a threatening reminder to the Ethiopians of the superior technology the Italians possessed. Cimmaruta also ordered some of the extra ammunition at Warder be sent over to the disputed fort.

The planes returned with the report that the Ethiopian soldiers appeared to number between 1500 and 1600 and the dubats about 550. Cimmaruta then wrote an identical note to both Shiferra at Wal Wal, and to Tessama Bante, the Ethiopian Commissioner at Ado, warning them of the increasingly ominous situation on the Italian-Ethiopian line. Shiferra had been summoned to Ado that day and was not at Wal Wal to receive the message. While he was gone, one of his subordinate chiefs, Fitaurari Alemaio, busily wrote a note to each of his four fellow chiefs which said:

> On their side they are now beginning to betray their officers and to pass over to us. We are at a distance of not more than three metres from the Europeans. Our weapons are loaded. We have no yet fired but are ready to do so. Pray that the Lord may have pity on us and that the God of Israel may grant that we be found again alive.[42]

While the situation went from bad to worse at Wal Wal, Haile Selassie's relations with the British were gradually disintegrating. The Emperor had not been pleased by the limited news he had heard about the standoff at Wal Wal. Not knowing what new orders to give Shiferra until he heard the British opinion of the situation, he summoned Sir Sidney Barton and asked his advice. Sir Sidney Barton immediately pleaded he needed more information and then hurried back to telegraph his superiors the news in London.[43] The Foreign Office had been fearful for the past month that just such a confrontation might occur, and hastily told the Colonial Office to contact Clifford at Ado as soon as possible. Since information from the British Commissioners had been so sketchy, both the Foreign and Colonial Offices remained unaware that Clifford had taken a strong pro-Ethiopian stance in violation of his orders. They soon learned the truth of the matter from Signor Vitetti, the Counselor at the Italian Embassy in London.

On December 3, Vitetti visited the Foreign Office to discuss the latest dispatch he had received from Rome. After narrating the highlights of the Italian version of the Wal Wal confrontation thus far, Vitetti said that he was confused "over Colonel Clifford's apparent espousal of the Ethiopian case in question exclusively at issue between Italy and Abyssinia,"[44]

The members of the Foreign Office expressed some surprise over Vitetti's allegations, but smoothly suggested that

> . . . it would be most regrettable if any question relating to these matters were allowed to react in any way upon Anglo-Italian relations. . . . the only opinion that could be expressed was that whatever Colonel Clifford's views might be, he could in no way commit His Majesty's Government.[45]

After the interview with Vitetti, the Foreign Office decided that the situation in the Ogaden had grown too dangerous for them to risk further involvement. They would tell the Colonial Office to drop the Zeila plan altogether, and leave the Ethiopians to fend off unwanted Italian advances by themselves. The deteriorating situation in Europe made it a dangerous time for international diplomacy. There was no reason to risk alienating Benito Mussolini and his Blackshirts over what was, to the Foreign Office, a worthless bit of desert.

Sir John Simon quickly ordered Eric Drummond in Rome to suggest an immediate territorial demarcation in the Ogaden to Signor Suvich, the Italian Undersecretary of Foreign Affairs. He then wired the same suggestion to Barton in Addis Ababa. Almost ten days after the Emperor had requested advice, Sir Sidney Barton received his instructions. On December 4, Barton obtained an audience with Selassie and brusquely came to the point. In response to the Emperor's request for advice concerning Wal Wal, he had been instructed to suggest an immediate demarcation between Ethiopia and Italian Somaliland as quickly as possible to solve the dispute. The Emperor was astounded at the radical shift in the ambassador's stance regarding the disputed Ogaden. And he knew this shift must have been caused by a change of policy in London which did not bode well for Ethiopia. Selassie now realized just how much faith he had put in the British and the successful conclusion of the Zeila negotiations. His faith had been misplaced. The British were going to desert him just when he needed them most.

The morning of Wednesday, December 5, the Emperor called together his three European advisors to confer on the Wal Wal situation. After a long meeting they concluded that Ethiopia's next course of action was to formally protest the Fascist occupation of the Ogaden to the Italian legation in Addis Ababa. By sending regular troops to Wal Wal, the Emperor had taken his first official military stand against the Italian encroachment. The note of protest would now be his first strong diplomatic stand.

At the battle lines at Wal Wal, the situation on December 5 was much the same as it had been the previous day. The air was filled with tension, but there was no shooting. The sun was past its zenith and at its most scorching. Soldiers on both sides, except those unlucky enough to draw sentry duty, were lounging in their tents or fort. Even in the tense atmosphere at Wal Wal, this was usually a peaceful time of day. But December 5 was not destined to be like previous days. Suddenly a series of rifle shots crackled through the camp and shattered the veneer of serenity.[46]

Men on both sides were unprepared, so each side accused the other of a premeditated attack. The Ethiopians believed that the Italian Somalis had ambushed a party of Ethiopian soldiers who had tried to obtain some water. One Ethiopian claimed he remembered hearing whistles and then commands in Italian to "take cover" and then "fire" seconds before the shots rang out.[47] The Italian side vociferously stated that the Ethiopians shot at one of their sentries positioned in a low tree, then followed it with a volley aimed at the dubat non-commissioned officers who were easily identifiable by their colored turbans. But irrespective of who started firing first, both sides sprang into battle with a vengeance. The pent-up hatred of many years was finally loosed in a cloud of dust and death.

The Ethiopian commanders were certainly unprepared for battle. Their machine guns still had their covers on. The second-in-command, Fitaurari Alemaio, was quickly hit as he stumbled out of his tent and died instantly. Other soldiers and their chiefs ran around in a panic trying to locate their weapons. Many were killed before they could reach their guns.

The dubats, too, had been unprepared for battle, and some of them had already been killed. Eight miles away at Warder, Cimmaruta had heard the first shots faintly while he had been getting ready to go to

Wal Wal for his daily inspection tour. Remembering a similar incident at the beginning of the confrontation which had proven to be inconsequential, Cimmaruta did not immediately sound the alarm. Then he heard the gun shots again in increased numbers and rushed outside the fort to hear better. The <u>dubats</u> who had been working in the vicinity immediately dropped their tools and grabbed their rifles.

Orders were given for the three planes to take off. One of the planes was to reconnoiter the battlefield and report back to Warder. The other two were to stay and aid the outnumbered <u>dubats</u>. The two armored cars were also ordered to Wal Wal, but cautioned not to open fire until they were sure it was an Ethiopian attack.[48]

Cimmaruta sped off in his truck towards the battlefield. When he finally gained access to the fort, the scene that met his eyes was bloody pandemonium. <u>Dubats</u> came running to him and begged for more ammunition, while their slain comrades were piled up in a corner. The Captain immediately sent four messengers to Warder to get more ammunition and reinforcements. He then began the gruesome task of frisking the dead bodies for their ammunition which he passed on to his other soldiers. As <u>dubats</u> came to him, Cimmaruta restationed them along the line which seemed weakest at that moment and exhorted them to continue fighting.

So far the battle was not going well for the Italians. The first twenty minutes had been so filled with confusion on both sides that neither one seemed to enjoy an advantage. Then the Ethiopian side began to achieve a semblance of order and the full force of their large contingent began to pressure the Italian line. The <u>dubats</u> battled bravely for a short time. Then, although the front line continued to hold, large sections of the back line started to retreat. This was partly due to fear, partly because their ammunition was running low, and partly because of the pressure of the superior Ethiopian numbers. The two Italian planes had thus far been frustrated in their bombing attempts because of the close intermingling of the two lines. But when the pilots saw some of the <u>dubats</u> begin to retreat, they flew over to the Italian side and dropped bombs in the path of the fleeing Somalis to force them to turn and fight. This maneuver was successful. Then the pilots flew back and began to drop bombs on the Ethiopian side. Very few of the bombs actually destroyed men or equipment, but they had quite a damaging psychological effect on the Ethiopian troops.

The two armored cars were much more destructive, and took a deadly toll among the Ethiopian contingent. The cars were not as effective as they might have been, however, as they had a difficult time maneuvering due to the various holes, trenches and wells which were scattered over the battlefield. Finally, after darkness fell, both the armored cars and the airplanes became useless, as they could no longer distinguish their Ethiopian targets from their own Somalis.

During the two hours after nightfall, the Italian side neither advanced nor retreated. They fired rarely, and only then when they were sure of hitting someone so as to conserve their precious ammunition. The Ethiopian side, shocked by the work of the planes and armored cars, and burdened with Shiferra's cautious leadership, did not press its advantage.

The extra ammunition ordered from Warder finally arrived, but no reinforcements came with it. Cimmaruta reorganized the dubats and then had them advance and reopen fire. He also ordered a few men to infiltrate the line and recapture one of the armored cars which was still in enemy territory.

The fighting continued on into the night. Finally, at 11:00 p.m., Fitaurari Shiferra ordered his men to retreat towards Ado and the Boundary Commission encampment. Shiferra justified his order because of the lack of ammunition, the heavy casualties the Ethiopian side had sustained, and the need to arrange transportation for the wounded.[49] This admission of defeat by their commander-in-chief demoralized most of the surviving soldiers, and the once proud and spirited Ethiopian troops "took flight in disorder."[50] After Shiferra left, the leadership of the remaining Ethiopian forces devolved onto Ato Ali Nur, a man with a more warlike resolve than Shiferra. But even his courage could not turn the tide of battle which now favored the Italians. He tried to overturn one of the armored cars, and lost 100 men in the process. The rest of his men became scattered in small groups surrounded by the enemy. Finally, about 2:00 a.m., Ali Nur also gave up the possibility of victory and hastily retreated towards Ado. Those men who were still caught behind Italian lines gradually slipped away during the night and straggled into Ado the following morning.

When Shiferra and his men first arrived at the Commission's headquarters late in the evening of December 5, they were a sorry sight. There had been no order to their retreat. And in their rush to fall back out of Italian range, they had left much of their equipment and many of their men behind. As one Ethiopian later testified, "The lorries assisted to transport a few of the wounded, but a fairly large number remained where they fell."[51]

During that long night, the Chief Ethiopian Commissioner, Tessama Bante, sent a telegram to the Foreign Ministry in Addis Ababa stating that "the Italians unexpectedly attacked our men who were at Wal Wal, employing aircraft, bombs, tanks, guns and machine guns. Persons were killed, but the exact number is unknown."[52] The exact number of casualties would never be determined due to conflicting reports. The estimates ranged from 107 to 300 dead on the Ethiopian side, with an unknown number of wounded. And on the Italian side there were at least 30 dead and 100 wounded. The Italian losses were all Somali dubats.

When Cimmaruta first heard that Shiferra and his men were retreating, he cautioned his men not to follow them and attack, fearing an ambush. But by early morning of December 6, there could be no question that the battle was over. The carnage of the night before became sickeningly visible, with the line of the Ethiopian retreat clearly marked by its litter of supplies and bodies. Once assured of his victory, Cimmaruta left Wal Wal for Warder to cable the good news to Governor Rava. The Italians were still in control of Wal Wal. They had won.

Ironically, it was Signor Mombelli, the Italian Chargè d' Affairs who told Haile Selassie the news of the battle at Wal Wal. Tessama Bante's telegram blaming the Italians for the attack arrived afterward. The Emperor then tried to have his Chargè in Rome lodge a protest in person to either Mussolini or Suvich. But the Chargè was repeatedly denied an audience. The Italians simply did not know what to say yet. The Wal Wal battle and resulting protests had caught them totally by surprise. The Italian occupation of the Ogaden had gone unquestioned for so long that the Fascist government had long past assumed the Ethiopians considered it a *fait accompli*. When Selassie finally protested officially their encroachment, Italy felt like a thief accused of a crime after thinking that the statute of limitations had run out. Even when Mussolini had decided to conquer Ethiopia, Eritrea was to be the main theatre of operations. The slow, piecemeal acquisition of the Ogaden was not part of the Duce's war plan. This lack of coordination of policies was the reason why the government in Rome was, initially, totally unprepared for the Wal Wal incident and the subsequent diplomatic furor.

Mussolini decided to play the role of the injured Great Power, and drew up a list of demands, including an apology and reparations, for Selassie to satisfy as atonement for the Wal Wal incident. When the Emperor asked Sir Sydney Barton Britain's advice on what to do about the demeaning list of Fascist demands, Barton coolly answered that the Ethiopians should comply totally to settle the matter quickly.

But Selassie's attempts to negotiate directly with Italy yielded only a useless exchange of notes. Only then in desperation, not in blind faith, did the Emperor of Ethiopia decide it was time to plead his case before the League of Nations. In his search for justice for his country, he placed his case before the court of the world. What he could not foresee was the critical situation building in Europe at that same time. The German Nazi threat was forcing the powers that most influenced the League of nations to act with special caution. And in the process, the rights of small, powerless states like Ethiopia became a secondary concern.

At the end of December 1934, Selassie sent a telegram to the League of Nations specifically invoking Article 11 of the League Covenant so that "every measure effectively to safeguard peace be taken."[53] Selassie's request for League intervention was received unhappily in Geneva. The countries represented had already realized that they would be in a no-win position if they grappled with the Wal Wal problem. If they sided with Italy, the small nations would accuse the international body of being a tool of the Great Powers.[54] On the other hand, if the League found Ethiopia to be in the right, as she surely was, Italy might flaunt their decision and walk out of the League, as Germany had done. Under such circumstances, it was no wonder the League Council found an excuse again and again for postponing discussion of the thorny problem.

During all the League postponements of the Wal Wal issue, the British continued to try to mediate a private solution to the quarrel. The Foreign Office definitely did not want a protracted League discussion which would reveal how deeply involved Great Britain had become in the question of the ownership of the Ogaden. Italy, too, wanted a quick settlement. Mussolini did not want a public dissection of his movements in East Africa as he was not quite ready yet to go to war against Ethiopia. Il Duce had to stop, or at least delay, a League discussion on Wal Wal to gain time to consolidate his position in Eritrea. As it was, Selassie's appeal to the League had become a source of acute embarrassment for the Fascist regime and exposed their aggressive designs against Ethiopia much sooner than they would have liked. Although she was certainly not ready to go to war in December of 1934, many countries were beginning to assume that Italy had contrived to bring about the battle at Wal Wal as an excuse to start the conflict.

As in the case of the Italians, the Wal Wal incident exposed the fact that the British, too, were also pursuing several different, uncoordinated policies in Ethiopia. Unfortunately for Haile Selassie and the Ethiopian nation, it was not until after the confrontation at Wal Wal had begun that the British understood the policies of the Colonial and Foreign Offices were in direct conflict with each other. The Colonial Office had sponsored a strong pro-Ethiopian policy, supporting the Anglo-Ethiopian Commission and the Zeila land trade. However, the Foreign Office's worry over Nazism increased their desire to improve relations with Italy. They decided to take a much more tolerant view of Italian rumblings about "civilizing" Ethiopia. The Foreign Office never protested Mussolini's proposed war in Ethiopia, much less attempted a move like supporting Ethiopia militarily, or closing the Suez Canal to Italian shipping. This paralysis of action speaks volumes on how afraid the British were of the increasingly unstable world situation. "Could we not have called Musso's bluff and at least postponed this war?" asked Winston Churchill later. "The answer I am sure is yes. We built Musso into a great power."[55]

After a two month delay, the League of Nations set up an Arbitration Commission in February 1935 to settle the Wal Wal dispute. But the Commission's discussions turned out to be a charade of international peacemaking. The Italians put such strong pressure on the Commission, that they were successful in shelving the important argument over the ownership of the Ogaden. And instead the Commission only concentrated its energies on the more insignificant question of who started the fighting at Wal Wal. Six months of fruitless wrangling resulted in a decision worthy of Solomon when the Arbitration

Commission announced in September 3, 1935 that neither the Italian nor the Ethiopian Governments"can be held responsible in any way for the actual Wal Wal incident."56

On the surface, the long-awaited decision by the Commission appeared to be in keeping with the rest of the indecisive League actions. However, an analysis of the confrontation shows that the Commission was right in its assessment. Although Italy was definitely guilty of illegally occupying Ethiopian territory, and Ethiopia was responsible for instigating the confrontation, neither government can be held responsible for ordering an attack at Wal Wal December 5, 1934. Ethiopian commander-in-chief, Fitaurari Shiferra, had given formal orders not to commence hostilities until he had further instructions from the Emperor--instructions which never came. When the first shots were fired, both he and his second-in-command were still in their tents, their machine guns still covered up. The evidence does not indicate that the Italians ordered the attack either. Governor Rava had counselled first Lieutenant Musti and later Captain Cimmaruta to keep the peace if possible. The time and circumstances of the attack appear to prove that Cimmaruta followed Rava's orders. The battle occurred late in the day when only a few hours of daylight remained by which the armored cars and planes could maneuver. To have made maximum use of them, an attack would have been launched earlier in the day. Indeed, no tanks or planes were present at Wal Wal when the fighting began and thus they did not participate in the first crucial twenty minutes of the battle. In addition, there was no Italian officer present when the fighting commenced, and the <u>dubats</u> were still outnumbered three to one with insufficient ammunition to sustain an attack. The Italian officers did not have much confidence in the loyalty of their <u>dubats</u>, and the latters' willingness to stand up under Ethiopian fire. This worry was later justified when the <u>dubats</u> did turn and retreat during the battle. They would have been routed had not Italian bombs forced them to stand and fight.

If neither the Ethiopians nor the Italians can be accused of starting the battle at Wal Wal, then the observation of one person that "a stray shot at a passing bird" precipitated the conflict would seem to be the answer. It is one possible answer. However, two separate testimonies, one Italian and one Ethiopian, attest to the fact that scattered rifle shots during the confrontation were a common occurrence without provoking hostilities. A more likely scenario may be that the battle erupted because of a small but definite fusillade which, at first, startled friend and foe alike, but then caused them to answer the fire almost immediately.

With both the Ethiopians and the Italians exonerated, there would appear to be no one left to blame for this planned fusillade. But there was another group well-represented on the battlefield--the Somalis. Given the facts that the Somalis, known for their volatile tempers, had continued to taunt and provoke their fellow tribesmen across the battlelines for ten consecutive days and that, historically, the ownership of the wells had long been the basis for conflict between the various clans represented, the strong possibility emerges that they were the ones who might have knowingly violated their orders to the contrary and commenced open warfare.

An Italian dubat may have fired first in a fit of pique at a tormentor on the other side of the thorn hedge which divided them. Or, with his perception clouded by exhaustion after the ten day stalemate, a dubat might have mistakenly thought one of those casual shots was aimed at himself or a fellow soldier and returned the fire. But a concerted attack, rather than an individual whim, is much less likely. The dubats knew their position was tenuous, that they were significantly outnumbered and that the armored cars and planes and extra ammunition were nowhere in sight. And they really had no good reason to attack. They already controlled the wells.

What seems much more likely is that Somalis from the Ethiopian side could have initiated the conflict. True, like the dubats, they were mercenaries, bought and paid for by the Ethiopian Emperor on more than one occasion. But the Somali chiefs were only nominally under Shiferra's control. They fought not only for money, but for the chance to avenge themselves on the Italians who had taken their homeland. They had been encamped at Wal Wal for ten days only because Shiferra had initiated a stalemate by refusing to attack that first day. During that time, the Somalis saw their supplies begin to run low and their men become ill and dispirited. And as they saw their own large force begin to atrophy under Shiferra's timid leadership, the Somalis may have feared they would have to ignominiously retreat without having tasted combat, if definite military action was not taken soon. For any and all of these reasons, the Somalis under Shiferra may have decided to throw Ethiopian caution to the wind and start shooting. They, of all the parties represented at Wal Wal, had the most to gain by attacking first.

On October 3, 1935, Mussolini's new Imperial Roman army trekked across the Eritrean-Ethiopian frontier and commenced their long planned conquest of Ethiopia. With the initiation of hostilities, the endless discussions in Geneva were finally shown to be the sham which everyone had long suspected. The League of Nations' hapless handling of the Italo-Ethiopian dispute eventually brought about its own ruin. Wal Wal was "the dangerous spark", as Samuel Hoare called it, that illuminated the weakness of the League. The arbitration of the Wal Wal dispute, or lack of it, by the League of Nations was a lesson for the world on the danger of appeasement as a tool of foreign policy. The actual battle at Wal Wal and the circumstances surrounding it, illuminated the need for a nation to have an integrated, global foreign policy. Sir Eric Drummond uncovered the problem when in plaintively questioning Sir Robert Vansittart of the Foreign Office he asked, "Can we . . . be certain that a clear-cut line of division between European and extra-European policy can always be maintained?"[57] Foreign policy and colonial policy could no longer be separated. A decision made concerning a small, unimportant country could and would have repercussions on relations with a more important nation. Nations could no longer risk giving "hostages to fortune" in one part of the world and assume that such a decision would not affect their foreign policy in another area. A lesson which should have been learned by the "Great War" had to be learned again at the desert oasis of Wal Wal.

NOTES

[1] Ivone Kirkpatrick, Mussolini: A Study in Power (New York: Hawthorne Books, Inc., 1964), p. 306.

[2] Arnold J. Toynbee, Survey of International Affairs 1935 (London: Oxford University Press, 1936), 2:134.

[3] In Somali language, turban is "dub" and white is "at". As part of their uniform, the Somali irregulars wore white turbans, therefore the origin of the term.

[4] League of Nations, Council, Official Journal (June 1935), pp. 751-53.

[5] Ibid., p. 751.

[6] Great Britain, Foreign Office, Documents on British Foreign Policy, 1919-1939, Second Series, Edited by E. L. Woodward and Rohan Butler (London: Her Majesty's Stationary Office, 1947), 14:3.

[7] Ibid., 14:67.

[8] Ibid., 14:3-4.

[9] Ibid., 14:9.

[10] Ibid., 14:9-10

[11] James Dugan and Laurence Lafore, Days of Emperor and Clown: The Italo-Ethiopian War 1935-36 (Garden City, New Jersey: Doubleday and Company, Inc., 1973), p. 97.

[12] Great Britain, Foreign Office, Documents 1919-1939, 14:20.

[13] Ibid., 14:23.

[14] Ibid., 14:25.

[15] Ibid., 14:33.

[16] Ibid.

[17] Ibid., 14:32.

18Ibid., 14:24.

19Ibid., 14:34.

20No information could be found as to whether the British section knew in advance that they would be supplied with such a large "escort." If they did, they conveniently neglected to tell the Foreign Office about it.

21Dugan and Lafore, Emperor and Clown, p. 90.

22Pitman Potter, The Wal Wal Arbitration (Washington: Carnegie Endowment for International Peace, 1938), p. 102.

23League of Nations, Council, Official Journal (February 1935), p. 269.

24Potter, Wal Wal Arbitration, p. 41.

25Roberto Cimmaruta, Ual Ual (Milano: Mondadori, 1936), p. 89.

26Potter, Wal Wal Arbitration, p. 43.

27Eric Virgin, The Abyssinia I Knew (London: Macmillan and Co., ltd., 1936), p. 23.

28At least seven dubats did desert to the Ethiopian side during the course of the confrontation.

29The reason for this delay cannot be adequately explained. Rome might not have transmitted this information deliberately, hoping to provoke an argument with the Commission when they arrived at Wal Wal, and expose British intentions towards the Ogaden. But more than likely it was simply incompetence that delayed news of the Commission's imminent arrival at Wal Wal. The officials in Rome never dreamed that the Commission would attach itself to a large, armed "escort."

30During the Arbitration Commission's hearings which occurred later, Cimmaruta was cross-examined on his ability to hear things over such long distances and gave a satisfactory answer. Potter, Wal Wal Arbitration, p. 109.

31Ibid., p. 160.

32Cimmaruta, Ual Ual, p. 113.

33League of Nations, Council, Official Journal (February 1935), p. 263.

34Ibid., p. 264.

35Potter, Wal Wal Arbitration, p. 161.

36The Princess Asfa Yilma, Haile Selassie, Emperor of Ethiopia (London: Sampson Low, Marston and Company, 1935), p. 272.

37Ibid.

38Dugan and Lafore, Emperor and Clown, p. 91.

39League of Nations, Council, Official Journal (February 1935), p. 262.

40Ibid.

41Ibid., (June 1935), p. 755.

42Potter, Wal Wal Arbitration, p. 45.

43Great Britain, Foreign Office, Documents 1919-1939, 14:34.

44Ibid., 14:39.

45Ibid.

46The Ethiopians claim the battle started at 3:30, the Italians say 5:00. There seems to be no reason for the discrepancy, and no way to prove one version is correct over the other.

47League of Nations, Council, Official Journal, (June 1935), p. 268.

48Later Ethiopian testimony agreed that the planes did not arrive until about ten minutes after the fighting started, and the tanks shortly thereafter, according to Potter, Wal Wal Arbitration, p. 80.

49League of Nations, Council, Official Journal, (February 1935), p. 268.

50Potter, Wal Wal Arbitration, p. 2.

51League of Nations, Council, Official Journal, (June 1935), p. 755.

52Ibid., (February 1935), p. 262.

53League of Nations, Council, Official Journal, (June 1935), p. 728.

54Actually the League had already bowed to Italian pressure and had withdrawn two maps in their chambers which showed Wal Wal to be within Ethiopian territory, according to the New York Times, 23 December, 1934.

[55] Leonard Mosley, <u>Haile Selassie: The Conquering Lion</u> (London: Widenfield & Nicolson, 1964), p. 196.

[56] Toynbee, <u>Survey</u>, 2:170.

[57] Great Britain, Foreign Office, <u>Documents 1919-1939</u>, 14:63.

AMERICAN NAVAL REARMAMENT, 1930-1940:
THE LEGISLATIVE DIMENSION

By MICHAEL A. WEST

As he savored the return of Democratic control of the House of Representatives on December 7, 1931, newly installed Majority Leader Henry T. Rainey must have felt vindicated as a political pundit. Although the Republicans weathered the bitter 1930 congressional elections with razor thin majorities in both chambers, Rainey was confident that their control of the House was too tenuous to survive the thirteen months until the 72nd Congress convened, for as he had written one of his constituents earlier in 1931:

> The chances are that the deaths which will occur between now and first Monday in December may give the democrats a clear majority in the House. Almost any Republican district will go democratic this summer, and ten or twelve Members of Congress will die between now and first Monday in December....[1]

And while Rainey's morbid prediction did not come entirely true, enough Republican members did succumb to enable the Democrats to regain control in the resulting special elections.

The Democratic organization of the House of Representatives also brought with it the elevation of Carl Vinson to the chairmanship of the Committee on Naval Affairs. In an appointment process dominated by the seniority system, the selection of the forty-eight year old country lawyer and ranking minority member on the committee since 1923 came as no surprise. While respected for his considerable expertise in naval matters and his conscientious committee work, there was little reason to suppose that his appointment represented a watershed in legislative efforts to build up and modernize the fleet. He seemed every inch the rural conservative, a man usually dressed in a well worn three piece suit set off by flashy necktie, who could customarily be found on the House floor lounging on a bench near a spittoon chewing on an inexpensive cigar or working a chaw of tobacco while regaling his colleagues with wry anecdotes--the very picture of the "good old boy" Southern politician.

And if surface appearances were not enough to raise some questions about Vinson's suitability for his new post, the fact that he represented Georgia's landlocked and predominantly agricultural 10th District made his selection appear entirely incongruous.

Closer observation suggested that these first impressions were deceptive, however. First, there was the robust, erect, six foot frame exuding the remarkable vigor of an indefatigable worker. Then there was a penetrating gaze beneath an impatient frown which bespoke a quick and incisive mind that chafed under delay or digression once a course of action had been chosen. A firm mouth mirrored a strong sense of purpose and tenacity in the pursuit of goals. Less tangible, but no less real, was a commanding presence which sought to dominate those around him. Masking this determination and sense of purpose were a wry smile and droll wit that deflated or diverted unwary opponents and earned him the nickname, "The Swamp Fox." A consummate power broker and superb legislative tactician, he kept his own counsel and jealously preserved his options until it was time to act. In sum, one could sense in him a combination of strong conviction applied to aims and subtlety and pragmatism in the selection of means.

These qualities, together with an unrivaled expertise on naval issues, were to make Carl Vinson one of the most remarkable committee chairmen in the annals of the House of Representatives, and the dominant legislative figure in the formulation of national security policy for over 35 years. During his first decade as chairman, however, he found himself fully occupied attempting to galvanize and direct congressional efforts to devise and enact comprehensive shipbuilding legislation. Vinson's success in this role was a major factor in bringing about one of the largest peacetime naval rearmaments in United States history.

The profound impact this naval rearmament had upon the conduct of American foreign policy in the late 1930s and its contribution to the global supremacy of the United States Navy during World War II has become a fertile ground for much study and interpretation. Less well appreciated, however, is the legislative aspect of that accomplishment and how it altered Congress's involvement in the formulation of national security policy. In fact, the following survey of the legislative dimension argues that the changes in the legislative process associated with these shipbuilding programs rivaled those in the sphere of naval and foreign policy. As will be seen, changes in institutional relationships within Congress and the legislative process played a major role both in the relative decline of American naval power in the 1920s and the "naval renaissance" of the succeeding decade.

Whatever doubts may have assailed him as he took over the reins of the Naval Affairs Committee, Vinson priorities were clear. Belonging to a small and dedicated band of legislators concerned about naval affairs in the early 1930s, he shared their belief that the most pressing national security requirement was the adoption of a consistent, comprehensive naval building program to redress a continuing erosion in

American naval capabilities vis-a-vis Great Britain and Japan. Sporadic U.S. naval construction since World War I failed to match the more balanced and coherent programs of its closest maritime rivals. It also raised the prospect of serious American qualitative deficiencies in the near future unless the bloc obsolescence of destroyers and submarines built during or immediately after the war was offset by a major replacement program. In addition, the dearth of naval orders at domestic shipyards resulted in the loss of skilled personnel who would be sorely missed in any future upswing in naval construction. Lastly, American shipbuilders were denied the opportunity to keep abreast with advances in the state of the art and incorporate the latest technology into their designs. Together, these developments raised grave doubts about the Navy's capability to safeguard vital American interests abroad, or to fulfill its assigned policy objectives in a period of increasing international instability.

This unfortunate situation did not occur because the Navy failed to appreciate the nature and extent of the problem. Indeed, Naval authorities had long argued that failure to adopt a comprehensive, long-term approach to shipbuilding would have dire consequences. Beginning in the mid-1920s, the General Board raised this issue with increasing stridency and repeatedly prepared and submitted plans for such a program.

These efforts were not sufficient, however, to overcome the combination of executive opposition, congressional inaction, and the absence of widespread public concern. The failure, then, was political.

"THEY'VE TAKEN OUR APPROPRIATIONS AWAY"

As he surveyed legislative remedies for fleet material deficiencies, Vinson must have been struck by the magnitude of the task before him. He knew that even in the best of circumstances, Congress was ill suited to make independent decisions on basic policy questions like a long-term, comprehensive naval building program. Nor did the political and fiscal climate in 1932 constitute the best of circumstances.

Compounding these difficulties was a major institutional change following World War I that significantly impaired Congress's ability to influence naval policy. This change involved the transfer of jurisdiction over annual Navy appropriations from the Naval Affairs to the Appropriations committees in Congress. The House Naval Affairs Committee exercised this jurisdiction from 1885 to 1920, while the Senate Naval Affairs Committee enjoyed a briefer span of control between 1899 and 1922. With appropriations, legislative and oversight functions in the hands of these sympathetic committees, it was not surprising that this period represented the golden age in Congressional-Navy relations, and that during those years, the American Navy grew from second class coastal defense fleet to the status of a great naval power.

But before long this arrangement prompted a rising chorus of criticism from those favoring more centralized budgetary control within the executive and legislative branches. Wide-spread concern over the unprecedented expenditures in World War I and sensational accounts of wartime profiteering brought matters to a head and resulted in the consolidation of all appropriations in the hands of the House and Senate Appropriations committees in 1920 and 1922. This came as a blow to the veteran members of the Naval Affairs committees. Chairman Butler of the House Naval Affairs Committee spoke for the majority of his colleagues when he observed, "Well, we might as well close up shop, now that they have taken our appropriations away."[2] Although this despair proved to be exaggerated, efforts by the Naval Affairs committees to effectively adjust to this change represented their single greatest challenge over the next decade.

On the positive side, the committees did retain their power to authorize appropriations for new programs. Consequently, the Appropriations committees could only provide funding for those new vessels, shore construction and major improvements within the amounts authorized. In practice, however, this was poor consolation for the inability of the Naval Affairs Committees to mandate funding at authorized levels.

In addition, there were a number of other practical problems this new situation created for the Naval Affairs committees, especially in their efforts to push a major shipbuilding program through Congress. First of all, it meant that congressional debate would have to occur twice--once on the authorization legislation and again on the annual Navy appropriation bill providing the actual funding. With something as controversial as a naval building program, consensus building was a formidable task once a session; but to attempt it twice was a doubtful proposition at best. Moreover, the separation of authorization and appropriations denied the committees the advantage of placing the building program within the annual appropriations bill that had to be enacted. Besides, there were fundamental differences in the orientation and approaches of the four committees. In general, the Naval Affairs committees represented Navy-related interests, emphasizing the need for a strong and effective Naval Establishment, and the funds necessary to maintain it. In contrast, the Appropriations committees tended to place more emphasis on protecting the Treasury from all comers, while carefully apportioning tax dollars among competing claimants.

The result, then, of the transfer of funding responsibility to the Appropriations committees was a fundamental change in legislative procedures. When naval construction was authorized and appropriated for in the same bill there was no ambiguity about congressional policy. And even when appropriations were limited to one year, as in the case of the 1916 Naval Building Program, Congress's intent was clear. But in the decade following 1922 this certainty was absent and congressional proponents of naval construction found themselves groping for a legislative mechanism to reestablish that relationship. The difficulty was that any proposal they devised would have to be capable of instituting the comprehensive, multi-year approach to naval construction they desired, yet without alienating the Appropriations committees by infringing on their jurisdiction. It seemed an impossible balancing act, and as a result, the failure of the Naval Affairs committees to fashion a satisfactory legislative mechanism before 1932 is not surprising.

NAVAL LIMITATION TREATIES

Looming over the legislative efforts of Carl Vinson and his pro-Navy colleagues were the naval limitation treaties negotiated at the Washington and London Naval Conferences. Support for naval limitation within the United States remained strong in 1931, and few questioned the desirability of continuing efforts to constrain naval competition among the major naval powers.

Only a decade before, the specter of a naval race had provided the impetus for a naval limitation conference at Washington in November 1921. Burdened by the war's crushing cost, and believing that the Anglo-German naval race had been a major cause of that conflict, Great Britain, Japan, Italy and France were amenable to American proposals for a substantial reduction in battleship tonnage. The result was an agreement upon a 5:5:3:1.75:1.75 ratio on dreadnought and aircraft carrier tonnage. The Washington Naval Treaty also provided for a ten year "holiday" on battleship construction and imposed a number of qualitative limitations on future capital ships. In return for Japan's acceptance of a lower capital ship ratio, the United States and Great Britain agreed not to fortify their possessions and naval bases in the Western Pacific. The rationale for this de facto grant of naval supremacy to Japan in those waters was the ratification of the Nine Power and Four Power treaties guaranteeing colonial possessions and territorial integrity of nations in the region, as well as preserving "Open Door" for China's commercial partners.[3]

The conference's failure to provide limitations on the construction of cruisers, destroyers, submarines and auxiliary vessels, however, spawned a naval race between major maritime powers in those categories. Concern over the costs and risks of that competition resulted in the ill-fated 1927 Geneva Naval Conference which, however, failed to produce any agreement among the powers.[4]

Despite this failure, several factors paved the way for another conference, that of London in 1930. First of all, elections in the United States and Great Britain brought to power chief executives committed to the extension of naval limitation to all classes of warships. Both Herbert Hoover and Ramsay McDonald viewed continued naval competition in unrestricted categories as a destabilizing influence in world affairs. Besides, the onset of the depression contributed to the willingness of maritime powers to reconsider naval limitation as a means of fiscal retrenchment. Equally important was the spirit of pacifism generated by the Kellog-Briand Pact of 1928 outlawing war as an instrument of national policy. That spirit was further strengthened in the United States by revelations that certain American shipbuilding interests had been instrumental in the failure of the 1927 Geneva Naval Conference.

Although the London Conference produced a treaty satisfactorily addressing outstanding naval issues between the United States, Great Britain, and Japan, this accomplishment was marred by the refusal of France and Italy to sign it; France was unwilling to grant naval parity to Italy or to acquiesce to Britain's two power standard in Europe. Still, the remaining three powers reaffirmed the existing ratios for capital ships, and agreed to extend the existing holiday on battleship construction through 1936. Most important, the treaty also set specific limits on cruiser tonnage "both light and heavy" and on destroyers and submarines. These provisions were to have tremendous influence on future naval construction as replacement programs, for the first time, could be accurately calculated.[5]

There were serious reservations about the Washington and London Treaties in naval circles. The British Admiralty resented granting parity to the United States, arguing that its worldwide responsibilities far exceeded American commitments that were primarily confined to the Pacific and Caribbean. The Imperial Japanese Fleet chafed over its lower ratios and sought to make its continued support of naval limitation contingent upon eventual parity with Great Britain and the United States. The French and Italians squabbled over their relative status vis-à-vis Great Britain and the naval balance in the Mediterranean.

The prevailing opinion in United States Navy held that the treaty system was responsible for preventing it from becoming the world's premier naval power after 1918, and for its relative decline throughout the next decade and a half. Equally galling was the belief that professional judgment and expert advice has been consistently sacrificed on the altar of political expediency in the pursuit of naval limitation agreements. Most of this brother officers concurred with Rear Admiral William A. Moffett's assessment of the treaties that "Uncle Sam" had been "hoodwinked and bamboozled" by a coalition of wily Europeans and inscrutable Orientals and ended up "losing everything but his shirt tail . . . ."[6]

Whatever the merits of these criticisms, they paled when compared to the chilling effect the agreements had on efforts to modernize the fleet. In a technical sense it can be argued that the treaties were not really responsible for the relative decline in American naval strength, since the United States never did build up to treaty limits, and nothing in the treaties forbade a replacement program for overage naval vessels. Nevertheless, the treaties perpetuated attitudes hostile to increased naval construction. The Navy persistently argued that treaty limits should be viewed as the baseline for a building and replacement program, and that they were part of an implicit political bargain involving a national commitment to maintain the fleet at those levels. Political leaders, on the other hand, instead viewed existing limits as temporary way stations on the path to greater reductions. In their minds, therefore, there was no obligation to build up the fleet to treaty limits as it would not be consistent with their desire to negotiate future agreements. Locked in a one-sided struggle against the twin political imperatives of naval limitation and fiscal retrenchment, the Navy's failure to fashion a realistic naval policy was foreordained.

1926-1932--EXERCISES IN FRUSTRATION

In seeking to devise legislation that could surmount these obstacles, Carl Vinson was at least spared having to start from scratch. He could draw upon congressional initiatives dating back to 1926.

By that time, the Navy Department and its allies in Congress reluctantly concluded that one year authorizations could not effectively address fleet modernization requirements. Except for the Eight Cruiser bill enacted in 1924, no new naval construction had been authorized since the Washington Naval Conference--in fact, none of the Navy's one year shipbuilding legislative proposals had even been introduced. The only ray of hope appeared in the guise of legislation authorizing a five year, 1,000 aircraft construction program recommended by the President's Aircraft Board--more commonly known as the Morrow Board after its chairman, Dwight W. Morrow. This bill represented a fundamental departure from previous one year authorizations as it called for a multi-year authorization broken down into specific annual increments. The speedy enactment of "The 1,000 Airplane Bill" in 1926 encouraged pro-Navy legislators to apply this approach to shipbuilding.

Their first opportunity came early in 1928 and was triggered by the abortive Geneva Naval Limitation Conference the year before. Angered by what he took to be British and Japanese intransigence, President Calvin Coolidge proposed legislation authorizing a five-year, 71 vessel naval building program. But strong opposition from peace and disarmament groups, combined with the high cost of the program killed any chance of its enactment. Nor did subsequent efforts in this direction fare any better. Pro-Navy bills died either on the floor or in committee.

In the wake of these defeats, pro-Navy legislators decided to abandon the multi-year authorization approach for the time being. Instead it was agreed that a single year authorization would be introduced, although care would be taken to place it within the context of a larger, longer range program. Each year thereafter, an annual authorization would be submitted to Congress until the total program had been enacted. It was hoped that this approach would escape the controversy generated by a larger multiyear authorization, and be more acceptable to the administration. But this approach, too, failed.

One reason for its failure was the personality of the House Naval Affairs Committee's chairman, Fred Britten. Strongly pro-Navy, Britten proved to be too combative and opinionated for any broad-based coalition building. Thus a change in committee leadership could not have come at a better time for Navy fortunes in Congress.

Even before he was installed as chairman, Carl Vinson called a meeting of the leaders of the House and Senate Naval Affairs Committees to examine the feasibility of a common approach to naval authorization legislation in 1932. Senators Frederick Hale and Claude Swanson and Representative Fred Britten all agreed with him that it was imperative to build the Navy up to treaty limits, that the best way to do so was via a comprehensive, steady ship construction program and that such legislation should be introduced in the next session of Congress. Unanimity broke down, however, when discussion turned to specifics, with Senator Hale favoring a general authorization of indefinite duration allowing the President to "build up the naval armament of the United States to the strength permitted," and Representative Britten arguing for the reintroduction of a specific one year authorization as part of a larger program as politically more expedient.

Carl Vinson was not impressed with either of these approaches. To him they represented a choice between the innocuous and the inconsequential, whose principal focus was to avoid or deflect pacifist opposition. But their greatest failing was that neither concretely addressed serious fleet material deficiencies that were becoming more critical with each passing day. What he had in mind was a comprehensive program broken down into specific annual increments whose execution would be mandated by law.

To Hale and Britten, Vinson's frontal assault seemed to be the recipe for certain defeat. The magnitude of his ten year program seemed sure to arouse the pacifists' ire, while simultaneously alienating those concerned about increased government expenditures. Moreover, they recognized that the inclusion of any provision mandating presidential compliance would be entirely unacceptable to President Hoover. Hale and Britten tried to convince the new chairman to adopt a more moderate approach, but the meeting broke up with no agreement on concerted action.

As matters turned out, Vinson, Hale and Britten were all partially right about President Hoover. Vinson correctly perceived that Herbert Hoover was opposed to a major naval construction program, and that his compliance would have to be mandated. Hale and Britten were equally correct in their assessment that efforts to require Hoover's compliance would only intensify his opposition to any naval construction legislation.

Actually President Hoover's attitude was merely the most recent manifestation of a consistent pattern of presidential opposition to naval construction efforts following World War I. During his tenure, however, this opposition reached its peak. By his words and deeds, President

Hoover sought to confine the Navy's mission to guaranteeing that "no foreign soldier will land on American soil."[7] Consequently, he rejected the Navy's planning emphasis on operations in the Western Pacific, and on the capability to protect American lives, interests and commerce around the world. Hoover felt that these aims were unrealistic, and the funding required to give the fleet such capabilities fiscally irresponsible. He was quite willing to recognize the naval supremacy of Japan in the Western Pacific, and to rely upon international agreements and diplomacy to protect America's vital interests there. In the unlikely event of war with Japan, the President felt that the industrial capacity of the United States would bring eventual victory.[8]

As if President Hoover's opposition was not enough to cope with, the stock market crash in 1929 and the onset of the Great Depression cast a further pall over efforts to enact naval shipbuilding legislation. The administration's response to the economic crisis was to make major spending cuts, with Navy requests being slashed to the bone. Officers took pay cuts, naval enlisted strength fell, and destroyers were rotated between active and reserve status because there was not enough funding or personnel to man and maintain them properly. Consequently, 1931 and 1932 marked the nadir of Navy capability and readiness in the interwar period.

The troubled state of the economy also riveted Congress's attention on domestic problems. The Democratic and Republican parties were all too aware that control of Congress and the Executive Branch would go to the party with the most attractive program for economic recovery. Both parties were for an "adequate" Navy, but purposely vague on the definition of that term. And each was vying with the other in promising greater cuts in government expenditures. A comprehensive naval shipbuilding and modernization program with a price tag of over $600 million simply did not fit into this agenda.[9]

And even if Vinson and his colleagues could have overcome the mood for fiscal retrenchment, they still would have faced a formidable challenge in the Geneva Disarmament Conference. Those talks provided their opponents with a persuasive argument that a naval construction authorization was not in keeping with the spirit of the conference, and might prevent the negotiation of an agreement in 1932. In addition, there was the reality of the Hoover one year moratorium on naval construction reached in late 1931.

In the face of these difficulties, then, neither Vinson nor his colleagues had much chance for success in 1932. Britten's bill never got out of committee, and Vinson failed to get the Democratic leadership of the House to schedule debate on his measure. Understandably, House leaders were more interested in the election of a Democratic President than in the dubious honor of presiding over the enactment of the largest naval construction authorization since World War I. Only in the Senate were pro-Navy forces successful and even there it was an empty victory;

after a delay of two months, Hale was able to secure Senate passage of his bill, only to have it languish in the House.

Still the efforts by Navy proponents in Congress in 1932 were not without results, as through hearings, floor debates, and media coverage they made people aware of the Navy's needs. In addition, Vinson was earning the respect of the civilian and military leadership of the Navy Department. Most important, however, the difficulties they had encountered in 1932 taught Vinson and his colleagues a number of useful lessons.

First and foremost, they had learned that tacit Presidential support was the absolute minimum required to enact a major naval construction authorization. Second, any successful naval construction proposal would have to be perceived as an integral part of the country's economic recovery efforts. Third, the enthusiasm for naval limitation and disarmament would have to abate somewhat before proposals to build to treaty limits could be enacted. And finally, pro-Navy leaders in Congress would have to agree on the authorization approach to be used.

FDR AND THE "DEMOCRATIC NAVAL PROGRAM"

On November 8, 1932, the first of these preconditions were met when the American electorate resoundingly rejected Herbert Hoover's bid for reelection, even though the new President Franklin D. Roosevelt at first sought to minimize his personal involvement in congressional efforts to enact major shipbuilding programs.

Certainly his love for the Navy had not been manifest during his campaign. He displayed little concern about the condition of the fleet and remained evasive when pressed for his definition of an "adequate Navy."[10] Moreover, he promised to outdo Hoover in slashing federal expenditures in the coming fiscal year. If he made good on his pledge to make deep across the board cuts, the Navy's primary worry would no longer be fleet modernization, but how to remain militarily effective.

Equally troubling was the president-elect's and Vinson's joint announcement of a "Democratic naval program" shortly after the election, in which Vinson associated himself with a program calling for a reduction in the Navy budget of $100 million, along with an annual ceiling of $30 million in shipbuilding expenditures over the next five years. In place of a treaty navy, the program contemplated a "compact, self-contained navy, powerful and effective enough to meet the country's needs."[11] Stripped of its rhetoric, this meant that the incoming administration was willing to accept second class naval status to balance the federal budget. There was no way the Navy could absorb a $100 million cut and carry out its assigned missions. Furthermore, a $30 million ceiling on ship construction over five years was actually below that appropriated in Hoover's last year in office and totally inadequate to correct the looming obsolescence of the Navy's submarines and destroyers.

Fortunately for the Navy, Vinson soon disassociated himself from this "Democratic naval program" and the President too came to see the hazards of such a radical change in naval policy. Nonetheless, the practical effect of this episode was to discourage serious efforts to enact major shipbuilding legislation in 1933. On the plus side, however, the President signaled his willingness to give indirect support to major shipbuilding legislation. He preferred to work behind the scenes and avoid personal involvement, since he wished to avoid the risk of alienating Democratic and Republican progressives who formed the backbone of his political support. But he knew that willing surrogates in Congress would do his work for him.

While this level of Executive support fell far short of the desires of Vinson and his pro-Navy allies, it was a tremendous improvement over outright opposition. In many cases the administration's tacit approval was decisive in clearing the way for shipbuilding authorizations. The quiet clearance of such legislation by the Bureau of the Budget spoke volumes to pro-Navy legislators, the Navy Department, and knowledgeable observers. Conversely, this indirect approach frustrated efforts to discredit congressional efforts to enact shipbuilding legislation by attacks on the President.

1933--THE N.I.R.A. ALTERNATIVE

Pro-Navy legislators discovered that, even in the case of the Great Depression, every cloud has a silver lining. It did not take them long to see that they had to find a way to make fleet modernization a part of national economic relief and recovery efforts. The Navy has recognized this early on, and explored the possibility of using public works funding to finance the construction and modernization of warships, but had been thwarted by President Hoover. Although the Navy became a major recipient of public works funds, they were primarily funneled through the Bureau of Yards and Docks, to provide employment at politically sensitive shore installations.

By mid-1932, however, the condition of the private shipbuilding industry prompted a reassessment of this policy. Commercial orders were drying up and nearly all of the scarce naval contracts went to public Navy yards. Unless something were done by the federal government to step up naval construction so that business could be given to private shipyards, they would have to lay off large numbers of skilled workers, and a few faced the prospect of going out of business altogether. This posed a significant threat to the Navy's ability to mobilize and sustain operations in wartime.

In the face of this, Hoover relented during the final weeks of his 1932 Presidential campaign. Using the authority provided in section 317 of the Economy Act, he approved the transfer of $1 million in public works funds for the construction of three destroyers.12 In doing so he established a precedent for making such funding available for ship construction and modernization on an ever larger scale.

Armed with this precedent, shipyard lobbyists, union representatives and other special interest groups descended on Washington, D.C. in the heady atmosphere of the FIrst Hundred Days of the Roosevelt Administration. Working closely with like-minded legislators and a sympathetic Navy Department, they were determined that the shipbuilding industry get a "fair share" of any relief and recovery funding. As a result of these combined efforts, the National Industrial Recovery Act (N.I.R.A.) contained a provision which authorized "the construction of naval vessels within the terms and/or limits of the London Naval treaty."13 On June 16, 1933, the day following the enactment of this legislation, President Roosevelt issued Executive Order 6174 providing $238 million for the construction of 32 naval vessels. Combining the N.I.R.A. vessels with those covered by residual authorization under the 1916 Navy Appropriation Act, the Navy announced on July 27 that contracts for 35 vessels had been awarded, with the split between private and public yards being 21 and 14, respectively. In all, total naval construction would double under the N.I.R.A. program, and this represented the greatest stimulus to the shipbuilding industry since World War I.

While the N.I.R.A. program fell short of correcting all of the Navy's material deficiencies, it did provide the essential momentum for the enactment of future shipbuilding legislation. After increasing their capacity, private and public yards would be very sensitive to significant cutbacks in workload. Likewise, their vendors and suppliers would have an interest in seeing that shipbuilding activity remained constant. These were factors that were bound to place a great deal of pressure on the president and Congress to approve further naval construction programs.

1932-1936--THE COLLAPSE
OF THE TREATY FRAMEWORK

The first solid evidence that something was seriously amiss had been the failure of the 1932 session of the Geneva Disarmament Conference to achieve any positive results. Concerned about the lack of progress in those talks, President Hoover proposed a general reduction by one-third in the strength of each nation's land, sea and air forces. But despite some initially favorable reaction, the Conference adjourned a month later without having taken any action on the Hoover proposal. Although it reconvened the following year, it never again commanded the same respect and support. This, along with the inability of the League of Nations and the Kellogg-Briand Pact to deter Japanese aggression in Manchuria, seriously undercut confidence in international remedies to preserve world peace and stability.

Nor did the news get better in the years that followed. In fact, the international situation was deteriorating. In Japan, the war party was gaining the upper hand in its struggle with the more moderate civilian politicians, and on December 24, 1934, the country formally renounced its adherence to the Washington Navy Agreement, effective at the end of 1936. This was followed, in 1935, by the conclusion of an Anglo-German naval agreement, which allowed the Germans to build their fleet up to 35 percent of the size of the Royal Navy.[14] This, in turn, led to the predictable expansion of the French and Italian fleets, making Great Britain's two power standard policy in Europe unattainable with treaty limits.

Despite these developments, the London Naval Conference convened in 1936 as scheduled. But agreement on quantitative limitations proved impossible, which led to a walkout of the Japanese delegation. Seeking to salvage something from the talks, a British draft treaty embodying certain qualitative restrictions was agreed to, but the Japanese refusal to abide by it made it into a dead letter. Thus, the interwar period of experiment in naval limitation came to an end.[15]

The political impact of this was effectively exploited by pro-Navy legislators. It surely made sense now, they argued, to begin a modest naval construction program to strengthen the hand of American negotiators at London, and as a prudent hedge against Japanese threats to American interests in the Western Pacific. It was an argument that was strengthened by Japan's lengthening trail of aggression in China, as well as by its vigorous naval rearmament efforts.

Ironically, then, the rubble of the treaty framework served as the bedrock for United States naval rearmament in the mid and late 1930s.

1934--THE VINSON-TRAMMEL ACT;
THE MECHANISM IN PLACE

Although 1933 was given over to efforts to promote fleet modernization through relief and recovery channels, proponents of shipbuilding legislation had not been idle. Both Senator Park Trammell, new chairman of the senate Naval Affairs Committee, and Representative Fred Britten introduced legislation providing blanket authorization to build the Navy to treaty limits. Carl Vinson had been dissuaded from introducing legislation of his own, but he had threatened to do so if ship construction was not contained in the N.I.R.A. package. Moreover, he made a public commitment to offer major shipbuilding authorization legislation in 1934.

Thus, it was a certainty that a multiyear, comprehensive ship construction authorization would be offered during the 2nd Session of the 74th Congress. The only question was who would get the credit for this legislation. The Trammell and Britten bills had been sent to the Navy Department for comment. The Department further refined them and was seeking clearance from the Bureau of the Budget for a positive endorsement of the recommended changes. The sticking point was that Lewis Douglas, the tight-fisted director of the Bureau of the Budget, was not disposed to put the administration's imprimatur on a piece of legislation that would end up costing about a billion dollars. Blocked by Douglas's opposition, the Navy and its legislative allies put pressure on President Roosevelt to override the Bureau of the Budget. Characteristically, he demurred, and the Navy resorted to an "end run" by providing Carl Vinson the draft legislation for him to introduce. The choice of Vinson was really quite simple. As chairman of the House Naval Affairs Committee, he was better able to secure enactment of such legislation than Representative Britten, or Senator Trammell.

Vinson's bill represented an improvement over the one he had offered in 1932 both in terms of political realism and of public relations. Like its predecessors, H.R. 6604 was primarily a replacement bill addressing the problem of bloc obsolescence of destroyers and submarines. Accordingly, it authorized replacement tonnage in those categories of 99,200 and 35,530, respectively, along with 15,000 for a carrier to replace the aging Langley. Moreover, it contained an unobtrusive proviso that, in effect, was an open ended authorization to replace any other vessels--battleships in particular--that might become obsolete during the life of the program.16 To make the bill politically palatable, the last section contained the obligatory escape clause allowing the President to modify the program in the event that the 1936 London Naval Limitation Conference should result in additional restrictions.

The main difference between H.R. 6604 and the earlier measures was the conspicuous absence of any mention of specific annual increments or mandated deadlines for the completion of the program to insure executive compliance. After witnessing President Roosevelt's expeditious implementation of the N.I.R.A. naval provisions, Vinson apparently had few qualms about reverting to a blanket authorization granting the President broad discretion over the execution of the replacement program contained in the bill.

Vinson's introduction of the Navy proposal placed the Bureau of the Budget in a difficult position. Instead of a Department proposal awaiting internal clearance, Director Douglas now confronted a shipbuilding authorization sponsored by a powerful chairman whose request for an administration position could not be easily put off. After formally referring H.R. 6604 to the Navy Department for comment on January 10, Vinson pressed for an early endorsement.

Douglas held out for a week before giving his grudging and indirect clearance on January 17. In order to salve Douglas's conscience, an ingenious rationale was devised to reconcile the passage of a major naval authorization with its budgetary implications. The administration's position would be that it did not object to the enactment of an authorization bill, but that it would make no commitment on either requesting funds for its implementation or fulfilling any shipbuilding schedule.

No amount of tortured logic, however, could obviate the pressing need for the authorization and appropriation of additional vessels for the 1935 building program. The "front end loading" of the combined 1934 and N.I.R.A. programs saw to that. As matters stood in January 1934, 54 vessels were under contract or laid down and private and public yards were handling the largest number of new orders since World War I. Subcontractors and vendors all across the nation benefited from this activity. The rub was that without new authorization legislation, the 1935 program would shrink to four ships as no residual authorization remained.[17] Obviously, the prospect of dropping from 37 to 4 ships was militarily, politically, and economically intolerable.

Aided by tacit administration support and testimony from the Navy Department, Vinson was able to guide H.R. 6604 through committee and House consideration in a mere 13 days! During brief floor debate on January 30, a number of amendments were adopted, including one to extend the authorization to cover additional aircraft requirements.

Efforts by Senator Trammell and his colleagues to expedite consideration of a companion bill were not as successful. For nearly a month, Senate anti-Navy forces were able to prevent floor debate through a number of dilatory tactics. Finally, Senator Joseph T. Robinson, Senate Majority Leader, secured a time limitation agreement and, after two days of florid debate, the measure was passed 65 to 18.

After the rejection of the initial conference report on March 21 on a point of order in the House of Representatives, a second conference report was agreed to on March 22. Despite being deluged with appeals to veto the Vinson-Trammell Act, President Roosevelt signed it into law on March 27. In an effort to appease opponents of the bill, he issued a brief statement explaining the difference between authorization and appropriation. His willingness to approve this legislation it suggested, should not be confused with actual funding of the naval construction authorized, and appropriations would not necessarily follow. But it is difficult to see how he expected to allay the fears of opponents in this fashion, since it was an open secret that the navy had already submitted a request for supplemental appropriations to fund the first year's increment of 20 ships.[18] Throughout the remainder of the decade, however, this was to be President Roosevelt's mode of operation--to avoid identification with ship construction authorizations, but to submit appropriations requests to implement them.

"THE GENESIS OF THE MODERN U.S. NAVY"

"It is considered desirable to recognize that the Vinson-Trammell Act was, in effect, the genesis of the modern U.S. Navy . . .," wrote one naval historian.[19] Although this assessment may be exaggerated, it would be difficult to overemphasize the contribution of the Vinson-Trammell Act in enhancing the readiness and material condition of the U.S. fleet at the time of Pearl Harbor. It eventually provided authorization for the construction of 8 battleships, 1 aircraft carrier, 4 light cruisers, 5 destroyer leaders, 46 destroyers, and 28 submarines--the core of the fleet's modern combatants in commission at the outbreak of hostilities. Succeeding authorizations in 1938 and 1940 dwarfed the size of the 1934 program, but their full effect was not felt until 1943 when the tide had already turned in favor of the United States Navy.[20]

Equally important, the Vinson-Trammell Act provided continuity between the N.I.R.A. program for 1934 and the increase in naval construction just prior to World War II. While additional building would probably have been authorized by Congress in the intervening years without the Vinson-Trammell Act, it is unlikely that the resulting program would have been as consistent or balanced. By shielding the naval construction program from incremental, short-term authorization amid the domestic and international turbulence of the mid and late 1930s, the Vinson-Trammell Act was able to ensure the maintenance of a comprehensive, consistent approach that facilitated sensible planning, budgeting and production. Furthermore, it permitted the Navy to adhere to a procurement strategy that avoided the bloc obsolescence characteristic of crash programs such as those undertaken in World War One.

Another major benefit was the ability to gradually increase and improve the production base of naval construction which had suffered badly during the 1920s. The Act accomplished the resuscitation of the industry by providing a steady workload over several years. This also allowed a limited number of design personnel to refine their plans and to incorporate new technology. Consequently, by the time emergency shipbuilding programs became necessary, basic designs could be frozen, so that production was simplified and construction lead time minimized. What was more, the experience of the war would demonstrate that these designs produced warships that acquitted themselves well in combat.

THE TRANSCENDENT LEGACY

When all is said and done however, the Vinson-Trammell Act registered its greatest and most enduring impact on the legislative process. It established a new harmony providing a comprehensive, consistent approach to naval construction and fleet modernization. Blanket authorization became standard practice and remained the pre-eminent legislative vehicle for military procurement for the next quarter century.

There thus was no need for the Naval Affairs Committees to contend with either the Congressional or public controversies normally associated with various efforts to initiate shipbuilding programs. Now it was simply left to the Appropriations committees to provide the funding necessary to carry out the administration's shipbuilding request contained with the annual budget submission. Once again, the ship construction increments were an integral part of the annual appropriations bills and enjoyed the relative security afforded by that status. Although the Appropriations committees could be expected to make some minor adjustments, major policy shifts were unlikely.

Thereafter, authorization legislation would only be required to close gaps or to increase tonnage levels in response to building programs by likely adversaries. It could thus concentrate on the enactment of an auxiliary authorization passed in 1937 and three successor Vinson acts of 1938 and 1940. Not that passage of these authorizations was all that easy, but the existence of a blanket authorization based on treaty limits provided the leverage for success in each of these struggles.

There was, however, a significant institutional cost associated with this new equilibrium, as the Naval Affairs Committees effectively legislated themselves out of the annual review of naval construction requests. Rarely have committees voluntarily elected to curtail their jurisdiction in this fashion, which raises the question of why the members were willing to make such a change. The reasons, it appears were the result of a combination of factors--the recognition that naval requirements demanded decisive action, an appreciation of the basic conservatism of the appropriations process, and Carl Vinson's realization that this new procedural framework could be used to maintain his personal dominance over the legislative efforts to implement the Vinson-Trammell Act.

Although this certainly was not a primary motive in his advocacy of a blanket authorization, there is good reason to believe that Carl Vinson actually welcomed the diminished role of the Naval Affairs Committees in the annual congressional review of naval construction requests. Never enthusiastic about widespread member involvement--including those on his own committee--in dealing with major naval policy questions, he apparently believed that such participation only resulted in greater parochialism, unnecessary delay, and, ultimately, poor legislation. Instead he preferred informal deliberations by a handful of responsible and knowledgeable senior members who were more inclined to make their decisions on the basis of fact and need. This kind of bargaining was an ideal medium for Carl Vinson , and one he could be expected to dominate through the force of his personality, expertise and energy.

Possessing a strong proprietary interest in the implementation of the Vinson-Trammell Act, Vinson became intimately involved in the decision-making process within the executive branch in determining the composition of the annual program and the level of funding requested. Once the President's budget was submitted to Congress, Vinson sought to persuade the Naval Subcommittee of the House Appropriations Committee to support the naval construction request. At times his interference was so obvious that on at least one occasion an exasperated subcommittee chairman was moved to forbid members to discuss the Navy appropriation with the wily Georgian.[21] But he was effective. When confronted by a navy request supported by Vinson, the House Appropriations Committee generally found acquiescence to be the better part of valor.

On the Senate side, Vinson's tactics were even more successful and resulted in the conclusion of an informal alliance between his committee and the Naval Subcommittee of the Senate Appropriations Committee. Chaired by Senator James F. Byrnes, a strong Navy backer in his own right, the Naval Subcommittee acted as a sympathetic court of appeals on cuts made by the House Appropriations Committee. With regard to the implementation of the Vinson-Trammell Act, Senator Byrnes left no doubt about his committee's position:

> Congress . . . in the Trammell-Vinson Act provided for the construction of certain vessels . . .
>
> The Appropriations Committee has no duty other than to comply with the act of Congress and to provide the funds to enable the Navy Department to carry out the policy which has already been determined by Congress . . . .[22]

Skillfully alternating between the application of his formal powers and prerogatives on behalf of the House Naval Affairs Committee and reliance upon personal persuasion, Carl Vinson came to dominate Congress's handling of Naval matters to a degree that has never been rivaled. Eliot Janeway was hardly exaggerating when he described Vinson's predominance shortly after World War II:

> For some years Vinson and his Capitol colleagues have lived together under a non-aggression pact. They knew that he doesn't care who makes the nation's laws, so long as he can build its Navy, and they have given him a blank check to operate as a one-man Committee of the Whole on naval matters. In return, Congress is assured from long experience, that the Vinson Navy measures which it votes for will never boomerang. The pact has been justified. In no other field does Congress wield more power, or do individual members suffer less embarrassment.[23]

Through his efforts to enact a blanket shipbuilding authorization, and the deft management of Naval appropriations in the years that followed, Carl Vinson was largely responsible for the American Navy's renaissance in the later 1930s. The measure of his success becomes even more apparent when it is remembered that in the short span of three years, he transformed Congress from being an intractable part of the problem to being a major contributor to the solution of the Navy's severe material deficiencies. And even more remarkable is the fact that Carl Vinson was able to preserve that happy relationship for over a quarter of a century.

NOTES

[1] Letter to Mr. Earl C. Smith, April 14, 1931, Henry T. Rainey papers, Box 3, Manuscript Division of the Library of Congress (Hereafter cited as MDLC).

[2] Albion, Robert Greenhalgh, "Makers of Naval Policy, 1798-1947" (Washington, D.C.: Office of Naval History, 1950), 304.

[3] The Washington Treaty for the Limitation of Armament, 1922, Chapter I, Articles II, IV, VII and XIX. A text of the treaty is found in Conference on the Limitation of Armament, Washington, November 12, 1921-February 6, 1922 (Washington, D.C.: Government Printing Office, 1922), 1573-1604.

[4] David Carlton, "Great Britain and the Coolidge Naval Disarmament Conference of 1927, "Political Science Quarterly, LXXII (December, 1968), 596.

[5] The London Naval Treaty of 1930, Part I, Articles 1 and 2. A text of this treaty is found in Proceedings of the London Naval Conference of 1930 and Supplementary Documents (Washington, D.C.: Government Printing Office, 1981), 203-220.

[6] Speech by Rear Admiral W. A. Moffett, Chief of the Bureau of Aeronautics, delivered over W.O.R., New York and at the Annual Dinner of the Naval Academy Graduates Association of New York, Commodore Hotel, New York City, on February 17, 1933, 1, located in the Dudley W. Knox Papers, 1933 File, MDLC.

[7] The Army Navy Journal, LXX (October 1, 1932), 1.

[8] Annual Report of the Secretary of the Navy for the Fiscal Year 1933 (Washington, D.C. Government Printing Office, 1933), 35.

[9] Michael A. West, "Laying the Legislative Foundation: The House Naval Affairs Committee and the Construction of the Treaty Navy, 1926-1934" (unpublished dissertation, The Ohio State University, 1980), 246-151 (Hereafter cited as West).

[10] Army Navy Journal, October 15, 1932, 1. Roosevelt did not return a questionnaire sent to him about his views on naval matters by the editors of the journal.

[11] New York Times, November 30, 1932, 1, 12.

[12] Robert E. Levine, "The politics of American Naval Rearmament, 1930-1938" (unpublished dissertation, Harvard University, 1972), 55-59.

[13] U.S. House of Representatives, Committee on Naval Affairs, Bill Jackets, H.R. 5755, 73rd Congress, 1933-1935, Record Group 233, National Archives.

[14] Ernest Andrade, Jr., "United States Naval Policy in the Disarmament Era, 1921-1937" (unpublished dissertation, Michigan State University, 1966), 375-378.

[15] Ibid., 395-397.

[16] While this open ended authorization would apply to all categories of combatants, its primary purpose was to permit replacement of capital ships. The London Treaty prohibited the laying down of any new dreadnoughts, but when it expired in 1937 many American battleships would be overage. Conscious of the controversy battleship generated and uncertain whether the existing building holiday would be extended, Navy proponents were understandably anxious to avoid making their construction a prominent feature of the bill.

[17] West, 373. One additional heavy cruiser was authorized under the 1929 "Fifteen Cruiser Act", but could not be laid down in 1935 because of the terms of the Reed-Matsudaira Agreement associated with the London Treaty.

[18] New York Herald, March 28, 1934, 1.

[19] Charles F. Elliott, "The Genesis of the Modern U.S. Navy, "U.S. Naval Institute Proceedings, XCII, March, 1966, 62.

[20] Calvin W. Enders, "The Vinson Navy" (unpublished dissertation, Michigan State University, 1970), 145-158.

[21] Interviews with Hon. F. Edward Hebert, February 17, 1974.

[22] Congressional Record, March 22, 1937, 2540.

[23] Eliot Janeway, "The Man Who Owns the Navy", Saturday Evening Post, December 15, 1945.

THE SECOND WORLD WAR - A PROBLEM IN RESEARCH

by HANS ADOLF JACOBSEN

Although forty years have passed since the end of the Second World War, numerous events in current politics remind us how strongly the present is still affected by those fateful decisions of 1939-1945, and how deeply the results of this global conflict have shaped our times. For instance: The division of Germany, Europe and Korea; the shift in the world's balance of power, the formation of several, partly antagonistic power blocs; the arms race, and the growing political importance of the Third World. In view of this it is not surprising that the question arises as to how this could have happened. What at the time seemed inextricable, unintelligible or even inconceivable can now be seen more clearly thanks to the efforts of the historians who have analyzed the motives, the causes and the course of this conflict, although details, of course, remain that need to be clarified.

Today the history of the Second World War--its most important outlines and dimensions--can be written more objectively than was possible shortly after the war ended. Indeed, the flood of publications--of surveys, memoirs, diaries, monographs, documentations and essays--has become immense in volume.

This situation makes it almost impossible for the individual historian to keep up with all the newly published accounts, let alone to analyze them. If he does not want to lose sight of the important aspects, he must concentrate on the essential, or lose track of the decisive lines of development.

If one would compile a list of publications on the history of the Second World War published to date (1985) by historians, one would notice that in regard to WW II the essential connections have been made; many points of controversy have been settled; a variety of aspects of the war have been analyzed in detail and the relevant strategic plans have been evaluated to the same degree as have the political-economic decision of all the parties involved in the war. One would, however, also find that certain weaknesses and gaps still exist (with the level of degree depending on the individual country). This applies especially to the comprehensive view of the war and the social conditions under which the people of the war-torn countries were forced to live and suffer.[1]

Taking into consideration the war's cause, its course and consequences, it is still difficult to classify the Second World War on the world-historic scale, that is, to understand the war as a phenomenon of Late-Imperialism; the Age of Revolutions; National Liberation Movements; World Wars or as an expression of Totalitarian Ideologies. To achieve this, one needs to make a clear distinction between the caesura of 1939-1945 and the period of 1914-1918, their respective categories of thought, social situations and goals as well as the treatment of the principle of unity and order in Europe, Asia and the rest of the world and the resulting political and economic problems.

MODES OF INTERPRETATION

If one analyzes the studies done to date by international historians on the History of the Second World War, one finds that one can distinguish between five distinct Modes of Interpretation. 1. The Military Mode; 2. The National-State Mode; 3. The Regional Mode; 4. The World-Historic Mode; and 5. The Ideologic Mode.

Military Mode

Without doubt, the Military Mode of Interpretation predominates among these categories. It is a form of evaluation and representation which understands war almost exclusively as a military confrontation--a phenomenon of fire and action achieved by means of an increased co-operation of all branches of the military--a confrontation between groups, nations, continents and world powers; a war which with the use of all available means, including the psychological, has its objective in the destruction of the enemy's military forces, often without taking into account any possible future political consequences. This mode conveys essential findings regarding the war's fundamental outlines, its character and changes as well as the extent of the war's expansion and its structure. The starting point is a description of the warring parties' state of defense readiness, the potential of the war economy, the reserves in manpower and material--their extent, possible increase and maximum output, most of the interest will be focused on the preparation, execution and final phase of the operations. This is followed by an examination of the function and effectiveness of the individual forces, for instance, of the Infantry, the Artillery, the Tank Forces, the Airborne Troops, the Airforce, the Naval Forces (submarines and surface vessels), the Signal Corps, the Systems of Transport, and the evolving techniques in the different phases of the fighting at the individual theaters of the war. Also critically analyzed are organization, function, strength, weaknesses and friction of the leadership structure (within the bounds of totalitarian, authoritarian and democratic governments) as well as the co-operation and the tensions between allies (coalition warfare), and how all this affected the fighting.

When the most essential details are settled, fundamental questions are answered, for instance: which high points and crises on land, in the air and at sea changed the war in a decisive way and in whose favor; thus, for instance, Dunkirk (1940), the Battle of Britain (1940/41), Rommel's campaign in Africa (1941/42), the German surprise attack on Russia (1941), Pearl Harbor (1941), the battles of Moscow (1941/42), Midway (1942), El Alamein (1942), Stalingrad (1942/43), Kursk (1943), Tunisia and Morocco (1942/43), the battles at sea in 1943 and in Leyte Gulf (1944), etc. What importance can be given to defensive and offensive strategy? What can be said about the battle of the home front, about the advantages of a one-front war, the difficulties of a war on several fronts and the insoluble problems of a war on all fronts? (In 1943 Germany tried to defend a landfront of some nine thousand miles, known as "Fortress Europe".) The interdependence of all branches of the service and the differences between continental, maritime and world-wide strategies are explored by the respective authors according to their intellectual ability. In order to summarize and examine all factors which caused either a military success or a defeat on the battlefields, numerous studies have explored the effect on the fighting made by the development and influence of psychological warfare, by technology, by the mobilization of industry and manpower, the ambushes "from behind" made by partisans or by commando operations.

As useful as this mode of interpretation might be to explain, for instance, a modern war, to give insight into war as a phenomenon of power politics, or to explain the ever-fluctuating course of military conflicts, the precarious one-sidedness of the premise involved must always be kept in mind. The greatest weakness can be found in the fact that military events are almost completely isolated from general politics. This severely limits the input needed to evaluate the war and often results in incorrect and invalid conclusions about "lost victories". The military struggle is often separated from its inherent political impulses to such an extent that it lacks the necessary connection that exists between politics and war. As a result the decisive question about the meaning of the war cannot be answered.[2]

National-State

In contrast the mode of interpretation using the national-state as its criterion explains the war and its manifestations by primarily using a nation's characteristics from its historic past and present. Utilizing the findings of the military mode (one mode builds on another), the beginning, the course and the conclusion of the war are more strongly brought into connection with a country's national, social and economic fate.

The advantages of this method of interpretation and its persuasive powers derive mainly from the fact that it illustrates the wide field of political goalsetting--forcing the enemy to comply with one's own political goals--showing the overall planning and military necessity--or as Clausewitz once formulated it: "the relationship between political purpose, given resources and military goals is significant because it is decisive." It explains how extensively the causes, motives, dispositions, goals and devices of war were determined and even formed by the warring nations' national and social-political concepts of order, and brings into focus the part the so-called "portrayals of the enemy" (syndrome of fear) played in it. This mode of interpretation recognizes the functional connections between domestic and foreign affairs, the nation's combined effort--at home and at the front--and the specific interrelation (for instance, between the munitions worker and the soldier), to accomplish the task set forth by politics. The significance of the accomplishments made during the war can be illustrated in the connection between social forces and the preservation of the political order. Obviously only with this mode can in principle the ethical side of the war, the question regarding the meaning of events, be answered correctly.[3]

Although legitimate, this mode of interpretation still signifies a certain limitation in scope, because the main interest is focused on partial findings and local manifestations. Consequently, the significance of factors other than those found on the national-state level, which also influenced events cannot sufficiently be considered. It especially complicates the very necessary comparison with the various other principles of order, the power of ideas and other nations' conceptions and rights. Moreover the importance of the national fate becomes overvalued. The fact that the national-state is only part of a larger world community is forgotten.

The Regional Approach

The focus of the regional approach is the political, social and cultural destiny of a region formed by geography, culture and history (for instance, Europe or Eastern Asia) and mutually competitive systems of order (bilateral or multilateral) either totalitarian, authoritarian or democratic in nature. This approach gives form to that which remains effective beyond the limits imposed by the national state. It reveals that which unites and that which separates, the constructive as well as the destructive; in it one recognizes both the varieties and the common aspects of civilization. The narrow-minded self-interests of individual nations and power groups, and the desire of nations to establish supra-national unions predicated on decisions freely taken is explained in this mode. Only this mode can show the decisive characteristics of the total revolutionary war, the civil war of the 20th century, in all its severity. It reveals that in this war it was less important to conquer provinces, strategic positions, religious symbols (such as Constantinople) or to change existing relationships of power, than it was to destroy value structures which had been declared obsolete and antagonistic in order to establish new systems of absolute power. Consequently more and more "resisters" or "Quislings" in setting themselves against their national environment or political order chose freedom, socialism or totalitarianism. And finally this mode of interpretation explains--take Europe as an example--how regional forces alone no longer sufficed to enforce decisions of world-political importance; to keep the balance of power-politics, or, as in Southeast Asia, to defend colonial holdings against the assault of enemy forces. The First World War had already shown that settling the conflict in favor of one power bloc required the intervention of a non-European super power. The war in Asia was also decided by the United States. Seen in this context, the most important turning point of the Second World War occurred in 1941, when the European conflict exploded into a world-wide war.[4]

The World Historic Approach

This leads us to the fourth mode of interpretation, the world historic approach. Without doubt, this approach makes the highest demands on both the scholar and the layman, since in this approach non-European history must equally be included to gain a valid overview of the war.

Literature and an abundance of material are perhaps responsible for the tendency to examine the development of certain regions with global events as a backdrop, rather than to write a world history of the war in which all parts are suitably proportioned. Worldwide interconnections of politics, economics and warfare, or to put it differently, international communications and interdependence, have become a reality. This trend has continued since 1941 and has decisively influenced the course of history to his date. Not only Germany or Korea, but the world was divided at the Elbe and at the 38th latitude.[5] It was characteristic of the actions of the warring powers that their thinking always focused on categories of global proportions, as for instance, in the design of the Axis powers for the partition of the world in 1940 and none less than Winston Churchill wrote about his impression in 1941 that he realized then that Hitler's and Mussolini's fate was sealed, and that Japan would be ground to powder between two millstones. "Nothing was left to do, but use our overwhelming might. No alliance in the world could withstand our united force."[6] The many political and military plans, operations, economic supply shipments (lend-lease) and most of all the deployment and the maintenance of the armed forces revealed how global American strategy really was. By the end of 1943 the United States had put into action 8,800 airplanes and 515 warships of all types in Europe, and 7,800 planes and 713 warships in East-Asia. A year later the deployment of the U.S. armed forces was as follows: 50% of the troops deployed outside the United States fought (or stood) on the European Continent; 17% in the Mediterranean; 26% in the Pacific, the rest (7%) in Africa, in the Middle-East, in China, Burma, India, Alaska and in the Caribbean Sea. At the same time, Great Britain deployed 50% of her forces overseas and 50% in Europe. Britain fought in the Atlantic, the Mediterranean, and from the Middle-East to India and Burma in order to protect her interests.[7]

The Ideological Approach

The fifth mode of interpretation, the ideological approach, is used by the Soviet Bloc. The war is judged sometimes using the class position as a premise by examining the benefits gained for the triumph of the most progressive class--Communism. Sometimes the premise is based on good conduct towards the USSR. Although the Marxist Science of History is "inseparably" connected with the "political struggle" of the working class, the party leadership always decides what the latest pre-determined truth really should be. Consequently it is still claimed that World War II started in 1939 because the growing internal conflict of Capitalism (according to its inherent law), had become more severe; that a struggle had started between the "Fascist Powers" (Japan, Italy and Germany)--Fascism being the most extreme and exploitative form of Imperialism--and other competing capitalist countries (Britain, France and the United States) for world dominance and new export markets; that the "reactionary forces" of the Western Powers had supported German rearmament probably in the hope of "appeasing" Hitler's desire for expansion by diverting him toward the east with the intent to weaken the troublesome rival and in the end dictate an "imperialistic peace".[8]

In contrast, the "peace-loving" Soviet Union, always true to her principles, had followed a policy of collective security and strategic protection of her western borders until war broke out (1941). She had done all she could to prevent a war. According to the views of Soviet historians, Great Britain and the United States sabotaged the creation of a "Second Front" in order to let the Soviet Union bleed to death. Both powers had wanted to save their strength because they would need it in the final phase of the war to carry out their designs of power politics in Europe. When, however, in 1943, with the military victories of the Red Army, the possibility arose that the Soviet Union would defeat Germany and march into Central Europe earlier than her allies, they decided to start the long promised but always postponed French landing operation.[9] Also the "reactionary forces" of these two countries had since 1941 conducted secret negotiations with Germany behind the back of the USSR. From the time of Rudolf Hess' flight to England (in May 1941) until the assassination attempt on Hitler's life on July 20, 1944, most of their measures had been designed to create a military bloc against the Soviet Union for the purpose of dominating her in the future.

The above is only a small selection of the most characteristic Soviet interpretations of the Second World War. More significant still is the Doctrine of the Superiority and Invincibility of Soviet Communism in the past and in the future, which is an example of the ideologic mode of interpretation. This doctrine has recently been re-affirmed in a resolution issued by the Central Committee of the Soviet Communist Party at the occasion of the 40th anniversary of the "Triumph of the Soviet People in the Great Patriotic War." It was done with great fanfare, propagandistic pathos and unmitigated self-assurance. The masters and dogmaticians of the Kremlin still proclaim that this victory--which had been "organized and achieved by the Communist Party"--was the "irrefutable" evidence for the "superiority of Socialism and its immense possibility--economic, social-political and intellectual--for the unity of party and people and the brotherhood of man among the nations of the Soviet Union."[10]

In holding with the above theme, it stands to reason that Soviet military science and strategy are superior as well. They also serve as a guarantee for the future defense of peace. Stridently the message proclaims: The victory of the Soviet Union has shown that it will never be possible to "defeat Socialism", because it is the embodiment of "historic progress".

Periodization

A weak spot in many accounts is still the periodization of the Second World War. Most authors focus predominantly on the military course of events. They subdivide the war into phases of "victorious Blitz campaigns" undertaken by the German Wehrmacht and her Allies from 1939 to 1942; the turning points of the war--the events of 1942 and 1943 in the Pacific, in Northern Africa, Russia and at Sea; and finally the German and Japanese defeats on many fronts and their surrender in 1945.[11]

Nor has there been a lack of attempts to present the events of the war aside by side in a simultaneous presentation of military operations and political and economic decisions (the nation-state approach). Detailed studies focused on special issues, such as for instance the persecution of the Jews, the politics of genocide, the resistance movements, the economy, armaments and war objectives.

A. Hillgruber accomplished the most meaningful classification of events in his successful survey of the major decisions of the war, by using world-political turning points and plans of reorganization as focal points.[12] The history of the Second World War done by the Militärgeschichtliche Forschungamt in Freiburg contains new conceptual approaches. Four volumes have so far been published. (1985). They make a partly successful attempt to relate military and economic events and policies of armaments to political objectives and in turn derive from this answers to the questions of military success and defeat.[13]

The historiography of the Soviet Union and the German Democratic Republic does not adopt such periodization. The Historians of these countries differentiate first of all between "just" and "unjust" phases of the war, based on whether or not the "socialist achievements" or interests of the Soviet Union were jeopardized. Therefore the war France and Britain fought in 1939 was not a "just" but an "imperialistic war of conquest". The transformation to a "just" war occurred with the peoples' growing resistance to German occupation, that is, with the beginning of the anti-fascist struggle for liberation. Communists played an especially valiant part in this first period of the war. The war turned into a "truly just" struggle when the Soviet Union entered in 1941 (This is seen as the second period of WW II lasting until 1942). Even for the "capitalist members of the anti-Hitler coalition" the war became "just and progressive", because they helped save the first socialist country in the world and with it safeguarded the future peace. This third period, to the end of 1943, includes the beginning of the expulsion of the "Hitler Wehrmacht" from Russian territory, the "main battle front" of the Second World War, and the increase of anti-fascist resistance movements. Concurrent with it, Allied counter-attacks started in the Far-East and in Northern Africa the initiative finally belonged to the Anglo-Americans.[14]

The Fourth period, to May 1945, includes the "liberation" of the nations of Eastern and South-Eastern Europe and the end of the war in Europe, while the Fifth period goes to the capitulation of Japan in September 1945. Admittedly the Allied invasion of France of June 1944 helped to hasten the German defeat. The decisive contribution to the destruction of "Fascism", however, was accomplished by Soviet troops.

WAR AIMS

In order to understand the course, the turning points and the final phase of the war and to explain and evaluate this merciless process of world history reasonably well, one must consider the fighting armies and guerrillas, the airplanes and warships, the multitude of weapons, the ever developing technology, the total mobilization of the economy, the unleashed passions. In short, one must consider the total military potential and understand it as an instrument of politics used to achieve a specific goal of power-politics and one must at the same time understand the total war and all its numerous elements as one unit. In this approach, it is not very useful to subdivide the period from 1939 to 1945 into battles and campaigns--victorious and lost--or to trace the changing fortunes of battles on different theaters of the war or to use isolated detail studies as a criterion for evaluation. It is more advantageous to start with an investigation of the de facto war aims of the great powers, the smaller nations, and the supra-national co-operation of groups (as for instance, the European resistance organizations and the movements for independence and liberation in Asia) and with it trace the unalterable interconnections between politics and warfare, their dimensions and imponderabilities.[15]

This raises several questions of varying importance: For instance, to what extent had the proclaimed war aims been discussed and agreed on by the parties involved? How did the problem of conflicting aims, which was evident to all parties involved, affect politics and strategy?

Aside from the propagandistic goals, several of the intended objectives must certainly have changed--been reduced, extended, expanded or reinstated--over the years, due to updated situation estimations, as for instance in 1941. Several objectives might not have been realized partly because of ineptness and lack of co-operation, or were successful as a result of compromises and compensations.[16]

In his fundamental studies of the Second World War, Hillgruber points out that Hitler followed a plan of several steps or phases (Stufenplan) in his quest for a position of world supremacy. This is still a point of controversy. Seen from the perspective of 1945, however, much favors this thesis, especially since the leadership of the National Socialist Party had programmatically chosen their final objectives back in the 1920s.[17]

Tensions, especially among the anti-Hitler coalition, but also the situation at the front, forced the leadership to postpone long range objectives. In the meantime more attention would be given to the cohesion of the alliance by accommodating its partners, and increasing the demands at a later, more propitious, time.[18] Quite evident was the tendency of the Anglo-Americans to postpone decisions of importance and consequence until the end of the war in the hope of reaching an agreement with the Soviet Union more quickly and easily then. Certain objectives might often have been prompted as a reaction to enemy strategy, while the numerous enemies necessitated an establishment of priorities which centered on "Germany first."[19] The military victory was, of course, the focus of the war aims and necessary to bring the enemy to the conference table and to force him to accept the victor's political decisions. In addition it also prevented the intervention of other powers.

After 1942/43 the National Socialist leadership continued the war for its own sake. According to Hitler's opinion, which he voiced in his inner circle, the primary antagonists could now no longer destroy each other. How National Socialist Germany could force the United States to her knees was from the very beginning of the conflict a mystery with seven seals. Radically and without alternatives for his enemies Hitler declared that: "Germany will be a world power or cease to exist."[20] Hopes for a split in the enemy alliance and thus for ending the war with more tolerable consequences proved to be an expression of the grotesque wishful thinking which possessed the "elites" of National Socialism. It showed once more that they were unable to evaluate their own surroundings and the world realistically, and thus to draw the political consequences.[21]

When these or similar questions are settled to any degree, it is important to add to the historical outline the military measures of all branches of the armed forces, all efforts exerted by technology, economy, arms industry, as well as all psychological data to recognize their importance as a part of the whole. And finally, to achieve a true history of the Second World War and not one that is based on many accounts which treat the conflict from the view of biased national-state developments and special interests, one must consider the difficult task of understanding the confrontation of nations from regional and world political perspectives and principles. The historian should try to give fair treatment to the truth and the demand for justice. He should also determine "how it actually was," and consider the human aspect, showing "the honor of men, their entanglement with guilt and fate, name that which is evil and dark and keep not silent that which is better."22

International historians have in the meantime, quite justifiably, explained the war's global topics. They traced, first of all, the political considerations, measures and methods of those major powers and their allies which in the 1930s challenged Asia and Europe in a breathtaking attempt of colonial conquest: Japan, Italy and Germany, the nations which had come too late, the so-called paupers, who now wanted to change the political status quo in their favor. Their respective actions remained, however, separated ones, mostly without mutual contact, although the success of one (and the failure of the League of Nations to put the aggressor in its place) might have encouraged the other in his decision to attack. What attempts there were to change a partner's decisions and have him participate in mutual strategic operations or in operations favoring the other partner often failed. It is therefore quite incorrect to claim that these three partners engaged in an organized, goal-oriented conspiracy against peace. They were allies, and although their power structures showed certain similarities, they nevertheless differed fundamentally in their structural elements. This is evidenced, among other things, in the barbarian policy of extermination pursued by the National Socialists in the occupied countries of Europe and the draconian yet dissimilar methods Japan applied in Asia. It can also be seen in the different attitude displayed by Berlin and Tokyo towards the rest of the major powers.23

Different social groups supported the policy of expansion in the respective countries. In Europe the restless and competing dictators who constantly inspired each other and their leadership elites made war in opposition to many military men. The opposite occurred in Japan where the militant army generals succeeded in their wishes against the Navy and the Foreign Office.

WAR GUILT

Regarding the question of war guilt 1939-1941, which is, of course, much less controversial than the one of 1914, historians have arrived at the following findings: the Second World War did not solely start because of a few power-mad, ambitious men and their supporting elites. None of the nations actively engaged in the conflict can claim to be completely free of some responsibility for this catastrophe. Fascist and National Socialist policy was aided--indirectly and mostly involuntarily--even by their enemies. The aggressors' war policy can, however, not be compared with this mostly "passive" culpability, which included among others the appeasement policy of England and France, who intended to keep the peace at any price; the egoism of the countries in South-Eastern Europe; the arrogance of--and the misjudgement of the situation by--the Polish statesmen. Above all the conduct of the Soviet Union in 1939, especially the conclusion of the Non-Aggression Pact, made it easier for Germany to attack Poland, which doesn't mean that Stalin had given Hitler the "green light" for the attack. The United States did their share as well to bring about the War in the Pacific. Their unyielding economic strategy restricted the space of action of the Japanese leadership more and more each month. Japan can, however, not be exonerated from her responsibility for December 7th, 1941.[24]

The experience of the "Cold War", military actions on non-European continents and the possible effect of modern weapons of destruction might alter the verdict of history that the theory and practice of National-Socialism with its complete disregard for the rules which makes it possible for nations to live together in peace represented an entirely isolated relapse into barbarism. Nothing will, however, alter the fact that the largest part of responsibility for 1939 and its consequences belongs to Hitler and his regime and their unrestrained policy of force and racial hatred.[25]

GRAND STRATEGY OF
JAPAN, ITALY and GERMANY

Japan, Italy and Germany, imbued with a "historic call of destiny", without doubt desired a regionally limited redistribution of land areas for raw materials and settlement purposes to protect their authoritarian and totalitarian regimes and militarily secure the conquered areas. In the final analysis, their objectives were an expression of post-imperialistic power-politics. Japanese, Fascist and National Socialist policy had one thing in common: Their expansionary drive received its impetus less from the surplus of capital, people and goods--as was the case during classic imperialistic times--but was a result of some kind of panic reaction to political depression, economic crisis and poverty.[26] In conclusion one must mention that the National-Socialist expression of post-imperialism--putting aside for a moment the expansionary phase 1939-1943, which in contrast to the overseas oriented expansionary phase of the pre-1914 German Reich, was continental in scope and directed mostly towards Russia--contained elements of goal-oriented plans and revolutionary programs symptomatic of the great ideologies of the 20th Century. The plans for a colonial Central-African Empire to obtain raw-materials, which had been proposed by Berlin and especially by the Foreign Ministry in 1940/41, were obviated by the failure of the German Campaign in the East in late-summer of 1941.[27]

The special objectives of National Socialist Germany, their thinking, planning, influence and decision making, have all been explored.[28] The same applies in essence to the other powers. The one exception would be Russia. We have been only sparsely informed about the proceedings in Moscow. Not much has become known about their internal directional struggles. In addition to the decisions made on a secret, propagandistic level to affect war aims, one must differentiate between official planning groups, groups of the opposition and public opinion. Official German war objectives, made public by the media revealed a tactic which Goebbels had mentioned frequently to his inner circle.29 The "New Order" of Europe under German control was only to be sketched in vague outlines, much was to be left open and undecided until the time when German plans could be realized without incurring any harmful psychological consequences. National Socialist propagandists tirelessly inundated the German people with the message that the war had been "forced" on Germany by the "Plutocrats and the Jews" and "World-Bolshevism" (1941). Berlin would in the future displace London and Paris as the center of the European civilization. While France was not deemed worthy of having a voice in the future Europe, the position of England remained ambiguous at first. Secret press direction in the summer of 1940 to commentators of the media stressed that Germany did not want to destroy the British Empire, only Britain's position of predominance. The struggle was not directed against the English people but against Churchill and his "clique". For quite some time Hitler considered a compromise peace with England, which would allow him -- something he had already aimed at prior to 1939--a free hand in the East. For several months Hitler had even envisioned a common German-British defense front against the United States. Then, over the years, Britain appeared to him increasingly to be the real "trouble maker of Europe" which had to be swept off the continent to get "at least a bit of quiet for some time". For that reason Hitler continued the struggle against Britain "with brutal energy" even as late as 1945. It was the chimera of a man who had already lost all touch with reality.30

The entrance of the United States into the war prompted the declaration of the Nazi war against "Roosevelt and the Jews behind him" in defense of any interference in European affairs. The Russian situation in 1942/43 forced the National Socialist leadership to re-interpret the "rise of Europe in the struggle against Bolshevism". Consequently, early in 1943, Goebbels informed foreign journalists of the principles concerning the creation of the new Europe, in the hope that this would have a psychological effect on the smaller countries. The slogans now called for voluntarism, and promised the retention of national individuality and a free choice of government for every nation. The slogans also contained the message that severe measures in the occupied countries would only last for the duration of the war. The "program" was designed to give the European countries positive objectives worth fighting for.31

Similar concepts had been developed much earlier by some conservative administrators of the Foreign Ministry, but they could not convince the higher levels of government. The practices of the National Socialist leadership in the occupied countries, however, stood in sharp contrast to these promises, and the real intentions were seldom hidden.32

In view of the heavy burdens on the homefront, large segments of the German population quite evidently hoped for a compromise peace with the British and the Americans in order to fight the common enemy in the East. Leading men of the German opposition to Hitler recorded their peace objectives in essays and notes. Among them was Carl Goerdeler, who in 1943 asked not only for a strong future alliance with Great Britain to protect the continent from Bolshevism, but also envisioned the creation of a confederation of nations which would guarantee peace and justice for all.33 These ideas, plans and alternatives received little response. Hitler and his closest aides, such as Borman or Goebbels, never lost sight of National Socialism's absurd final objectives, which determined politics and warfare and with it all action on the German side.

Compared with Hitler's and his supporters' objectives, Mussolini's objectives were certainly more limited although not less ambitious.34 Based on Fascist ideology and power politics, and directed towards Africa and the Balkans, Italy's expansionism was already apparent in the 1930s when Italy conquered Abyssinia and occupied Albania. These actions were most likely prompted by economic and political considerations as well as by the dictator's desire for prestige.

The gradual approach to National Socialist Germany, which was publicized with the formation of the "Axis" in 1936--more for propaganda reasons than for substance--or by joining the Anti-Comintern Pact in 1937 and the "Pact of Steel" in 1939, indicated that Mussolini oriented himself by his programmatic promises for the future. Of the three feasible foreign policy alternatives--to co-operate with the western powers, to pursue a policy of neutrality and use Italy as fulcrum of the European power balance, or to become an ally of the neighbor to the north--Mussolini chose the latter. This decision was aided not only by certain ideologic similarities (anti-Bolshevism, principle of action) but most likely also by the realization that only an alliance with Germany would give Italy the opportunity to expand her power base without being accused--as in 1915--of betraying an alliance. The Italian predominance in the Mediterranean and the status of the Fascist State in international politics could be strengthened and revalorized only by choosing this course of action. Mussolini's decision to join the war on Hitler's side on June 10, 1940, after the earlier phase of "non-belligeranza" might have been prompted by the thought of preventing unlimited German hegemony in Europe and by the desire to hunt for booty--the German General Staff referred to the Italians contemptuously as "harvest helpers"--and receive some of the spoils of war.35

It was characteristic of the German-Italian war coalition that neither partner informed the other of their war objectives or co-ordinated operational planning in a meaningful way. The Duce, the man of action, saw in the alliance a defense of Europe against Asia, or world-Bolshevism, and participated in the struggle in order to gain glory and status for the Italian nation, an objective which he--like most dictators--soon identified with his own personal reputation. Impressed by the early successes of the German Wehrmacht and in the hope that the war would be brief and victorious, it was his misfortune that he tried to imitate Hitler's successes in "parallel wars". He failed to realize in due time that Fascist Italy lacked the military and economic strength and the support of the General Staff and large parts of the population to successfully enforce this overextended policy. He finally did understand the bitter truth that Italy was only a German appendage, that since 1941 Italy had been unseparably connected with Germany's fate and that even in the event of a mutual victory, Italy would not receive the status worthy of an equal partner, but rather receive the treatment alloted to an "allied province". Yet however presumptuous Mussolini's objectives might have been, they focused less on the racist and destructive aims inherent in a peace of total victory, or <u>Siegfrieden</u>, but opted more for a peace of negotiations and compromise intended to preserve and strengthen the Fascist systems.

ALLIES OF THE "AXIS POWERS"

The allies of the "Axis Powers" pursued diverging objectives. Their leadership elites--some of them democratic (Finland); clerical-authoritarian (Slovakia); authoritarian (Rumania) and conservative (Hungary)--fought against Russia (not Britain and the United States) in the hope of securing positions of future independence for the price of temporary and limited subordination to the hegemonial power. Misled by the prospects of a quick "final victory" by the powerful neighbor, Slovakia believed--without considering how unpopular this was among the people--that participation in the Eastern campaign would help enforce her territorial claims against Hungary. Finland's geographic position between the great powers was different. She had the choice between becoming a battlefield or getting the chance to regain the territory lost to the Soviet Union in 1940. Finland decided to "fight for freedom". In the meantime Antonescu, the Rumanian leader, had declared a "Holy War" in order to re-capture Bessarabia and the Northern Bucovina.36

Without exception these were limited national and territorial objectives. On a psychological level, Rumanian hatred for Russia, or the anti-Soviet attitude wide-spread among the Finns, might have fueled the flames. But with Hitler's increasing military demands, which severely strained these countries' capacities, and with the counter-offensives of the Red Army, which signalled the turn of the tide in Eastern Europe, the critical attitude toward the German ally increased. Soon the men in power searched for ways and means to rid themselves of the burdens incurred by the alliance, while anti-government groups prepared the fall of their respective governments in order to end the war or even to declare war on Germany.37

In the early thirties, militant Japan was the first of the great powers that upset the status quo. It started an expansionary drive into Asia, an action prompted mainly by economic, strategic and imperialistic considerations and by the overpopulation on the Japanese mainland. Japan severely violated the tenets of the League of Nations. In 1933 Japan left the system of collective security for the purpose of pursuing a policy of aggression. This became apparent in 1937/38 when Japan started her long range objective: the creation of a "Greater East Asian

Co-prosperity Sphere", an area of political federation, economic integration and cultural co-operation under Japanese leadership. This projected plan for a "New Order" was interspersed with stirring anti-colonial slogans such as "Asia for the Asians". Japan's "living space" was to extend to India in the south-west to Australia and New Zealand in the south-east and to the Pacific Islands (New Caledonia) in the east.[38]

The course of the war revealed the greatest weaknesses of such an ambitious program. Domestically, the centrifugal forces predominated, which became apparent in the controversies that arose over which direction the expansion should take. (Continent versus South-East Asia). The creation of a political consensus was plagued from the beginning by complicated collective decisions. The alliance with the other Axis Powers showed signs of weakness. It was troubled by conflicting aims which became apparent in military discussions on the objectives and priorities necessary to defeat the common enemies. Most decisive was the circumstance that the Japanese lacked the power to defend the conquered territory against the Allies and their supporters, and the fact that the often proclaimed Pan-Asiatic solidarity was nothing but a scrap of paper. The plan for a regional economic union, autarchic in nature and largely protected from international commerce, proved to be one of the numerous miscalculations made by Tokyo which led to defeat in 1945.

PEACE AIMS

We know today that in 1942/43 Great Britain, Soviet Russia, the United States and their allies (including the European resistance organizations and Third World independence movements) gained the military initiative on all theaters of the war and began to dictate the action.

The Allies, forged by Hitler's and Japan's attacks into one war coalition, put aside their differences and focused on one fixed primary objective: Militarily to force Italy and Japan, but "Germany first" quickly and completely into an unconditional surrender, and to that end to keep the alliance functioning, regardless of any heterogenous forces within the different countries and resistance movements.[39] One must always keep in mind, however, that the Second World War can only be evaluated correctly as an interaction of conflicts occurring simultaneously and interconnectedly at sea, in the air and at the "invisible front" with global interdependence at the major theaters of war. In addition--and on this question not much disagreement has existed--the occupied countries had to be liberated and their national independence guaranteed.

The Allies intended above all to re-organize, that is to temporarily control the defeated countries'--and most of all National Socialist Germany's--political systems so that they could never again threaten the neighboring countries with the "scourge of war". The status quo of 1937 was to be re-established and a new system of collective security to be formed. Premised on the Atlantic Charter it would be designed to strengthen international peace and create world stability. This completed the general formulation of the constructive peace aims.[40]

Not all partners of the Allied coalition had fought for these objectives and even if they had, they did so for various reasons. The two major Allies, Great Britain and the United States, held diverging views on many issues aside from those connected with grand strategy.[41] The aim of Poland's politicians was the liberation of their country from German occupation, which had threatened its very existence. They hoped above all for the rebirth of the Polish state with secure borders and ethnic solidarity. And they hoped that after the war Poland would never again be pushed around by the major powers. Their dilemma soon became apparent: The fight for liberation was only possible with the help of the Soviet Union, and Moscow had its own plans for the post-war fate of Poland.[42]

Denmark, Norway, Belgium, Holland, Luxembourg, Greece and Czechoslovakia desired to return to the status quo ante with assurance of protection from any renewed aggression. France desired the reconstruction of her democratic Republic and the establishment of France's position of predominance in post war Europe. Many resistance fighters and enemies of the Vichy regime saw in General Charles de Gaulle the personification of a victorious France.[43] India and the countries of South and East Asia had fought for their independence, for a separation from their colonial masters and for self-determination. All this amounted to a change in the status quo in their favor. In China the problem was domestic in nature--a decision between the Nationalists under Chiang Kai-shek and the Communists under Mao Tse-tung. For North and West Africa the Atlantic Charter kindled a spark of hope. The intellectual elite of the Moroccan Nationalist Party (Istinqlal) referred to it in its petition of 1943. In the same year, Azikiwe of Nigeria published his historic memorandum "Atlantic Charter and British West-Africa", in which he demanded that Article III be applied in regard to West Africa. For the nationalist movements of Asia and Africa the United Nations and the binding principles on which it was premised represented the best guarantee for their national independence.[44]

While anti-colonialism was one of the most important principles of American foreign policy, Great Britain tried to prevent the dissolution of her colonial empire, until shortly after the war when Britain under the Labour government had to accept it as a reality. It was one of the prices she had to pay for her military victory over the "challengers".[45] The Soviet Union agreed to the creation of a new system of collective security most likely because she viewed it more as additional protection from aggressors and less as a tool intended for the protection of national sovereignty, the re-establishment of the status quo and peaceful global co-operation. As early as 1944 the Soviet Union had introduced into the Eastern European countries liberated by the Red Army social policies of a revolutionary nature.

Next to the Soviet Union the United States was the major victor of the Second World War. It had finally become the leading world power. For several years after 1945 it could use its superiority and dominate the world with its monopoly of nuclear weapons and its extraordinary economic power. Whether the United States was sufficiently prepared for such a difficult task is, according to the evidence available to date, still questionable. Nevertheless the leading politicians in Washington realized that the United States neither could nor would return to the isolationism of the post-World War One era. In view of its experiences with the Soviets, and after a period of miscalculations in that connection, it seemed necessary that the United States engage itself world-wide, using its financial and economic powers. Only in this manner could conditions become more stable and a peaceful future for all continents be guaranteed.[45a]

The answer to the National Socialist, Fascist, and the Japanese challenge by the "unnatural" coalition was military victory. But it created a new political dilemma: the "Cold War" with all its consequences. The Alliance had disintegrated. Disagreement about the future ways and means to be used in the political reorganization of Europe, questions regarding world peace, and the Soviet policy in Eastern Europe had caused its demise. The ideological contrasts which up to that point had been largely concealed by one of the partners, and not sufficiently recognized or underestimated by the other, were too pronounced. After the Red Army had created a <u>fait accompli</u> in the countries which she had "liberated"--a fact more important than all the resolutions promulgated during the war--it became quite apparent that although the common enemy had been defeated in the war, the causes fought for had been quite different.[46]

The process of de-colonization could no longer be halted in Asia after the predominantly Communist-led resistance forces had helped to defeat the Japanese and together with the Nationalist leadership had seized political power in 1945.[47]

The decisions made and the measures taken during that time cannot be evaluated from the perspective of the Cold War, however. They were the consequence of their particular moment in history when the sum total of all experiences becomes effective. George Kennan quite correctly pointed to the "fears, moods, dreams, hopes and illusions, outbursts of anger, the strain of the exhausting war effort, the inhibitions and the psychoses of military thinking" which possessed the "actors of this drama". Only he who uses these viewpoints as a premise for the understanding of history, will be able to evaluate sufficiently the events and the decision-makers of that period, and analyze the historical development which after 1945 changed our world into a unified political and economic scene, posing questions which no other generation ever had to face.[48]

ABOUT THE HISTORIAN'S ENGAGEMENT

Much credit is due to the large number of historians who have researched and evaluated the connections suggested in this essay, although the trend toward detailed studies has perhaps been more pronounced than the attempt to present an overall picture with all the relevant factors. Several "official" accounts of the history of the Second World War have been published. Quite understandably the national-state interpretation predominates in these publications.[49] In these accounts events have been analyzed and evaluated premised on timely points of interest, certain political viewpoints, or the concepts mutually arrived at by some groups of authors. Such studies revealed how differently the factors that determined successes or defeats in the war have been assessed. Of course many controversies still exist. Some will only be laid to rest with the discovery of fresh primary material. Others will have to wait, due to the world's existing ideological differences.

Shortly after the war, young historians primarily in West Germany, Belgium, France, Great Britain and the United States started to do research in this significant but difficult subject. It was done during a time when it was very difficult to get primary material, especially since the victorious powers intended to open their archives only 30 years after the respective event had happened. The first systematic evaluation occurred mainly in connection with documents of the German leadership (notes, reports, diaries) used in the war crimes trials at Nuremberg, such as Wehrmacht or Foreign Ministry files. In the course of it the co-operation between historians in Germany and in other countries played an important part and step by step aided in the creation of a network of historians. From the very beginning historical research received much impetus from this group. Many fundamental studies could not have been undertaken without this co-operation.

The American military historians soon became well known in this connection. One of these well known historians is Charles Burdick, at San Jose State University in California, who since the 1950s has been holding a special place among them. He belongs to that group of historians who, with remarkable success and expert knowledge of the often very complicated subject matter, have written several long and short accounts on the subject,[50] and who aside from that have advanced the co-operation between German and American historians in a manner that can hardly be surpassed. It has been decisive that Burdick has inventively and diligently searched for new source material, that he has helped his German colleagues in the most altruistic way, gained the confidence of the people he interviewed (especially among the German generals) and examined the former German Wehrmacht's war documents which used to be deposited in Washington. Probably no other non-German historian of rank has the same knowledge of the German generals (and officers), has the corresponding contacts to them and has been appreciated by them as a historian who is always searching for objectivity. None less than the former Chief of the German Army General Staff, Lieutenant Colonel (ret.) F. Halder, a man who is usually rather restrained in his opinions, wrote in the preface of an anthology written in honor of the 75th birthday of General Hubert Lanz, which Burdick published in the early 1970s, that this American became internationally renowned because of "the depth of his search for the truth, his psychological understanding, and his recognition of the essential". It must be mentioned that it was first of all his goal-oriented working style, his humanity, his admirable patience in listening to many reminiscences, which opened many doors for him and gave him insights which others could never gain. In addition Burdick contributed much to the mutual understanding between the former victors and the defeated, by attempting, as did the British Military Historian B. H. Liddell Hart, to do justice to the conduct of the German soldiers in the years from 1939-1945--not an easy undertaking.

It should not be kept a secret that the critical colleague did not and could not agree with every opinion that came from the friend's pen. This does in no way lessen Charles Burdick's achievements. In his attempt to give fair credit to the German military accomplishment, he forgave rather than accused. Some of his theses at times even caused a certain astonishment, as, for instance when he did not sufficiently emphasize the ideologic-aggressive element in National Socialist politics and warfare, and when he mostly parenthesized the precarious relationship that existed between National Socialism and the Wehrmacht. The German military leadership, by commission and omission, did contribute to the German defeat, not to mention the shameful behavior of some of its officers toward the National Socialist policy of genocide. Burdick's tendencies might be explained by the fact that his strength lies more in the writing of detailed military studies of the operational and biographical type, and less in the examination of questions regarding National Socialist policies. Many military historians share this tendency. As has been pointed out earlier in this paper, they evaluate the war by using primarily the military mode of interpretation.

In his studies Charles Burdick focused on the German military planning preceding the war; the planning for the offensive in the West 1940, and the measures and deliberations for the conquest of Gibraltar (Operation "Felix" and "Isabella") from 1940 to 1942. This account published in 1968 is an excellent case study of German operational strategy in the decisive months of the Second World War, researched with remarkable thoroughness, using all the available primary sources. In it Burdick has superbly reconstructed the fluctuating deliberations, the probing in Spain, the military preparations and the task of the National Socialist leadership connected with this operation. To date this study has not been superseded. "Operation Sunflower", a smaller study, published three years later, is an excellent contribution to the studies of the coalition warfare of Germany and Italy in 1940 and 1941, focusing as it does on the German decision to support the Italians in Africa, and on the question why in the end the operations of the Africa Corps under Rommel's leadership failed. Burdick quite correctly points out that strategic miscalculations were mostly responsible, but that so was the fact that these divisions were not adequately prepared for the special conditions encountered in desert warfare.

In the nineteen fifties, the historian who wanted to study the war had great difficulty in obtaining the necessary source material. The archive of the <u>Munich Institute Für Zeitgeschichte</u> was still under construction. In Göttingen, the university's <u>Forschungsstelle für Zeitgeschichte des Instituts für Völkerrecht</u> (under Dr. Seraphim), was systematically collecting the documents of the post-war trials. Soon it became more and more possible to acquire documents form private sources including diaries, letters, and copies of directives of the German Armed Forces of all kind. Most useful, however, were the German military documents which in the meantime had been deposited at the American Historical Division in Karlsruhe. German officers under the direction of Franz Halder worked in the so-called Control Group on numerous manuscripts regarding questions about the operational leadership on all theaters of the war. At first the authors had to rely on their memories, first drafts and memoirs. After a while they gained access to the captured German documents and their opinions could be founded more solidly on fact.

Young West German historians had only limited access to these documents, and an often not-quite-legal access at that, since perusal of these documents depended on permission from the American authorities. When permission was not given, ways and means were frequently found to circumvent these obstacles, especially when the historian could gain the confidence of the German clerk, who in turn would loan him the material "privately".

In a remarkable article, Charles Burdick described the activity of this U.S. Army agency, and sketched the problems which arose shortly after the war, when victor and defeated worked together and when the attempt was made to turn soldiers into historians. Although there still exists a need to answer certain questions in connection with the German contribution to the American historiography of the Second World War, especially regarding the significance of the operational studies (a large scale project which Charles Burdick and Donald Detwiler have published in the early 1980s), Burdick has made many interesting contributions which deserve to be honored more comprehensively in the future.

The research of the history of the Second World War has, without doubt, been advanced by the dedicated work of many scholars. Across the borders, they have set valuable criteria for the future with their exemplary co-operation. One of them is Charles Burdick. He deserves much recognition for his significant contribution and for the extraordinary support he has given to his fellow historians.

NOTES

[1] See G. Schreiber, Der Zweite Weltkrieg - Probleme und Ergebnisse der Forschung (I), in Neue politische Literatur, vol. 29/4 (1984), pp. 453 ff; La Seconda Guerra Mondiale nella prospettiva Storica a trent' anni dall 'epilogo, Como 1977; Deutschland im zweiten Weltkrieg. Bibliographie der Geschichtswissen-schaftlichen Literatur der DDR, bearb. v. M. Piesche (in "Bulletin der Arbeitskreises Zw. Weltkrieg" No. 1-4, 1982 (East Berlin); Janet Zieglers, WWII Books in English 1945-65, Stanford 1971.

[2] See e.g.: B. H. Liddell-Hart, Geschichte des 2. Weltkrieges, 2 vols., Düsseldorf 1972; B. Collier, The War in the Far East 1941-45, London 1969; A. Seaton, Der russisch-deutsche Krieg 1941-1945, Frankfurt 1973.

[3] See e.g.: K-D. Erdmann, Der Zweite Weltkrieg, München 1980; Geschichte des grossen Vaterländischen Krieges der Sowjetunion 1941-1945, 6 vols., Berlin 1962-1968; Deutschland im zweiten Weltkrieg, Berlin (E) 1974-1980, 4 vols.; G. Bocca, Storia d'Italia nella Guerra Fascista 1940-43, Ban 1969; Winston S. Churchill, The Second World War, 6 vols., Boston 1948-53; R. Buchanan, The United States and World War II, 2 vols., New York 1964.

[4] Among the numerous accounts see: K.D. Bracher, Europa in der Krise. Innengeschichte und Weltpolitik seit 1917, Frankfurt 1979; Handbuch der Europäischen Geschichte, ed. by Th. Schieder, vol. 7. Europa im Zeitalter der Weltmachte, Stuttgart 1979 (nach Ländern geordnet); G. Wright, The Ordeal of Total War, New York 1968; I. Lukacs, Der letzte europäische Krieg, 1939-1941, Stuttgart, 1978.

[5] See M. Howard, History of the Second World War, London 1971; P. Calvocoressi, and Guy Wint, Total War. Causes and Courses of the Second World War, New York, 1972; R. Cartier, Der Zweite Weltkrieg 1939-1945, 2 vols, München 1975; L. Gruchmann, Der Zweite Weltkrieg. Kriegführung und Politik, München 1971; H.A. Jacobsen, Der Weg zur Teilung der Welt. Politik und Strategie 1939-1945, Koblenz-Bonn 1979 (2nd edition).

[6] See W.S. Churchill, The Second World War, 6 vols., Boston 1948-1953.

[7] See: M. Matloff, Snell, Strategic Planning for Coalition Warfare, 1941-42, Washington, 1953; 1943-1944, Washington 1959, pp 398 & 555, and F.C. Pogue, George C. Marshall, Organizer of Victory, 1943-1945, New York, 1973; I. Ehrman, Grand Strategy, vol. VI, 1944/45. London 1956.

[8]See: Geschichte des Grossen Vaterländischen Krieges (footnote 3 above); Vtoraja Mirovaja voina. Kratkaja istorija, Moscow, 1984, and Wörterbuch der Geschichte, L-Z, Berlin (E), 1983.

[9]See: O. Rsheschewski, Unternehmen "Overlord", Moscow 1984; D. Ose., Entscheidung im Westen 1944, Stuttgart 1982; M. Hastings, Overlord. D-Day and the Battle of Normandy, London 1984.

[10]See: Sowjetunion heute, No. 1/1985, pp 1-2; M. Koslow, Der Zweite Weltkrieg und die Gegenwart. Zum Erscheinen des 12. Bandes der Geschichte des Zweiten Weltkrieges 1939-1945, in Militärgeschichte (Berlin /E), 6/1983, pp 734 ff; W. Ostrogorskij, Zwei deutsche Staaten - zwei Einstellungen zum 40. Jahrestag des grossen Sieges, in: Nowosti, Moscow, Jan. 22, 1985.

[11]See footnotes 1-3; Ploetz. Geschichte der Weltkriege. Mächte, Ereignisse, Entwicklungen 1900-1945, xed. by A. Hillgruber and J. Dülffer, Würzburg 1981; also D. Irving, Hitlers Krieg. Die Siege 1939-1942, Munich, 1983.

[12]See A. Hillgruber, Der Zweite Weltkrieg 1939-1945, Kriegsziele und Strategie der grossen Mächte, Stuttgart 1982 (to date perhaps the best brief survey of the war's significant decisions).

[13]See: Das Deutsche Reich und der Zweite Weltkrieg. ed. by Militärgeschichtliches Forschungsamt (10 volumes planned in all) vol. 1-4 Stuttgart 1979-1984 (to 1941).

[14]See footnote 8 (Wörterbuch der Geschichte).

[15]See: Hillgruber footnote 12; Jacobsen, footnote 5: also G.L. Weinberg, World in the Balance, Behind the Scenes of World War II, Hanover-London 1981.

[16]See footnotes 12 and 13.

[17]See: A. Hillgruber, Hitlers Strategie, Politik und Kriegführung 1940-1941, Frankfurt 1965 (Neuaufl. 1980) and Schreiber, op. cit. (footnote 1); N. Rich, Hitler's War Aims, 2 vols., New York 1973-1974.

[18]Regarding the war objectives of the USSR see A. Fischer, Sowjetische Deutschlandpolitik im Zweiten Weltkrieg 1941-1945, Stuttgart 1975; and Hillgruber, (footnote 12).

[19]CF.: Hillgruber; R. Beitzell, The Uneasy Alliance: America, Britain, Russia, 1941-1943, New York 1972; J. Burns, Roosevelt, The Soldier of Freedom 1940-1945, London 1971.

[20]Cf. Hillgruber, Footnote 12.

[21] Ibid., N. Rich, Fn. 17; Weinberg. World in the Balance (Hitler's Image of the United States), pp 53 ff.

[22] Cf. R. Wittram, Das Interesse an der Geschichte, Göttingen 1958. p. 26.

[23] Cf. Hillgruber, Fn. 12; Rich, Fn. 17; G.K.Kindermann, Der Ferne Osten, Munich, 1970; S. Jenaga, The Pacific War, 1931-1945, New York 1978.

[24] Cf. W. Hofer, Die Entfesselung des Zweiten Weltkrieges, Düsseldorf 1984; E.M. Robertson, ed., The Origins of the Second World War, London 1971; W. Benz/H. Graml, Sommer 1939, Die Grossmächte und der Europäische Krieg, Stuttgart 1979.

[25] Cf. Fn. 24; (also Hillgruber, Fn. 12.)

[26] Cf. Fn. 4 (Schieder, pp. 171 ff).

[27] Cf. K. Hildebrand, Vom Reich zum Weltreich. Hitler, NSDAP und koloniale Frage 1919-1945, Munich, 1969.

[28] Cf. Fn. 12 (Hillgruber); E. Jaeckel, Frankreich in Hitlers Europa. Die deutsche Frankreichpolitik im Zweiten Weltkrieg, Stuttgart 1966; W. Boelcke, ed., Deutschlands Rüstung im Zweiten Weltkrieg. Hitlers Konferenzen mit A. Speer 1942-1945, Frankfurt 1969; F. Forstmeier/H.E. Volkmann, ed., Kriegswirtschaft und Rüstung 1939-1945, Düsseldorf 1976.

[29] Cf. Jacobsen, op.cit. (Fn. 5), p. 232 f.; W. Boelcke, ed., Wollt Ihr den totalen Krieg? Die geheimen Goebbels-Konferenzen 1939-1943, Munich 1969.

[30] Cf. Joseph Goebbels Tagebücher. 1945, Hamburg 1977, 3.5.45, p. 116 f.

[31] Cf. Erlass vom 15.2.1943, in O. Buchbender, Das tönende Erz, Deutsche Propaganda gegen die Rote Armee im Zweiten Weltkrieg, Stuttgart 1978, p. 315 ff.

[32] Cf. Rich, op.cit. II (Fn. 17).

[33] Cf. Meldungen aus dem Reich. Die geheimen Lageberichte des Sicherheitsdienstes der SS 1938-1945, ed. by H. Boberach, Herrsching 1984, p. 5061 (4.5.43); 5104 (4.12.43); 5619 (8.16.43). G. Ritter, C. Goerdeler und die deutsche Widerstandsbewegung, Stuttgart 1956 (3rd ed.)

[34] Cf. M. Knox, Mussolini Unleashed 1939-1941. Politics and Strategy in Fascist Italy's Last War, Cambridge-London 1982; D.M. Smith, Mussolinis Roman Empire, London-New York 1976; F.W. Deakin,

Die brutale Freundschaft. Hitler, Mussolini und der Untergang des italienischen Faschismus, Cologne, 1964.

35Cf. Das Deutsche Reich und der Zweite Weltkrieg, op.cit. (Fn. 13), vol. 3.

36Cf. inter al.,: F.V. Adonyi-Naredi, Ungarns Armee im Zweiten Weltkrieg, Neckargemünd 1971; M.D. Fenyo, Hitler, Horthy and Hungary. German-Hungarian Relations 1941-1944, New Haven 1972; G. Fricke, Kroatien 1941-1944, Freiburg 1972; Hillgruber, op.cit. (Fn. 17); Handbüch der europäischen Geschichte, (Fn. 4)

37Ibid., Hillgruber, (Fn.12).

38Cf. Kindermann, (Fn. 23); W. Craig, Als Japans Sonne untergang. Das Ende des Krieges im Pazifik, Vienna and Munich, 1970; John W. Dower, War Without Mercy, New York, 1986.

39Cf. inter al: G. Kolko, The Politics of War: Allied Diplomacy and the World Crisis of 1943-1945, London 1969; W. Kimbell (ed.), Franklin D. Roosevelt and the World Crisis 1937-1945, Lexington 1973; R. Dallek, Franklin D. Roosevelt and American Foreign Policy, 1932-1945, New York 1979. And from a Soviet point of view, see V. Israeljan, The Anti-Hitler Coalition. Diplomatic Cooperation between the USSR, USA and Britain during the Second World War, 1941-1945, Moscow, 1971.

40Ibid.; See also D. Yergin, Shattered Peace, The Origins of the Cold War and the National Security State, Boston 1977.

41Cf. Matloff (Fn. 7); A.Bryant, Sieg im Westen (1943-1946), Düsseldorf 1960.

42Cf. V. Vierheller, Polen und die Deutschlandfrage 1939-1949, Cologne, 1970; W. Jurgielewics, Poland's Contribution to the Victory over Fascism 1939-1945, in: Military Technique. Policy and Strategy in History, Warsaw, 1976, pp. 640 ff; G. Rhode, Polen von der Wiederherstellung der Unabhängigkeit bis zur Ära der Volksrepublik 1918-1970, in Handbuch der Europäischen Geschichte, (see Fn. 4), 978 ff, 1040 ff.

43Cf. R.V. Albertini, Frankreich vom Frieden von Versailles bis zum Ende der Vierten Republik, in Handbuch der Europäischen Geschichte (Fn. 4), pp. 438ff, 457 ff. See Albertini as well for the political history of the other European states (Denmark, Norway, Belgium, Holland, etc.)

44Cf. G. Arnold, Modern Nigeria, London, 1977; P. Bertaux, Afrika, Von der Vorgeschichte bis zu den Staaten der Gegenwart, Frankfurt, 1966, pp. 251 ff.; as well as Kindermann (Fn. 23).

[45] For general background, see L. Woodward, British Foreign Policy in the Second World War, 5 vols., London 1970; R.A. Blasius, ed., Dokumente zur Deutschlandpolitik, Britische Deutschlandpolitik 1939-1941 (English texts), Frankfurt 1984.

[45a] Cf. W.H. Harriman and A. Abel, Im geheimer Mission. Als Sonderbeauftragter Roosevelts bei Churchill und Stalin 1941-1946, Stuttgart 1979; G.L. Weinberg, World in the Balance. Behind the Scenes of World War II, Hanover-London, 1981, pp. 27 ff.

[46] See the literature cited in Fn. 39.

[47] Cf. J.H. Boyle, China and Japan at War, 1937-1945, Stanford, 1977.

[48] Cf. G.F. Kennan, Memoirer eines Diplomaten, Stanford 1967, and Russia and the West under Lenin and Stalin, London 1961, p. 379.

[49] Cf. notes 7, 13, etc.

[50] See the list of his publications.

THE EVACUATION OF THE KUBAN BRIDGEHEAD, A MODEL RETROGRADE MOVEMENT

by DAVID MIDDLESWORTH

During the course of World War II, many military actions received world-wide attention. One that did not receive such attention, but nevertheless represented one of the most successful military operations of the War was the evacuation of the Kuban Bridgehead. More than a quarter of a million German troops and supporters evacuated the Taman Peninsula on the southern front in Russia. The evacuation occurred shortly after the German catastrophe at Stalingrad, and, indeed was motivated to a large extent by that experience. The German field commanders on the Taman Peninsula wanted to avoid either a grand encirclement of the Army Group A, or suffer severe casualties. Both of these objectives were satisfied by the success of the withdrawal. The evacuation served as an excellent example of the precision with which a large complicated movement of men and material can be conducted. Furthermore, it demonstrated the close cooperation and support of the German Army, Navy and Air Force, since all played an important role in the ultimate success of the evacuation of the Kuban Bridgehead.

The chief objectives of the southern extremity of the attacking German forces in Russia in 1942 were the Caucasian oil fields and the control of the Black Sea ports of Novorossiysk and Batumi. The plan called for German advances across the Kerch Strait over the Taman Peninsula into the Caucasus. The ports of Novorossiysk, Taupse, Sochi, Sykhumi and Batumi were all objectives of some importance. Not only would the Soviet Black Sea fleet be denied its last bases (permitting the German Caucasus front to be supplied by the sea), but an even greater prize might be won: Once the last Soviet coastal strip on the Black Sea was occupied by German troops, Turkey would possibly join the Axis. This might have far-reaching consequences upon the Allied conduct of the war. The British-Soviet position in Northern Persia would collapse and the southern supply route for American military aid to Stalin by way of the Persian Gulf, the Caspian Sea and up the Volga River would be severed.[1] In addition, the Baku oil fields would be open to the German forces.

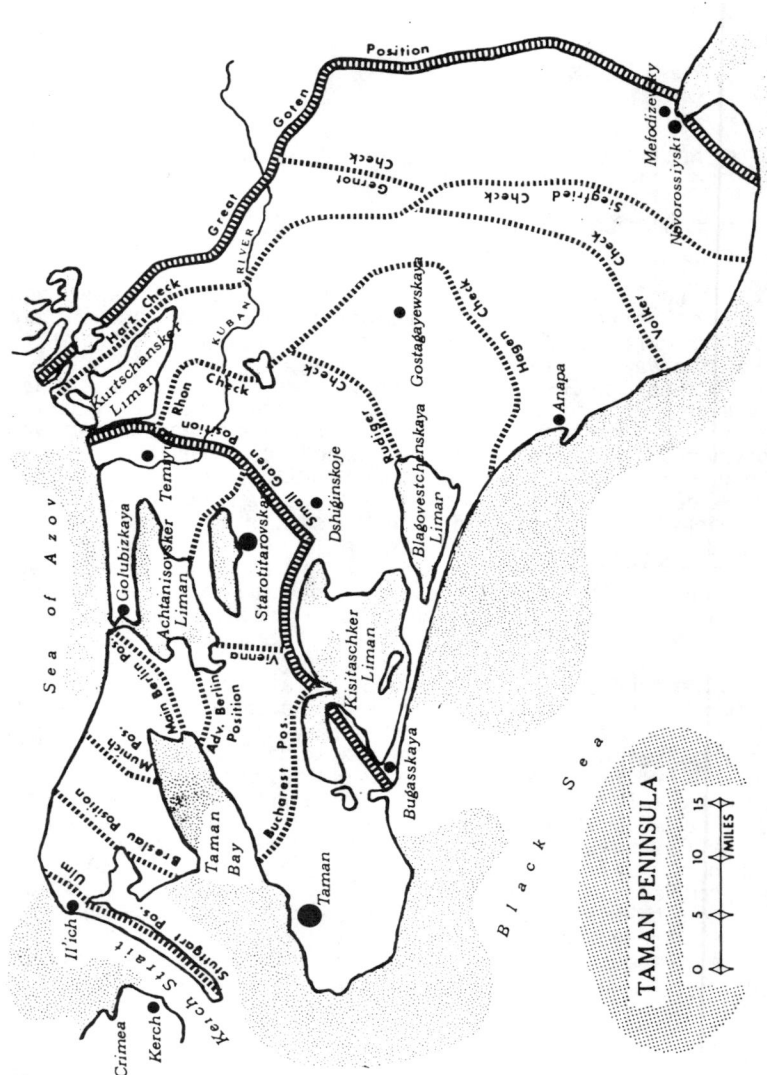

In early September 1942, Hitler assumed direct command of Army Group A along with his other responsibilities as Supreme Commander of all German fighting forces and Commander-in-Chief of the German Army. He did not appoint another commander for Army Group A until November 1942 when he named General Ewald von Kleist.[2] By that time, of course, Hitler had become almost totally involved with the perilous condition of the German Sixth Army in Stalingrad. This may explain, in part, why he chose to appoint a new commander after all. However, an even more plausible explanation may be Hitler's known aversion to ordering retreats, which became the destiny of Army Group A.

By November 1942, Army Group A had driven far into the Caucasus Mountains in its vain attempt to reach the Baku oil fields on the Caspian Sea. They had earlier failed to acquire the much needed oil from their capture of the Maykop oil fields in the Fall of 1942, because the Russians had successfully destroyed the fields by the time the special German Oil Brigade had reached them. After having lost the Maykop oil facilities, Hitler's next objective was the Baku oil fields. But Army Group A never reached Baku, although a small advanced group did reach the Caspian Sea.

Hitler's obsession with oil competed with a newer one, the prestige of holding Stalingrad, whose Russian garrison was now surrounded by strong German forces. In the early fall of 1942, the city of Stalingrad became a critical objective in Hitler's strategy. He had avoided the time-consuming, house-to-house fighting in Leningrad and Warsaw, but he was determined to pursue this form of fighting in Stalingrad. The result of this tremendous depletion of personnel and material forced Hitler to pull troops away from the Caucasus to strengthen the German forces in Stalingrad. Although originally the Caucasus had been the prime military target, now the city of Stalingrad eclipsed the former objective.

In September and October 1942, the bitter house-to-house fighting began in Stalingrad. (The Russians' tenacious resistance ultimately contributed to the annihilation of the German Sixth Army as a fighting force.) In addition, the Russians were massing forces around Saratov for their impending offensive against the Germans in Stalingrad.

Although German Luftwaffe reconnaissance reports had not confirmed other German intelligence reports of this Russian concentration, even Hitler suspected the Russians might attack across the Don River toward Rostov.[3] Eventually, German intelligence confirmed the Russian concentration around Saratov. All indications pointed to a Russian attack against the Rumanian Third Army.

On November 18, 1942, the Soviets began their two-pronged attack on the German and Rumanian forces surrounding Stalingrad. The Russians chose the area defended by the Rumanian Third Army to initiate this attack. Soviet T-34 tanks succeeded in breaking through and penetrating 30 miles behind the Rumanian lines. In the south, the Soviets again chose an area occupied by Rumanian forces, the Rumanian VI and VII corps, to launch their offensive. The Soviets succeeded in penetrating the Rumanian-held line, and eventually reached Kalach after a German motorized division, the 29th Motorized Infantry Division, had been recalled to establish a defensive position on the southern side of Stalingrad. This German unit could have prevented the Russian breakthrough, but German Intelligence at this time was unable to determine the true intentions of the Soviets. Thus, Hitler fell prey to the Soviet strategy of encirclement at Stalingrad. Field Marshall Erich Von Manstein, the newly appointed Commander of the Army Group Don, (composed of the Fourth Panzer Army, Sixth Army, Third and Fourth Rumanian Armies) came within 25 miles of Stalingrad. General Friedrich Paulus, Commanding General of the Sixth Army in Stalingrad, however, continued to honor Hitler's express orders not to attempt a breakout. When the order to breakout did come after all, it came too late, resulting in the loss of an entire German Army with over 90,000 men. The battle for Stalingrad had cost the German and Rumanian forces over 300,000 casualties.[4]

After the debacle of Stalingrad, the entire German Southern Army front faced a similar fate. The Russian offensive threatened to turn the left flank of Army Group Don, seize the Donets and Dnieper River crossings behind it, and drive on to Rostov. If this Soviet strategy succeeded, Army Group A would be separated from Army Group Don and another Army, the 17th under Army Group A, would be surrounded and cut off. This scenario contained the seeds for a German loss greater even than Stalingrad. What would be at stake then was no longer the fate of 200,000 to 300,000 men, but of a million and a half soldiers.[5]

Finally, on January 21, 1943, Hitler reluctantly authorized Army Group A to withdraw to the Taman Peninsula in order to establish a bridgehead in the Kuban River area. Hitler's directive demanded the complete demolition of all facilities on the Kuban Bridgehead. It was to be carried out ruthlessly, using forced civil labor, including women's battalions.[6] He assigned chief responsibility to the 17th Army under Army Group A. The 17th Army, commanded by General Erwin Jaenecke,[7] conducted six offensive battles at this bridgehead from February to September 1943. After maintaining a defensive position for almost eight months, Army Group A issued the order to evacuate the Kuban Bridgehead on September 3, 1948.[8] Although Hitler opposed the construction of any defensive position, because he believed it made his generals less aggressive, he had no alternative in the Kuban area. Even Hitler was cognizant of the impact of a second Stalingrad. Defensive fortifications had been carefully prepared throughout the spring and summer months. As a result, the evacuation of the Kuban Bridgehead unfolded as one of the most successful retrograde movements in military history.

Although Hitler had not allowed the evacuation until the September 3rd order, the 17th Army had already made the preparations for the evacuation. The evacuation plan called for an elaborate series of defensive positions, beginning with the so-called "Great Gothic Position." This defensive line ran from the northern section occupied by the XLIX Mountain Corps under General Rudolf Konrad, through the center section occupied by the XLIV Light Infantry under General Maxmillian Angelis, to the southern section occupied by the V Army Corps under General Karl Allmendinger.[9] The "Great Gothic Position" was the longest defensive perimeter, with each successive retrograde movement reducing the German line accordingly. (See map). It was separated from the next major defensive position, the "Small Gothic Position," by seven minor checkpoints. Behind that, a series of strong points were in various formative stages, each one named after a German city. These stations were constructed in a manner which afforded the retreating German forces with the optimum means to withdraw units from the fighting front that were no longer needed.[10]

The Russian attack precipitated the evacuation on the key harbor of Novorossiysk. This harbor on the Black Sea had been a critical Russian objective. In April 1943, this port had been the target of a Soviet assault, which failed only in the face of stiff German resistance. The second and successful Soviet attack which occurred on September 10, 1943 initiated the actual German evacuation of the Kuban Bridgehead. Novorossiysk had been the most modern port of the Soviet Black Sea Fleet, and its recapture remained vital both in psychological as well as strategic military terms. Its modern harbor installations were capable of handling shipping of all sizes up to and including battleships.[11] The harbor was surrounded by foothills ranging in height from 1,500 to 1,800 feet.

In the beginning of 1943 Hitler had not envisaged a complete evacuation of the Caucasus. Although the city of Stalingrad with the remnants of the Sixth Army was lost, Hitler still maintained that the Caucasus could be held until he could initiate a new offensive. This strategy of a renewed initiative required that Germany retain Novorossiysk, which would confine the Russian Black Sea Fleet to one port, Batumi. The retention of the Black Sea under German control represented even wider implications for German strategy because if Rostov in the north fell to the Russians, the German Army Group A in the Caucasus would be cut off from their primary supply line. If the Russians had been successful in closing the "Rostov bottleneck" in early 1943 and occupying the Taman Peninsula, all the German forces in the Caucasus would have been trapped.[12] The only other supply line was across the Kerch Strait which led into the Taman Peninsula and the port of Novorossiysk, and it became, therefore, highly important for the Germans to maintain control over these areas. In addition, the German presence in the Kuban as well as the narrow Kerch waterway would seal off the Sea of Azov. This meant that another entrance to the Black Sea would be denied the Russians. Moreover, Hitler appreciated the strategic importance of retaining the harbor facilities of Novorossiysk not only because the harbor was the best on the Black Sea, but also because Novorossiysk was located on the southern part of the Taman Peninsula (Kuban Bridgehead) which protected the entire Crimea. The Crimea, in turn, served as a geographical buffer to the Reich's only source of natural oil, the Rumanian fields at Ploesti. These fields represented a rich prize to whomever controlled them.[13]

Stalin, for his part, also appreciated the importance of capturing Novorossiysk and the immediate surrounding area. The significance he attached to the capture of Novorossiysk may be seen from the units chosen for the assault, which included the Special Landing Corps and the 81st Guard Artillery Regiment, both elite formations. On September 10 the Russians launched their assault by feinting an attack on Novorossiysk, while simultaneously attacking another point, Osereika, located on the southern tip of the harbor where the main attack actually occurred. This latter operation achieved greater success than the attack on Novorossiysk, since the German coastal defenses here were weaker than their artillery fire power in the harbor itself.[14]

The Russian landing operations in Novorossiysk required significant improvisation, particularly in terms of obtaining a suitable number of landing craft. The Russian commanders demonstrated ingenuity and a talent for organization by their use of old fishing boats that were converted into landing craft. Although the operation appeared to be a grave threat to the entire 17th Army, we now know that the attack did not seriously change the planned evacuation of the Kuban Bridgehead, except to accelerate the time plan by a few days.[15]

The official Soviet history celebrates the recovery of Novorossiysk as a great victory; a view which tends to discount the practical results of the operation.[16] What did the Russians actually receive from their successful recapture of Novorossiysk? They took possession of a mined harbor that made it impossible for any ship other than small boats with light draught to enter for six months. The railroad facilities were destroyed, the city was a burning mass of rubble, and the Russian elite troops had incurred heavy casualties.[17] The Russian landing attack at Novorossiysk which lasted from September 10-15th did not seriously alter the German evacuation timetable. With the effective withdrawal of all German forces from Novorossiysk to the "Great Gothic Position," the actual evacuation could proceed. The Russians were not even aware the Germans had evacuated Novorossiysk until the "Great Gothic Position" had already been occupied. The German field staff also received some encouragement from this initial encounter, and the overall troop morale was high, given the absolute minimum number of casualties.

The Russian attack on Novorossiysk did alter the original German timetable by five days. The Germans had intended to evacuate Novorossiysk before the Soviets landed on September 8, 1943. The Germans, however, gained one advantage by being forced to fight in Novorossiysk. The Russians had employed their elite formations, which had been badly mauled so that as a result their participation in future operations was seriously impaired.

The Soviet offensive continued to press the planned German evacuation from September 15th through the 26th. This period witnessed a series of conflicts between Soviet and German forces from the "Great Gothic Position" to the "Small Gothic Position." Between these two major defensive lines, the German engineers had prepared seven minor defensive lines. As the German forces withdrew, the German engineer troops continued to mine the evacuated areas. The detonation of these mines took an increasingly high tool among the Russian horses used for supply. Soviet attacks grew stronger as more support from tanks and aircraft arrived, thus increasing the threat of breaking through the German and Rumanian forces, severing the continuous German defense line.[18]

On September 16th the German forces withdrew to the "Small Gothic Position." The 10-day withdrawal from the "Great Gothic Position" had run smoothly with no major difficulties. The fighting front under the V Corps in the south had been reduced from 10 kilometers to 30 kilometers. This reduction in area allowed the 17th Army to evacuate five divisions, leaving a total German strength in the Kuban area of six divisions (50th, 98th, 370th Infantry Divisions, 97th Light Infantry Division, 4th Mountain Division; and the Rumanian 19th Infantry Division. The Soviets had also been able to withdraw eight of their divisions as a result of the shortening of the front. However, this still left them with 13 fighting divisions, three brigades, four tank groups and two Navy battalions, an overwhelming numerical superiority.[19] This example of Russian numerical superiority was accepted in the German Army daily reports with no great alarm, since they had become accustomed to these unfavorable odds.

The last and most dangerous stage of the evacuation commenced with the fighting for the "Small Gothic Position." This last stage would determine the success or failure of the evacuation. Up to this point, the evacuation had proceeded without any major obstacles, but now the Soviet leadership concentrated all of its efforts on preventing the remaining German and Rumanian forces from evacuating safely to the Kerch Peninsula. It was obvious to both sides who possessed the superior number of men and material. This placed even greater pressure on the Soviet leadership to prevent a successful German withdrawal. On the other hand, the days became increasingly filled with tension and apprehension for the German leadership because they were forced to remain always one step, one move, ahead of the attacking Russians. One miscalculation, blunder or irresolution could threaten the chances of the remaining six divisions to evacuate safely. Although the pressure was mounting, a fiercely competitive attitude among the German officers toward the attacking Russians contributed to an increasing sense of excitement.

The evacuation of the German V Corps began on September 26th. General Konrad, Commanding General of XLIX Mountain Corps, was designated Commanding General for all troops committed in the "Small Gothic Position" by General von Kleist, Commanding General, Army Group A. The V Army Corps Headquarters with the Commanding General, General of the Infantry, Karl Allmendinger, was transported to the Crimea with orders to assemble troops and material that were to be moved during the final phase of the evacuation.[20]

On September 26th, the German defense line ran from the mouth of the Kuban River on the Sea of Azov, south to Temryuk, and from Temryuk southwest along the high ground on the western rim of the lowland marsh of the old Kuban River in front of Woroschdenije. The line then skirted the southeast rim of the Kisilashsky Marsh to the south side of the Taman Peninsula on the Black Sea. This was approximately a 72 mile defensive perimeter. The northern sector, the area between Temryuk and the mouth of the Kuban River, was especially vulnerable to Russian attacks because of the great width of the Kuban River mouth (200 yards) which permitted coastal landings from the Sea of Azov. This had been clearly demonstrated by the attempted Russian landing on the 25th of September when the Russians made a landing three miles northwest of Blagoveschtschenskaya in division strength. The purpose of the landing was to threaten the position by hindering German troop movement on the Taman-Soljonoje Road. This road ran behind the German front line, and was being used to withdraw men and material. The Russians landed one Navy Infantry Brigade with orders to establish a bridgehead on the Bugassker Marsh.[21] This operation involved 6,000 Russians who were transported in 50 landing boats. The conflict lasted the entire day, at the end of which the German and Rumanian forces finally were able to contain the Russian landing force south of the Bugassker Marsh and thus to permit themselves to withdraw safely to the "Rüdiger" checkpoint.[22]

The center sector provided some excellent observation points which enabled the German defense to observe Russian activity deep into the rear. This was possible because of the numerous hill crests which rose to heights of 300 feet. The wide left flank also provided numerous observation points of the flat Kisilashsky Marsh. This southern marsh was dried out in September because of a rainless summer. This meant the Russians could drive heavy armor vehicles across it, although the terrain was not entirely dependable since parts of it would not support armor traffic. The southern coast of the Taman Peninsula west of Wesselowka provided a natural defense against Russian landings, because of the steeply rising coastline. The narrow strip of land that ran from Anapa to the Soljonoje Lake was capable of supporting heavy vehicles, although the road was only passable during the dry season.

By September 26th most of the construction on the defensive positions had been completed by the German V Corps Army Engineers. Between the "Small Gothic Position" and the final embarkation point were eight additional positions: "Vienna", "Bucharest," "Berlin Advance,"

"Berlin Main," "Munich," "Breslau," "Ulm," and "Stuttgart." The defensive line was 72 miles long with 15 miles of completed anti-tank trenches and with another 45 miles partially constructed.[23]

Time was of the essence, as the evacuation was scheduled to be completed in two weeks. The tempo of the evacuation was adjusted according to the particular defensive strength of each individual position. The "Small Gothic Position" was to be maintained for six days. The "Vienna Position" and "Bucharest Position" were to be held only for a short time before the occupation of the "Berlin Advanced Position." In contrast, the "Golubizkaya Checkpoint" was to be held until the entire left flank of the XLIX Mountain Corps had withdrawn through that narrow passage of land. Also, this position had to be occupied until the southern flank had reached the "Berlin Advance Position." The "Berlin Main Position" was especially important because it had to be occupied until the mass of the remaining troops had been actually transported across to Kerch. The Germans could not afford to have troops and vehicles congesting the embarkation points, contributing to any unnecessary delay or confusion.[24]

At this point, General Konrad initiated a bold departure in the German retreat. He ordered the entire front to swing north toward the "Berlin Advance Position." This sudden change was in lieu of establishing an embarkation point at Taman, as the Russians had anticipated. Consequently, the Russian Commander was caught off guard. Moreover, the narrow sea between Kerch and Kosa Chushka was not as dangerous as the wider stretch from Taman to Kerch; and finally, the "Berlin Advanced Position" in the northern part of the Taman Peninsula was far easier to defend.[25] Konrad's dramatic tactical changes demonstrated the agility of the German leadership, and it also kept the Russian Commanders in a state of confusion.

The Soviets, for their part, tried to apply such pressure at the center of the "Small Gothic Position" so that most of the German defensive strength would be sapped, thus leaving the two flanks vulnerable to sea landings from either the Black Sea or the Sea of Azov. Powerful land operations combined with landings behind the German front lines certainly would have created a dangerous situation for the German forces. This Soviet pressure caused serious concerns for the German forces, as evidenced by a report of German losses on the 30th of September by th XLIX Mountain Corps.[26] However, in spite of these casualties the general German timetable was not altered.

The retrograde movement from the"Small Gothic Position" to the "Vienna Position" meant that the harbor of Taman would fall into Russian hands. The German engineers estimated that the destruction of the harbor and city would take 36 hours. This meant that Ssennaya was the only remaining harbor, and it was only held one more day until October 3rd. The remaining troops and materials would be moved over the bridges and landing piers at Il'ich, which were quickly utilized. Also, the west bank of the Kosa Chushka Peninsula provided an embarkation point for the German forces.

On October 1st, the remaining German and Rumanian forces and materials in the Kuban Bridgehead consisted of the following:

    65,000 men
      800 motorcycles
  1,100 passenger vehicles
  2,000 trucks
     600 tracked vehicles
     600 trailers
  5,400 horse drawn vehicles
10,000 horses
     900 artillery pieces of all kinds[27]

Their evacuation was to be completed in eight days if the operation ran according to plan. All divisions were again ordered to abandon everything non-essential in order to save essential space and time. General Konrad and his staff had to prevent a last minute bottleneck at all costs. The success of the entire evacuation depended on the German leadership's ability to out-guess and out-maneuver the attacking Russians. This retreat was therefore subject to last minute alterations whenever observed Russian activity indicated that a position should either be evacuated or held. For this reason the Germans had to specially alert for any changes they could detect in Russian formations. It also meant the careful coordination of German Army, Navy and air support, especially toward the final embarkation period.

The commander of the German Black Sea Fleet during the evacuation was Vice Admiral Gustav Kieseritzky, with headquarters in Simferopol in the Crimea. He was in charge of the Ukraine, Crimea and caucasus Sea Commands. The responsibilities of the German Black Sea Fleet during the evacuation of the Kuban Bridgehead included the following: transport troops and materials from the various harbors on the Taman Peninsula back to Kerch; ferry army engineer troops and materials across the Kerch Strait; protect all escorts and ferrying traffic against Soviet sea and air attacks; protect the flanks of the German Army on the Taman Peninsula against Soviet landing attempts; lead offensive attacks against the Russian rear guard and attack Russian harbors.[28] This list of responsibilities demonstrates that a very significant role was played by the German Navy in the evacuation. It also implied close cooperation with land operations.

In addition to these specific duties, the Black Sea Fleet was responsible for providing sufficient landing craft to ferry German and Rumanian units across the Kerch Strait during the evacuation as soon as they became no longer necessary for the defense of the Kuban Bridgehead. This required the Navy to possess an accurate figure of how much weight they would be required to ferry across the Kerch Strait, and then to have the required number of boats available to handle the task. Delays of any type could be critical, and as a result, the information had to be accurate. The Navy was also charged with the responsibility of assessing weather conditions for various naval operations, and with the repair and salvage of their own craft and their captured Russian vessels. It was a dual responsibility of the Navy and Air Force to coordinate their activities because the Black Sea and Sea of Azov offered no natural protection to ships. Daytime travel required a fighter escort, whereas nocturnal passages presented additional anxiety, since neither the German nor Russian charts indicated the many shallow sand bars. Tricky currents also threw many barges off course, at times dangerously close to Russian sea mines. Anapa remained the most vulnerable port, with its decrepit system of piers that could not withstand the severity of the winds which cut straight across the harbor. Moreover, Anapa had no natural defense. Although several types of naval craft were available to convoy the troops and material across the Kerch Strait, the Navy barges were deemed the most suitable because they were more seaworthy and possessed greater carrying capacity. The speedboats, on the other hand, were fast but had such a small carrying capacity they were relegated primarily to patrol and security functions.[29]

The small harbors of the Taman Peninsula (Anapa, Temryuk, Taman and Ssennaya) were, in the course of the summer, improved by the German Army Engineers. Their capacity in April 1943 of 100 tons per day had been increased by August 1943 to 8,000 tons per day. The responsibility for mining the harbors in the Taman Peninsula after the German forces had been evacuated belonged to the 30th Evacuation Fleet. The German Black Sea Fleet also had the responsibility of clearing Russian sea mines. The German Navy mastered the situation, losing only three Navy barges in all from mines. This relatively low damage rate was the result of the excellent mine-sweeping operations of the 30th Evacuation Fleet.[30]

The German Naval gunfire was coordinated closely with the Army artillery, with the former used primarily near the harbors. Moreover, certain coastal sections which were difficult to defend with ground artillery were also protected by offshore Naval gunfire. Although the role of the German Navy in the Kuban area was subordinate to that of the Army, it is evident that the total success of the evacuation was, in large part, due to the effective defense and transport services provided by the German Navy.

Although the Soviets achieved intermittent air superiority, the Germans received air support from both German and Rumanian Stuka groups. In addition, the German railroad artillery battery located at Kolonka on the Kerch Peninsula was employed during the final phase in front of the "Munich Position." The Russians massed three divisions in front of the narrow position with 40 to 50 tanks. The tanks posed a great potential threat because the flat terrain was particularly suitable for armored warfare. Although the Russians experienced an initial advantage with these tanks, the anti-tank ditches constructed by the Germans in front of the "Munich Position" proved to be an insurmountable obstacle for them. Also, the Soviet thrust came under such effective artillery fire from the German Bridgehead in close collaboration with the railroad battery at Kolonka that the Russians eventually called off the attack. In contrast the Russian artillery support was ineffective because their batteries had to fire from flanking positions, utilizing observers located at a considerable distance on the hills to the west of Achtanisovskaya.[31]

In the early hours of October 8th, the Russian Air Force, utilizing attack bombers accompanied by fighter aircraft, attacked in waves which resulted in momentary air superiority. General Konrad immediately reported this threatening situation to 17th Army Headquarters, emphasizing that the evacuation schedule would be jeopardized if the Russian air superiority continued. 17th Army Headquarters promised that all available fighter aircraft would be sent to the bridgehead. The promise was kept; German and Rumanian Stuka support was coordinated with German artillery later that day. They inflicted severe damage, shooting down twelve Russian planes while the ground anti-aircraft artillery brought down three more planes. General Konrad expressed his personal gratitude to the 1st Air Corps: ". . . for their faithful help in the past weeks which had led to a complete joint success."[32] Helped by this air support, the retreat to the "Breslau Position" was successfully completed by the evening of October 8th, which was followed by Russian artillery fire on the Kerch Peninsula, while the German forces retreated from the "Munich Position" to the "Breslau Position." This effort was so successful that Russian artillery continued firing on the already evacuated "Munich Position" as late as 5:00 a.m. the next morning. On October 8th no embarking operations had been scheduled, insuring that all available shipping would be available for the final evacuation.

On October 8th German Intelligence intercepted a Russian radio message which confirmed an earlier German suspicion that Russian troop morale had suffered greatly in the past few days. The Russian leadership continued to issue harsh and uncompromising commands to advance, which were met, however, with an anemic reception on the part of the Russian infantry. These men had been subjected to tremendous artillery bombardments which had created an atmosphere of exhaustion and depression.[33]

Although the German Air Force commitment was small in relation to the size of the entire evacuation, nevertheless it also played a key role in the Kuban Bridgehead Evacuation. The newly trained Rumanian Stuka Group proved itself under German tactical supervision. Without the able assistance of both air reconnaissance and fighter bomber commitments, the evacuation could not have succeeded. Notably, and fortunately for the German forces, the Russian Air Force did not deploy more of their planes. A German air reconnaissance report on July 10, 1943 indicated that the Russians possessed five to six times more planes than the Germans.[34] However, all airfields on the Taman Peninsula had been completely destroyed by the evacuating Germans, forcing the Russians to use airfields deep in the Caucasus near Krasandor. The presence of the Germans and Rumanian Stuka formations served to neutralize not only the Russian air support, but also the Russian Navy, which remained passive throughout the evacuation, in spite of significant strength in the Caucasian ports of Batumi and Poti.35

The Germans demonstrated ingenuity in the extensive use of smoke-generator units. The commitment of these units proved most effective for the evacuating troops. German losses were minimized as a result of the persistent smoke-screen activity at Kosa Chuschka and Il'ich. The loading and ferrying operations were protected so thoroughly that they were able to maintain a nearly perfect schedule.36

Shortly after dusk on October 9th, all available landing craft were positioned at their designated embarkation points. In spite of the tension which existed for the German command and troops at this decisive final moment, the prevailing attitude was one of calm deliberate activity. The reason for this in part stemmed from the knowledge of all concerned that the coordinated efforts of the Army, Navy and Air Force had been orchestrated down to the last detail. From 5:30 p.m. on, all vehicles and weapons rolled across the piers. Every quarter hour the "Transfer Command East" (Weiterleitungsstab Ost) reported the progress of the loading operations. All vehicles were loaded by 7:15 p.m. The 97th Artillery Division provided cover for the remaining German troops along with the 560th Special Battalion in the "Ulm Position" which formed an arc around the piers at Il'ich. In addition, German heavy artillery on the Kerch Peninsula continued to support the evacuating troops. The departure of the last units occurred without Russian pressure. General Konrad and his staff departed in the last craft arriving on the Kerch Peninsula at 2:00 a.m., October 10, 1943, thereby completing the evacuation of the Kuban Bridgehead.

The landing of the last German forces in Kerch ended a withdrawal movement that had begun on January 5, 1943 in the high Caucasian Mountains, eventually covering over 420 miles. The <u>Battle Report</u> of the XLIX Mountain Corps gave the following reasons for the success of the mission:

> The evacuation of the Kuban Bridgehead has thus succeeded according to plan. The valor of the troops, well prepared positions, superbly organized artillery fire, carefully prepared logistical support, favorable weather and perceptive leadership have resulted in a daily increasing sense of security and calm and in a daily weakened and even more tired enemy as a result of his casualties. The enemy was so demoralized that he could not muster the strength for a last strike although success appeared to be within his grasp. He could not

prevent a single German soldier from leaving the Bridgehead.37

Three German corps had successfully completed the evacuation of the Kuban Bridgehead in spite of 39 Russian divisions employed to prevent the evacuation. The operation indeed was a success, due to the expert leadership of the German officers, ranging from General Jaenecke of the 17th Army and General Konrad of the Mountain Corps down to a Captain Paul Schroeder of the 30th Naval Evacuation Fleet. They were all compelled to remain continually alert in the face of superior enemy forces. The Soviet Command, on the other hand, failed to take advantage of their superiority in the air, sea and on the ground. According to the German military leadership, one of the most important reasons for the German success stemmed from the great difference in morale between the German and Russian troops. Although they were retreating, the German troops felt part of a highly successful team, while the Russian troops were not only harassed by their own officers, but were constantly frustrated in their attempt to prevent the Germans from evacuating. The modern structure of the German Army with its subordination of class prejudice and social barriers, which for instance allowed officers and men to share the same food, contributed to the positive attitude maintained throughout this evacuation. This retreat has been considered by some observers as "an achievement almost without parallel in military history. A chapter in the war marked by gallantry, dedication and readiness for sacrifice on the part of officers and men, and not with weapons only, but equally so with spades along with horses and mules."38

The ferrying of the 17th Army across the Strait of Kerch must indeed be evaluated as a great military maneuver. In the relatively brief span of 34 days, the German Navy transported 227,848 German and Rumanian troops, 28,486 non-German workers, 72,899 horses, 21,230 motorized vehicles, 27,741 horse-drawn vehicles and 1,805 guns.39

The 17th Army together with German Naval and Air Force units continued to keep the Soviet Black Sea forces in check until April 1944. This prevented the Soviets from using the Crimea as a staging base against the Rumanian oil fields. Basically, a small number of German Stukas, from 120 to 160 planes, served as the backbone of the German air support. The fate of Colonel-General Erwin Jaenecke and the 17th Army was determined finally in the Spring of 1944. Hitler dismissed Jaenecke in April 1944 over the latter's demand for "freedom of action" in the defense of Sebastopol and its fortress. In the end, the number of 17th Army troops killed and wounded between April 8 and May 13, 1944 was 57,500. An additional 20,000 remained unaccounted for during an assessment of the evacuation figures. The Russians, on the other hand, tended to view the Crimea as one large POW compound which explains, in part, their lack of initiative in terms of taking a more offensive posture in this theater of World War II.40

NOTES

[1]Albert Seaton, The Russo-German War 1941-45, (New York: Praeger), 1970, 0. 266.

[2]Ewald von Kleist was born on August 8, 1881 in Braunfels. For a biographical sketch, see Wolf Keilig, Das Deutsche Heer, Vol. 3, p. 166 and Deutsche Soldatenkalendar 1974; pp. 51-60.

[3]Alexander Werth, Russia at War, (New York: E. P. Dutton, 1964), p. 564. Hitler did not know that a Soviet counter-offensive had been drawn up in the Fall of 1942 which called for the encirclement of the German Sixth Army in Stalingrad. The second phase of the offensive called for the Soviets to move toward Rostov and Novorossiysk to cut off the Germans in the Caucasus.

[4]Seaton, The Russo-German War, 1941-45, (New York, Praeger, 1970), p. 336.

[5]Julius Braun, Enzian und Edelweiss: Die 4. Gebirgsdivision, 1940-44, (Bad Nauheim: Hans-Henning Pdozun), 1955, p. 658.

[6]Albert Seaton, The Russo-German War, 1941-45, p. 379.

[7]Erwin Jaenecke was born on April 22, 1890 in Freren, see Keilig, Vol. III, p. 150. Rudolf Konrad was born on March 7, 1891, see ibid.

[8]17 AOK Führungsabteilung, Anlage 2C KTB Nr. 7, Sonderband Krimhild, Oberkommando der Heeresgruppe A., Friedrich Forstmeier, Die Räumung des Kuban-Brückenkopfes im Herbst 1943. Darmstadt: Wehr und Wissen Verlagsgesellschaft mbH, 1964.

[9]Karl Allmendinger, infantry officer, general staff corps, was born on February 3, 1891 in Abtsgemünd, see Keilig, VOl. III, p. 4. Rudolf Konrad was born on March 7, 1891, see ibid., p. 150.

[10]Stephanie Van D'Elden, "A Retreat Can Be Victorious," an unpublished research paper on an after-action report of the XLIX Mountain Corps obtained by Van D'Elden's husband, Major Karl Van D'Elden, during World War II. Hereafter the report will be referred to as the XLIX Mountain Corps Battle Report.

[11]Rudolf Konrad, "The Kuban Bridgehead Operations of XLIX mountain Corps (1943)" (Microfilm D-364), p. 10. General Konrad was the Commanding General of the XLIX Mountain Corps.

[12]Alexander Werth, Russia at War, p. 564.

[13]Alan Clark, Barbarossa: The Russian-German Conflict, 1941-45, (New York: William Morrow and Co., 1965), p. 281.

[14] V Army Corps, After-Action Report, July 1943, German Field Commands (Microfilm Series 311, Roll 729).

[15] Ibid.

[16] Erwin Jaenecke, "Die Räumung des Kuban-Brücken-Kopfes," Deutsche Soldatenkalendar, 6. Jahrbuch (München: Lochausen, 1958), pp. 96-100.

[17] 17 AOK, KTB Nr. 7. Beilage 1, Anlage II. Tagesmeldungen vom 10-16.9.1943. Forstmeier, p. 48. The Russians had indeed occupied Novorossiysk, but the cost in men and material was high. The 17th Army reported the Russian casualties and material losses at 2,726 counted dead, 1,318 prisoners, 102 deserters, 177 tanks destroyed, 54 rendered immovable, 24 landing boats sunk. German losses were also serious: 492 dead, 86 missing, 2,232 wounded and 274 seriously ill. In addition to these losses, the V Army Corps morning reports indicated a high number of men lost because of malaria.

[18] Tagesmeldung (September 17, 1943), (Microfilm T-730).

[19] Forstmeier, Friedrich. Die Räumung des Kuban-Brückenkopfes im Herbst 1943. Darmstadt: Wehr und Wissen Verlagsgesellschaft mbH, 1964. p. 57.

[20] V Army Corps, After-Action Report.

[21] Forstmeier, p. 52.

[22] 17 AOK, Tagesmeldung (September 25, 1943) (Microfilm T-730).

[23] Ibid., p. 59.

[24] XLIX Mountain Corps Battle Report.

[25] Konrad, p. 34. As each successive position was occupied, a corresponding reduction in the total number of German defense forces was made possible. The evacuation plan was organized in the following manner:

1. Small Gothic Position	6 divisions
2. Vienna-Bucharest-Golubinskaya Position	3 1/2 divisions
3. Berlin Advanced Position	2 1/2 divisions
4. Berlin Position	2 divisions
5. Munich Position	1 1/2 divisions
6. Breslau Position	1 1/2 divisions
7. Ulm Position	1/2 division

[26] These losses included the following: 4 officers, 11 non-commissioned officers, 45 troops dead; 9 officers, 49 noncommissioned officers, 176 troops wounded; 5 non-commissioned officers, 37 troops missing. XLIX Mountain Corps Battle Report. Van D'Elden, p. 46. Also, the landing attempt by the Russians on September 25th illustrated this same strategy.

[27] XLIX Mountain Corps Battle Report. Van D'Elden, p. 52.

[28] Forstmeier, p. 85.

[29] Ibid., p. 90.

[30] Ibid.

[31] Ibid., p. 92.

[32] XLIX Mountain Corps Battle Report. Van D'Elden, p. 74.

[33] Forstmeier, p. 30.

[34] Ibid., p. 141.

[35] Paul Carell, Scorched Earth, The Russian-German War, 1943-44 (Boston: Keith Brown, 1966), p. 455.

[36] XLIX Mountain Corps Battle Report. Van D'Elden, p. 72.

[37] XLIX Mountain Corps Battle Report. Van D'Elden, p. 75.

[38] Carell, Scorched Earth, p. 145.

[39] XLIX Mountain Corps, Morgenmeldung (October 9, 1943). Forstmeier, p. 211.

[40] Carell, Scorched Earth, p. 477.

PREPARING TEENAGERS IN HITLER'S GERMANY FOR WAR:
THE TRAINING OF THE 12th SS
PANZER DIVISION "HITLER YOUTH"

by CRAIG W. H. LUTHER

The decision to establish an elite military formation composed almost exclusively of youngsters from the Hitler Youth emerged from the context of crisis that confronted Nazi Germany by the beginning of 1943. Following the twin disasters of Stalingrad and El Alamein, and the Anglo-American demand for Germany's unconditional surrender issued at Casablanca on January 24, 1943, the Reich, under the able direction of Albert Speer, began to mobilize for total war. Anxious to make a special contribution to the expanding war effort, representatives of the Hitler Youth and Heinrich Himmler's SS gathered at Hitler Youth headquarters in Berlin on February 16, 1943, for a planning conference. Among those present were Artur Axmann, the leader of Germany's youth, and SS-Gruppenführer[1] Gottlob Berger, the Chief of the Waffen-SS[2] Recruiting Office. The conferees agreed to accept 17-year-old volunteers (class of 1926) from the Hitler Youth for the creation of a new Waffen-SS division. These boys, they reasoned, would provide a living symbol of the commitment of German youth to the Reich's total war effort.[3]

Recruitment of the Hitler Youth Division commenced at once, and by early summer 1943, the first boys were arriving at the Beverloo troop training grounds northwest of Brussels, Belgium, to begin basic training. Because of the youthfulness of the recruits, those in charge largely dispensed with conventional military drill, concentrating instead on an innovative training program calculated to familiarize the youths with actual combat conditions. The formation of the divisional officer corps posed a particular challenge, for the rapid expansion of the Waffen-SS, coupled with limited training facilities and heavy losses at the front, had created a serious shortage of SS officers and non-commissioned officers. The division, however, did receive a nucleus of experienced officers, NCO's and technical specialists from the elite SS Leibstandarte Panzer Grenadier Division; veterans of the eastern front, they would impart spirit and substance into the new formation--initially designated the 12th SS Panzer Grenadier Division "Hitler Youth"--shaping its identity as a combat unit.

With its extreme youthfulness, the Hitler Youth Division represented one of the more unusual combat units established in Nazi Germany during the Second World War. The following narrative, gleaned in part from interviews with former division members, offers a detailed account of the division's training--of an effort to transform teenagers into soldiers in the Third Reich--and of its preparations to play a major role in the defense of Hitler's fortress Europe against the expected Anglo-American invasion.

* * *

The problem of fleshing out the divisional officer corps would persist throughout the entire training period. Most urgent was the need for additional company, platoon and squad leaders. To serve as squad leaders, a number of youths who had performed well in the pre-military instruction camps staffed by the Waffen-SS received training at the SS NCO school at Lauenburg. Several weeks after the start of basic training, other recruits who had demonstrated the requisite aptitude participated in special NCO courses within the division itself. The outcome of this approach was certainly unique, for the divisional non-commissioned officers, were, in part, the same age or barely a year older than the boys they would lead into combat.

To fill vacant company commands, the division had no alternative but to turn to young platoon leaders, and, under the guidance of Knight's Cross holder Hauptsturmführer Wilhelm Beck, the division organized a special officer training course. The shortage of technical specialists caused particular concern, especially following the commencement of unit training early in 1944.[4] Several "raids" at the Army Personnel Bureau in Cottbus, however, managed to secure the transfer of some 50 Wehrmacht officers, most apparently with a technical background, to the Hitler Youth Division.[5] Yet despite these efforts, the division would enter combat in June 1944 with a shortage of 144 officers and 2,192 NCO's--given an authorized strength of 664 and 4,575, respectively.[6] The 48 percent shortfall in NCO's was particularly crippling, and for a formation lacking the peculiar motivation and thorough training of the Hitler Youth Division might have had disastrous consequences. Conversely, the paucity of small unit commanders was bound to undermine efforts to hone the division into a professional fighting force, and to adversely affect its performance in battle.

Despite such obstacles, by the end of July 1943, most of the top officers--the regimental and battalion commanders--had been assigned. The great majority were quite young--in their late twenties or early thirties; the company and platoon commanders were younger still--mostly in their early twenties.[7] The rank and file recruits, moreover, and a portion of the NCO's, were barely 17 years of age at the start of the training period.

The Hitler Youth Division was indeed a youth division--a fact that not only discomfited the Reich Youth Leader, Artur Axmann, but

Propaganda Minister Dr. Joseph Goebbels as well. Goebbels feared that Allied propaganda might interpret a division made up of teenagers as a sign of desperation. His fear did not lack substance, for Allied propaganda broadcasts and leaflets did refer sarcastically to the "Baby Division," with a "milk bottle" as its symbol![8] Hitler's attitude was quite different, and at his mid-day military conference on July 26, 1943, he lectured Himmler on the utility of military formations consisting of young boys. Referring to the youthful recruits in the Hermann Göring Panzer Grenadier Division, Hitler exclaimed:[9]

> The youngsters from the Hitler Youth fight fanatically . . . young German lads, some only sixteen. Most of these Hitler youths fight more fanatically than their older comrades . . . The enemy reports that they only got hold of them after every man had fallen . . . The Hitler Youth Division will fight the same way, like the rest of youth. They are already uniformly aligned. The enemy will be utterly amazed.

By August 1943 the first 10,000 recruits had arrived at the Beverloo training grounds.[10] Basic training commenced immediately, and, with the gradual arrival of additional recruits, the division was almost full strength by the end of September. The organization of divisional sub-units also began at once--a process largely completed by mid-September. Most of the sub-units were quartered and trained at various locations east and southeast of Antwerp. The division's two Panzer grenadier (motorized infantry) regiments, for example, underwent basic training at Beverloo. The artillery regiment also occupied quarters near the Beverloo training camp, in the area of Mol. The reconnaissance, signals and medical units were situated in Turnhout; the divisional headquarters located just outside the city. The armored regiment, however, was assigned the former French tank training grounds at Mailly-le-Camp, some 20 miles south of Chalons-sur-Marne and roughly 150 miles from divisional headquarters.[11]

The decision to organize the division as a Panzer grenadier formation had come as a surprise to the divisional command, which seized the occasion of a visit by the Inspector General of Panzer Troops, General Heinz Guderian, to request reorganization as a full-fledged tank unit. The request brought swift results, for on October 21, 1943, Hitler ordered that the division, along with the formations of the I and II SS Panzer Corps in general, be reorganized into Panzer divisions. A corresponding directive from the Waffen-SS operational headquarters followed on the 30th.[12]

One problem the 12th SS Panzer Division "Hitler Youth," as it was now officially designated, could do little about was its subordination to an unduly complex chain of command. As an SS division, it looked to the Waffen-SS operational headquarters in Berlin on matters concerning personnel and equipment. For training purposes the division was subordinated to General Freiherr Leo Geyr von Schweppenburg's Panzer Group West--a training staff with no operational responsibilities. Operationally, it came under the control of the I SS Panzer Corps, itself in the process of organization, and the 15th Army.[13] Commanded by General Hans von Salmuth, the 15th Army defended a critical stretch of the Atlantic coastline from Antwerp to the Orne. Finally, German ground forces in the western theatre, from the Zuider Zee in Holland to the French Mediterranean coast, came under the supreme command of Field Marshal Gerd von Rundstedt, the Commander-in-Chief West (Oberbefehlshaber West, or OB West). With the arrival of Field Marshal Erwin Rommel and his Army Group B staff in the fall of 1943, the German command structure in the West would grow even more complex, generating fundamental disagreements over strategic policy and undermining efforts to devise a uniform plan for the defense of the Atlantic coastline.

The commencement of basic training, however, confronted the Hitler Youth Division and its 35-year-old commander, Oberführer Fritz Witt,[14] with more immediate concerns. Because few of the distinctive SS camouflage uniforms were immediately available, most of the boys began training in their civilian clothes or in Hitler Youth uniforms. Army and Luftwaffe personnel transferred to the division also served initially in their old uniforms. A more serious obstacle was the shortage of heavy weapons and armored fighting vehicles. The artillery regiment boasted but a few field howitzers; the armored regiment just four Panzer IV and two outmoded Panzer III tanks filched from the Leibstandarte. Damaged in Russia, the tanks had gone first to the Allkett tank factory in Berlin for repairs, then to the Hitler Youth Division. By the end of November, the regiment would have an additional ten Panzer IV's available for training purposes. Ammunition of all types and gasoline were also in short supply; trucks, personnel carriers and motorcycles practically non-existent. Eventually, the division would be outfitted with a colorful assortment of captured Italian vehicles, but these would not arrive until December 1943-January 1944; once pressed into service, the Italian trucks and half-tracks broke down repeatedly.[15] Hence, after a corps-size communications exercise near Dieppe had demonstrated the complete unreliability of these vehicles, the divisional command requested their replacement with more efficient German models--a conversion only partially completed by early June 1944.[16] The paucity of training personnel, especially for instruction in heavy weapons use, posed an additional problem. Another concern was the physical immaturity of many of the young recruits, which rendered tasks such as lifting or moving heavy equipment particularly burdensome.

Clearly, the goal of transforming teenagers into an efficient fighting force posed a formidable challenge--one that would require patience, understanding and an innovative approach. Most of the boys had fathers, or older brothers, serving in the Wehrmacht or the Waffen-SS, many of whom had been killed or wounded. With fathers at the front, the task of bringing up the youngsters had been left largely to their mothers and the Hitler Youth. The destruction wrought by the carpet bombing of

German cities had caused additional hardship for many. Sensitive to the special wartime conditions under which these boys had grown up, Witt required unit leaders to assume a fatherly responsibility for their young charges, and to help fill the gaps in their education. Many officers and NCO's, in fact, took a special interest in the boys, providing support in family matters, assisting with official business such as letters to authorities, and even comforting them when homesickness struck. In one case, a young recruit overcome by homesickness simply ran away, only to be nabbed by the military police on his way home to Germany and returned to the division. Desertion, of course, was a serious offense, yet the youth's regimental commander simply boxed the youngster's ears and returned him to his company.[17] Divisional policy in general promoted an unusually close relationship between unit leaders and enlisted men. The result of such a bonding process would be poignantly evident during the Normandy campaign, when many young soldiers would risk their lives to retrieve the bodies of fallen leaders.

As much as possible, the youngsters' parents were included in the educational process, and the ties to the Reich Youth Leader carefully maintained.[18] Discipline was strict--the youths forbidden to drink, smoke or patronize the local brothels. Any relationship with girls, in fact, was prohibited for those under 18.[19] The boys received sweets instead. To promote physical development, they also received special rations, thanks to an agreement between the German High command (Oberkommando der Wehrmacht, or OKW) and Oswald Pohl, the Chief of the SS Economic and Administrative Main Office. The weekly ration, which, according to Pohl, was considerably more substantial than that allotted to workers in heavy industry, consisted of:[20]

> 3.5 liters of fresh milk
> 1,750 grams of bread
> 200 grams of meat
> 140 grams of lard
> 120 grams of sugar
> 245 grams of other nutrients

The discipline of the boys was generally good, though youthful exuberance and immaturity did cause occasional problems. Some serious incidents occurred when recruits "used weapons to even scores in personal disputes. One such incident sent a young soldier to the hospital, but his adversary was excused on grounds of immaturity--of engaging in 'child's play.'"[21] A more common breach of discipline was theft, which appears to have occurred with alarming frequency. The boys stole from civilians and fellow soldiers alike, finding valuables in letters and packages a particular enticement, and forcing Witt to order close surveillance of the mails.

Despite repeated warnings by Witt, some lower echelon officers and NCO's evinced little sensitivity for the youthfulness of their recruits, and persisted in practicing bizarre punishments for minor disciplinary infractions--punishments that included electrifying door handles, shaving heads and forcing the boys to clean their weapons between one and three in the morning. Less than two months before the Allied invasion of western Europe, on April 12, 1944, Witt complained in a special directive that "many unit leaders still do not seem to grasp . . . that their principal duty is to shape our young soldiers into straight and decent [gerade und anständig] SS men." He ordered platoon and squad leaders to live in the same rooms with their troops to demonstrate concern for the welfare of the youths.[22]

Actual military training witnessed a number of innovations designed to exploit the natural enthusiasm of the seventeen year olds. Training personnel limited formal military drill to the essentials, and excluded entirely from the training program such traditional methods as weapons practice on the firing range and marches with heavy packs. As the Waffen-SS did in general, the division placed great emphasis upon sports to harden the youths physically. To familiarize them with actual battlefield conditions, most training took place in the field, often with live ammunition. Even instruction in weapons use was conducted in the field under realistic battle conditions.[23] In one exercise, the heavy machine guns fired over the heads of the advancing infantry while the 81mm mortars lobbed their shells barely 50-100 yards in front of them.[24] Although such activities prepared the recruits for the rigors of combat, they also resulted in occasional mishaps; by the beginning of April 1944, the division had suffered 15 dead--most, no doubt, through training accidents.[25]

On the suggestion of General Geyr von Schweppenburg, the division also emphasized close combat training and the proper use of camouflage. Most of the training personnel had learned the art of camouflage from their Russian opponents, and now passed on their knowledge and experience to the young recruits. Gradually, the boys became masters of camouflage, capable of "reading" terrain, taking advantage of the natural cover it provided, and concealing helmets, vehicles and weapons with branches, leaves or straw.[26] The recruits of the two Panzer grenadier regiments devoted particular attention to reconnaissance, night fighting and flexible shifting from attack to defense. Training personnel also stressed the critical importance of proper radio discipline, and the division boasted a special radio monitoring unit for intercepting enemy communications; it would perform valuable service during the Normandy campaign.

To toughen the recruits mentally, build confidence and enhance knowledge of weapons and equipment, the division occasionally resorted to curious procedures. The commander of one infantry battalion devised a special exercise that required his soldiers--fully equipped with weapons and accoutrements--to leap into a sand pit 30 feet deep. Through such an activity the boys learned never to hesitate to do what was necessary in a combat situation. One recruit recalled how his instructor, to demonstrate the explosive effect of a hand grenade, detonated the weapon atop his head, on his helmet. The instructor was not hurt, for the grenade splinters travelled laterally and upwards. In another exercise, the youths disassembled and rebuilt their machine guns with their eyes bound, or in the dark.[27] The young soldiers were fascinated by their weapons and vehicles and handled them with the special care and enthusiasm not unlike a present-day teenager caring for his first automobile.

The organization and training of the division's tank regiment commenced at the end of July 1943. Upon arrival in Mailly-le-Camp, the prospective tankmen joined the special training companies established for tank commanders, gunners, loaders, drivers and radio operators, respectively.[28] The majority of tank commanders were from the class of 1925, and had successfully completed their college entrance examinations, or <u>Abitur</u>. Like the infantry recruits, the Panzer trainees received little formal military drill, concentrating instead on weapons and combat training in the field. The shortage of tanks and gasoline disrupted and slowed the training process, and the few available tanks often had to be distributed to the individual companies for only a few hours at a time. Thanks to the personal initiative of Obersturmbannführer Max Wünsche,[29] the regiment commander, the tank crews did have the opportunity to work 8-14 days in tank production at an armament plant in Nürnberg; others took part in gunnery and anti-aircraft training courses, or received instruction in driver training at the Waffen-SS technical training institute in Vienna.[30]

Despite the rigorous schedule, the young tankmen took advantage of their stay in France to visit local sites of historical interest. Not far from Mailly-le-Camp were the Verdun battlefields, where, 27 years before, their fathers' generation had fought its most desperate struggle. Duly impressed, the youths toured the battered forts and the still thoroughly cratered landscape on the outskirts of the city. A happier excursion took them to Rheims, one of France's cultural treasures with its historic buildings and inspiring Gothic cathedral.

Though the boys had undergone eight years of incessant ideological schooling in the Hitler Youth, and four additional weeks of intensive indoctrination in the pre-military instruction camps, Witt still considered weekly sessions in ideological training a necessity within the division as well. He found two principal reasons for this--the German collapse in 1918 and the struggle against Bolshevism. Every soldier, he felt, had to realize what Germany was fighting for, and it was the responsibility of officers and NCO's alike to make sure that the weekly ideological theme was hammered home. These themes included "Germany's demand for living space," and "the enemies of Germany are the enemies of Europe"--National Socialist platitudes no doubt familiar to the boys from the age of ten, when they had first entered the Hitler Youth. The indoctrination sessions also included lectures in which the youngsters were reminded of the destruction wrought by the Anglo-American bomber offensive against Germany. From their quarters in Belgium, in fact, the boys could often hear the drone of the Allied bomber fleets high overhead as they approached the cities and factories of the Reich. The purpose behind such indoctrination was "to make every man of the division a convinced carrier of our ideology, i.e., that every last man of the division understands what he is fighting for, and to transform the Hitler youth into an SS man, who lives according to the fundamentals of the SS as a fanatic warrior."[31]

Despite the shortages in training personnel, equipment and supplies, by January 1, 1944, the division had made substantial progress in its training efforts. It now had 40 Panzer IV tanks at its disposal and more on the way, for on November 3, 1943, Hitler had ordered that all armored divisions in the West be equipped at once with 93 Panzer IV's.[32] By the beginning of 1944, moreover, most of the 12th SS Panzer Division's artillery, anti-tank guns and machine guns had also become available; trucks, motorcycles and armored personnel carriers had arrived in significant numbers. The division had conducted training exercises on the squad, platoon, company and battery level, and, though far from fully operational, some of its elements were now ready for tasks of a minor nature--such as providing security or cover (Sicherungsaufgaben).[33]

As basic training neared completion, unit training (Verbandsausbildung) commenced, and was well underway by early February 1944.[34] Because coordinated unit exercises demanded the presence of the Panzer regiment, it moved in mid-January from Mailly-le-Camp to Beverloo. The potential vulnerability of a large troop training ground to attack from the air, however, quickly compelled Witt to shift the regiment into the area around Hasselt, a short distance from Beverloo.[35] The regiment had now received most of its Panzer IV tanks, but only eight of the newer and heavier Panther models that would equip one of its two tank battalions.[36] The Panther battalion's 3rd Panzer Company, quartered in the village of Winterslag, was one of the units that waited impatiently for its armored fighting vehicles; while it waited, training continued--on foot. The endless marches through the Belgian countryside, one recruit remembered, became even more distasteful after the company commander,

> invented his famous flag and signal system. This signal system would be used in an emergency, when no contact by radio was possible. To master such a system in combat, however, demanded intensive training--a procedure roughly as follows: The company marched from its billets into the countryside. Once there, the recruits were divided into tank crews, and the crews widely separated. They then began to advance on foot. While the company or individual platoons moved forward in accordance with the given signal, our commander followed the spectacle from his command car atop a small rise. First platoon forward, third platoon forward . . . . and so it went kilometer after kilometer through the knee-

high brush, and we wondered repeatedly what it was all for . . . . Now though the signal system included signs for halt and reverse, these commands had not yet been practiced, and after hours of marching one crew suddenly became mischievous. Arriving at a [small] stream it signalled, 'Company halt, swamp!' That went like a sigh of relief through the widely separated tank crews, and we immediately took cover, which, considering the high brush, was hardly difficult. Our commander had already motored on to the next small hill and was unaware of our action. After a short wait, he came roaring up in his command car to find the company. It took some time, however, until he tracked down the first crew. His ensuing rage still rings in our ears . . . [but] all our commander's efforts to determine who had given the, in his opinion, 'idiotic halt order' were unsuccessful. With some satisfaction the company renewed its advance.[37]

On February 6, 1944, elements of the Panzer regiment conducted a training exercise attended by Guderian, Geyr, and the commander of the I SS Panzer Corps, Sepp Dietrich. The tankmen won high praise, which led to the accelerated outfitting of the division with Panther tanks.[38]

For the 3rd Panzer Company the arrival of its first Panthers later that month proved something of an event. One young loader, perhaps overwhelmed by the prospect of his first exercise with live ammunition, absent-mindedly slammed an armor piercing round into the breech of the cannon, despite an order to load with a high explosive shell. To his horror the lad soon discovered that an armor piercing round had a greater muzzle velocity; it sailed over the target, located on a small forward slope, and crashed into the field beyond, where other companies were busy with their own training exercises. Happily, the only injury was to the young man's pride, and after a thorough "dressing down," his punishment consisted of dragging a heavy hatch cover from the training ground all the way back to his quarters.[39]

In March, the division conducted another major training exercise, this time with infantry and several tank companies. The Commander-in-Chief West, Rundstedt, observed the exercise, and once again the division won recognition for its high state of preparedness. Pleased with the progress of his command, Witt declared on March 16, 1944, that the "training situation happily is a good one. Our Hitler Youth boys during these eight months have been transformed into young men who know the military craft." To celebrate this "miraculous transformation," he ordered the replacement of candy rations with cigarettes and tobacco.[40]

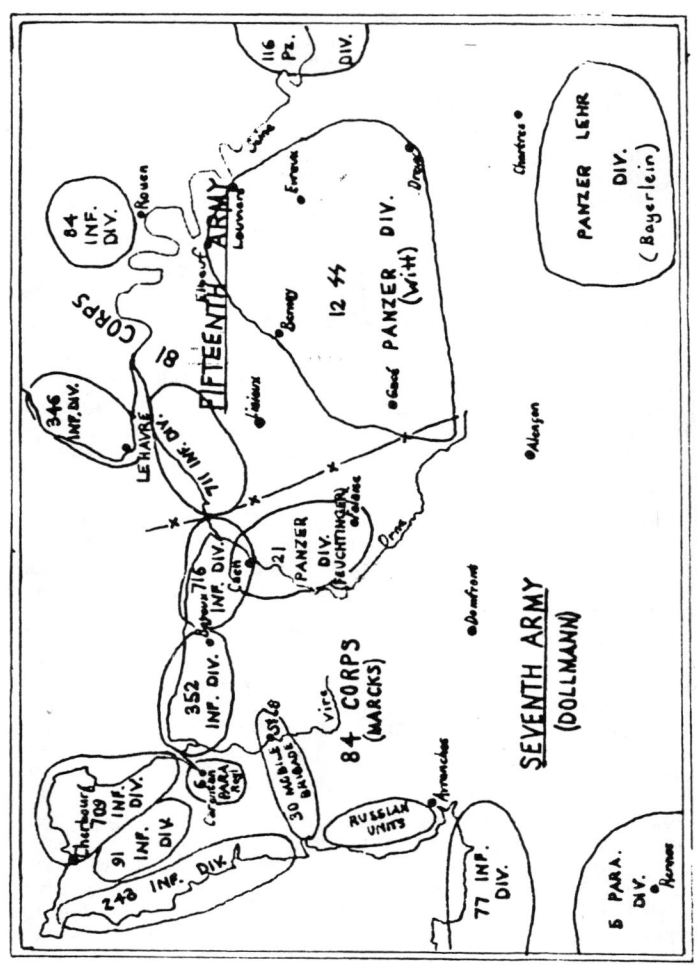

NORMANDY
GERMAN DISPOSITIONS--JUNE 6, 1944

By early April the I SS Panzer Corps considered the 12th SS Panzer Division ready for action. Problems persisted, however, as the division noted in its monthly status report. Fuel for training purposes remained in short supply. The Panzer regiment suffered from a shortage of armored command vehicles, and had yet to acquire the majority of its Panther tanks; the artillery regiment's 1st Battalion still lacked its armored observation vehicles. In addition, some sub-units were not yet fully motorized, and the division was still in the process of exchanging its Italian vehicles for German ones.[41] Despite such concerns, the division remained confident that it would be fully prepared in time to meet the expected enemy invasion of western Europe.

The beginning of spring 1944 brought the transfer of the 12th SS Panzer Division from Belgium to France. The encirclement of General Hans Hube's 1st Panzer Army by Russian forces in the Ukraine in late March had led to the OKW decision to dispatch the II SS Panzer Corps (9th and 10th SS Panzer Divisions) to the rescue.[42] As a result, the 12th SS Panzer received instructions to move into the area vacated by the 10th SS between the lower reaches of the Seine and the Orne around Lisieux. This decision came as an unwelcome surprise to Fritz Witt and his staff, for it would place the 12th SS directly behind the Normandy coast, where, in the event of an Allied invasion, the division would immediately face the full weight of enemy air and naval power. Witt's chief operations officer, Sturmbannführer Hubert Meyer,[43] immediately notified Panzer Group West of the planned move, about which the staff had no prior knowledge. The next day, after conferring with OB West, Geyr assigned the division a sector farther back from the coastline, in the area south and southwest of Rouen.[44]

On April 1, 1944, the trains transporting men and equipment began to roll southwest towards Normandy--a process that would take some two weeks to complete and require about 90 trains in all. The division's new quarters encompassed a rather large area, stretching from Elbeuf, near the Seine, all the way to Sees, south of Argentan, and from there to Dreux, located west of Paris. The Panzer regiment settled near the Seine crossings in the area Elbeuf-le Neubourg-Louviers, from where it could rapidly intervene against an enemy landing either north or south of the river. For the same purpose, the division's engineer battalion was also situated near the Seine, astride the Eure from Pacy to Autheuil.[45] The special task of the engineers was to keep the crossings open for the tank regiment. The artillery regiment's sector was south of Evreux, at Damville; the reconnaissance battalion assigned the sector around Rugles. Commanded by Obersturmbannführer Wilhelm Mohnke,[46] the 26th SS Panzer Grenadier Regiment was positioned south of the tank regiment, around Houdan, while the division's other motorized infantry regiment, the 25th SS Panzer Grenadier Regiment, commanded by Standartenführer Kurt Meyer,[47] took up quarters in the western sector of the divisional area: Bernay-Orbec-Vimoutiers-Sees. From these positions, Meyer's infantry could move rapidly in a westwardly direction toward Caen and Falaise. Finally, the Flak battalion was ensconced near Dreux to provide anti-aircraft cover for the local airfield; the divisional headquarters was established at Acon, roughly in the middle of the divisional sector.[48]

The transfer to Normandy proceeded smoothly, with the exception of an incident involving the French underground and the division's reconnaissance battalion. Elements of the battalion had entrained and begun to move south from Turnhout on the evening of April 1. Following some ten minutes behind the Anvers-Paris express, they crossed the Franco-Belgian frontier at Baisieux, arriving in Ascq (near Lille) at exactly 10:45 p.m. A few hundred yards from the Ascq train station, and in the path of the convoy, an explosion shook the tracks, causing the derailment of two flat cars and the disruption of some cargo and equipment. But damage was negligible, and despite hostile small arms fire, the battalion incurred no casualties.

The commander of the troop transport, Obersturmführer Walter Hauck, immediately ordered the town searched for weapons and the seizure of the entire male population between the ages of 17 and 50. A thorough search of the streets and houses netted several groups of 20 to 30 suspects, who were led in swift succession to the station and lined up along the railway track near the damaged train. Up to this point, Hauck had apparently acted in accordance with a strict new set of guidelines issued by OB West on February 3, 1944, to combat French underground attacks against German military personnel and installations. Such attacks had increased alarmingly in recent months; in Ascq alone the Resistance had recently conducted two similar attempts to sabotage German rail traffic, forcing the local German military authorities to dispatch a guard unit there to provide additional protection--a move, no doubt, that failed to have the desired deterrent effect.

The tragic conclusion to "l'Affaire d'Ascq" is difficult to reconstruct. According to French trial records, Hauck, in extreme agitation, ordered the groups of suspects to be shot in the roadbed beside the railway cars --a task allegedly carried out at once. A fourth group was only spared a similar fate through the intervention of the German Feldgendarmerie (military police), who, alerted by the frantic telephone calls of a French railway employee, arrived from Lille to put an end to the killings. German sources insist that the roundup of suspects was conducted in a proper soldierly fashion, and that only after several men had attempted to escape had the Germans opened fire. In the ensuing confusion at least 77 men lost their lives--all Frenchmen. The search of the town, moreover, had uncovered large quantities of weapons, explosives and radio equipment. A subsequent investigation by the Germans led to the capture of a number of participants in the sabotage actions in Ascq; following a military trial, seven of them were condemned to death on June 16, 1944. While in Normandy, and even during the fighting there, the 12th SS Division would experience no further problems with the French Resistance; on the contrary, relations with the local population were often cordial in nature.[49]

While the division settled into its new quarters, Fritz Witt and his chief operations officer contacted local forces and their commanders in an effort to acquire a picture of the state of German preparedness in Normandy. They drove first to St. Lô, where they conferred with the commander of the LXXXIV Army Corps, General Erich Marcks. Marcks was pessimistic, for his corps was weak in strength but responsible for the defense of the Normandy coastline from the Orne to the base of the Cotentin Peninsula at Avrances. The Anglo-American invasion, he insisted, would come in June, perhaps between the Orne and the Vire and on the east coast of the Cotentin Peninsula; yet he doubted the ability of his own meager forces to turn back the invaders.

Deeply concerned, Witt and Hubert Meyer decided to inspect for themselves the vital sector of the Normandy coastline from Bayeux to the Seine--an undertaking that only confirmed the initial briefing by General Marcks. The inadequate strength and depth of the coastal defenses convinced both Witt and his chief of operations that an enemy landing in Normandy could not be prevented, and that a successful outcome of the battle would hinge in large measure upon the timely commitment of the Panzer divisions at the invasion front.[50]

The 12th SS, to provide for its commitment along the French coastline from the Somme to the area west of Caen, received instructions from Panzer Group West to prepare three different approach routes. Approach route "A" foresaw a commitment of the division between the Somme and the Seine; "B" its deployment between the Seine and the Orne; and, "C" an advance to the coast west and northwest of Caen. Later, Geyr also ordered the division to prepare an approach march for a deployment farther west--at the mouth of the Loire. The staff of the 12th SS prepared the various contingencies in great detail, dividing the divisional elements into march columns that represented fully operational battlegroups. To enable each battlegroup to move at a uniform pace, the wheeled vehicles were separated from the tracked vehicles, and the latter assigned to a separate marching column. As a precaution against attack from the air, all vehicles were to maintain 100 meter intervals during the approach march; to prevent the division from becoming too strung out, each approach route comprised four major thoroughfares--three for the wheeled and one for the tracked vehicles. Once completed, the plans were distributed in sealed envelopes to all regiments and independent battalions, and copies provided for Panzer Group West.[51]

As the warm spring days of April and May followed in swift succession, the division completed its final preparations. Although shortages of gasoline persisted, unit training progressed at a vigorous pace. To avoid attack from the Allied fighters and fighter-bombers that now roamed the skies over Normandy, most training was conducted at night, the boys sleeping during the day.[52] As an added precaution, all vehicles, including the tanks, were dug in and carefully camouflaged. With the threat of invasion growing ever more imminent, the division conducted frequent alarm exercises, as well as maneuvers calculated to meet the challenge of an enemy airborne assault. To combat an airborne attack, all sub-units provided for the all-around defense of their respective quarters. In mid-May, Witt transferred his Flak battalion into the area around Louviers, where it assumed the air defense of the local Seine bridges; although the destruction of the bridges could not be prevented, the battalion's 88mm guns sent four or five heavy bombers tumbling out of the sky in the remaining weeks before the invasion.[53]

By May 1944, the great majority of the division's heavy weapons and vehicles had arrived, and, in field maneuvers attended by the Inspector General of Panzer Troops, Heinz Guderian, the 12th SS Panzer Division demonstrated that, after nine months of determined preparation, it was reaching a state of complete operational readiness. In the first days of June the final Panther tanks arrived and their crews worked feverishly to ready them for combat. Thus, the division had reached a strength that included some 20,500 men, 177 tanks, 52 pieces of artillery, more than 1600 machine guns and over 300 armored personnel carriers and scout vehicles.[54] Clearly, it represented one of the better equipped and more thoroughly trained German formations of the Second World War.

The months of training, against the backdrop of a military situation that had grown progressively more critical for Germany, had transformed the 17- and 18-year- olds of the 12th SS into a professional fighting force of unusual quality and élan. The youngsters were convinced that Germany's fate would be determined by the outcome of the invasion battle, and they waited impatiently for the opportunity to prove themselves at the front. Already the front had drawn perceptibly closer, for daily the enemy bombers passed overhead on their way to smash the bridges across the Seine or the rail installations around Paris upon which the resupply or reinforcement of Rundstedt's divisions in Normandy depended. Letters from home often brought news of family members killed or wounded by the saturation bombing of German cities, or killed at the front. One young soldier lost his mother in a bombing attack on Berlin; two months later, his parents' home was struck again and his father reported missing.

On the night of June 4-5, the division shifted elements of its Panzer regiment into the cantonment areas of the 25th and 26th SS Panzer Grenadier Regiments. A new issue of gasoline had just arrived, prompting Witt to order joint exercises of armor and infantry--an activity that the insufficient stocks of gasoline had hitherto sorely limited. The exercises were necessary, and with poor weather predicted for the English Channel, the likelihood of an imminent enemy descent appeared remote. Field Marshal Rommel himself, assured by the reports of his chief meteorologist in Paris, had left his headquarters at La Roche-Guyon on June 4 to meet with Hitler at the Obersalzberg. Such optimism, however, had no basis in fact, for by the evening of June 5, 1944, an immense armada of 6,483 ships--including six battleships, 23 cruisers and 104 destroyers--was approaching the Normandy coastline. All day long the wind-swept, surging sea had carried the invasion fleet towards its destination--a movement undetected by the Germans, whose coastal radar stations had been put out of action by the Allied air force, and reconnaissance aircraft long swept from the skies.

Following the Allied landings in Normandy on June 6, advance elements of the 12th SS Panzer Division "Hitler Youth" began to reach the invasion front on the morning of June 7. For the next month, the youngsters of the division tenaciously anchored the eastern sector of the German front. Deployed in the diminutive Norman villages and verdant countryside north and northwest of Caen, they thwarted all enemy attempts to capture the city until July 9, 1944. A major strategic prize, the Allies had hoped to capture Caen in the initial days of the campaign. Indeed, the historian Chester Wilmot wrote that, during the struggle for Caen in late June, the 12th SS "fought with a tenacity and a ferocity seldom equaled and never excelled during the whole campaign."[55] But delaying the enemy was the best the 12th SS could do, and the price for even that came high, for when the fighting in Normandy concluded in late August 1944, the division had practically ceased to exist.

* * * * *

DIENSTGRADÜBERSICHT/COMPARATIVE RANKS

Waffen-SS	U.S. Army
Reichsführer	---------
SS-Oberstgruppenführer und Generaloberst der Waffen-SS	General
SS-Obergruppenführer und General der Waffen-SS	Lieutenant-General
SS-Gruppenführer und Generalleutnant der Waffen-SS	Major-General
SS-Brigadeführer und Generalmajor der Waffen-SS	Brigadier-General
SS-Oberführer	---------
SS-Standartenführer	Colonel
SS-Obersturmbannführer	Lieutenant-Colonel
SS-Sturmbannführer	Major
SS-Hauptsturmführer	Captain
SS-Obersturmführer	First Lieutenant
SS-Untersturmführer	Second Lieutenant

NOTES

[1] See table at end of chapter for comparative rank listing.

[2] The armed, or military branch of the SS.

[3] National Archives Record Group, T-175/108/2631249-51. Berger to Himmler, Geheim! Betr.: Aufstellung der Division Hitler-Jugend. 18.2.43; see also Meyer, Kurt. Grenadiere. Schild Verlag. München-Lochhausen. 1956. p. 204.

[4] The Divisional Escort Company (Begleitkompanie), for example, experienced "special difficulties" in training its light infantry gun platoon; for no officer with requisite knowledge of the weapon was available. Bundesarchiv-Militärarchiv, RS 3-12/1. Tagebuch Divisions-Begleit-Kompanie der 12. SS-Pz. Div. "H.J." 1943-1945. 24.2.1944 (Bundesarchiv-Militärarchiv, hereafter cited BAMA).

[5] Meyer, Hubert. Foreign Military Study P-164, "12. SS Panzer-Division 'Hitlerjugend,' Juni bis September 1944," p.3 (hereafter cited P-164); Meyer, Hubert. Kriegsgeschichte der 12.SS-Panzerdivision "Hitlerjugend." Munin Verlag. Osnabrück. 1982. Band I. pp. 18-19.

[6] BAMA RH 10/321. Zustandsbericht 12.SS Pz.Div. "H.J.," Meldung vom 1.6.1944.

[7] T-175/18/2521572, 2521760. Führerstellungbesetzung der 12.SS Pz.Gren.Div. "H.J.," 31.7.1943.

[8] Rempel, Gerhard. The Misguided Generation: Hitler Youth and SS: 1933-1945. Unpublished doctoral dissertation. University of Wiscovnsin. 1971, p. 646.

[9] Heiber, Helmuth (ed.), Hitlers Lagebesprechungen. Die Protokollfragmente seiner militärischen Konferenzen, 1942-1945. Stuttgart: Deutsche Verlags-Anstalt. 1962. p. 334.

[10] For the division's 25th SS Panzer Grenadier Regiment there are two surviving company lists. The lists show that the great majority of the rank and file recruits from these two companies came from the class of 1926, and had backgrounds in vocational training. T-354/154/3798022-28: Kompanieliste 3./Pz.-Gren.Rgt.25, Kompanieliste 10./Pz.-Gren.Rgt.25.

[11] Meyer, H., Kriegsgeschichte, p. 20.

[12] T-175/111/2635155. Führerhauptquartier, 21.10.1943; T-175/108/2631204-5. SS-Führungshauptamt. Betr.: Umgliederung der SS-Panz.Gren.Div. "Hitlerjugend." 30.10.1943.

[13] Meyer, H., P-164, p. 4. The I SS Panzer Corps would not become operational until the spring of 1944.

[14] At 35 Witt became one of the youngest divisional commanders in the German armed forces. He had fought with distinction in the major campaigns of the war, and had earned many of Germany's most coveted military honors, including the Iron Cross first and second class, as well as the prestigious Knight's Cross. A humane yet hard-driving commander, he was held in high esteem by officers and enlisted men alike; and despite a youthful, almost boyish physiognomy, was typical of the dynamic breed of young SS officers who commanded from the front line. Witt would serve as commander of the 12th SS until his violent death early in the Normandy campaign on June 14, 1944. Berlin Documentation Center, SS Personalakten, Fritz Witt: Dienstlaufbahn, Lebenslauf, etc.

[15] The engineer battalion for one appeared to devote a good deal of time to the repair of its broken down vehicles. T-354/155/3798847, 3798863. Darstellung der Ereignisse, SS Pz.Pi.Btl.12.

[16] BAMA Zustandsberichte, 12.SS Pz.Div., 1.11.1943, 1.1.1944; Meyer, H., P-164, pp. 4-5; Meyer, H., Kriegsgeschichte, pp. 17, 21.

[17] Gurowski, Günther. Fragebogen zur Geschichte der 12. SS Panzerdivision "H.J." im Normandie Feldzug; Grabher-Meyer, Rudolf, Fragebogen (both questionnaires in possession of the author).

[18] Axmann conducted formal inspections of the Hitler Youth Division on a number of occasions, including December 1943, and March and April 1944. Die 3. Kompanie. SS-Panzer-Regiment 12, 12.SS-Panzerdivision "Hitlerjugend." Eigenverlag. Kompanie-Kameradschaft. 1978. pp. 13, 25, 31

[19] National Archives Record Group 238: Records of Proceedings (revised) of the Trial by Canadian Military Court of SS Brigadeführer Kurt Meyer., pp. 552-53 (Meyer testimony under oath).

[20] Rempel, The Misguided Generation, p. 644; Meyer, K., Grenadiere, p. 208; T-175/70/2586532-3. Pohl to RFSS, Verpflegung der Angehörigen der SS Pz.Gren.Div."H.J.", 25.6.1943.

[21] Rempel, The Misguided Generation, pp. 649-50.

[22] Ibid., p. 651-52; T-354/154/3797992-3. Witt, Kdr. Tgb. Nr. 237/44, "Sonderbefehl." 12.4.1944.

[23] Meyer, H., P-164, p. 6.

[24] Interview by the author with Günther Burdack, May 21, 1983, Bad Hersfeld, West Germany.

[25] BAMA Zustandsbericht, 12. SS Pz. Div., 3.4.1944.

[26] Gurowski, Fragebogen.

[27] Burdack interview; interview by author with Heinz Berner, June 1, 1983, Normandy, France.

[28] The regiment, however, would not approach its full strength in personnel until late December 1943, with the arrival of some 600 recruits from the SS Tank Instructional Battalion of the SS Tank Training and Replacement Regiment in Dondangen, Latvia. Die 3. Kompanie, pp. 13-14.

[29] Tall, slim, blue-eyed and blond, with handsome regular features, Wünsche was a charismatic leader. He had joined the SS in July 1933, and came to the Leibstandarte in October 1934. Thereafter, Wünsche attended a series of officer training courses at Jüterbog, the SS Junkerschule Bad Tölz, and at Dachau. On April 20, 1936, his birthday, he was promoted to the rank of Untersturmführer and given command of an infantry platoon in the Leibstandarte. Following a promotion to Obersturmführer in September 1938, Wünsche was transferred to Hitler's personal escort detachment (Begleitkommando des Führers), where he served as an orderly--a position he also filled during the Polish campaign in 1939. As a platoon and company commander in the western offensive of 1940, he won the Iron Cross first and second class. During the Balkan campaign Wünsche served as divisional adjutant and continued to see duty as a staff officer with the Leibstandarte on the eastern front in 1941. In Russia he demonstrated his intelligence, versatility and toughness as a soldier--taking temporary command of units whose commanders had been killed or wounded, flying battlefield reconnaissance in a Fieseler Storch, and even serving briefly on two occasions as the Leibstandarte's chief operations officer. In February 1942, Wünsche took over the division's assault gun battalion and played a significant role in the successful defensive battles that winter. Following the withdrawal of the division from the Russian front, he attended the Kriegsakademie in Berlin, and in October 1942, took command of a tank battalion of the Leibstandarte's Panzer regiment. By late January 1943, Wünsche was back in action--successfully leading his tank unit in the defensive battles around Kharkov. In recognition of his soldierly abilities, he was awarded the Knight's Cross on February 28, 1943. SS Personalakten, Max Wünsche: SS Stammkarte, Dienstlaufbahn, Lebenslauf, etc.

[30] Meyer, H., Kriegsgeschichte, pp. 21-22.

[31] Rempel, The Misguided Generation, pp. 656-57; MacDonald, B.J.S., The Trial of Kurt Meyer. Clarke, Irwin and Company Limited. 1954. p. 16; T-354/156/3800397-8. 12. SS Pz. Div., Abt. IIa. Die weltanschauliche Schulung in der SS-Panzer-Division "Hitlerjugend," 22.11.1943.

[32] Hubatsch, Walther (ed.), <u>Hitlers Weisungen für die Kriegführung 1939-1945</u>. Dokumente des Oberkommandos der Wehrmacht. Bernard und Graefe Verlag für Wehrwesen. Frankfurt am Main. 1962. p. 234.

[33] BAMA Zustandsbericht, 12. SS Pz.Div., 1.1.1944.

[34] BAMA Zustandsbericht, 12. SS Pz.Div., 5.2.1944.

[35] <u>Die 3. Kompanie</u>, pp. 15-16.

[36] BAMA Zustandsbericht, 12. SS Pz.Div., 5.2.1944.

[37] <u>Die 3. Kompanie</u>, pp. 20-21.

[38] Ibid., pp. 22-23; Meyer, H., <u>Kriegsgeschichte</u>, p. 22.

[39] <u>Die 3. Kompanie</u>, pp. 24-25.

[40] Rempel, <u>The Misguided Generation</u>, p. 655.

[41] BAMA Zustandsbericht, 12. SS Pz.Div., 3.4.1944.

[42] Among the formations swept into the pocket was the SS Panzer Division Leibstandarte, by now but a shadow of its former strength. Following its rescue the division was moved to Belgium to refit.

[43] The 30-year-old Meyer (no relation to Kurt Meyer) had served as a company and battalion commander in the Leibstandarte, and had been decorated with the Iron Cross first and second class. In September 1943, he completed a General Staff training course at the Kriegsakademie, qualifying him to serve as a chief operations officer in an armored division. SS Personalakten, Hubert Meyer.

[44] Meyer, H., <u>Kriegsgeschichte</u>, p. 40.

[45] T-354/155/3798863. Darstellung der Ereignisse, SS-Pz.Pi.Bt. 12.

[46] Mohnke had fought in Poland, France and in the Balkans. Wounded repeatedly, he had earned the Iron Cross first and second class. In early 1942, he served briefly as the commander of the Leibstandarte's armored detachment, which was then in the process of initial organization. Mohnke would end his military career in April 1945 amidst the rubble and flames of Berlin, where, as the commander of an SS battlegroup, he conducted the defense of the government quarter of the city. Harsh and austere in appearance, Mohnke was a man of violent emotions, distant and even brutal. He was not popular among his fellow officers or enlisted men. Severely wounded in the Greek campaign, he had lost a foot, and most likely, acquired an addiction to morphine. He was, however, a man of some courage--a statement supported by his many wounds and willingness to assume the responsibility of a

regimental command despite his severe physical handicap. SS Personalakten, Wilhelm Mohnke: Lebenslauf, Dienstlaufbahn, etc.; MacDonald, The Trial of Kurt Meyer, p. 30; interviews conducted by the author with former 12th SS Division members.

47Standing approximately 5'10", broad shouldered and athletic with penetrating grey-blue eyes, Kurt Meyer combined the cool "Draufgängertum," or recklessness, of the Landsknecht with the ideological fanaticism of the political soldier. In September 1939, Meyer entered the Polish campaign at the head of an anti-tank unit of the Leibstandarte, launching a spectacular combat career that would make him a legend and earn him the sobriquet "Panzermeyer." As the commander of a motorcycle company in France, and of the reconnaissance battalion of the Leibstandarte in the Balkans and Russia, Meyer demonstrated an instinctive grasp of the technique of modern mobile warfare. A dare-devilish motorcycle man, he suffered 18 broken bones and four concussions in the course of his military career. By early 1943, his reckless but effective style of combat a 'outrance had gained him the Iron Cross first and second class, the Knight's Cross and the Oak Leaves to the Knight's Cross. His unorthodox methods in Russia, where he sometimes ventured far behind Russian lines with his reconnaissance unit and then blasted his way out, were legendary. Yet despite his ruthless adherence to the SS virtue of "toughness" (Härte), Meyer was genuinely loved and honored by his young soldiers.

Because members of the 12th SS murdered well over 100 Canadian prisoners in the initial days of the Normandy campaign, Kurt Meyer was tried by a Canadian military court at Aurich, Germany, in December 1945; found guilty on three of five charges, Meyer was sentenced to be shot. However, Major General Chris Vokes, the commander of the Canadian Army Occupation Force in Germany, was of the opinion that Meyer's responsibility for the murders was "vicarious rather than direct", as a result, he commuted Meyer's sentence to life imprisonment on January 13, 1946. Meyer was released in September 1954. In his final statement before the court Meyer said, "I have here, during these proceedings, been given an insight into things which, in the aggregate, were unknown to me up to now. I wish to state to the court here that these deeds were not committed by the young soldiers. I am convinced of it, that in the division there were elements who, due to the year-long battles, due to five years of war, had in a certain respect become brutalized." A Canadian participant in the trial wrote that, "there was a profound sense of relief [when the trial] was all over. We had come to admire [Kurt Meyer] for his qualities and proficiency as a soldier; we respected his courage and his dignity throughout the trial." SS Personalakten, Kurt Meyer: Dienstlaufbahn, etc.; National Archives Record Group 218: Supplementary Report of the SHAEF Court of Inquiry; National Archives Record Group 238: Meyer Trial Proceedings, p. 557; MacDonald, The Trial of Kurt Meyer, pp. 190, 195, 198; interviews conducted by the author with former 12th SS Division members.

48Meyer, Kriegsgeschichte, p. 40; Public Archives of Canada, Ottawa: Special Interrogation Report, Brigadeführer Kurt Meyer, HQ Cdn. Forces in the Netherlands, 24 August 1945; interviews and questionnaires completed by former division members also provided valuable information.

49On August 6, 1949, Hauck and seven other former members of the reconnaissance battalion were sentenced to death by a French military tribunal in Metz; eight additional men were sentenced to death in absentia. One man received 15 years hard labor. However, thanks in part to the efforts of the French defense lawyers, two of the men eventually received pardons. The others were released from captivity in 1954. Hauck, Walter. L'Affaire D'Ascq. Paris Editions Internationales. 1949. Acte d'Accusation, Tribunal Militaire Permanent Metz. Expose des Faits, pp. 13-20 (Hoover Institute Library); Meyer, H., Kriegsgeschichte, pp. 556-57; Meyer, H., P-164, p. 11.

50The 12th SS Panzer Division was one of the ten Panzer or Panzer grenadier divisions that the Wehrmacht had assembled in the West by June 1944. These units represented the German mobile reserve in the western theatre.

51Meyer, H., P-164, pp. 12-13; Meyer, H., Kriegsgeschichte, p. 42.

52Returning from a divisional communications exercise on the eve of the invasion, Obersturmführer Rudolf von Ribbentrop, the commander of the 3rd Panzer Company and the son of the German foreign minister, was badly wounded in a Spitfire attack. Die 3. Kompanie, pp. 32-33.

53Meyer, H., P-164, p. 14.

54Operational as of June 6, 1944, were 94 Panzer IVH, 63 Panther G, 12 Panzer 38(t) and eight command tanks. The Panzer 38(t) was a Czech tank that the Germans had continued to manufacture as late as 1942. Although obsolete by 1941, the Panzer 38(t) continued to see service as an artillery observation vehicle. The shortage of some 2,300 officers and NCO's was made good numerically through the addition of some 2,360 enlisted men not originally included in the division's organizational tables. According to Kurt Meyer, the 12th SS also had roughly 500 Italians, Russians and ethnic Germans attached to its support units. BAMA Zustandsbericht, 12. SS Pz.Div., 1.6.1944; BAMA RH 19IX/3, Generalkommando I.SS-Panzer Korps, Ia Tgb. Nr. 44/g. Kdos.; Record Group 218: Supplementary Report SHAEF Court of Inquiry, Exhibit 8, p. 16.

55Wilmot, Chester. The Struggle for Europe. Harper and Row. New York. 1952. p. 343.

INNERE FÜHRUNG AND THE PROBLEM OF TRADITION
IN THE EMERGENCE OF THE WEST GERMAN ARMED FORCES

by DONALD ABENHEIM[1]

The foundation of the West German armed forces (Bundeswehr) in 1955-6 was without precedent, since never before in German history had a democracy created its own army. The relationship between the West German soldier and Germany's military past stood foremost among the dilemmas confronting the founders of the new army. The Nazis had taken the existing heritage of the German soldier and grafted it onto their own ideology in an effort to create a new cult of tradition overnight. Germany's defeat in two world wars further made the step towards a West German contribution to Atlantic defense a bold and difficult one, an enterprise that could only take place with the reform of the future soldier's political self-image and his position in state and society. In effect, the creators of the new West German army in the 1950s and 1960s had to reconstruct from the nation's military past traditions and symbols which the Nazis had not fully destroyed. The founders of the Bundeswehr had to determine what of this heritage remained valid in the present. This effort soon evolved into the concept of Innere Führung.[2] Although there has been a long debate about its meaning, one can suggest that Innere Führung has been the Federal Republic's ongoing attempt to reconcile the citizen with the soldier, and to overcome the traditional anatagonism in the German past between democracy and the military. The creators of Innere Führung saw their task as adjusting the relationships of everyday military life to the new political realities of West Germany, while assuring the Bundeswehr's readiness for action. This promise of reform encountered formidable political and social obstacles, which made the new army a source of constant debate during its first fifteen years of existence.

Throughout the 1950s and 1960s, the West German armed forces struggled with the political, social and material burdens of their sudden creation in the wake of the Korean War. These problems reached a high point in the late 1960s, with the revival in the Federal Republic of political radicalism on the left and the right. Such events renewed longstanding anxieties among West German critics of the new army that the German military might try to regain its former preeminent social and political position, a fear that grew acute during 1969.

On 19 March 1969, the Vice Chief of Staff of the West German Army, Major General Hellmuth Grashey, spoke in the Moltke Hall of the armed forces staff academy in Hamburg-Blankenese to former students of the school. Grashey's comments were in keeping with his reputation among his admirers as a man of dynamic qualities, destined for high positions in the Bundeswehr leadership. To others, he was a troupier, a traditionalist alien to the spirit of reform essential for the successful integration of the West German forces into society. Although not intended for the public, the gist of Grashey's speech found its way into Spiegel magazine.3

The Vice-Chief of Staff was deeply concerned about the state of the army. One day, he predicted to his audience, the general staff (greatly reduced from its past political and symbolic influence) would regain its former role as the prime-mover of military life. Grashey described the army's ills as stemming from three sources: the swollen civilian administration (die Bundeswehrverwaltung), the parliamentary commissioner (der Wehrbeauftragte), mandated by parliament to oversee the implementation of the reforms at the troop level, and the concept of Innere Führung itself. Grashey's most disturbing claim was that the program of military reform begun in the early 1950s had been nothing more than a "mask," a means for the government of West Germany's first chancellor, Konrad Adenauer, to "sell" rearmament to the Social Democrats. Now that the Federal Republic seemed threatened by radicals from the left and the right, with an incipient break-down of discipline visible in the ranks, the time had come for the Bundeswehr to "cast off" the mask of reform. Besides, Grashey observed, Innere Führung was nothing more than a new name for an old concept, a battle-proven tradition of the former German armies: the care of the leader for his men.4

Immediately following Grashey's speech, Colonel Eberhard Wagemann, a staff officer closely associated with the reforms, stood up to contradict his superior on the spot. Wagemann was also the chief author of many important ministerial directives on the reforms, who told the audience of his fellow staff officers that Grashey's statements were simply untrue and did not represent the position of the Ministry of Defense. Grashey responded by berating him in front of the audience.

The Vice-Chief of Staff's "verbal assault" on the institutions of reform was the most spectacular in the history of the Bundeswehr, ushering in months of controversy that coincided with the end of the Christian-Democrat-Socialist Grand Coalition in Bonn. Although many people in West Germany shared Grashey's skepticism about the effect of reform on the army's fighting power, he was the highest-ranking officer to make these assertions in an official forum. He later chose the path of early retirement once the furor surrounding his speech had passed. His statements are important for the history of the Federal Republic and the reforms that became synonymous with the new West Germany army. Did the West German government seek to correct the military abuses of political power in the past, or did it merely employ an elaborate ruse to mask the restoration of the old order? The debate on this question has been long and bitter. An integral part of it has been the nature of military tradition in the Bundeswehr[5], a topic of such importance that it finally compelled the West German Ministry of Defense to publish a decree on military tradition in July 1965.

The account that follows contains a brief overview of the events leading to the decree, which was the first of its kind in German history and the subject of controversy ever since. The issues involved in the preparation of the decree over a period of eight years and their effect into the 1980s highlight the dilemmas that the leadership of the Bundeswehr has faced for thirty years. The creation of the Bundeswehr's policy on military tradition provides clues and insights that disprove Grashey's claim that the reforms were a fraud.

I.

The start of the Korean war in June 1950 prompted the Western allies to carry forward the arming of the new Federal Republic of Germany within a united European army. Konrad Adenauer and his military advisors recognized the imperative to break with Germany's military past, much as the advocates of reform in Prussia had tried to do after 1806, and as the Weimar Republic had more fatefully failed to do with the Reichswehr in the 1920s. The political and social conditions of the 1950s were vastly more difficult, however. The political and military disasters of the recent past and the Nazi perversion of so many German traditions and institutions created enormous domestic and international obstacles. It was necessary now for the Bonn government to cooperate internationally with Germany's former enemies while at the same time overcoming the formidable domestic opposition to a new army.

The close identification of the military with the Nazi past, the traumatic effects of the 20 July 1944 attempt on Hitler's life, the charges against the professional soldiers at the war crimes trials, and the popular disgust with all things military after 1945 prevented Adenauer's government from resurrecting the Wehrmacht as it had existed before 1945. The chancellor and his military advisors had to take stock of past mistakes and integrate the new army into the transformed setting of a pluralistic, democratic society within a nascent united Europe, a task that was made no easier by Germany's division into east and west along the front-line of a world-wide ideological confrontation. Added to this were the realities of post-war life: cities filled with rubble; the Wehrmacht leaders on trial and branded as criminals, with thousands of former officers imprisoned in east and west; and the popular response to Adenauer's army of ohne mich. With these obstacles before them, Adenauer's government began to plan for the new army in the Fall of 1950.

Summoned by the chancellor in the late summer and early fall of that year, a group of former Wehrmacht officers (some identified with the military resistance to Hitler) met in the Abbey Himmerod in the Eifel mountains to draft a planning document for the new armed forces, a paper that would also be the basis of negotiations with the western allies.6 Described years later by Adenauer's chief security advisor as the "Magna Carta of the Bundeswehr", the Himmerod memorandum contained the chief political, operational and ethical issues facing the future West German soldier. In addressing the inner structure (inneres Gefüge) of the new force, the group at Himmerod recognized that the profoundly altered conditions of post-war Europe required the creation of "something fundamentally new, without any borrowing from the forms of the old armed forces."   The West German contribution to European defense must find a compromise between the need for "new meaning" in military life and for "less rigid forms," while nonetheless respecting peoples' wishes for a more traditional image of the soldier in society.7

Historians, reflecting on the Himmerod memorandum, have suggested that the document's proposals for the inner structure contained obvious contradictions. The call for new and less rigid forms that would nonetheless be acceptable to those with a "more traditional image" of the soldier revealed uncertainties and differences among the men at Himmerod. Such contradictions were no surprise, when one considers that the authors of the passages on the inner structure included, among others, General Hermann Foertsch, and Major Graf Wolf von Baudissin. Foertsch, the brother of the second Generalinspekteur der Bundeswehr, had been closely associated with the ideological training of the Wehrmacht, and was later denied a commission in the Bundeswehr. In contrast, Baudissin quickly became known over the next ten years as an outspoken advocate of reform in the West German armed forces.8

Observers of the ethical debates within the Bundeswehr began early on to describe soldiers as either "reformists" or "traditionalists." As the initial troops were mustered into the Bundeswehr in 1956, the first Generalinspekteur, Lieutenant General Adolf Heusinger, worried aloud that, with the rapid tempo of rearmament, the new army would become a battleground between officers adhering to tradition and advocates of reform.9 From today's perspective, one can say that Heusinger's fears proved unfounded. This apparent cleavage in the professional officer corps long seemed a problem to observers, but never grew as serious as the political divisions in the professional officer corps of the Weimar Republic and the Third Reich. No general emerged in the 1950s to lead a putsch against the Federal Republic. But the debate between professional soldiers about the purpose of their existence in the nuclear age and the role of military tradition within that controversy became more intense as the process of creating the West German army continued during the 1950s.

Such debate grew after 1950 during the years of preparation for the new European army. Until August 1954, the planning for reform proceeded within the framework of the European Defense Community. This work took place in Bonn and Paris under Theodor Blank, a parliamentarian, reserve officer, and Catholic trade union official whom Adenauer had chosen to oversee this shadow defense ministry--the Dienststelle Blank. By its very nature, the program of military reform in the Adenauer government was a liberal Antitraditionskonzept[10] intended to eradicate the authoritarian and militarist practices of the past. The reform signified Adenauer's hope that he could win the cooperation of those in society who before had distrusted or opposed the military.

The effort to transform this general desire for reform into specific measures, which got underway in early 1951 with the arrival of Baudissin in the Amt Blank, included a wide variety of social groups and professional organizations. Baudissin's work, however, was but one aspect of hundreds needed for raising the new armed forces. The scope of this essay precludes an examination of this issue, but public interest in the reforms and Baudissin's tireless advocacy of them won him much public attention. Of course, his ideas also provoked opposition within the Amt Blank, West German society and the Atlantic alliance. More important, this effort took place under conditions of political uncertainty, scarce resources and international friction. As time passed, the planning for reform fell victim to conceptual vagueness and bureaucratic disputes, which have had an enduring and fateful effect.[11] As part of this problem, questions of military tradition were implicit not only in the planning for reform of the political and social position of the armed forces in the state, but in operational tasks as well. The discussion of these issues in the early 1950s was dominated by a confusion about the character of military tradition and by a recognition of the need to define it. An explicit policy on this question became increasingly necessary after the first soldiers joined their units in 1955-6.[12]

This requirement grew more pressing once the French National Assembly eliminated the European Defence Community on 30 August 1954. The West German planners quickly had to modify their proposals to suit a national army. As it emerged by 1955, the concept of reform focused on the need to re-examine all military traditions, to retain those of value, and to discard the rest.[13] The changing nature of warfare in the mid-1950s, with its emphasis on mechanization, small unit engagements, the emerging role of nuclear weapons on the battlefield, and the importance of ideology, underscored the need for a soldier capable of operational initiative and ideological conviction. The answer to this dilemma was the "citizen in uniform," whose democratic beliefs and military skill would allow him to survive on the modern battlefield.[14] The blind obedience and barracks-square drill depicted in Hans Hellmuth Kirst's novel, 08/15, were to be a thing of the past.[15] Political education of the future soldier would assume equal status with military training, for the idea of Innere Führung addressed the ideological aspects of the cold war no less than the integration of the soldier into West German society.[16]

Once the process of mustering the first troops into the Bundeswehr began in 1956, the Ministry of Defense had to introduce the concept to the new officer corps, most of whom were Wehrmacht veterans. This series of seminars began in the Spring of 1956 at Sonthofen and included the first major official statement of policy on military tradition. These presentations were later edited and published in the Handbuch Innere Führung, the standard military text on the reforms-- a kind of reader, but by no means was it a military regulation with binding effect.[17]

In his speech at Sonthofen on "Military Tradition and its Meaning in the Present", Baudissin (now a colonel and senior Ministry staff officer for Innere Führung) put forth ambitious suggestions for emphasizing those traditions in the Bundeswehr that oriented officers towards the ideas of the Prussian reformers of the early 19th century and the 20 July 1944 plot against Hitler.[18] As he had done before, Baudissin repeated his call first found in the Himmerod memorandum for a radical break with the immediate past. He insisted that soldiers distinguish between the maintenance of spiritual and ethical values that should be described as traditions, and the preservation of forms and externals that should be called conventions. Often the two got confused as most soldiers seemed only to concentrate on the externals, rituals and symbols of military life. Early on, the planners in the Amt Blank had done away with many conventions of the old German armies, among them the famous steel helmet, the field-grey uniform, and the high marching boots. Members of certain veterans organizations and conservative journalists critical of the reforms excoriated the replacement of the old uniform with the "American" as a violation of German military tradition. This criticism became especially loud once the East German People's Army introduced the field grey army uniform of the Wehrmacht almost without change save for the absence of Nazi insignia.

Baudissin reminded his audience of August Bebel, who, in 1898, had called for the abolition of parade-ground soldiers and the orientation of military life solely to the requirements of battle. Rather than focusing on externals, he told his audience that a desire for peace, humanity, a chivalrous attitude, loyalty, and above all, a sense of moral responsibility for one's fellow man were traditions that should obtain in the Bundeswehr. The abuses of the past now dictated that military obedience conform to ethical boundaries. The Prussian reformers of the 19th century had confronted the need for compromise between blind obedience and the requirement for soldiers to weigh humanitarian and political needs in carrying out their mission. Indeed, contrary to the impression left by the Nuremberg trials, Prussian-German history revealed a surprising degree of freedom in military service, where soldiers had disobeyed orders out of conscience, and acted on their own in the face of events. This tradition had been undermined by an over-technicalization of the military craft. The Nazis had done all they could to destroy it; the Bundeswehr would have to revive such tradition. The former chief of the general staff, Ludwig Beck, and his fellow participants in the 20th of July had pointed the way that the new forces must follow.

In part as a reflection of his own heart-felt beliefs and partially as a response to those whom he viewed as reactionaries, Baudissin chose the Prussian reformers and the men of the 20th of July for the formation of a new military tradition. This was a fundamental part of his effort to preclude the Bundeswehr from making a direct connection, through the maintenance of conventions and traditions, with the Reichswehr and the Wehrmacht.

II.

In the following months, as new units were created with great speed under difficult conditions, a growing number of veterans organizations approached the Bundeswehr with the hope of establishing official lineage and honors. Several veterans groups and commanders requested permission from the Ministry to restore aspects of Seeckt's observance of tradition, in which Reichswehr companies, squadrons and batteries had maintained regimental lineage and honors from the old armies. A prominent example had been the Potsdam Infantry Regiment No. 9, which took over the lineage and honors of certain Prussian regiments. This system, that became a prominent feature of Reichswehr and Wehrmacht, was closely associated in the popular mind with the ambivalent attitude of the German military to the first republic.[19]

The calls for the revival of a key part of the old traditions forced the Bundeswehr leadership "to make good on its promise of a new beginning,"[20] while challenging it to preserve the good will of many former professional soldiers. Although reasonably innocent in appearance, the requests from the veterans groups filled the military leadership and their parliamentary advisors with uneasy memories of the 1920s.[21] A Ministry staff paper of October 1957 by Colonel Hans Meier-Welcker (later head of the Bundeswehr historical office) spoke of the need to recognize the desire of former and active-duty soldiers for the maintenance of tradition, a wish shared by civilians in garrison towns who fondly recalled units once stationed there. To meet these wishes, however, the armed forces leadership would have to reconcile diverse points of view. The new system of military tradition "must have a beneficial effect on the spirit of the Bundeswehr,"[22] while corresponding to Germany's actual political and international status. This maintenance of tradition also had to "aid the old soldier to have a positive attitude toward the Bundeswehr," yet at the same time it should not "provoke the public, but win their approval."[23].

Turning to the issue of lineage and honors, Meier-Welcker suggested that, for the time being, Germany's political situation, that is to say, its division, precluded former units from central and eastern Germany from awarding lineage and honors to the Bundeswehr. The technical problems of such a transfer were difficult enough, if only because there were far too many old units. However, two greater political arguments spoke against such a transfer as well: public anxiety among critics of rearmament about military revanchism, and the fear that the transfer of unit traditions from the Communist zone would signal the acceptance of the status-quo.[24] A transfer of the lineage and honors from the Waffen-SS and units with such political names as "Hermann Goering" and "Feldherrnhalle" was out of the question. Once this study reached his desk, Generalinspekteur Heusinger agreed with Meier-Welcker that the Bundeswehr consider some joining of lineage and honors between old and new. He directed Meier-Welcker to prepare a plan linking the traditions of former units in garrison towns with Bundeswehr units now there.[25]

But as is so often the case in a bureaucracy, events outpaced the ability of staff-specialists to plan for them. The requests from the veterans were overtaken by the initiative of local commanders, who, lacking guidance from above and eager to improve the sagging morale of their new troops, acted on their own with local veterans organizations. In one instance, the unit commander in question believed that his self-initiated transfer of lineage and honors from a traditions association of a Reichswehr cavalry regiment from Stolp, Pomerania was a proper way to keep alive memories of the imperial and Reichswehr garrisons now in the Communist east. In addition, the troops had reacted positively to the lineage and honors and the commander hoped that the step would improve espirit de corps.[26]

Baudissin visited the unit at the same time these events were taking place. In a conversation with officers in the Kasino, he pointed to the unit crests on the wall that recalled the garrisons of Danzig and Stolp (home of the Death's Head Hussars and Cavalry Regiment 5). To highlight the possible political difficulties inherent in these innocent decorations, Baudissin asked the officers how they would have reacted to similar crests in a Polish officers' club of 1937. It would have struck Germans of the time as an expression of Polish designs on the Free City of Danzig. Plainly, the effort in the Bundeswehr to "keep alive memories of the lost eastern territories" could easily be misinterpreted by critics. This official sensitivity to anything resembling revanchism was compounded by the high number of refugees from the east who had joined the Bundeswehr in the 1950s.

Although the military leadership did not immediately forbid such lineage and honors outright, they realized that they would have to act. General Heusinger and his Innere Führing staff saw that this proliferation of an ad-hoc cult of tradition on the unit level must be controlled. This step became especially necessary, because many of the Ministry's civilian advisors opposed a symbolic connection with the former German armed forces. In response, in June 1958, Heusinger directed that the transfer of lineage and honors could only take place with the permission of the Ministry. For the time being, the staff was to defer action on such requests, this being, in reality, a bureaucratic tactic to deny them.[27] As the years passed, the Ministry routinely postponed action on these requests. The staff gave the excuse that they could not take action "until a further arrangement" had been made by the military leadership.[28]

This "further arrangement" was the ministerial decree on tradition, work on which had started in 1957. In the next several years, the leadership of the armed forces concentrated on this paper that was to address a full range of issues connected with the military past. This document was unprecedented in German history, and took eight years to complete. This long delay--a cautionary policy in effect--allowed the proliferation of a local adoption of tradition to spread unchecked, against the directives of higher headquarters. This state of affairs only contributed to the greater debate about the valid aspects of Germany's military past in the late 1950s and early 1960s.

III.

The decision in the Ministry of Defense to establish a policy on military tradition went against the wishes of many in West German society. To them, it seemed that such a decree would be nothing more than a typical bureaucratic expression of the over-regulation of German life. Participants in the official discussion of the issue often protested that the Ministry should allow the Bundeswehr to form its own tradition without interference from above. However, the difficulties with lineage and honors, and the constant scrutiny from a suspicious civilian world anxious about the fate of the reforms, compelled the active involvement of the Ministry and a variety of outside personalities. These included leading officers of the Bundeswehr, the civilian advisors to the Ministry, parliamentarians, historians and journalists.[29] Although a noteworthy feature of the civil-military relations of the Bundeswehr, the pluralistic combination of so many viewpoints meant that it would take nearly eight years to write the decree.[30]

In preparing the ministerial decree, the staff specialists had to confront not only the question of lineage and honors, but a broader set of historical interpretations as well. Outstanding among these were the legacy of the 20 July 1944 plot against Hitler and the relationship between history and tradition in general.

Baudissin's choice of the 20 July 1944 as an ideal had been a bold attempt to resolve the dilemma of command and obediance, of the military oath, and the right to resistance. By capitalizing upon the courage, morality and personal example of the resistance, he sought to forge a spiritual link between the Prussian reformers, the 20th of July and the reforms in the Bundeswehr.[31] Some historians of the Federal Republic have described this use of the 20th of July by the Christian Democratic government as an attempt to garner a moral advantage in the face of the Social Democratic resistance to Hitler. The refusal of the SPD to vote for the enabling legislation in March 1933, or the sufferings of Kurt Schumacher, provided considerable moral weight to the Socialists in post-war politics.

There is surely an element of truth in calling the 20th of July something of a conservative God-send, offering as it did proof to the post-war world that there had been decent Germans in the officer corps and landed aristocracy innocent of collective guilt. Yet the plot had been very real as well, and to many of the key leaders of the <u>Bundeswehr</u>, it had meant personal suffering, and the humiliation, torture and death of comrades and relatives.32

Still, during the early 1950s, the new veterans organizations displayed a hostile attitude towards making heroes of the military resistance. This judgment echoed the Nazi condemnation of the conspiracy. These organizations later revised their stand on the issue to recognize the ethical motives of both the soldier at the front and the members of the resistance. This inclusion of both categories of heroic self-sacrifice became a compromise solution framed by the setting of the 1950s. It was, in fact, an important foundation stone upon which the <u>Bundeswehr</u> was built.33

During the planning phase for the new armed forces, journalists and commentators often asked Theodor Blank for the official view on the 20th of July. Sensitive to press reports of disagreements in his office, and to the public criticism that he employed only breakers of oaths, Blank answered that each man had to decide the issue of the 20th of July for himself. This was a response that was taken up and repeated in the official discussion for years thereafter.34 After 1955, the officer examination boards made the 20th of July a major criterion in the selection of new officers. The members of the boards asked the applicant if, after ten years reflection, they could explain the 20th of July, and understand the ethical motives of the participants. The response to this question was an important means for judging the individual's attitude towards the reforms of the new army.35

As the 1950s ended, the writing of the traditions decree required the Ministry to prepare an official position on the military resistance to Hitler. The struggle to find a common formula on this issue was a chief cause of delay in the publication of the decree.36 The civilian advisors to the Ministry strongly advocated making the 20th of July the principal source of tradition for the <u>Bundeswehr</u>, speaking of the event in the same manner as had the officer screening boards. But the draft passages of the decree prepared by the Ministry sought to strike a balance between resistance and obedience. Whereas in earlier drafts the 20th of July was a "touchstone" for the ability of the new army spiritually to come to grips with the past and develop its own tradition, later ones included greater emphasis on the need to honor those who had obeyed.37 Some officers, however, did not feel the need to wait for some definitive word from the Ministry. Thus, on 20 July 1959, the fifteenth anniversary of the attempt on Hitler's life, Heusinger issued an order of the day commemorating the event as a "bright spot in Germany's darkest time."38 The soldiers of the <u>Bundeswehr</u> stood "in honor before the sacrifice of those men, whose consciences were called [to act] by their knowledge. They are the best witnesses against the collective guilt of the German people. Their attitude and spirit are an example to us all."[39] The publication of this order of the day marked an important milestone in the evolution of the valid heritage of the Bundeswehr, but did not bring debate to an end.

IV.

During the next four years, the staff experts continued their struggle to define a usable past for the Bundeswehr. Disagreements about the nature of history and tradition and the objection of parliamentarians doomed these attempts, however. In the interval, the difficulties caused by the rapid expansion of the Bundeswehr became more glaring. Several events took place that drew attention to the difficulties with the reforms and brought their effectiveness into serious doubt.

In early 1963, news of abuses by NCO instructors against paratroops trainees at Nagold near Stuttgart, which led to the death of a recruit, caused an outcry about Innere Führung and training in the armed forces.[40] This was followed by yet a greater scandal in June 1964. The parliamentary commissioner for the reforms in the armed forces, Vice-Admiral Hellmuth Heye, published a series of articles in Quick, warning of the dangerous inner state of the armed forces.[41] "If we don't turn the rudder now," Heye wrote, "the trend is unmistakable towards a state within a state."

These events on the political scene, which nourished popular fears of militarism, made the completion of the traditions decree all the more necessary. In mid-1964, the Inspector of the Army demanded the staff of the Bundeswehr "cut the proliferation of local Traditionspflege." At this time, Colonel Dr. Eberhard Wagemann took over responsibility for the decree in the staff. In a summary for him on the obstacles encountered thus far, a civilian staff expert wrote in October 1964 that "the pluralism of the authors writing the decree prohibits a formulation [of tradition] upon which all can agree." In the view of the author, the paper had become an attempt to base the program of reform upon historical antecedents; "but without the bending of historical facts, this can scarcely be achieved. One ignores history 'as it was' in favor of history 'as it should have been.'"[42]

As the work on the decree proceeded, the debate resumed about the military resistance in the Third Reich. In a passage expressing the virtues of Auftragstaktik (mission oriented orders) and Clausewitz's ideal of freedom in obedience, Generalinspekteur Heinz Trettner crossed out the sentence "Hitler and his paladins were the first to disrespect [freedom in obedience]", commenting that "this is so obvious that it does not justify saying it."[43] He apparently did so because he wanted to avoid Hitler's name in the text. In response to Trettner's deletion, the civilian advisors to the Ministry remained steadfast and insisted that the sentence be retained.

In order to overcome the impasse, Wagemann worked out a compromise passage "The Nazi regime was the first to disrespect [freedom in obedience]," a formulation that avoided Hitler. In order to gain Trettner's assent to the new version, Wagemann argued in a note that

> . . . the sentence does not contain a polemical accusation. Rather, it is the sole sentence [in the decree] that reminds us of the conflicts to which the entire military leadership was subjected in World War II. One must recall Heusinger's <u>Befehl im Widerstreit</u> or the suicide of several generals in the war. Without this sentence, the <u>Bundeswehr</u> . . . will not distance itself in its field from the unprofessional violation [of military affairs] of the Nazi regime which cost us the war and millions of soldiers. At the same time, the <u>Bundeswehr</u> will miss the opportunity for the future to turn back interference by the political leadership as unprofessional.[44]

Wagemann's appeal won Trettner's blessing, but the latter portion of his comment displeased Minister of Defense Kai-Uwe von Hassel, who wrote tersely, "everyone seems to have overlooked this sentence [about political interference]. If the Staff Officer for Training and Education [Wagemann] intends to mean the political leadership in the Ministry and the <u>Bundeswehr</u>, then he is to be relieved. I want a report on this immediately."[45] The controversy only subsided after Trettner assured the Minister that Wagemann had meant the unprofessional interference of a criminal regime in a possible future war, not that of a "legitimate democratic government."[46] This exchange between the Minister and his staff illustrated the enduring tension between soldier and civilian in the <u>Bundeswehr</u> and the potential for disagreement about the valid traditions of the new army.

V.

Wagemann and his staff successfully completed the draft decree in late June 1965. Signed by Hassel on 1 July 1965, and presented to the public shortly thereafter, the first portion of the document contained the principles the <u>Bundeswehr</u> had to apply to its "valid heritage."[47] It stated that the democratic order of the Federal Republic and the mission of the <u>Bundeswehr</u> to serve the Republic and its people loyally and bravely were the fundamental measure of tradition in the West German armed forces. Tradition was not to offer an escape from "critical self-examination" through blind admiration of the past. Rather, only those soldiers who had also fulfilled their responsibility as human beings could serve as examples for the present.[48]

Part two on the "valid heritage" of German military history (Wehrgeschichte) confronted the prejudices against the term itself and referred to the enduring values in Germany's past. In a passage that later provoked criticism, the authors of the decree observed that "to each person is given his father, mother, hour of birth, fatherland, mother-tongue and his own position in history." The decree contained the statement that what today was considered worthy of tradition had usually first been a novelty. One had to maintain an open mind to new ideas and a lack of prejudice; these were the qualities necessary for a progressive tradition. German military history "contained in peace and war countless soldierly achievements and human accomplishments which deserved to be passed on." But war was not to be justified as an "opportunity for proving one's self," especially in view of the technological development of modern weapons. The opportunity for such a test of one's self lay in the readiness for battle and the soldierly skill that deterred war.

The fulfillment of one's duty had always been among the most important aspects of German soldierhood. It was also one of the bases of personal freedom. The ideals of obedience and fulfillment of duty were embodied in the loyalty of the soldier to the master--the Dienstherr in this case, the Federal Republic. This loyalty was expressed in the oath that bound both soldier and master to one another. In this connection, paragraph 14 of the decree contained the important statement on the military resistance:

> According to German military tradition, the achievement and dignity of the soldier rests to a large degree on his freedom in obedience. The training for self-discipline, the call for shared responsibility and the kind of command exemplified in mission-oriented tactics gave this freedom ever greater room [to develop.]
> [The Bundeswehr] must once more tie itself to this freedom in obedience. One's own responsibility in the risk of life, position and reputation has always given a human dimension to the soldier's obedience. Answerable in the end only to their conscience, the soldiers of the resistance proved themselves to the final degree to be opponents to the injustice and criminality of the National Socialist rule of force. Such loyalty to conscience must be preserved in the Bundeswehr.49

The authors of the decree in subsequent passages called for the kind of political thought and responsibility advocated by the Prussian reformers of the early 19th century. "The value of [the soldier's] service is largely determined by political aims." This insight required that soldiers educate themselves. At the end of this section, there followed a list of virtues that later aroused public criticism for being nothing more than "school book platitudes." These virtues included honesty, respect for human rights, tolerance, and loyalty to one's conscience. Such qualities formed a lens through which the soldier of the Bundeswehr must examine military tradition.

The third section of the decree included specific guidance for the maintenance of tradition. These passages contained the final answer to the problem of lineage and honors and the relations with veterans of the old armies. With respect to the tangibles in the cult of tradition, the authors wrote that symbols were living expression of the German military heritage. Those with particular meaning were the black, red and gold flag of the Federal Republic that signified the responsibility of the citizen and the striving of all Germans for unity, law and freedom. These ideals were also expressed in the national anthem, the eagle in the German federal coat of arms, and the iron cross, "the embodiment of ethically bound soldierly bravery."

The Bundeswehr could awaken the "consciousness of tradition" in its soldiers at the swearing of the oath, the presentation of weapons to young soldiers, promotion ceremonies, the playing of the tattoo on memorial days, and the launching of ships. Military tradition was to be made vital through historical instruction by officers and NCOs, who should use concrete examples. With the permission of the Ministry, troops units and barracks could be named for "personalities whose attitude and achievement had been exemplary." Soldiers could also collect historical artifacts to acquaint themselves with tradition, but memorabilia with swastikas could not be displayed. Flags of the old armies could be trooped at ceremonies, but not those of the Third Reich.

Paragraph 26 in the decree included the final answer to the problem of lineage and honors: "The traditions of former troop units will not be awarded to units of the Bundeswehr." The authors of the decree then attempted to make their position more palatable to former soldiers by observing that it would be possible to have comradely relations without an official inheritance of lineage and honors. Bundeswehr units should include in their social activities all former soldiers in the vicinity, both in groups and as individuals. However, the authors stated that "it must remain clear that the Bundeswehr distinguished itself in its political position, its mission and its structure from the armed forces of earlier periods."

The final paragraphs of the decree spoke of the honoring by the Bundeswehr of the "soldierly achievement and sacrifice of the veterans" and the need for "an exchange of experience and meetings" between former and active soldiers. This practice would increase mutual respect. Former soldiers were to be invited to official functions and celebrations, but these ceremonies had to "adhere to the demands of taste." Finally, the decree specified that "all events for the maintenance of tradition were to serve [the purposes of] education and further bind the Bundeswehr to its present mission."[50]

The public reaction to the decree was generally positive, with the majority of the press displaying an understanding for the difficulties the Ministry had faced in the task.[51] The decision to honor the men of the 20th of July and to prevent the handing down of lineage and honors elicited many positive responses in print, although there also was criticism of the lack of concrete historical examples in the decree. The reception of the document at the unit level is less easy to characterize. As one high-ranking commander wrote, "Many officers apparently expected both somewhat more and something different from the Ministry's traditions decree."[52] The absence of concrete historical examples for instruction at the unit level allowed commanders to prepare their own.[53] In many cases, these were much like the syllabus for a college-level history course, constructed around various themes with readings on aspects of military history. The responsibility for such instruction in military tradition rested chiefly with unit commanders.

VI.

The appearance of the decree on tradition brought to a climax the military tradition controversy in the Federal Republic that had begun with rearmament in the 1950s. The debate on military tradition subsided during the remainder of the 1960s. One can suggest that the decree symbolized an ongoing process whereby the West German state struck a balance between the soldier and society, striving to integrate the military into West German life. In its most fundamental sense, the decree signified a compromise for the war-time generation. And as long as this generation remained preeminent, this compromise made some sense.

By the mid 1970s, however, it began to show cracks. Several events followed that shook the compromise and made a new effort to define tradition necessary. A bitter controversy over the visit of dive-bomber ace Hans-Ulrich Rudel to a German Air Force base in 1976, and the violence over military ceremonies in public during 1980, led to demands first for a revision, and later for the complete abolition of the traditions decree of 1965. The compromise created by the war-time generation during rearmament became the object of growing protest, itself part of a far greater questioning of the tenets of West German society. In addition, new historical scholarship during the past fifteen years had drawn attention to the connections between the Nazis and the professional military, making the Wehrmacht seem an invalid source of tradition in the eyes of many.[54]

In the wake of these developments, Minister of Defense Hans Apel rescinded the 1965 decree in April 1981 as a prelude to a new directive on military tradition. Apel's effort appeared in September 1982, on the eve of the break-up of the social-liberal coalition. His "Guidelines for the Understanding of Tradition and the Maintenance of Tradition in the Bundeswehr" was one of his last acts as Minister of Defense.[55] The overall tone of the guidelines emphasized that soldiers derived their traditions from democratic examples. The authors of the decree observed that the Basic Law was the foundation of all tradition in the armed forces (this in contrast to the earlier decree's emphasis upon the mission of the armed forces). The authors also insisted that all aspects of German history--pleasant or unpleasant--be fully discussed in the <u>Bundeswehr</u>. They wrote that German military history had developed with deep breaks in its continuity. The armed forces had been in part ensnared in the guilt of National Socialism and in part had participated innocently. The authors stated that "such an illegal regime as the Third Reich cannot be the a basis of tradition." This was rather a different answer to the issue of the <u>Wehrmacht</u> than had appeared in 1965 after years of debate. Notable for its absence from the 1982 decree was any mention of the 20th of July 1944 plot. Although it appeared in earlier drafts of the decree, one can say that the authors deleted the military resistance to Hitler because of an apparent unwillingness to include personalities and events from the period 1933-45 in any form. While the authors retained the ceremonial swearing-in and the tattoo, these were no longer to be combined in one event. The tattoo was to be reserved for special occasions.

This statement of a valid heritage also divided spirits and provoked controversy. Once Minister Apel left office, the new Minister, Manfred Woerner, announced that he would immediately rescind Apel's decree in favor of new ones. He then refrained from doing so, however. The publication of new guidelines was later postponed by the political imperatives of seeing the missile deployments through in 1983 and by the scandal over the reputed homosexuality of General Guenter Kiessling in 1984. The controversy over the visit of President Ronald Reagan to the military ceremony in Bitburg in 1985 delayed the appearance yet again, reflecting the enduring political difficulties with the heritage of the past in West German life.56

The changing interpretation of military tradition in West Germany reveals the degree to which the West German military has mirrored developments in the society and state that created it. The founders of the <u>Bundeswehr</u> established the new force with the promise of reform, one which was difficult to fulfill. Looking back in the mid-1980s, Baudissin believed that these reforms had failed to live up to their original hopes. Grashey and his fellow critics of reform claimed that <u>Innere Führung</u> had been nothing more than a political mask and a hindrance to efficiency in battle, although the controversy that surrounded these statements in the late 1960s has long since abated. From the perspective of one who has both served with the <u>Bundeswehr</u> and studied its history from the sources, it seems fairly plain that, though Baudissin's wishes of the 1950s may have gone unfulfilled, he is overly pessimistic in his judgment, while Grashey and his sympathizers are simply wrong. The reforms have been flawed in detail and the victim of circumstance, but they gave the <u>Bundeswehr</u> a quality that the armed forces of countries with a longer democratic tradition have not attained.

Military tradition has been only one aspect of the program of reform, although it is a highly visible and interesting one, especially to scholars. In trying to formulate a policy on military tradition, the founders of the Bundeswehr sought honestly to come to grips with their history and traditions while balancing the demands of a pluralistic society with those of the soldier. The writing of the 1965 traditions decree reflected the considerable obstacles to rearmament as well as the political necessity for compromise. This imperative for compromise in the formation of the self-image of the Bundeswehr led many critics to observe that the Federal Republic missed its opportunity to create truly democratic soldiers in the 1950s. But this kind of statement serves the needs of contemporary politics more than those of historical scholarship. The reforms fell victim to the political imperative to create the West Germany army virtually overnight, as well as to the inherent problem of quickly altering traditional patterns of human behavior and experience.

The changes in world politics, strategy and technology, the dictates of personnel, the necessity to come to terms with the burden of the past and the need to integrate the soldier into society all have had their effect on the Bundeswehr from its first years into the present. That the Bundeswehr could have done better with its soldiers and the fashioning of their self-image is probably true; that it has done much better than its predecessors in the 20th century seems fairly well substantiated by events, a reality that should be measured against the practical rather than the ideal. This thirty-year record of an army within an alliance, whose leaders sought to learn from the past, should today provide the Bundeswehr with its greatest military tradition.

NOTES

[1] The author wishes to thank the West German Ministry of Defense for its generous support in providing materials for this essay. The opinions expressed herein are the author's, and do not represent the position of the Department of the Navy nor the Department of Defense. In particular, this article is based on the manuscript of Norbert Wiggershaus and Hans-Joachim Harder, "Tradition und Reform", which was unpublished in 1983-1984 during the author's research, and has since appeared in print: Tradition und Reform in den Aufbaujahren der Bundeswehr (Herford, 1985), Vol. 2 in Entwicklung deutscher militärischer Tradition. Citations in the text below are from the unpublished manuscript, as the published version differs in detail from the former.

[2] Among the many works on Innere Führung are: Bundesverteidigungsministerium (BMvg), Führungsstab der Bundeswehr (Fue S) B I 6, Handbuch Innere Führung: Hilfen zur Klärung der Begriffe (Bonn, 1957); BMvg, Fue S I, Zentrale Dienstvorschrift (ZDv) 10/1, Hilfen für die Innere Führung (Bonn, 1972); Wolf Graf von Baudissin, Soldat für den Frieden: Entwürfe für eine zeitgemässe Bundeswehr (München, 1969); Heinz Karst, Das Bild des Soldaten (Boppard, 1964); Carl-Gero von Ilsemann, Die Bundeswehr in der Demokratie: Die Zeit der inneren Führung (Hamburg, 1971); Ulrich Simon, Die Integration der Bundeswehr

in die Gesellschaft: Das Ringen um die Innere Führung (Heidelberg, 1980); Anfänge westdeutscher Sicherheitspolitik, Militärgeschichtliches Forschungsamt, eds. Vol. 1 (München, 1982); Peter Wuellich, Die Konzeption der Inneren Führung der Bundeswehr als Grundlage der allgemeinen Wehrpädagogik (Regensburg, 1981); BMvg., Bibliographie der Inneren Führung 1950-1980, Streitkräfteamt, eds. (Bonn, 1980).

[3]Interview with General Ulrich de Maizière, June 1984; with Major General Dr. Eberhard Wagemann, March 1984; with Lieutenant General Carl-Gero von Ilsemann, March 1984. This incident is also in Spiegel No. 15, 7 April 1969, p. 33 and in Ulrich de Maizière, Führen im Frieden: 20 Jahre Dienst für Bundeswehr und Staat (Bonn, 1974) pp. 139-40.

[4]Simon, Integration, p. 64ff; Carl-Gero von Ilsemann, Die Innere Führung in den Streitkraeften (Regensburg, 1981) p. 225; Interview with Ilsemann, March 1984.

[5]Among the several works, see Wiggershaus and Harder, cited in nt. 1; Hans Herzfeld, "Die Bundeswehr und das Problem der Tradition" in Studien zur politischen und gesellschaftlichen Situation der Bundeswehr Vol. 1, George Picht, ed. (Berlin, 1965); Georg Macioszek, Das Problem der Tradition in der Bundeswehr; eine empirische Untersuchung unter Offizieren des Heeres (Hamburg, 1969); Martin Esser, Das Traditionsverständnis des Offizierkorps: eine empirische Untersuchung zur gesellschaftlichen Integration der Streitkräfte (Heidelberg, 1982). The article by David Clay Large, "'A Gift to the Future?' The Anti-Nazi Resistance Movement and West German Rearmament" in German Studies Review, VII, October 1984 provides a useful introduction to the issue of military tradition, but should be compared with the above works for a more complete interpretation. For a discussion of military tradition in the German Democratic Republic, see Alexander Fischer, "Tradition und Traditionspflege in der NVA" and Wilfried v. Bredow, "Die Last der Traditionen" in Deutsche Studien, Sonderheft, January, 1981.

[6]The discussion of the Himmerod memorandum is from Norbert Wiggershaus and Hans-Juergen Rautenberg, "Die Himmeroder Denkschrift von Oktober 1950: Politische und Militärische Überlegungen für einen Beitrag der Bundesrepublik Deutschland zur Westeuropäischen Verteidigung" in Militärgeschichtliche Mitteilungen, Vol. 21, 1977, p. 135ff. The ideas presented in this portion of the essay are based on interviews with General a. D. Ulrich de Maizière, April and June 1984; General a.D. Johann Adolf Graf von Kielmansegg, June 1984; Generalleutnant a.D. Wolf Graf von Baudissin, May 1984; Generalmajor a.D. Dr. Eberhard Wagemann, March, June 11984; General a.D. Carl-Gero von Ilsemann, March, June 1984; Brigadegenral a.D. Heinz Karst, March 1984; Oberstleutnant Dr. Hans-Joachim Harder, February 1984; Oberst Dr. Norbert Wiggershaus, April 1984; Oberstleutnant Dr. Helmuth Schubert, April, July 1984.

[7]"Himmeroder Denkschrift," p. 185.

[8] For more on Baudissin, see his Sodat für den Frieden, cited in nt. 2.

[9] Bundesarchiv-Militärarchiv (BA/MA), Bw 2/ 282, "Vortrag vor der Gesellschaft für Wehrkunde, 4.II. 1956, 'Aktuelle Probleme des Aufbaus der deutschen Streitkräfte,'" cited in Norbert Wiggershaus, "Zum Problem der Tradition im Vorfeld des westdeutschen Militärbeitrages, 1945-1955/6," manuscript, 1983.

[10] Interview with Wagemann, June 1984.

[11] Dietrich Genschel, Wehrreform und Reaktion: die Vorbereitung der Inneren Führung (Hamburg, 1972); Heinz Brill, "Das Problem einer wehrpolitischen Alternative für Deutschland" dissertation, (Göttengen, 1977); Interviews with de Mazière, April and June 1984; Kielmansegg, June 1984; Brigadier General Dietrich Genschel, March 1984.

[12] Claus Freiherr von Rosen, "Tradition als Last: Probleme mit dem Traditionsangebot der Gruppe 'Inneres Gefüge' (1951-1958) im Leitbild 'Staatsbürger in Uniform' für die Tradition der Bundeswehr" in Tradition als Last: Legitimationsproblem der Bundeswehr, Klaus M. Kodalle, ed. (Köln, 1982).

[13] Vom Künftigen deutschen Soldaten: Gedanken und Planungen der Dienststelle Blank, Dienstelle Blank, ed. (Bonn, 1955) pp. 19-27.

[14] Ibid., p. 28ff.

[15] Ibid.; Hans Hellmuth Kirst, Null-Acht Fünfzehn (München, 1954ff) 3 Vols. Kirst's works are especially interesting, since they appeared at the height of the public discussion about the reforms. Kirst had been an officer and a Nationalsozialistischer Führungsoffizier (NSFO or National Socialist Leadership Officer) a kind of political commissar introduced into the ranks after the 20th of July 1944. For more on the political effects of Kirst's writings, see Hans Speier, From the Ashes of Disgrace: A Journal from Germany, 1945-1955 (Amherst, 1981) p. 262.

[16] Vom künftigen . . ., p. 35ff.

[17] Handbuch, cited in nt. 2. The official regulation finally appeared in 1972 as Zentrale Dienstvorschrift 10/1, cited in nt. 2.

[18] Handbuch, p. 47ff; Interview with Baudissin, May 1984.

[19] For more on Seeckt's concept of military tradition, see Hans von Seeckt, Die Reichswehr (Leipzig, 1933). On Seeckt, politics and tradition, see Herzfeld, cited in nt. 2; Walter von Rabenau, Seeckt: aus seinem Leben 1918-1936 (Berlin, 1940); Hans Meier-Welcker, Seeckt (Frankfurt, 1967); Karl-Dietrich Bracher, Die Auflösung der Weimarer Republik (Stuttgart, 1955); Hanns Demeter, "Die Pflege der Traditionen

der alten Armee im Reichsheer und in der Wehrmacht," Feldgrau Sonderheft 7, 1956.

20 Interview with Harder, July 1983.

21 Interviews with Wagemann, March 1984; de Maizière, April 1984.

22 BA/MA, Bw 2/3949, "Chef des Stabes (Ch.d.S.) Führungsstab der Bundeswehr (Fue S) Aktenzeichen (Az) 35-08-07, 'Die Pflege der Tradition in der Bundeswehr,' 25 Oktober 1957." (The writer also consulted a copy of this document in private hands.) Unless found in other official archives or in private collections, all sources cited from the Bundesarchiv-Militärarchiv are in Hans-Joachim Harder, "Die Traditionspflege in der Bundeswehr," manuscript, 1983 upon which this section is largely based.

23 Ibid.

24 Interviews with Baudissin, May 1984; de Maizière, April 1984.

25 BA/MA, Bw 2/3949, "Fue S B, Vermerk, Traditionspflege, 10 Januar 1958; Schreiben, Heusinger an Dr. Meier-Welcker, 13 Januar 1958."

26 BA/MA, Bw 2/3949, "Schreiben, Kommandeur, Pazerbatallion (PzBtl) 2 an Befehlshaber, Kommando Territoriale Verteidigung (KTV) 17 Maerz 1958; Interviews with Baudissin, May 1984; with de Maizière, June 1984; with Wagemann, June 1984.

27 BA/MA, Bw 2/3949, "Weisung, Generalinspekteur (GenInsp) an Führung Heer, Luftwaffe, Marine, Territoriale-Verteidigung und Inspekteur Sanitätswesen, 16 Juni 1958."

28 BA/MA, Bw 2/3928, "BMvg, Fue B I 4, A3 35-08-07, an alle Kommandeure und Chefs selbsständiger Einheiten, 17 Dezember 1958."

29 Harder, "Traditionspflege," p. 28.

30 Interview with Wagemann, June 1984.

31 For an excellent discussion of the 20th of July in the Bundeswehr, see Norbert Wiggershaus, "Zur Bedeutung und Nachwirkung des militärischen Widerstandes in der Bundesrepublik und in der Bundeswehr" in Der militärische Widerstand gegen Hitler und das NS Regime 1933-1945: Vorträge zur Militärgeschichte, Vol. 5 (Bonn, 1984) and Gerd R. Überschär, "Gegner des Nationalsozialismus, 1933-1945" in Militärgeschichtliche Mitteilungen No. 35, 1984, pp. 141-196. The article by Large cited above should be noted, but must be complemented by Wiggershaus and Überschär for a more accurate picture.

[32] Interviews with Baudissin, May 1984; de Maizière, June 1984; Kielmansegg, June 1984. For Baudissin's viewpoint on the fortieth anniversary of the Attentat, see his "Ohne den Widerstand wäre der Neubeginn unmöglich gewesen" in Frankfurter Rundschau, 19 July 1984. For Kielmansegg's views, see his "Gedanken eines Soldaten zum Widerstand" in Widerstand, cited in nt. 31.

[33] Hans Speier, German Rearmament and Atomic War (Evanston, 1957) p. 31; Interviews with Baudissin, May 1984; de Maizière, June 1984; Kielmansegg, June 1984; Karst, July 1984; Schubert, June 1984.

[34] "Wortlaut des Interviews das der Bundestagabgeordnete Theodor Blank dem Vertreter des Nordwestdeutschen Rundfunks Hans Wendt am 8. November 1952 gewährt hat" Presse- und Informationsamt der Bundesregierung, 9 November 1952, consulted by the writer; Wiggershaus, "Zum Problem," pp. 84-89.

[35] Interviews with Brigadier General Freiherr Harald von Uslar-Gleichen, May 1984; Major General Wilhelm Ranck, May 1984.

[36] Harder, "Traditionspflege," p. 13.

[37] BA/MA, Bw 2/3949, "Vermerk, Leiter, Fue B I zur Vorlage, Entwürf Traditionserlass beim GenInsp am 11 März 1959, 13 März 1959."

[38] Zentrum Innere Führung, Zentrales Unterrichtsarchiv, (ZIF/ZUA) 0.4.7.1.2., "Zum 15 Jahrestag des 20. Juli, GenInsp Bw, Bw B I 6, Az 35-20-17-50, 20. Juli 1959" Gerd Schmueckle and Wolfram von Raven in Minister Strauss' office wrote this order of the day. Interview with General Gerd Schmueckle, March 1986.

[39] Ibid.

[40] ZIF/ZUA, 2.6.5.4., "Die Vorfälle in Ausbildungskompanie 6/9 in Nagold, BMvg, 31. Januar 1964."

[41] For a collection of the articles, see Hellmuth Heye, In Sorge um die Bundeswehr: Sonderdruck wichtiger Quick Berichte (München, 1964).

[42] BA/MA, Bw 2/4238 "Dr. habil. Ibach, Fue B I 4, Sprechzettel für Oberst i.G. Dr. Wagemann, 27. Oktober 1964."

[43] BA/MA, Bw 2/4238 "Handschriftliche Notiz des GenInsp Trettner an Kopie des Erlasses an Minister von Hassel, 13. Mai 1965."

[44] BA/MA, Bw 2/4238, "Fue B I 4, Az 35-08-07, an GenInsp über Chef des Stabes Bw. 24. Juni 1965."

45BA/MA, Bw 2/4238, "Handschriftliche Notiz des Minister von Hassels an Fue B I 4, AZ 35-08-07, 24. Juni 1965."

46BA/MA, Bw 2/4238, "Originalexemplar des Erlasses, Unterschrift und schriftliche Korrekturen von Hassels, 1 Juli 1965."

47ZIF/ZUA, 3.1.2.2., "BMvg Pressereferat 'Mitteilungen an die Presse,' Nr. II/86 14 Juli 1965;" ZIF/ZUA, 3.1.2.2. "BMvg, Fue B I 4, AZ 35-08-07, 'Bundeswehr und Tradition' 1. Juli 1965; "Information für die Truppe, Beilage zu Heft 9/1965."

48"Bundeswehr und Tradition"

49Ibid.

50Ibid.

51"Bundeswehr und Tradition" in Vorwärts, 28 July 1965; "Tradition--nicht nur Bewunderung" in Rheinische Post, 16 July 1965; "Traditionspflege" in Christ und Welt, 23 July 1965; "Die Pflege der Tradition in der Bundeswehr" in Neue Zürcher Zeitung 17 July 1965; "Richtlinien für die Traditionspflege der Bundeswehr" in Frankfurter Allgemeine Zeitung 16 July 1965.

52"Gedanken zum Erlass 'Bundeswehr und Tradition,' Kommandierender General (KG) I Korps (Generalleutnant Meyer-Detring) Dezember, 1965; "Quellennachweis-Gedanken zum Erlass 'Tradition und Bundeswehr,' KG I Korps, Januar 1966" both consulted by the writer.

53"BMvg, Fue S I 4, 'Hinweise für die Unterrichtung über den Erlass "Bundeswehr und Tradition"'" 18. Oktober 1965." consulted by the writer.

54Manfred Messerschmidt, "Kein gültiges Erbe" in Süddeutsche Zeitung, 21/22 February 1981; Manfred Messerschmidt, "Das Verhältnis von Wehrmacht und Staat und die Frage der Traditionsbildung" in Aus Politik und Zeitgeschichte: Beilage zum Parlament 25 April 1981; Interview with Professor Dr. Manfred Meeserschmidt, February 1984.

55"BMvg. Fue S I 3, Az 35-08-07, 'Richtlinien zum Traditionsverständnis und zur Traditionspflege in der Bundeswehr'" 20 September 1982. consulted by the writer.

56For the discussion of the tradition issue in late-1985, see "Fettnäppchen aus dem Panzerschrank" in Stern, 24 October 1985; Ulrich Mackensen, "Ein Schritt Zurück" in Frankfurter Rundschau, 4 November 1985; "Neuer Traditionserlass für die Bundeswehr; Schlimmer Rückfall" in Die Zeit, 8 November 1985; "Woerner: Neuer Traditionserlass" in Die Welt, 12 November 1985.

As of this writing (December 1986), the Ministry of Defense had prepared the revised guidelines on military tradition based upon the suggestions of the Council on Innere Führung. Drafts of the new guidelines included some mention of the 20th of July and the Wehrmacht. In effect, the new work seemed to be a compromise between the wording of the 1965 decree and the one of 1982. The publication of this third document was delayed yet again due to the desire of the Christian-liberal coalition government to avoid unnecessary political controversy.

BIBLIOGRAPHY: CHARLES BURTON BURDICK

Compiled By NANCY J. EMMICK

PUBLICATIONS

BOOKS

Contemporary Germany: Politics and Culture. Edited by Charles Burdick, Hans-Adolf Jacobsen, and Winfried Kudszus. Boulder, Colorado: Westview Press, 1984.

The Frustrated Raider: the Story of the German Cruiser Cormoran in World War I. Carbondale: Southern Illinois University Press, 1979.

Furchtlos und Treu: Zum Fünfundsiebzigsten Geburtstag von General der Gebirgstruppe a.D. Hubert Lanz. Köln: Markus, 1971.

German Military Planning for the War in the West, 1935-1940. Thesis. Stanford, California: Stanford University, 1954.

German Prisoners-of-War in Japan, 1914-1920. Charles Burdick and Ursula Moessner. Lanham: University Press of America, 1984.

Germany's Military Strategy and Spain in World War II. Syracuse, N.Y.: Syracuse University Press, 1968.

The Japanese Siege of Tsingtau: World War I in Asia. Hamden, Conn.: Archon Books, 1976.

The Political Institutions of the German Revolution, 1918-1919. Charles Burdick and Ralph H. Lutz. New York: F. A. Praeger (for the Hoover Institution on War, Revolution, and Peace, Stanford University, Stanford, California), 1966.

Ralph H. Lutz and the Hoover Institution. Stanford, Calif.: Hoover Institution Press, 1974.

Unternehmen Sonnenblume: der Entschluss zum Afrika-Feldzug. Neckargemünd: Vowinckel, 1972.

War in Asia and the Pacific, 1937-1949. Edited by Charles B. Burdick and Donald S. Detwiler. 15 Volumes. New York: Garland, 1980.

- Vol. 1 - Introduction & Guide: Japanese and Chinese Studies and Documents.

- Vol. 2 - Japanese Military Studies, 1937-1949: Political Background of the War: Japanese and Chinese Studies and Documents.

- Vol. 3 - Japanese Military Studies 1937-1949: Command, Administration, and Special Operations: Japanese and Chinese Studies and Documents.

- Vol. 4 - Japanese Military Studies, 1937-1949: Naval Armament Program and Naval Operations: Japanese and Chinese Studies and Documents.

- Vol. 5 - Japanese Military Studies, 1937-1949: Naval Armament Program and Naval Operations: Japanese and Chinese Studies and Documents.

- Vol. 6 - Japanese Military Studies, 1937-1949: The Southern Area: Japanese and Chinese Studies and Documents.

- Vol. 7 - Japanese Military Studies: The Southern Area: Japanese and Chinese Studies and Documents.

- Vol. 8 - Japanese Military Studies, 1937-1949: China, Manchuria, Korea.

- Vol. 9 - Japanese Military Studies, 1937-1949: China, Manchuria, Korea.

- Vol. 10- Japan and the Soviet Union.

- Vol. 11- Japan and the Soviet Union.

- Vol. 12- Defense of the Homeland and the End of the War: Japanese Military Studies, 1937-1949.

- Vol. 13- Japanese Military Studies, 1937-1949: The Sino-Japanese and the Chinese Civil Wars.

- Vol. 14- Japanese Military Studies, 1937-1949: The Sino-Japanese and the Chinese Civil Wars.

Vol. 15- Japanese Military Studies, 1937-1949: The Sino-Japanese and the Chinese Civil Wars.

Washington Square, 1857-1979: The History of San Jose State University. Charles Burdick and Benjamin F. Gilbert. San Jose, Calif.: San Jose State University, 1980.

World War II German Military Studies: a Collection of 213 Special Reports on the Second World War Prepared by Former Officers of the Wehrmacht for the United States Army. Introduction and guide by Charles B. Burdick, Donald S. Detwiler, and Jürgen Rohwer. New York: Garland, 1979.

BOOK REVIEWS

(A Partial Listing)

Activity Reports of the Commander of the German Army-Personnel-Office Schmundt, Rudolf Presented by Burgdorf, Wilhelm, 10-10-1942 to 10-29-1944 by D. Bradley and R. Schulzekossens, Military Affairs. Vol. 50, 1986, pp. 110-111.

German Navy World War II by E. P. Vonderporten. Journal of Modern History. Vol. 45, 1973, pp. 544-545.

Guilty: Hitler's Generals by C. Stewart. Military Affairs. Vol. 33, 1969, pp. 344-345.

History of the German-Army, 1916-1945 by W. K. Nehring. Military Affairs. Vol. 34, 1970, p. 109.

Hitler and His Generals: Hidden Crises, January-June 1938 by H. C. Deutsch. Review of European History. Vol. 2, 1976, pp. 113-118.

Hitler and Middle Sea by W. Ansel. Journal of Modern History. Vol. 45, 1973, pp. 544-545.

India in Axis Strategy: Germany, Japan, and Indian Nationalists in World War II by M. Hauner. American Historical Review. Vol. 88, 1983, p. 739.

Italy in World War II: Bibliography by J. Schroder. Military Affairs. Vol. 43, 1979, p. 218.

No Mans Land: 1918, the Last Year of the Great War by J. Toland. Military Affairs. Vol. 45, 1981, pp. 151-152.

Politics and the Military in Modern Spain by S. G. Payne. Military Affairs. Vol. 31, 1967, p. 153.

Promise of Greatness: War of 1914-1918 by G. Panichas. Historian. Vol. 32, 1970, 00.488-489.

The Secret Daily Reports of the German High-Command in the 2nd World War, 1939-1934, Vol. 12, January 1, 1945 to May 9, 1945 by K. Mehner. German Studies Review. Vol. 9, 1986, pp. 165-166.

Security of Dictator: Hitler's Bodyguards and Protective Measures at Residences and Headquarters by P. Hoffman. Military Affairs. Vol. 41, 1977, p. 95.

Soldiers of Destruction: SS Deaths Head Division 1933-1945 by C. W. Sydnor. Journal of Modern History. Vol. 51, 1979, pp. 191-192.

Tradition and New Beginning: International Research on 20th Century German History by J. Hutter, R. Meyers, and D. Papenfuss. Military Affairs. Vol. 41, 1977, p. 101.

U-Boat Strategy: German U-Boat Tactics, 1900-1945 by H. Jeschke. Journal of Modern History. Vol. 45, 1973, pp. 544-545.

Die Wehrmacht in Kampg .44 Kampf um rom Inferno am po der Weg 362 Inf. Div. 1944-1945 by H. Griner. Military Affairs. Vol. 34, 1970, p. 69.

PERIODICAL ARTICLES

"Amerikanische Studenten." Alte Kameraden. Vol. 19, January 1971, p. 11.

"Army Intelligence Reserve." Army Reserve Magazine. Vol. 7, July 1961.

"Austro-Hungarian Missions in the Pacific at the Outbreak of the Great War." Research Studies. Vol. 51, 1983, pp. 12-24.

"L'Avion a Reaction Allemand." Revue D'Historie De La Deuxuime Guerre Mondiale. Vol. 44, November 1961, pp. 21-38.

"L'Axe Rome-Berlin et la Campagne Italo-Grecque 1940-41." Revue Historique De L'Armee. Vol. 16, September 1960, pp. 71-86.

"The Day of Versailles, June 28, 1919." The Tower . Spring 1968, pp. 46-57.

"Die Deutschen Militärischen Planungen Gegenüber Frankreich 1933-1938." Wehrwissenschaftliche Rundschau. Vol. 6, December 1956, pp. 678-685.

"Dora, the Germans' Largest Gun." Military Review. Vol. 41, November 1961, pp. 72-78.

"The Errant Flyers." Military Review. Vol. 39, June 1959, pp. 53-57.

"Foreign Military Records in the National Archives." Prologue. Vol. 7, 1975, pp. 213-220.

"The Franco-Italian War, 1940." Cosantoir, The Irish Defense Journal. Vol. 30, January 1970, pp. 21-25.

"The Frustrated Raider." The American Neptune. Vol. 24, October 1964, pp. 272-279.

"The Gibraltar Armband." The Army Quarterly and Defense Journal. Vol. LXXXXI, January 1966, pp. 214-218.

"Gruen: German Military Planning for Ireland, 1940-1941." Cosantoir, The Irish Defense Journal. Vol. 34, March 1974, pp. 77-80.

"A House on Navidad Street: The Celebrated Zimmwemann Note on the Texas Border." Arizona and the West. Vol. 8, March 1966, pp. 19-34.

"'Ilona' and 'Gisela': Hitler's Military Plans and Spain, 1942-43." Military Review. Vol. 44, June 1964, pp. 48-57.

"Library and the Academic Community." Library Resources and Technical Services. Vol. 8, Spring 1964, pp. 157-160.

"'Moro': the Resupplying of German Submarines in Spain, 1939-1941." Journal of Central European Affairs. Vol. 3, June 1970, pp. 256-284.

"Operation Cyclamen, Germany and Albania." Journal of Central European Affairs. Vol. 19, April 1959, p. 23.

"Les Plans Militaires Allemands pour la France 1940-1942." Revue Historique L'Armee. Vol. 27, 1971, #4, pp. 31-37.

"Planungen für das Einrücken deutscher Kräfte in Spanien in den Jahren, 1942-1943: Die Unternehmen 'Ilona' und 'Gisela'." Wehrwissenschaftliche Rundschau. Vol. 13, March 1963, pp. 164-178.

"Le Plus gros cannon du Monde." Revue Historique L'Armee. Vol. 19, August 1963, pp. 103-106.

"Prisoners as Soldiers: the German 999th Penal Division." The Army Quarterly and Defense Journal. Vol. 102, October 1971, pp. 65-69.

"Selected Bibliography of German Books." (relating to the Second World War) <u>The American Committee on the History of the Second World War: Newsletter</u>. No. 3, December 1969, pp. 8-9.

"The Tamback Archive." <u>Military Affairs</u>. Vol. 36, December 1972, pp. 124-126.

"Tower of Military Learning." <u>Army Information Digest</u>. Vol. 19, March 1964, pp. 56-59.

"Die Unterlagen über Einheiten des Deutschen Heeres im Zweiten Weltkrieg." <u>Wehrwissenschaftliche Rundschau</u>. Vol. 16, January, February, Marchx 1966, pp. 55-58, 112-116, 172-176.

"Volunteers Without Honour." <u>Cosantoir, The Irish Defense Journal</u>. Vol. 31, February 1971, pp. 56-58.

"Von Schwert zur Feder: Deutsche Kriegsgefangene im Dienst der Vorbereitung der amerikanischen Kriegsgeschichtsschreibung über den Zweiten Weltkrieg." <u>Militärgeschichtliche Mitteilungen</u>. Vol. 10, 1971 II, pp. 69-80..

CHAPTER IN BOOK

"Werner Heisenberg und die Politik," in Heinrich Pfeiffer's <u>Denken und Umdenken</u>. München: R. Pieper, 1977.

Additional scholarly articles have appeared in numerous foreign language publications.

CONTRIBUTORS

DONALD ABENHEIM

Donald Abenheim earned his B.A. and Ph.D. at Stanford University. His M.A. in German History was earned under Charles Burdick at San Jose State in 1977. Currently Abenheim is a member of the faculty at the Naval Postgraduate School, Monterey, California. His Stanford dissertation, from which his contribution has come, is being revised for publication as a book.

NANCY J. EMMICK

Nancy J. Emmick is an associate librarian at San Jose State University (SJSU), San Jose, California. She is the history librarian and a part time history instructor at SJSU and is the proprietor of a library consulting firm in Santa Clara Valley. She taught a credit course in Irish History, under the auspices of the Minneapolis Community College, while escorting the students through Ireland. She also developed and taught a credit course on online database searching through the SJSU Continuing Education system. Nancy received her B.A. and M.A. in history and her M.L.S. in Librarianship from SJSU. She has published several articles including a three year study titled, "A Survey of Academic Library Reference Practices", RQ, Fall 1984; "Release Time for Professional Development: How Much for Research?, ACRL's Third National Conference Proceedings, June 1984; "The Jobline: A Valuable Resource for Librarians," Special Libraries, January 1984; "Nonprofessionals on Reference Desks in Academic Libraries," The Reference Librarian, Spring/Summer, 1985; "Employment Interview Information Available Online," Online Review, February 1986. She has also presented papers at many conferences including the Pacific Coast Branch of the American Historical Association on "Historians and Librarians: A Productive Partnership," August 1986. She is a member of both library and historical associations and is now the President of the California State University Librarians Chapter of the California Library Association which constitutes the 19 California State University campuses.

DOREEN GAMA FARR

A native Californian, **Doreen Gama Farr** attended schools in the San Jose area, including San Jose State University. As part of her undergraduate program, she studied ancient and medieval history while living in Florence, Italy for a year. Doreen graduated from the University in 1973 with a Bachelor's degree in History, and then earned a Master's degree in 1981 from the same institution. She was employed as a counselor for Westmonst College in Santa Barbara, during which time she taught a course on Italian Fascism. Currently, she is occupied full-time as a homemaker and mother. She is married to James Farr and they have two sons.

JAMES FARR

Born in San Francisco, **James Farr** attended a number of schools as an undergraduate, taking a B.S. in Finance in 1969 from Syracuse University. He returned to school after several years, studying history at San Jose State University with Charles Burdick. In addition to providing wise counsel, Dr. Burdick acted as a reader for Farr's Master Thesis. In 1982 he received a doctorate in United States History from the University of California, Santa Barbara. Blowing with the winds of academic need, Farr has taught a variety of courses in American history and related fields, both at Santa Barbara and San Jose State. He has published articles in The Journal of Negro History and California History. Dr. Farr is married to Doreen Gama Farr and has, in his own estimation, two wonderful sons.

HANS-ADOLF JACOBSEN

Born in Berlin in 1925, Professor **Hans-Adolf Jacobsen** is Director of the Department of Political Science, University of Bonn. His publications are numerous and have been translated into Spanish, Swedish, Italian, French, English, Polish, Russian, Dutch, Japanese, and Korean. His fields include German Foreign Policy, East-West Relations, the Soviet Union, China, Japan, and Security and Disarmament Problems. He lectures worldwide. Professors Jacobsen and Burdick became acquainted as graduate students in post-war Germany.

S. J. LEWIS

S. J. Lewis was born in Stockton, California in 1948. He received his A.B. and M.A. degrees in history from San Jose State University. He studied modern European history at the University of California Santa Barbara, where he received his Ph.D. in 1983. A career civil servant, Dr. Lewis has served as an archivist at the National Archives and as a historian at McClellan Air Force Base and at the U.S. Army John F. Kennedy Special Warfare Center at Fort Bragg, North Carolina. He is currently on the faculty of the U.S. Army Command and General Staff College, Fort Leavenworth, Kansas. Dr. Lewis is the author of Forgotten Legions German Army Infantry Policy 1918-1941 (1985).

CRAIG LUTHER

Craig Luther received his B.A. in history and music from Claremont McKenna College in southern California in 1974. He completed his M.A. in modern European history at San Jose State University from 1974-76. During 1979-80, the author undertook a year of study and research in West Germany under the auspices of the Fulbright Scholarship Program. Thereafter, he began work on the Ph.D. in modern European history at U.C. Santa Barbara--completing his oral and written examinations "with Distinction" in July 1982. In 1981 and 1983 the author made additional research trips to West Germany and Normandy, France, on behalf of his doctoral dissertation: a study of the 12th SS Hitler Youth Tank Division. Since May 1984 the author has worked as an Air Force historian at McClellan Air Force Base, Sacramento, California. The author's publications include articles concerning German military affairs in the Balkan Studies Journal and the British Army Quarterly, as well as a book (co-authored) on Germany's most well-known military commander -- Field Marshal Erwin Rommel.

DWIGHT MESSIMER

Dwight Messimer is a graduate of San Jose State College (B.A., 1966) and San Jose State University (M.A. 1979). His specialty is 20th century military history with an emphasis on naval history and naval aviation. He is the author of three books, all published by the Naval Institute Press. They are No Margin for Error (1981), Pawns of War (1983), and In the Hands of Fate (1985). The latter two were republished by Doubleday for the Military Book Club. Messimer has also published several articles on naval history. Those articles have appeared in Proceedings, Naval Aviation News, and The American Neptune. He is currently working on a book about the German commercial submarine U-Deutschland.

DAVID MIDDLESWORTH

David Middlesworth received a B.S. in Business Administration from San Jose State University in 1962. He studied German language in Stuttgart, Germany in 1964/65 while teaching for the United States military, entered a combined B.A./M.A. program in history at San Jose State in 1965 and completed this program under Charles Burdick in 1967. In the fall of 1967, he entered a Ph.D. program in history at the Ohio State University in Columbus, Ohio. After completing the course work requirements and passing the general examinations, he received a Fulbright graduate fellowship to spend one academic year researching a doctoral dissertation, "The Democratic Influence of Karl Renner in Austria, 1945-50." He completed the dissertation in 1973 while teaching at San Jose State University. After receiving the doctorate, he was unable to obtain a tenure track position in a college or university in the post-Vietnam era, and as a result entered the business world where he has remained since 1973. He has been married for 24 years, and has three lovely children.

URSULA MOESSNER

Ursula Moessner met Charles Burdick in 1974 while attending one of his Graduate Seminars on Modern German History. History, taught Burdick style, was a most fascinating and engrossing experience for her. His enthusiasm was catching and it converted her to the study of Military history. Burdick advised her on her M.A. thesis. Later she collaborated with him on a book about the German Prisoners of War in Japan during the First World War. The book was published in Japan in 1982 and in the U.S. in 1984. Moessner has taught European history, translated several books and articles and is presently working on a book about a specific phase of the air war during the Second World War, which will be published in Germany in 1987.

STEPHEN M. PAYNE

Stephen M. Payne is a graduate of the Public History Program at the University of California, Santa Barbara. He has taught local history and California history for several years at San Jose State University. His publications include the book <u>A Howling Wilderness: The History of the Summit Road Area of the Santa Cruz Mountains, 1850-1906</u>, an article, "Over a Century of Tradition and Progress: A History of Santa Barbara's fishing community," in <u>Santa Barbara by the Sea</u>, as well as another book in progress, <u>Harvest of Change: Santa Clara County, California</u>.

JOACHIM REMAK

Joachim Remak is Professor of History at the University of California at Santa Barbara. He received his Ph.D. at Stanford, where he also served as an instructor in Western Civilization in the fifties with Charles Burdick. They soon became friends as well as colleagues. Among the books he has written or edited since are <u>Sarajevo, The Story of a Political Murder</u>; <u>The Gentle Critic: Theodor Fontane and German Politics</u>; <u>The Origins of World War I</u>, and <u>The Nazi Years</u>.

ALLEN WACHHOLD

Allen Wachhold was born in Fresno, California in 1948. He attended local schools there, graduating from Fresno City College in 1968. In 1970 he transferred to San Jose State University, where he received a B.A. and M.A. in History. He earned his Ph.D. at the Univesity of California, Santa Barbara in History in 1984. His dissertation topic was, "Frank A. Golder: An Adventure in Russian History." He has published five articles from this project. His most influential professors were Charles Burdick and Irma Eichhorn of San Jose State and Joachim Remak of U.C. Santa Barbara. His favorite book is Montaigne's <u>Essays</u>. He has traveled to England, France, West Germany, and Greece. He enjoys running, swimming, crosscountry skiing, backpacking, bicycling, tennis, and basketball. He is married and lives in Santa Barbara, California.

JAMES P. WALSH

James P. Walsh is Professor of History at San Jose State University. He received his B.S. and M.A. degrees from the University of San Francisco and Ph.D. from the University of California, Berkeley. Twice he has served as Senior Fulbright Lecturer in the National University of Ireland. His books include: <u>Ethnic Militancy</u>, <u>The Irish: America's Political Class</u>, <u>The San Francisco Irish: 1850-1976</u>, <u>San Francisco's Hallinan: Toughest Lawyer in Town</u>. Walsh frequently lectures in Ireland on American social history.

MICHAEL ALLEN WEST

A Professional Staff Member of the Committee on Armed Services, U. S. House of Representatives, **Michael West** has served with the committee since June 1974 and performs budget review of the Department of Defense operation and maintenance accounts and policy oversight of readiness, civilian personnel, and environmental issues. He received a B.A. degree from San Jose State University in 1970 and did graduate work in military history at the Ohio State University. He received an M.A. in 1972 and Ph.D. in 1980 with a dissertation topic "Laying the Legislative Foundation: the House Naval Affairs Committee and the Construction of the Treaty Navy, 1926-1934". West resides in Fairfax, Virginia with his wife Elizabeth and two sons, Allen and Jeremy.

GERALD E. WHEELER

Gerald E. Wheeler is Emeritus Professor of History at San Jose State University. He joined the Faculty in 1957 and retired in 1983. During his years at the University, he served as Chairman of the Department (1969-1976) and as Dean of the School of Social Sciences (1976-1983). He received the A.B. (1948), M.A. (1949) and Ph.D. (1954) degrees from the University of California, Berkeley. He is the author, with P. E. Coletta, of <u>Outline of World Naval History</u> (1956); author, <u>Prelude to Pearl Harbor: The United States Navy and the Far East 1921-1931</u> (1963); author, <u>Admiral William Veazie Pratt, U. S. Navy: A Sailor's Life</u> (1974).

U 41 .W37 1987

War, revolution, and peace

MAY 1 1 1989